# THE PHILOSOPHY OF
# MIND
# TRAVEL

# PSYCHOTIC
# LOGICIAN

ISBN
978-1-957378-38-1 (Hardcover)
978-1-957378-37-4 (Paperback)
978-1-957378-36-7 (eBook)

# TABLE OF CONTENTS

Existence (A Very Short Introduction) ........................................................v

Prolegomena To Any Future Complete Deduction of Existence .............. vii

On Reference Use In Language ................................................................. xii

    Section 1  An Introduction to Mind Travel ..................................... 1

    Section 2  The "Psychosis" of Mind Travel ................................... 37

    Section 3  Adventures in Mind Travel ......................................... 100

    Section 4  Jobs in Mind Travel .....................................................140

    Section 5  Dreams of Mind Travel ...............................................180

    Section 6  The Degeneracy of Mind Travel ................................201

    Section 7  Abstract Mind Travel ..................................................256

    Section 8  The Rationality of Mind Travel ................................. 288

Index  Tools for Mind Travel or
        (The Operation of Mind Travel)................................. 295

Movie Script Idea
(Also, A Lesson In Abstract Reworks And Combinations) ..................... 310

The Grain Silo Story
(How It Didn't Happen) ........................................................................ 360

The Purple Bishop Idea......................................................................... 362

(This Is The Observer Speaking…) Inserts Throughout Book ...............365

Philosophical Roast or (Heuristics of Mind Travel)............................... 415

# EXISTENCE (A VERY SHORT INTRODUCTION)

Do absolutely anything you want, just as long at you don't infringe upon the rights of anyone else, as outlined by each mind.

Thus, we have the necessary and sufficient conditions for absolute freedom (a one rule utopia):

Deontological Anarchism

*FADE IN.*

# PROLEGOMENA TO ANY FUTURE COMPLETE DEDUCTION OF EXISTENCE

1.  There exists two relations that exist in all of existence:

    (i)  The internal relation (subjectivity)
    (ii) The external relation (objectivity)

2.  There exists two realities that exist in all of existence:

    (i)  The mental reality (immaterial existence)
    (ii) The physical reality (material existence)

3.  There exists three points of reference that exist in all of existence:

    (1) A *thesis* point of reference
    (2) An *antithesis* point of reference
    (3) A *synthesis* point of reference

4.  There exists two points of reference that exist in subjectivity, the mental reality, and the thesis and antithesis points of reference:

    (A) The conscious mind
    (B) The subconscious mind

5.  There exists three points of reference that exist in objectivity, the physical reality, and the synthesis point of reference:

    (a) Complete conscious mind
    (b) Complete subconscious mind
    (c) Complete unifying awareness mind

6.  There exists two observable points of reference through which the thesis, antithesis, and synthesis refer to one another:

    (x) The absolute observable reference
    (y) The relative observable reference

7. There exists two forms of knowledge:

   (X) A priori knowledge
   (Y) A posteriori knowledge

8. There exists four forms of organizing all of existence that relate to one another:

   (α) Parts
   (μ) Whole
   (β) Part in parts
   (Ω) Whole in whole

9. The complete dual opposites in existence, that refer to every opposite in existence:

   -Infinite
   -Finite
   -Finite Infinite and Infinite Finite
   -Infinite Infinite and Finite Finite

10. The two complete logical relations that exist which refer to everything in existence:

    ① The complete logical existential reference ($\forall$x)
    ② The incomplete logical existential reference ($\exists$x)

11. There exists five dimensions that make up all of existence:

    First Dimension: Relative observation of time
    Second Dimension: Relative observation of space
    Third Dimension: Absolute observation of space
    Fourth Dimension: Absolute observation of time
    Fifth Dimension: Absolute observation of time and space

12. The causal relationship between the four dimensions of time and space are:

    #1: Observation of time preceding space (the past)
    #2: Observation of space preceding time (the future)
    #3: Observation of space and time not preceding each other (the present)

13. The observation of time correspond to one another through two forms of relative and absolute temporal relations:

    (→) Relative time (the arrow or direction of time through which the past precedes the present, and the present precedes the future)
    (↔) Absolute time (no direction of time, since the past, present, and future are unified and no arrow exists)

14. The observation of space correspond to one another through two forms of relative and absolute spatial relations:

    (↔) Simultaneous causal spatial relation (spatial state A, and spatial state B are causally connected through an absolute moment)
    (→) Non-simultaneous causal spatial relation (spatial state A, and spatial state B are causally connected through a relative moment)

15. There exists three absolute moments in existence, and one relative moment in existence:

    Relative moment: space and time measured through relative observers in a differentiated form.
    Absolute moment #1: space and time measured through a singular or absolute point in which an observer measures time through a first causal moment. (the beginning of the universe) (scientifically seen through the big bang)
    Absolute moment #2: space and time measured through a singular or absolute point in which an observer measures time through a final causal moment. (the end of the universe) (scientifically seen through the big crunch)
    Absolute moment #3: space and time measured through a singular or absolute point in which all observers measure time and space at the same causal moment, existing between Absolute moment #1, and Absolute moment #2 through all relative moments. (the fate of the universe) (scientifically seen through the absolute point of reference (absolute rest))

16. There exists two forms of possible spatial and temporal connectivity through the relative and absolute observations:

    Connectivity #1: a wormhole connecting two observable points within any universe. Space and time form an arrow: the wormhole connects two spatial existences, through a temporal existence (it takes relative space and time, since it takes time to connect space within a universe (takes time to go through wormhole))

Connectivity #2: a splice point connecting two observable points within all of existence. Since splice points connect all universes in existence, they are not observable through the space and time of any given universe, because they exist outside the causal laws of any given universe.

17. A complete unification of all differing relations that exist (as shown above), completely deduces all of existence, since every form of reality has been demonstrated as through its correspondence to everything:

    Formation of reality: completely deduced existence (existing form)
    Non-formation of reality: nothing deduced existence (nonexistence form)

18. Existence and nonexistence unify every relation shown above, through the following logical form, that unifies all existing forms, but does not refer to nonexistent forms, since nothing cannot exist outside existence (outside of a universe, there is the possibility that other universes exist (thus, something that is nonexistent in a given universe (like other universes within universes) can only be referred to through a unified form of reality; however, outside of all of existence, there is not nothing, since anything outside of all of existence, is existence in some form. Hence, even nothing is something (even nonexistence is existence).

19. The completed form of knowledge through which a complete deduction of existence can be seen through the logical resolution of Russell's Paradox:

    Let $R$ be the set of all sets that are not members of themselves. If $R$ is not a member of itself, then its definition entails that it is a member of itself; if it is a member of itself, then it is not a member of itself, since it is the set of all sets that are not members of themselves.
    The paradox: $R \in R \leftrightarrow R \notin R$

**Set of all universes: $\forall x$**
**Set of a given universe: $\exists x$**

Let $\forall x$ be the set of all universes that are not members of $\exists x$. If $\exists x$ is not a member of $\forall x$, then this means that it is not a member of $\exists x$ (itself). If $\exists x$ is a member of itself, then this means that it is a member of $\forall x$.

($\varphi$) $\exists x \in \exists x \rightarrow \exists x \in \forall x$
($\Omega$) $\exists x \notin \forall x \rightarrow \exists x \notin \exists x$

- $(\exists x \in \exists x \rightarrow \exists x \in \forall x) \leftrightarrow (\exists x \notin \forall x \rightarrow \exists x \notin \exists x)$

Equivalent semantical syntax:

- $\omega \leftrightarrow \Omega$

Thus, the two are logically equivalent to one another, since they can be deduced from each other. Thus, they do not contradict each other.

Reason for contradiction: The paradox does not differentiate between the set of all sets, and the set of all sets that are not members of themselves. Both are denoted by R, and hence, contradict each other, since they should be differentiated from each other by a different logical sign.

Semantical logic referring to all of existence:

$(\text{Part} \in \text{Part} \rightarrow \text{Part} \in \text{Whole}) \leftrightarrow (\text{Part} \notin \text{Whole} \rightarrow \text{Part} \notin \text{Part})$

If a part of existence exists within itself, then the part of existence exists in the whole of existence. This means that, if a part of existence does not exist in the whole of existence, then part of existence does not exist in itself.

Therefore, Russell's Paradox ceases to exist. And hence, everything in existence is referred to without contradicting itself.

What is written in this prolegomena is a basic guide through which everything in existence can be deduced from. Through this, anyone can know reality in its completed form. Whomever succeeds in this task, unifies everything in existence, knows everything, and is made an absolute being. Such a feat is the ultimate achievement of human reason.

"May others come and do it better."
-Ludwig Wittgenstein

# ON REFERENCE USE IN LANGUAGE

There are 5 points of reference through which a *conscious* observer can speak through in existence.

*Subconsciously*, the observer is not speaking since the speaker is not referring to any point of reference inside itself and outside itself.

1.  Internal Subjective Reference

    The speaking observer: I am speaking to *myself.*

2.  External Subjective Reference

    The speaking observer: I am speaking to *you.*

3.  Internal Objective Reference

    The speaking observer: I am speaking to *him.*

4.  External Objective Reference

    The speaking observer: He is speaking to *himself.*

5.  External Objective Subjective Reference

    The speaking observer: He is speaking to *me.*

Thus, every reference point through which a conscious observer can speak through has been identified:

(i)   Myself
(ii)  You
(iii) Him
(iv)  Himself
(v)   Me

Therefore, if all five reference points have been identified and spoken through by the observer, then the observer is consciously self-aware of everything inside itself, and outside itself.

Thereof, subconsciousness vanishes, and transcends to a self-aware conscious observer. The differentiation of all internal, external, subjective, and objective points of reference in existence are unified by *Me* and hence, I am consciously self-aware of *Myself.*

Author's Note: During the course of the book you may sometimes see a small number right beside a part of what I wrote (located on the right side of the book, for example[99]). The number beside what is written denotes a break in the flow of what is written, in order for me to comment further upon what I wrote. These numbers relate to the index of the book, where you will find the number shown in the book, corresponding to its number in the index, which are further remarks that I wish to make the reader aware of, without breaking the overall flow of what is written in the book. I leave it up to the reader whether they decide to ignore the small numbers until a time which better suits the way they want to read about through the book, or whether they want to read the inserts in the index whenever they become situated within what is written. The inserts always start with, "(**THIS IS THE OBSERVER SPEAKING:…**)" and are my simple way of showing the reader any further comments that I wish to convey about what is being discussed in the book. These comments range from a philosophical/logical analysis of what is being discussed in the book, to other points of view that I have relating to the matter that it is referring to.

Viewer discretion advised.

To whom it may concern.

"Into every tidy scheme for arranging the pattern of human life, it is necessary to inject a certain dose of anarchism."

– Bertrand Russell

# SECTION 1

# An Introduction to Mind Travel

I am climbing a fence that is roughly seven to eight feet high. Aaron is above me and is trying to help me up. Abe is not far behind, but he, being a much better climber than me, reaches the top first. I get to the top and I look up at the sky. I wonder if other people have done this before. It's not that hard of a thing to do. I decide that this would be a good place to take a girl to hang out. I think I will call up Colleen and ask her if she wants to chill sometime, and climb up onto the roof of the planetarium. She smokes cigarettes and I don't, but I will definitely buy a pack and pretend to smoke if that gets me the chance to take her out.

I throw down another huge swig of shitty/generic vodka as I look around the room. Benjamin is there and Charlie is somewhere else. A see a guy eyeing me from a distance, but decide that if he asks who I am, I will just say I came here with "Scott". We leave the party and are in an open field. There is about two feet of snow on the ground and I see Benjamin and Charlie walking about ten yards in front of me. We get to a place on campus where there is construction and a huge crane. We try and climb up the crane but then decide it's too difficult to do in our near blacked out stupor. We hear a noise and bolt. The only way out of the construction area is to climb up a fence. Charlie jumps on the fence, and it immediately collapses, ending with him lying on his back with the fence on top of him. Benjamin and I laugh and walk over the fence to get the hell out of there.

I am at Blake's frat party, the same fraternity that I attended rush at a few months ago. They seemed to like me at the rush party and so I was given an invitation to come back to their formal dress party. I don't know what "formal" dress attire means so I just show up to the party wearing kakis and a button down collard shirt, untucked. When I enter the house I immediately become aware of what formal dress attire means. Since I was the only one in the house who wasn't wearing the proper attire, I had to make a way in which

I could stand out. We smoke cigars in the backyard as people get called into their interviews. I heard from a source that the proper/expert way of smoking cigar is to ash it as least as possible. My ash is around two and a half inches long when it perks the interest of a fraternity brother. "That's the way you smoke a cigar!" I am happy that he noticed. I think back to the day when the different fraternities around campus pick the people who they want to be in their frat. I get to the building and find that I have an envelope with my name written on it, with the name of the fraternities that have chosen me to be with them. I look in the envelope and find that it is empty. "What does it mean if there is nothing inside?" I ask the person at the desk. "Oh…damn…" "Does that mean nobody chose me to be in their frat?" "Yeah, pretty much." I look over to Abe and say, "Fuck yeah!" and give him a high five.

I look over at the place where the DJ is playing music with the DJ pads. I want to try it out. "Hey could I scratch that record for a minute or two?" "No" "Why not? Come on man I just want to try it out." "No kid, fuck off!" I am too drunk to know what that means so I reach over the table and try to scratch the DJ pads from the opposite side of the table. "I said fuck off!" The kid pushes me in the chest and I fly backwards and my whole body hits a wall. I am temporarily stunned, and have the air knocked out of me. I look at the kid who pushed me and the expression on his face is something like, "damn, I didn't think his body would fall that far back." I see three women dancing on a table. I notice that if I dance on the table I will be the only man who does this which would make me unique. I start dancing on the table and get my shirt halfway off when I see Blake leave the room. I have not talked to him in a while so I decide to see what he is up to. As I leave the room, I make sure to go back over to the DJ who pushed me, and tell him what I really think. I extend my hands over the table and place them on the scratch pads and yell, "FUCK YOU!" to him. "You crazy fuck!" he responds as I run out the door.

Aaron bets me that I won't run around the center Field naked and I decide that I will prove him wrong. I take off my clothes and do two laps around the field, pumping my fist in the air and happy that I have proven him wrong and that I can cross streaking out on my bucket list. I contemplate going streaking with a bunch of other college kids along Pearl Street. It is Halloween and the streaker's wear pumpkins over their heads. I heard stories that there are a few unfortunate one's each year that get arrested by the cops and are charged as sexual offenders. This dissuades me from doing it, but I still watch them go by. I am with Abe and we see that there is a woman standing five feet from us also watching the streaker's. Abe begins to laugh and he taps me on the shoulder to show me what is so funny. The woman watching the naked people run by, unknown to her, has her left breast hanging out of her shirt. Another man sees this and starts laughing with us. We give each other high fives.

We are walking along Pearl Street and a guy wearing a strap on dildo approaches us. He talks to us about something and makes a point to tell us that he does not have an STD. I then grab the dildo and he is confused, and walks away. "Why the fuck did you touch that?" "I don't know. He said he didn't have an STD." We walk up to a tarot card reader. I ask Aaron to give me five dollars so the guy will read my fortune. The man describes exactly what I am going through and doing with my life and this makes me happy and content.[1]

I decide that I want to dress nicely for a party that Emma and her roommates are throwing. I know that if I do this my roommates will ask me what I am getting all dressed up for, so I make up a story about going over to a judges house to get my medical marijuana card certified. They buy this for some reason. I pregame with a handle of Brunette's Vodka and go to the party. I see Mia and I go up and talk to her. Olivia and Tom tell me that I should kiss her. I decide that I will ask her instead of just doing it/forcing her to do it. Feeling confident because of the bad ass attire I have on, I say to Mia, "can I kiss you?" She says no and I am thankful that I asked.[2]

Olivia and Tom still think I should have just kissed her for some reason. I smoke cigarettes and weed out on the deck. Aaron recently has gotten into a bad habit of breaking my cigarettes whenever I take one out to smoke because they are apparently bad for you, so I say, "Don't fucking break this cigarette you mother fucker!" He doesn't break it and that makes me happy for the both of us. I get back inside and I see Emma. She has a crush on me. I take out my phone for some reason and as she approaches me, she puts her hand on the cell phone and it breaks in half. "God fucking dammit" I think to myself. I decide to tell Mia's friends that I like her, but that they have to promise not to tell her. They all agree not to tell her, but end up telling her the next time they see her. Fucking women.[3]

I see a laundry shoot that goes from the kitchen all the way up to the top floor, which only happens to be about three feet away from each other. I think it would be a good idea if I went through the laundry shoot, starting at the top, and getting through the end of it at the kitchen. There is a glass window that turns sideways that enable me to get through it. I get stuck for a few minutes, but Tom helps me get through it by pulling on my feet. I go back to my dorm with my brother who has decided to pay me a visit and sleep on my dorm room floor. Three hours previous to this he was at a party and a girl wanted to fuck him. He tried to make a move but then the girl's brother came out and said that if he touched her he would fuck him up. It was then at that point, drunk out of his mind that he decided to drive to my college and visit me. I see Tristin in my dorm hall and I challenge him to a fight. We set it up so that we only do body shots, and we have two judges who will watch the fight and see who wins. He immediately charges after me and has his arms around my waist. I am confused as to why he doesn't throw any punches and so I start punching him in his rib cage. I don't land any hard blows because I want it to be a fair fight and with him not hitting me in any way I think that it would be to one-sided if I punched as hard as I could. The judges of the fight say that the fight was a draw.

I sink another cup in a game of beer pong, and Brad and I give each other high fives. We have sunk seven out of ten of our opponent's cups without them even having a turn yet. Our goal: to go ten cups and not even allow our opponents the chance to have a turn. We fail to reach our goal but are still happy to win. Sitting on the couch is Miranda, who Brad likes. When we are black out drunk, we break into his apartment complex's swimming pool and go for a swim. I get back and see Miranda sitting on the carpet, with a shirt on, but no bottom. No pants, no underwear, nothing. I laugh at this, but I am not sure what Brad thinks.[4]

As a I walk around campus at twelve at night, smoking cigarettes and buzzing from some alcohol shots, I decide that I will break into Folsom Field. I easily climb the gate and I walk out onto the bleachers. I sit in the stands chain smoking, and I walk around the whole stadium, keeping watch to see that I go unnoticed. I do go unnoticed and feel a sense of satisfaction that I broke the rules and got away with it.

I walk up to a girl smoking by a door with a friend and ask, "Is this Scott's house?" "I don't know. Just go in and have fun" she responds. I approach the situation the same as I approached the last 16 times I have done this. Get in, consume as much alcohol as possible without being noticed, and get out. I am getting to now be a pro at this, but when a guy asks me who the hell I am, I respond, "Is this Scott's house?" he tells me he doesn't know anyone named Scott. "You need to leave immediately" he says and I comply.[5]

Aaron walks up to a tree in the Quad and sees a raccoon that has just climbed up to the top. He decides that he will climb up the tree and try and get close to the raccoon, close enough perhaps, so that he can blow smoke rings around its head. He gets to the middle of the tree and the raccoon starts hissing at him. I laugh and tell him to keep getting closer to it, but he thinks it will just piss it off more and attack him so he climbs back down.

Having just consumed six shots in ten minutes, I tell Charlie and Benjamin that I want to go somewhere else. I piss some crazy bitch off and she tells me I need to leave her house immediately. Before I close the door behind me, I see that the door is covered with a brown blanket, and I will be damned if some crazy bitch thinks that she can just kick me out of her house and not remember me in some way. I rip the blanket off the door and start running down the sidewalk with Charlie and Benjamin running after me. We get to a part of campus that has a long staircase leading up to a pole that extends about three feet from the building. I want to show my stolen prize to the world so I tie the blanket to the end of the pole and let it drape down. At least two to three weeks after that, the blanket is still there. The only thing sweeter than this would be if the girl saw it and said to herself, "that looks a lot like the brown blanket that went missing from my door."[6]

I talk to a friend, "Calvin" on Facebook and he tells me a funny story: my ex-girlfriend got caught having sex with someone who she teaches tennis to. I think this is funny and so I decide to call her up. "No, I didn't do that!" "Why would he make that up?" "Because he is a guy. Guy's lie." I tell her that I don't care, I that I just think it is really funny. Once I hang up on her, I contemplate stealing a chair from a fraternity house that we were in and bringing it back to my dorm room as a prize. I don't do it, but I tell my friends that I did.

I self-reflect about all the lies that I told to people to get them to think more highly of me. I tell the story of when I shit in my dorm hall to some people at a party and they interrupt me, saying, "Tucker Max! That's Tucker Max!" to which I respond, "I'm not Tucker Max! I'm Psychotic Fucking Logician!" I should have changed the part where Tucker's feet kick shit up onto the walls with a more original version like, "I ran through my dorm hall to get to the bathroom, but I trip and hit the wall, and I lose control of all my bodily functions, causing me to shit on the wall and puke violently on the floor."

My friends want me to come to a coffee shop tonight for open mike night. When it is my turn to go on I tell them a story about how I went to a nude beach in France when I was twelve with my cousin and grandparents. Everyone laughs and thinks it is the funniest story they have ever heard. I am pleased, considering that I came up with it in about ten minutes. The next week I get nervous because I don't have a funny story to tell to people, so I just tell my friends that I won't go up. Emma goes up and tells everyone that I have a funny story to tell. Dammit. I tell the story about when I ran my face into a doorknob, giving me a black eye. I laugh, but nobody else does. Depressed, I never go back to the coffee shop again.[7]

I decide that I need to get my confidence up and develop more of an "I don't give a fuck attitude" about how I see the world. I tell Aaron that I will go into the sauna in the men's bathroom in the rec center, completely naked and sit in it for a while. He thinks this is funny and decides to join me. I get into the sauna, and nobody says anything. Before this, I had seen lots of people, mostly older men, go into the sauna wearing nothing, so I figure this is not that unusual. Aaron comes in a minute later, causing one guy to say, "Jesus guys, what's up with not wearing any clothes?" I leave before I start to sweat and have a sweat print of my ass on the sauna benches.

Josh from high school comes to visit me and Aaron and he tells me that he has perfected, "The Secret". I ask him if it is anything like the "I don't give a fuck attitude" and he responds, "Yeah, it's a lot like that." We get some acid from a drug dealer who I have named in my phone as, "Dave Acid". We each take a hit and it doesn't kick in ever for me, and it takes few hours for Josh. We follow Aaron into a friend's dorm hall, and Aaron, right after finishing a candy bar, throws the wrapper into the air and says, "I don't give a fuck!" to which Josh responds, "Yeah…that's not the secret." I think this is funny. Aaron's friend has just gotten accepted into a fraternity. The same fraternity that I got rejected from. All three of us give him shit about being in a fraternity and how gay it is, and he just sits there, saying nothing. I feel bad, saying I didn't mean it but this gives him no encouragement.[8]

I see a rubber string strapped around my arm and a guy holding a needle, injecting something into it. I wake up from my temporary black out state to remember that I had taken shrooms mixed with chocolate that Aaron gave me for my birthday. He claims that I really did do heroin and that the guy hooked me up with some because it was my birthday. I intricately describe how it took place, and one of the guys who gave me the heroin told me to listen to a CD that he had called a, "visualized haircut", which gave you the sensation of getting your haircut, without actually doing it. The CD begins and I agree with everything that the person tells me. A loud laughing sound then becomes apparent to me and I see the entire room go up in flames. I see Aaron's head on fire, and when it goes out, his hair and head look like coals that still have red flames on it. When my perception returns to normal, I see that everyone in the room is laughing. Aaron asks me, "what did that Devil guy say to you?" because apparently that is what the visualized haircut made me think.[9]

As I walk towards Donnie's house to chill, I begin to question my existence. So, I say, "Devil if you are real and it turns out that Christianity is correct, then I give you permission to take control of my body in exchange for everything that I have ever wanted." I immediately begin to feel shitty about what I just did, but just shrugged it off. I have paranoia about this, and I came to believe three things that were made on top of the deal I made with the Devil. If it were ever the case that I, "ever injected heroin, did DMT, or married Mia" then he could have control of my body in exchange for me living 10,000 trillion years doing whatever I wanted. In my state of believing that I had just injected heroin, I believed that the deal was now up. I became docile and accepted my fate, believing that when I went to sleep that night, I would have a dream that felt to me like 10,000 trillion years, and then when I wake up I would be controlled or maybe be in hell. I wake up and find that nothing has happened. I am neither happy nor sad. I take an Adderall and study for my history test which I get an A- on. This makes me happy. I text Aaron and he tells me that I was just hallucinating that I took the heroin. This makes me angry. Reminiscing about the earlier part of the night after eating the chocolate shrooms, I am sitting under a tree with Aaron and someone else smoking pot out of a bong. There are four or five people covered in blue painting and wearing piercings and jewelry that sit alongside us. Aaron and the other person don't see them, but I do.

I stare off into Brad's room as he and Rick sit in the other room watching TV. A hand reaches forward towards me extending its entire arm. I see a person wearing blue painting all over him with jewelry, further extending his arm towards me as to say, "Take my hand." I am filled with anxiety over the situation so I talk to Brad and Rick and tell them that I could go far away into a different universe right now if I wanted to. "What should I do?" "Do whatever you want. That is so sick." I go back into the room but the arm holding the blue guy in its hand was gone. "LSD is a crazy drug" I think to myself as I further try and induce a trip. Maybe the guy was a Mayan person who was trying to guide me into a trip, or maybe I was just an acid head hallucinating his balls off.[10]

My roommate wakes me up and I am sitting in a chair looking up at the ceiling. A moment earlier I was in another realm with unicorns and other crazy mystical objects around me enveloping my perception like a merry go round. I am a little upset that he woke me up from such a peaceful state but, I decide it's all good and take another hit from his vaporizer, trying to bring about another psychedelic state while the Robotussin is still in my system.[11]

I am facing a man in a black leather jacket, and he is holding my medical marijuana papers in his hand. "I've seen this paperwork before." "What..." "Not just this medical paperwork but this exact copy, same name, same doctor, same everything." I don't know what to say but what I think is, "you are either a fucking moron or really shitty at your job." I am not sure if the punishment is more severe or not if you call police officers profane names or flip them off, but I better not risk it. My ninth-grade doubles tennis partner comes walking in the door, which turned out to be the exact same CU security officer that busted me twenty minutes earlier. I contemplate asking him how he was able to get a respectable job after being charged with criminal charges in high school for sporting pictures of guns on his Myspace page, but I think the answer would just make me have less respect for the way the justice system operates in society. Although I could see in my tennis partner's eyes after he told me to take out the pot he had found in my desk drawer, that he was shocked and felt a relatively decent amount of sympathy for me when he realized who I was. If only he remembered me twenty seconds ago, this whole situation would have been a lot less fucked up.[12]

I dial my phone for Max, who I hadn't seen since last semester. He gives me directions to his house, and I try to coherently tell him that I will be there soon. I make some friends along the walk to his house, who I ensure will have a fun time at a sick party if they follow me. A group of five, six or seven people follow me to Max's door. "Yo Max, what's up bro! I got some people with me who wanna party with us". It would be a lie to say that Max was not used to this type of behavior from me, seeing that I spent nine months as his roommate when we were freshman. "Sorry, there's no party, you can't come in." This disappointed the people who I had led to his house, but I was happy because I was about to smoke weed with the master himself. We smoke out of his bong and I get the spins. I run over to his kitchen sink and begin to puke inside of it. "Psychotic Logician! Goddammit!" I wake up the next morning on his couch, with one of his bitchy roommates yelling in my ear that I am a fucking asshole. I call Max an hour later, asking if I was with him last night, and that I had not known where I had woken up to justify why I had lost my shit earlier in the night.[13]

Me, Victoria, and Donald are inside a building's stairwell with a window looking over the Quad. There are thousands of people crowded within it and the time is nearing four o'clock. We wonder why suddenly there is a new wave of people coming into the quad in such large groups, but do not wonder why they are people there in the first place. A professor walks by us as Donald says, "Is there a concert going on?" to which the professor stops and gives us a look like we are the dumbest people she has come across in a while. "It's 4/20" she says and walks away. We laugh because she didn't know what we were really referring to. We make our way down to the center of the quad and meet up with Audrey. I remember the last time I saw her when we tried to smoke weed out of her pipe, but she broke it as she was loading it. "I just broke my pipe. I can't do this." Me and four of my friends looked at each other with a kind of, "that fucking sucks for all of us" look and showed our way out of her house. I am on drug tests at the time and so I must settle for smoking, "spice" instead. I hear that spice is what the football players and other athletes who get drug tested smoke, and so I thought that it must be better than not smoking anything. I empty one of my cigarettes of the tobacco and load the spice in it. The time hit's 4:20pm and I see everyone in the crowd hit their pipes and pieces at the same time, making the whole area very silent for about four to five seconds. People begin to cheer, and a huge cloud of smoke rises slowly above the entire quad. I smoke my spice cigarette joint and feel envious of the people that were smoking real weed. In about ten to fifteen minutes people begin to make their way out of the quad and disperse around the campus and other parts of it. I see a cop wearing sunglasses standing with his back against a stone wall that leads to "The Hill". "Everyone is so calm. Makes you wonder why they even need cops." Victoria said to which I agreed.[15]

I become very irritated when I see a cop put his lights on behind me. What the fuck could this be about? My car is wrecked to shit on the outside. It doesn't have any side mirrors, the back passenger side light is cracked, my driver's side door is crunched in, and there is a piece of metal sticking out like a wing from the side of the passenger door. I role down my window as far as my crunched door will allow me to as the officer approaches my car. "I need to see your license please" he said, "we got a complaint from someone yesterday that you were urinating in public, and we are going to write you a court subpoena." "Oh." I sat there contemplating my thoughts about how the fuck I am going to explain this to my parents, and just dreaded the utter bullshit that I would have to go through in getting caught up in the legal process again. The officer returned a few minutes later and said, "I don't have the proper paperwork to give you a court order so you should consider yourself lucky. Next time don't urinate in public." "Ok, will do." Grateful that I lucked out with this situation, I now had the Adderall euphoria to look forward to. Note to self: next time don't drunk drive to your Adderall dealers house and piss in the parking lot and then return the next day to the exact same spot to get some more. Central City cops are obviously very bored, seeing as that they had the parking lot staked out the entire day, waiting for when I came back.[15]

"Go for it" Aaron said to Abe as he is about to perform a stunt. I see him standing on a ledge at the top of some stairs of a university building. About three to four feet away is a small deck with iron bars attached to it. Abe is a master at doing stunts and this should be cake for him. He jumps from the stairs to the deck and makes it. Halfway done, he still needs to jump from the deck back to the stairs because it is about a ten-to-twelve-foot drop from the deck to the ground. "You got this" I say as he tries to turn himself around to face the stairs from which he came. I see him jump back and make it without incident. "Let's find some more places to fuck around on, this is way too easy."

I am disappointed that the show is censored. If it wasn't, this would be one of my first times seeing a girl naked on a screen in front of me. Eddie's parents are asleep upstairs, and it is our Friday or Saturday night ritual to watch "Howard Stern" on the E! Channel. I have a blanket over me as Eddie and I begin to masturbate to the show. No Kleenex needed, I have not yet developed to the point that anything comes out once I finish.

I look out the window and see lights shining onto something. It looks like the pyramids in Egypt, and for a second, I think they are. I find out later that this is "Red Rocks Amphitheater". Donnie, Brad, and I arrive at what looks like an open space, roughly the size of a football field. Donnie is driving and we start doing donuts in what is actually a gravel parking lot. The pipe gets passed to me and I take a hit. I am higher than I have ever been before in my life. We drive along a one lane road surrounded by brightly lit buildings on both sides of us. Twenty minutes later we drive by the same place again. This reminds me of a French neighborhood that I had seen before when I went to France when I was 12. We arrive back at Brad's house three hours and one hundred miles later.[16]

I am semi freaking out. I have never driven high, and I am not exactly sure how to get back to my house from where I am. Rick draws me a map on a paper towel and I figure this is good enough. Blitzed out of my mind, I begin the journey. I will later tell Rick that once I left his house it felt like only a second has passed from the time I left his house, to the time I got home. As cool as this sounds, it is not true. I am sitting at a green light. I regain my awareness of the present moment and begin to drive. I am extremely paranoid that I will get pulled over, but I was assured by the other people at the party that if you don't have any weed on you, the cops can't do anything. Making my way up the canyon I try my hardest to stay focused. I reach my house, unscathed with the attitude that I will never drive high again.[17]

I never thought watching Barney would be so entertaining. I am high as a kite and having a very fun time. The next thing on the agenda for the night: watch a bunch of Disney movies, baked out of my mind. Life is good.[18]

"Fuck that guy!" I want to go back and kick his ass, but the bartender might call the police. Twenty seconds ago she was pushing me out the door, one of only a few frames I have of the night, due to my black out drunkenness. I just bought shots for the whole table and I see a cute girl playing an arcade game in the corner of the restaurant. I buy her a shot of Jagger and she drinks it, even though she might be under 21. The stories I tell the group of people I am with revolve around me being in a mental institution and the crazy shit I saw. That is, this experience of being in a mental institution, that never actually took place. "Could we have three more shots of Wild Turkey?" I ask one of the bartenders. She agrees, but before she pours the shots the other bartender cuts us off. "You already have a huge bill, and you are very drunk." I try and persuade her, but she doesn't budge. She hands me the bill: $120. I have $135 in my pocket, thanks to the big night I had yesterday waiting tables. As I pay the bill a man sitting at the bar begins to get pissed off at me. I am confused. What exactly did I just do or say that is pissing this guy off? I watch him get out of his seat and approach me with the intention of kicking my ass. I later learn that he is the boyfriend of a girl who I used to work with at this same bar. Questioning him about it a few years later, the man still remembers who I am and that he wanted to fight me. Edwin and Carl look on and laugh as they examine the situation I am in. A random guy trying to pick a fight with me, the bartender yelling at me to get the hell out of here, and me, attempting to control the situation by asking exactly what the fuck I did to piss this guy off. "He said that you were being disrespectful to the bartender" Edwin tells me. "What the fuck?" I think to myself. I gave them all the money I had. $120 for the bill and the other $15 I had for a tip. I wanted to leave more but I am poor at the current moment. Carl attempts to calm me down, saying it's not a big deal and to forget about it. I walk with Edwin and Carl back to Edwin's house with my main intention: get blitzed out of my skull and forget all about this situation. I do just that.[19]

Not feeling much, I ask my brother what exactly alcohol is supposed to do to you. I have just had four shots of whiskey, diluted in grape soda, and don't exactly know what to expect from this substance. Dwayne begins puking in the sink. My brother and I laugh at this. Two of my brother's other friends have just left, right after indulging in a few drinks and a couple of bowls of weed. "I don't really feel anything" I say. "You are standing on a chair right now, you are drunk" he responds. I see he has a point. The first time you drink is a lot like the first time you smoke bud. You don't recognize the high at first, but when people start telling you all the irregularities of your sober self, then it kicks into your head that the substance is having somewhat of an effect on you. It is important that we don't fuck around too much. My brother and I are housesitting for a couple of my parent's friends and if they find out that we are drinking and smoking pot in their house, they will be a little more than pissed. A few hours earlier I am sitting in what is essentially an interrogation. I sit facing five other people who begin questioning me about my entire stint in the Boy Scouts. I try my best to answer their questions, 95% of my answers being bullshit. "Do you have any personal hero's" one interrogator asks. I think for a moment, I had been warned that this question would be asked and instead of going with my honest answer, mainly being, "No", I instead answer with, "The soldiers in the military." They like this answer and I pass the test. At 15, I am now officially an Eagle Scout, and I am about to house sit with my brother and drink for the first time in my life.

What makes no sense to me is why the fuck these goddamn professors don't know what the fuck I am talking about. To me it is so blatantly obvious but to them and the rest of the world it comes across as "obscure". Stephen Hawking called Immanuel Kant's, "Critique of Pure Reason", obscure, but that doesn't change the fact that it is still a work of genius. A few days earlier I had just turned in a revolutionary paper that I believe has answered a major problem of philosophy. I never use the word, "prove" in the paper, but instead write that the problem has been, "demonstrably shown to be true". My professor isn't convinced and so approaches the rest of the class about it. I never understood what compels teachers to single out a student and make an example of them to the rest of the class. Yes, they do not mention the students name to the class, and instead say, "this student wrote…", but when the student who actually wrote what the professor is talking about to the rest of the class realizes that the professor is talking about him, this makes him the only person in the class who completely understands what the professor is actually talking about. The rest of the students in the class may have a laugh at the expense of the anonymous person being referred to by the teacher, and the teacher thinks this is ok, just as long as the person remains anonymous. "So, this student believes that he can "prove it." And after showing this student's work to other professors who agree with me that this paper is just, "typical undergraduate work", what advice would you give to this person who believes he has proved something?" I know who the professor is referring to, but nobody else does which apparently justifies the singling out of someone to prove a point to the other people in the class. Caught up in my own thoughts, I don't listen to the advice that the other students give. It is the last week of the semester and I believe I have come up with a brilliant response to the professor's willingness to, not only use me as an example to prove a point to the class (apparently the professor thinking me not proving a point in my paper, provided a way in which he could prove a point to the class), but also show that I really did prove something in my paper. My final paper is on the topic, "how do you resolve a disagreement between people and get them to agree on what is true?" A few days earlier, we had a class discussion on the topic, and I decided to share my view with the class. "I think, ultimately, if both people are truly convinced that something is true, even if they disagree, then they are both right", I propose to the class. Immediately another student raises his hand and says, "It is absolutely not true that two people can both be right when they hold contradictory viewpoints." The professor laughs at this, obviously agreeing with him. I now had my opportunity to state exactly what I thought about the subject. A few days after the due date, I am still working on the essay, trying to perfect what I want to say. Obviously waiting in anticipation to read how I could possibly justify such an irrational position, the professor email's me asking for me to turn in the paper. I title the paper, "Proof that

Psychotic Logician has no idea what he is talking about", the joke being, if I did indeed prove my point in the paper, then I proved something, and if I didn't, then I still proved something. He never responds.[20]

I ponder at the comments left by the professor on my "Minority Report and Free Will" paper, which, again, I feel like I have solved a major problem in philosophy. What grabs my attention is not the comments that he wrote, but rather that it says, "A" on the paper, lightly scribbled out, and replaced with, "B". I later talk to him about this, and he looks just as confused as I am, but says nothing. I wonder about the first time I have elicited this type of reaction from my college professors. I am sitting in a lecture in my "Philosophy of Science" class, when the professor, to his credit, instead of using me as an example to show how ridiculous a thing someone could actually write to try and pass off as truth, asks the class, "How many of you believe that science will ever provide certainty of truth?" I wish to remain anonymous, so I sit there, never raising my hand, observing the reactions of the rest of the class. Nobody raises their hand. "I don't think science will ever provide certainty. I don't think anyone in this class does...well actually one person did" the professor says. I like this because instead of attempting to disprove my proof like the other professor did, he merely was pointing out a view that someone possessed that very well could be as reasonable as the opposite of it. His comment on my final paper of the semester was, "I don't think we can change the world". I like this because it shows that he possesses a viewpoint like I do, and that if it indeed is the case that we can change the world, then my viewpoint, rather than something to be scoffed at, is something that is quite insightful.[21]

Providing insight is something that I made my intention to do in the philosophy classes that I took in college. It was either hit or miss. If you could splice together Plato's intellect, and Wittgenstein's logical deduction ability, the result would be my philosophical abstraction. In my proper mind state, I could tap into the sixth sense ability to perceive the immaterial. My goal: to provide a complete theory of how it is possible to gain absolute irrefutable knowledge. I am sitting in class and the professor claims that there is no way to know for sure that you are not a brain in a vat, or in the matrix, or something of that sort. I am not convinced. The paper is supposed to be five pages, single spaced, defending one of four epistemological positions, those being, skepticism, foundationalism, coherentism, or infinitism. Apparently only one of these four is correct. The flaw: if it is true that only one of these four can be true, then doesn't that itself entail that, A) skepticism is the only one that can be completely refuted, because the fact that someone is skeptical about something, itself show that they possess knowledge of something, and B) the other three have to all be completely contradictory to each other, because if they were in some way able to be reconciled, then that would provide a framework where all four of these viewpoints can be shown to be unified together, and produce knowledge. I ponder how interesting of a solution this might be. However, in order to do this, I must first show that each one of these viewpoints, by themselves, is wrong, and therefore only correct when viewed in relation to one another. I begin to get a glimpse of how this is possible: a theory of knowledge which has an infinite number of justifications that all cohere together and has a foundation. Skepticism fits into this theory through the understanding that even if you doubt something to the point that you cannot doubt it anymore, you are obeying the theory because the reasoning behind your doubt stems from this theory's basic framework. I like this. I write a 16-page, single spaced essay in which I examine this abstract subject and turn it in a week late. I am irritated and impatient because the professor takes so long to respond. Two to three weeks later, I receive an email back from him in which he says, "I stopped reading this halfway through…" Goddammit. I had finished the essay with, "therefore, you can know for certain that you are not a brain in a vat." Even though he skipped half the essay, he did write his comments at the end of the essay, and so, I think, must have looked at this part. If he did see it, he obviously didn't care.[22]

I catch a break with an essay I write in my "Major Social Theories" course. I put forth an argument showing that Plato's theory of justice stems from its accordance with the "Form of the Good", and even include a brief symbolic logic deduction, showing why this is the case. I think it is funny that the professor didn't understand the symbolic logic part, but I am even more pleased that she liked what I wrote so much. She responds with, "This is every bit of what I expect from one of my students to write. A+" An A+, of course, not being an actual grade that colleges use, but I was happy to see that she went out of her way to tell me how much she liked it.[23]

I am now in a shitty state. I have run out of Adderall and my Thomas Aquinas class essay is already a few days late. A few weeks earlier I had written my first draft, expounding on Aquinas's "Second Proof" of God's existence. I show how a first cause can and does occur in the universe. The professor seems to sympathize with this viewpoint and writes back to me, "this can actually be quite good." Unfortunately, I have no amphetamine inspiration that allows me to find the internal discipline required to reread the first draft, make a few changes, and turn it in. Instead, I opt to go with a shorter essay I wrote a few days earlier, while I was on the last bit of Adderall I possessed. I see the paper as a brilliant attempt to show how through a philosophical interpretation of quantum physics, one can come to understand how a first cause is possible, and that God, indeed, does exist. The professor doesn't see it this way. "This is a very obscure essay" he comments back to me and gives me a B- for the essay. Well, fuck me. If he can't see how much I dumbed down the paper to put it in the most basic terms possible, then I guess what I consider to be an easy to follow, purely logical deductive valid argument, is considered to be a bunch of horseshit by someone with a PhD.

When reading some of the papers that were assigned in my philosophy classes, I laugh at the complete unoriginality and uninspiring/not insightful ideas that are proposed by philosophers with PhD's. I grow angry when my beautifully abstract papers are seen as meaningless to "philosophers" (apparently if you have a PhD then that automatically makes you a philosopher). So, I then decide to move onto something a little more concrete and definite in its logic, that being, mathematics. I major in philosophy and mathematics at the same time, and figure if my insights do not receive notice in philosophy, then perhaps they will in mathematics. More importantly, I figure, if I have Adderall, I can make a killing. Back in my days of tripping balls, I would attain philosophical perceptions that can closely be related to mathematics. I later found out, upon reflection, that all mathematics is philosophy, but not all philosophy is mathematics. Therefore, the more philosophical intuitions I receive, the more it will begin to encompass all mathematical knowledge. For example, if you want to understand the foundations of mathematics, this closely relates to the metaphysics of wholes and parts and how they relate. My goal: to reach an understanding of mathematics that is just as certain and irrefutable as Descartes, "I think, therefore I am", which I had heard before, but never truly understood what it meant until I tripped acid for the second or third time. Staying awake for five straight days, I begin to ponder how it is possible to find an all-encompassing foundation for mathematics. I read Bertrand Russell's "Introduction to Mathematical Philosophy" in which he states that there could exist a logical understanding of mathematics, through which one could come to know sound inferences, without knowing a single word of the mathematical vocabulary. I agree. At this time, being awake for that long of a time, rather than making me hallucinate like a mother fucker, makes me more capable of tapping into my abstract intellect. I write down my ideas until I reach a fundamental understanding: a central concept through which, by a single deduction from it, any mathematical knowledge can be deduced. However, I fuck up. Instead of deducing major mathematical breakthroughs, I instead use this time to become familiar with the vocabulary that I was not aware of before (which were taught in my mathematics class at the time, but I slacked off and didn't really know any of the vocab at all). I lose sight of the concept two hours later. I will be damned, however, if I do not rededicate myself to achieving a similar understanding in the future.[24]

The time for college finals arrive and I decide to cram for them within a week, nonstop. I have used up all my Adderall, but I luck out when Eddie gives me his two-month supply of Ritalin, that his psychiatrist prescribed to him as test doses. By the fifth day, I have blown through all but a weeks' worth. However, I am now in a position where I set out to go. I see a concept that I understand through the P vs NP problem. The mathematics book I am studying from says something like the following: "the thing about this problem is that it should not even be that hard to solve." That is what is important to know about abstracting to a logical foundation for all mathematics, mainly, that it is very simple. I look up information on the "Riemann Hypothesis", and completely understand it. I fully grasp its meaning, in spite of the fact that I possess no knowledge of any of the high up complex mathematics required in order to solve it. It is 8:50am and my discrete mathematics final begins at 10:00am, so, unfortunately, I have to abandon my search into gaining more knowledge of difficult mathematical problems. Since I have been awake for five days with no sleep, I forget all my important deductions, and receive a D in the class. This makes me very disappointed. I do, however, retain a very important understanding: there is the potential that I might be God.

I decide to skip the 4/20 festivities and instead seclude myself in the library reading Hegel. It speaks to me. Everything he writes about somehow pertains to exactly what I am experiencing. And what am I experiencing? I intuit that there are two sides to my observation of reality, one thesis, and one antithesis. In the previous week or so I started to become more aware of something that was going on around me, but never thought it could actually be a description pertaining exactly to me. I come to the following understanding: the thesis side of me is the Jesus, or "Christ" consciousness; the antithesis side of me is the Satan, or "Antichrist" consciousness. As I sit in the library, Hegel talks me through exactly what is occurring within my mind. The two consciousness's begin to transcend to higher and higher levels, until they are finally fully developed and set within the perception of my mind. In the library, the Antichrist consciousness becomes fully developed. As I walk to my friend's house to smoke some weed, I hear comments from the people that I pass along the sidewalk. "Look at this fag" one said, and "This guy is totally gay" another thought. Looking back, I believe this to somehow pertain to the Antichrist being gay/having "no regard for the desire of women." I, however, still had regard for the desire of women. I am now at my friend's house, and we smoke a bowl. This is just what needed to happen for the Christ consciousness to become fully developed. "This may sound crazy to you" I say to my friend, "but we have never met before." He is freaked out by this, so he goes into his room and never comes out. I never see him again. I see in my perception people surrounding me. "What the fuck is going on?" The people in my head are confused as to why I cursed/how I cursed. Just like how I retained my heterosexuality in reference to the Antichrist consciousness, I retained my ability to blaspheme in reference to the Christ consciousness. This was a sign for things to come.[25]

"Little to be known to anyone at this time, but there exists a third consciousness" I write on a piece of paper. But who/what is this third consciousness? I learn that this is the synthesis of the thesis and antithesis consciousness's. This synthesis being me, Psychotic Logician. I learn more about how this third consciousness develops. The more I am able to unite my understanding of the two contradictory perceptions together, the more I become fully aware of who I truly am. Once I reach the perception that I know and am certainly and inconceivably aware that I am God, then I have then completely unified the two consciousness's together, to fully attain the complete third consciousness. I laugh at the ridiculousness of the situation and realize that the reality of the situation is a complete joke. Everyone in the world is convinced of something that happens to be complete bullshit, mainly, that I am either one consciousness or the other, and certainly not both together. "Now he is trying to say that there is a third consciousness" I hear one person stating. Upon reflection, I see that what this person was completely ignorant of what was the following understanding: First, if it turns out that I am just bullshitting everyone and making the third consciousness's existence up, then this would be evidence that I am the Antichrist consciousness, trying to deceive everyone. Hence, why wouldn't everyone just think I am the Antichrist consciousness? Second, if it turns out that I am not bullshitting everyone and not making the third consciousness's existence up, then this would be evidence that I am the Christ consciousness. Third, and finally, the Christ consciousness is claiming something to be true, just as the Antichrist consciousness is claiming something to be true, the only difference is the intention, the Christ to speak truth, and the Antichrist to speak false. However, if it turns out that I am not the third consciousness, then the Christ consciousness would be false, and the Antichrist consciousness would be true, because it would be the Christ consciousness that was claiming something to be true that was actually false, and the Antichrist consciousness that was claiming something to be false that was actually true. If, however, it turns out that I am the third consciousness, then what the Christ consciousness would be claiming would be true, and the Antichrist consciousness would be claiming something that is true. Hence, the $3^{rd}$ mind is true, because both the thesis and antithesis have set up their intentions to accord with truth, such that if the $3^{rd}$ mind did not exist, it would be the Christ consciousness that was deceiving, and hence, be the Antichrist consciousness, and the Antichrist consciousness that was not deceiving, and hence, be the Christ consciousness. If the $3^{rd}$ mind did exist, it would be the Christ consciousness that was not deceiving, and the Antichrist consciousness that was not deceiving either. Therefore, the $3^{rd}$ mind exists, because there only exists one way in which the Christ and Antichrist consciousness's would be equivalent to each other, mainly, that they are both the same if it doesn't exist, and are both the same if it does exist. Hence, their intentions are the same in reference to the existence or nonexistence of the third mind.

I nonchalantly go about my business in reference to the games that people play with me. People make a federal case out of me getting a haircut. I take this to mean that if I keep my hair long, like Jesus had long hair, then I am more likely to be the Christ consciousness, and if I cut my hair short, I am more likely to be the Antichrist consciousness. Observing how people act towards me, I understand that they are basically there to put forth suggestions to my mind that will cause me to think in a certain way about one consciousness versus another. A woman comes into the restaurant where I work and puts up three or four crosses around the dining room. My paranoia becomes even more like it represents reality when I hear on the radio, "Everyone, are you prepared for the rapture?"[26] I am depressed why people just can't get along and must always be so divided against each other. Thinking back to how my ideas of how two opposing sides to an argument can both be correct, was mocked in my college classes, I come to think that this has something to do with the fact that people don't think it is possible for there to exist a unified third perception, or in basic terms, an agreement. Even more so, I find it very upsetting why people act as puppets to the authorities who they believe are in charge, without understanding that they themselves can make a difference and through their own free will, change how something appears to be. For example, if people really were told that I contained two consciousness's that were at odds with one another and that I was to really only become one of them, all that people would need to do in order to refute this, would simply be to act in a way that doesn't accord with what they are being told. If Heaven exists, and Hell exists, then why would people act in a way such that it would reinforce Hell's existence? Why not do everything in their power to bring about a future that would attempt to try and bring about Hell's nonexistence? In this respect, acting in accordance with the very thing that something highly negative predicates its existence upon, seems highly irrational.

Fearing that I may be a pawn being used to accomplish the desires of an authority figure or figures, I decide that two can play at this game. What becomes blatantly obvious to me is that the Christ side believers really don't give a fuck about the Antichrist side believers and vice versa. I, however, do give a fuck about everyone and want reality to be a representation of something more sympathetic and compassionate for all differing sides to a disagreement. To those who say that what is nice and good is not always true, I say, "then you are essentially saying that truth is not necessarily always good, and has an aspect of it that is bad? If negativity is a part of truth, then why the fuck would anyone want to come to know the truth?" To say that evil has a definite existence that will always reside within the goodness of truth, is to suppose that the goodness of truth really isn't really as good as it is claiming to be. I wonder why anyone would wish negativity onto another person. If seeing something evil happen to something or someone in the world brings another person feelings of goodness, then the person who derives positivity from this is merely manipulating the perfection of truth to accord with an egocentric attitude that essentially says, "I'm right and get to reap the rewards; you are wrong and get to reap the punishment; good for me, sucks for you." Notice that in this type of attitude, no feelings of sorrow, remorse, or sympathy exists between the person who ends up on the high end of the totem pole, towards the person on the low end.[27]

Dozing in and out, I sit on my couch as the suboxone begins to take effect. I had gotten this drug from Donald, and it is supposedly what they give to heroin addicts to help them taper off the drug. You could give this stuff to some tweeker after smoking fifteen hits of crystal meth and it would knock them on their ass within an hour. It's not just the pleasant feeling of dozing off into a peaceful sleep that is the best part of it, rather it is the mellow, mood brightening, barely noticeable euphoria that creates the setting for you to fall into and experience the twelve to fifteen hours of nonexistent dream space that envelops your reality.

I sit around a table with four of my friends, passing a pipe between us. Donnie gets the idea of wanting to bring his high to a greater level. He leaves temporarily and comes back holding in his hand a can. I watch as he takes a hit from the can and passes it to me. It reads, "Air Dust Cleaner" on it and I decide to try it out.[28]

I try ephedrine for the first time, and it hits me hard. 75mg and it kicks in within 15 minutes. I take another 75mg and masturbate before I go into work. It feels good. Different than any other stimulant I have ever tried. I am at work, and I am hearing voices up the shit. I tell myself that I can disprove the Bible if it ever came to a time when the Christian God ever told me to bow to him. Just don't bow and the Bible is false. I take another 75mg on my lunch break and go back to work rolling tits. I think this might be the best stimulant I have ever taken. Good euphoria and concentration. However, one problem: I start hallucinating bad. I see that the bar codes on the aisle that I am working on change every time I look at them. The voices tell me that I am possessed even though I still retain my free will, despite hallucinating hardcore. I begin to freak out that I might be wrong about how I see reality. The voices tell me that I am the Antichrist consciousness. I am displeased. It gets to a point where I think (incorrectly) that there is only one possibility as to the relation that I stand in to truth. This mainly being, that you can either side with the Antichrist or Christ sides. The Jesus in my mind tells me that I must call out to the entire store that he is God, lord and savior. If I yell this to the store then that is equivalent to me bowing to him, and if I don't do it, then I am going to hell. Upon reflection, I think that the Jesus in my head is highly irrational. I yell out to the store, "Jesus Christ is lord and savior and if you want to be with him then call out to him." Why is the Jesus in my head so out of touch with how reality is, not just in reference to existence as a whole, but also in reference to the qualities of the true Jesus? After I shout this out to the store he tells me that everything that I do is to serve him. I get off work and begin to read the Bible. He tries to speak to me through what I am reading. I am reading Job because I want to gain more knowledge of how to best serve Jesus, even in spite of bad shit potentially happening to me. As I begin to read, I come across a point in the Bible in which the Father is disappointed with the Son (Jesus), and that I am somehow responsible for this separation. Through the Bible, it speaks to me in such a way that Jesus tells me I am a hypocrite. It tells me that I am no longer one with the Christian God anymore. It is at this point that I realize that I am not the hypocrite, but rather the person who claims to be Jesus in my mind is a hypocrite. He told me that everything I do from the time I metaphorically bowed to him is in service to him, and then an hour later somehow, I fucked this up. I now realize that the Jesus in my head is a liar. What's even more fucked up is that you can read the Bible in such a way that evil speaks to you through it. But if this is supposedly God's word then how is this possible? I am displeased. I think that if the Jesus in my head is the real Jesus, then the Bible does not even come close to be a representation of truth. The voices tell me that the Bible is true, even though, apparently, people reincarnate and live past lives through history. I think that if this is true, then that is a pretty big thing that the Bible doesn't mention.[29]

I look up on Facebook the girl who I have a crush on. It shows on her profile a half an inch by half an inch profile pictures of some of her friends. I see a girl wearing a red dress and I am intrigued. I click on the picture, and it takes me to the girl's profile. She is a brunette with what I can only describe as the most beautiful (at that point in my life) face I have ever seen. After that I no longer am interested in the girl who I had previously liked, but rather am now completely obsessed with the girl in the red dress. Every day after this I go to the girl's profile and peer into perfection. I see the girl's interests and other things about her that she has posted on her profile. I begin to base my existence, my entire purpose for living, on somehow completely revolving around this girl. I am happy. She gives me hope and a reason for living. She posts on her profile a new picture every week or two. I see a new aspect of her every time she does this. I see clearly that she is a princess, and I begin to equate being with her as the absolute pinnacle of what it means to be free. I think that I need to become the ultimate version of myself to even come close to being worthy of being with her. This, a few months later, will come to fuck me royally.[30]

My roommates leave the dorm room, and I am hanging out with a girl that I have no interest in whatsoever. I think that if I tell my roommates that I had sex with her then they will come to respect me more. As evidence that I fucked this girl, as I walk back to my dorm room, I begin to scratch my back, making scratch marks, which I will later tell my roommate that she did this to me while we were having sex. My roommate buys this, and I am content.

Tripping hard, I see in front of me a city with buildings. This city is being held by somebody's hand on the front dash of my roommate's car. He tells me that when he dies, he is 100% positive that he will go to heaven. This interests me. Either he has completely figured out what is equivalent to understanding absolute truth, or he is just pretending to be so convinced (or just honestly mistaken). I don't know what to think, but it fascinates me that someone could literally think to the core of their being that they know how reality is.

Meeting her at a friend's party, I am not sure how I started talking to her. I think if I would have gone through with the proposition she asked me, then this would have been equivalent to some prostitution to a certain degree. "If you drink your own cum then I will blow you" she says to me. The deal is that when I am about to cum, I will ejaculate in a cup and proceed to drink it in front of her. I get the idea that if I end up going through with this, I will just cum in her mouth and tell her that I fucked up. Whoring myself out through this situation just to have a decent looking chick blow me, I think it would be a degradation to my soul, from which I may not ever recover. She later tells me that she will not do this, and my first response is to tell her that the point is not that she would actually go through with this, but that she even considered to do it in the first place. If I did decide to just cum in her mouth, then she might file sexual assault charges against me, and this would piss me off.

Considering that she was kind of a freak for starters, I think that if I tell my friends an innocent lie, they will be impressed. "I will smoke with you sometime" is what I told my friends she said. They think this is a crazy thing for her to say but buy it. Although I made this up, I think that if I get back in contact with her, this may lead to a self-fulfilling prophecy. If porn stars like Ms. T might like to party, then I am correct about this.

I'm playing in a waiting room with the toys that they have for children. I am very happy. My parents are with me, and I do not really understand what is going on. A nurse comes into the waiting room, grabs me, and takes me away from my parents and my toys. This upsets me greatly. I scream as the nurse takes me away from the toys I was having fun with, and my parents. Still screaming, the nurse puts me on a bed and puts a hospital gas mask on me and I no longer remember anything. Getting your tonsils removed is a bitch of a procedure, especially when you are an innocent child. Around ten to fifteen years later a friend of mine's mother tells me that her son is getting his tonsils removed.

Mother: So how is it?
Me: It was really scary if I'm being honest.
Mother: Well, we certainly don't want to hear about that.
Me: I guess.
Mother: Tell my son how much ice cream they give you.
Me: They give you a lot, I think.[31]

I think back to the reason why I am sitting in this court room and awaiting my presence in front of the judge. The DA wants to have a meeting with me before it is my turn to stand in front of the judge.

DA: So how do you want to plead?
Me: I'm not sure. I don't even think that I did anything wrong.
DA: It says here that you threw your cigarette out the window, which the law considers to be littering and a fire hazard.
Me: But I didn't actually throw the cigarette out. I was just ashing it and while I did this the cigarette hit the window and made some sparks fly out the window.
DA: If you plead guilty, the best I can do for you is a couple hundred dollar fine.
Me: That sounds good, but I still don't think what I did was illegal.

I tell the cop when he pulls me over that I didn't throw the cigarette out and that it was just ash. He responds by telling me that if he sees any sparks fly out of the window, he will just assume that I did. Well, fuck me, I guess. I tried using this same logic when I appeared in front of the judge, but she, just like the other people in the law that I dealt with previously, didn't understand how the situation actually went down.

Judge: How do you plead?
Me: I'm not exactly sure how to plead, your honor. All I did was ash my cigarette out the window. I didn't throw it out and liter.
Judge: What exactly is the difference?
Me: Well, there actually is a big difference –
Judge: How do you plea, Mr. Logician?
Me: I guess I'm pleading guilty.

The fact that the judge didn't understand the difference between ashing your cigarette out the window and throwing your cigarette out the window, shows how little she knows about the case that she was presiding over. If the judge presiding over my case was a smoker, or who at least possessed a shred bit of knowledge regarding the difference between tobacco that has already been burned, and tobacco that is still in the process of being burned, I think my plea would have gotten a lot more sympathy.

I feel great. 50mg of Adderall with a low tolerance is like two hits of pot on your second time smoking. You know what to expect, and the fact that you have a better open-mindedness about the drug, makes the euphoria even greater. Just like you are smarter if you know a little about a lot, in comparison to a lot about a little, you get higher if you have a low tolerance to a little, than if you have a high tolerance to a lot. This makes me realize, which I put into practice, that if you have a low tolerance and take a lot of something, sure your tolerance will skyrocket, but until that time occurs, you will roll tits. I finish watching "Moulin Rouge" and drive into work. I see the snow blowing across the highway from the meadow, and I turn into the left lane. My problem: I am going roughly the speed limit and there is ice on the road. I begin to slide into the lanes of the cars going in the opposite direction. Nothing is going through my head, other than that this is a bad situation. I see a car swerve out of my way, and then I become anxious when my car turns horizontal to the upcoming traffic when I see that a van is coming right towards my driver side door. Wham! My cigarette falls out of my hand, and out of the window. I get out of my car to talk to the other driver and see that my entire driver side door is completely crunched in. I am now in the other driver's van. I see three things: First, I see that the van is completely fucked up in the front.

Second, I see a news station about sixty to seventy yards away parked on the side of the road. Third, I see an ambulance come to the scene of where my car and the van are. I am made aware that earlier that day, some person got in an accident at around the exact same area that I just did, and that person died. Apparently, that was the reason why the news station was present at that same place and time as when I just so happened to have gotten in an accident. The driver of the car, a woman who has two kids with her, takes down my insurance information and I luck out, we are insured with the same insurance company. Victoria will later tell me that she saw my accident, apparently at the opportune time so that she didn't get caught up by the massive stop to traffic that occurred shortly after the woman with the van ran into me (or me running into her by sliding?). I am not even upset, thanks in part to the fact that I am still riding the Adderall euphoria. A woman from the ambulance comes over to the car. "Is everyone alright?" she asks. "Yes, I'm fine. It wasn't that bad of an accident. I just got my door crushed in, but I am not injured" I reply. The woman with the two kids tells the ambulance woman that they are fine as well. The ambulance woman tells us that the Channel something news is doing a story on someone who was killed earlier that day, and that this is the second time she has come back with an ambulance today. I am grateful that the police do not get involved. I also wonder if me or my car, or both will be on the news that night. I forget about this and enjoy my work shift at the sports grill.

On Adderall, when I feel like I have nothing to lose, getting into a car crash really isn't that big of a deal. So what if I may only be able to roll my window 2/5 of the way down. Every scratch on my car has become a memory, with which I could tell a story. My first ever accident wasn't really an accident, but a minor hit that would become the first of at least five minor accidents, which my car possesses a scar of, with no people getting hurt. I am proud of this. As I drive my car to work, I notice that I am having a good time. There is snow on the ground, and I have just gotten five hours of sleep, and if I had a breathalyzer, I would blow way over the legal limit. I round a corner and my car slips on the snow/ice and fishtails into a wood fence, smashing the passenger back lights. I tell my parents that someone did a hit and run in the parking lot of my work, and they buy it. Nice.

I am drifting around a corner that has me end up 180 degrees opposite from where I start the drift. At the end of the corner sits a ten-foot drop. Eli, Ron, and Edwin witness the pro style type drift, usually only reserved for actual instances of how well they perform this maneuver in, "Fast and Furious: Tokyo Drift". I am now facing the bottom of a hill, and since there is ice covered in snow on the road, I misjudge my speed. I begin to slide all the way down to the bottom of the road, at the end of which is a five to six foot slope. "It's gonna hit!" I say as we brace for impact. Wham! Fuck. We all start laughing very hard, and then we go back to school. I survey the damage and see that the front bumper is bent upwards. I lose the bumper a few years later when I park too far forward at my buddy's house. The bumper gets lodged underneath a bunch of rocks and as I go in reverse (I can only think that they must have been, or were too heavy for the force of my car to move them), the front bumper rips off. Everyone in the car laughs, and my attitude, like always, stays neutral in relation to how beat up my car becomes. I somehow, duck tape my driver's side mirror to my car and it sticks to the side with the help of a few wires connecting it to the car. It drapes down and I see a police officer notice this. "What is this?" he says referring to the mirror. Nothing more has been said despite being pulled over with both mirrors missing.

If I speed, I will apparently get home quicker. This thought enables me to curve around corners at twenty to twenty-five miles per hour over the speed limit, potentially even greater. Interesting and nice. I drive around a corner and begin to skid on some gravel on the road, or something less than that. My car enters a ditch, within which there is a huge area of mud. I try to drive forward, and my tires spin out in the mud. I try to drive in reverse and the same thing happens. I get very pissed off at the fact that I couldn't just drive the goddamn speed limit and not drive into a freaking ditch from which you cannot escape. I thought about the fact that I had just bought $100 worth of Adderall from Eli, and this fuels my anger at myself for being so dumb. I call my dad and tell him where I am to see if he can come pull me out of the ditch with my mom's Expedition. As I sit there, it never even occurs to me that if a cop drives by and sees a car in a ditch, he will probably stop and see what the hell is going on. And this is exactly what happens. I see him turn on his lights and the first thing that came to my mind was where would I put the Adderall if he were to search my car? This happened to me once when I got baked after work and decided to drive high to Eli's house to pick up my fix. As soon as I turned on the highway, I didn't even see the deer in front of me when I hit it. I see blood spray up as it takes out my front passenger side headlight, as well as leaving little bits of hair on the side of my car. No more than two to three seconds after hitting the deer, I keep driving and some other animal, I am not exactly sure what it is, but it looked like a skunk or a black cat or some mystical creature that was sent down to earth to fuck with me while I am driving high, ran out in the middle of the road. No more than two miles away from my house after I got the shit from Eli, a cop pulled me over for driving with a headlight out. My twenty or so amphetamine pills were in the center console, which had felony written all over it if he searched my car. I got 15 months of probation in college for one pill, imagine what twenty would do.

Cop: You seem a little nervous.
Me: Yeah, I just hate being pulled over by the police.
Cop: Is there anything in the car I need to know about. Weed or anything else like that?
Me: No, sir.
Cop: Have you been drinking. You just seem really on edge.
Me: I just get uneasy when I get pulled over by a cop that is probably what justifies your suspicion.
Cop: Ok. I'll be right back.

He went back to his car, and a couple minutes later asked me to step out of my car. I did and I walked over to where he was standing near the back of my car.

Cop: I just wanted to make sure that you were not stumbling or walking crooked when you got out of your car and walked over here. Here's your license and registration. Have a good rest of your night.
Me: Thank you so much.

I offered to shake his hand because I was so grateful, but he told me he doesn't give handshakes. This was fine with me. I was just happy to not have gotten completely fucked.

So, after seeing the cop when my car was in the ditch, I walked over to his car to see what he was thinking about in reference to the situation.

Cop: Have you been drinking?
Me: No, I have not.

Just hearing me say that little amount of words, convinced him that I was not drunk. He radioed this information into his radio microphone in his car. I can only think that he just thought I was some dumbass who went to fast around a corner and lost control. If this was what he was thinking, then to the best of my analyzation of the situation, he would be correct. I told him that my dad was coming to pull me out, but the officer instead called a tow truck, which was a good idea because anything less than that would not have worked. I sat in my car, waiting for the tow truck and my dad to arrive and pondered what I should do with the Adderall. Throwing it out of the car never even crossed my mind as an option. I was determined to make this a successful night in some way, and if I threw out the Adderall, then I would have not only ended up with my car in a fucking ditch with a few points taken off of my license and a hefty fine with court fees, but also would have driven the forty five minutes to Eli's house only to not get my mood brightening agent, aka, what I indulge in to make my life suck a little less, I was going to flip an even bigger bitch. I was anxious about turning the inside of my car's light on, because I didn't want to attract attention to myself in any way, and the cop, being about fifteen yards away, might potentially notice that the light was on and then perhaps come to believe that I might be doing something suspicious. *Sometimes paranoia is a good thing, at least in reference to potentially saving your ass at some point.* I ended up putting the pills in the ash tray, hiding them in their little baggie behind the cigarettes that were already put out inside it. My dad showed up, followed by the tow truck who got me out without incident. It cost a couple hundred dollars for me to make use of the tow truck. My dad paid it, but then got reimbursed soon after. I ended up getting a reckless driving ticket which took two points off my license, and fees in the excess of $400, which, considering I was only making roughly $250 - $300 a paycheck washing dishes, this screwed me over. A penny saved is a penny I could use to get fucked up and have fun. Sure, drugs are fun (quote from Maxim magazine), but if it gets to a point that you start screwing with your own ability to keep it on the down low and not draw attention to yourself like running into a ditch or hitting a deer with your car, then you should just admit that you are too much of a dip to live that kind of lifestyle. For example, as I am writing this, currently, I am rolling on methamphetamine.[32] I think back to the semi-sketchiness of the deal made between me and the dealer. After I get my dose from the dealer, I notice that one of the guys is wearing either a cold weather face mask or a bandanna to cover his face.

Meth, according to National Geographic, is the most dangerous drug in the world. In this respect I get why the dealer's friend didn't want me or my friend to see his face. Or maybe he just didn't want to reveal the meth scars under whatever it was that covered his face. The higher up in the drug trade you go, and the more illegal the drug becomes, the more that people want to keep their identity protected, especially from people they don't know. But why does meth even get that big of a name for itself as being dangerous? After all, some psychiatrists prescribe it to patients with hardcore ADD, under the medication name, "Desoxyn." I also learned from someone, who, I believe to be a reliable source, that the biggest abusers of meth in the United States are soccer moms. I guess that is the way they can put up with a bunch of screaming kids in their car. In a meth high your concentration goes up, which, must make it appealing to cleaning ladies, and probably professional poker players, although in the latter case I am not entirely sure how many people do it. Apparently, poker is considered to be a sport by those who take to it as a job for a living. There was even a petition going around before the 2004 Summer Olympics that tried to campaign for poker being an Olympic sport. I laugh when I hear proponents of the "poker is a legitimate sport" side trying to get people to recognize it as such. They mention that your muscles get tense; it is mentally draining and requires real skill to get good at it like other sports. Poker, it seems, would to be a meth heads paradise. Just like other stimulants like Adderall and Ritalin that are abused by college students to help them study, stimulants used for gaining an advantage over other people in card games, should, if one is to treat a card game like poker for example to be a sport, then why do they not drug test people at the World Series of Poker? Or any other professional tournament for that matter, if you wish to cut down on performance enhancers? I like meth, but I like Adderall and Vyvanse more. Vyvanse in my opinion stands alone as the best stimulant, even over Adderall, because the euphoria is better when it starts to kick in and lasts longer. I once had such a high tolerance to Adderall, that I took 120mg extended release and went to sleep fifteen minutes later. The most important things that I look for in a speed high are the following: A) it makes you euphoric and feel really good. The more of a brightening of your mood, the better the drug will work for you. B) It gives you very good focus and clarity of thought. I once took between 200-300mg of Adderall in a few hours and stayed up writing philosophy all night. After what must have been at least five to six hours, I realized that I was biting my cheeks the entire time, and I never realized it until I came down a little. Eating food for the next week was a bitch and hurt like hell. The point is that I was so focused on writing philosophy that I completely didn't even notice anything else that was happening to me or around me, except for my writing. C) How long it lasts. It seems in this respect that meth seems to last the longest, however, if you have a low enough tolerance to amphetamines, then depending upon how rational the dealer's prices are that you are getting it from, $100 worth of Adderall or Vyvanse may last you just as long as $100 worth of meth. I saw a video describing how college kids take pills to study, and it said that one girl took one, 20mg pill of Adderall, and it kept her up for two days. When I was in college, around 600-700mg lasted me for five days, but that was when my stimulant tolerance was not as high as it is now (My record now is 600mg in one day, and I don't even roll nearly as much (at least in reference to the euphoria) as I used to when my tolerance was lower). I was sitting in on a conversation with a guy who I knew from my high school class at a bar once. The topic of the conversation turned to Adderall and other stimulants and the kid was apparently looking at the situation from a superior outlook that told him that the most amount of Adderall he ever took at one time was a lot.

Me: So how much Adderall have you taken at once or in a day?
Guy: I took 120mg once. Beat that.
Me: The most I ever took at one time was around 220mg – 230mg within a five second period.
Guy: Touché.
Me: The most I have ever taken in one day is 330mg. The amount that you were talking about, I have taken that much at one time at least 30 – 40 times.
Guy: Jesus, I don't know what to tell you other then maybe just you should just move on to ice.
Me: I have taken crystal meth and I think that Adderall is better.[33]

I heard a story about a famous mathematician who always was on some form of speed when he was working on his mathematics (I think it was Paul Erdos). He said something that I believe sums up how fun and cool amphetamines can be. He said that when he was on the speed, he would look at a piece of paper to do mathematics on and said that he had a ton of ideas coming into his mind. When he was not doing mathematics on speed, he said the paper was just blank and he didn't really know where to begin. I relate to this in a huge way (to say the least), because of all the philosophy I have written in my life, I think only two essays, which together were a total of five or six pages (out of 1700-1800), I have written sober, without the aid of some stimulant. In other words, I can't philosophize worth shit without proper inspiration (Philosophy with speed = lots of ideas; Philosophy without speed = blank page).

I have proper inspiration right now, so I will now write the conclusion to this introduction. I'm not sure if there is a psychological theory as to the root source of why people lie, but I would have to say, purely by examining my own life, lying is innate ability I was born with. Or maybe it was that I was raised into telling lies from infancy, due to the fact that I always thought I needed to come across to people in a better way than how I actually am. I remember back to when I was taking an alcohol class in college and the instructor told the class to go around the room, and each person has to say three things about themselves, two true things, and one false thing. Then the rest of the people in the class had to guess which one of the things the person said was false. I decided, like the reason why I decide to lie to begin with, that this would be a perfect time to say something about myself which would make me stand out as a cool person, with the incentive of the other people in the class thinking very highly of me. I say two things about myself, which I don't remember if they were true or not, and then end with, "I was valedictorian of my high school class." Some people in the class chose this one as the thing that was false, but I was proud when I told the class that it was actually true. I had told people in my own graduating class in high school the same thing, which I covered up for by telling them I was probably going to lose the number one ranking status because I was about to get a C in a class. The thing about being a good liar is that you can actually make yourself believe in the lies that you tell. To the extent that you are better able to make yourself believe in the bullshit that you come up with, corresponds to the amount of lies you can make other people believe. I used to be a master at coming up with stories from scratch, constructed purely by my own imagination, and work them into a situation which I would tell someone. In all these instances, my intent was to entertain and amuse the person who I was talking to. I was fueled by the comments the people gave back to me regarding the impact that the story had on them. I think back to middle school, entertaining my friend Eddie, which, whenever we slept over at each other houses every week or so, our favorite activity to do was for him to listen to me tell stories that he enjoyed hearing very much. I did this a lot when I was in the boy scouts as well. I developed a reputation as the kid whose tent you wanted to come into at night to hear the crazy shit he talks about. The details are very important in making up a lie, it is what sells it. One night I was telling a story in the boy scouts about a nude beach that I went to in France. I said that I was watching a woman play beach volleyball and when she dove for the ball, sand got into her vagina, and she had to dig it out with one of her hands. One of my fellow scouts was very intrigued by this and asked for all the details about the girl so that he could better visualize what I was talking about. I made something up, trying to come make the details of the girl come across as something which he would like to fantasize about.

One of most notorious of the lies that I have told growing up occurred in high school. Later on, you will read about a time when I got stuck in a grain silo. I ended up using this as the backdrop to an even more ridiculous situation that I came up with. The object of the story was to make people laugh because the teacher wanted the students to write a paper about something humorous. The paper was such a hit with the students and the teacher, that they wanted me to publish it in the school newspaper. Not thinking about the consequences of what this potentially might bring about, I agreed. Whenever people came up to me to ask if it was true, I would always respond by saying it is "definitely" or "very true". Having such a high ego in relation to the story and its impact that I saw it had on people, I even told the teacher that it was true, to which he responded with one of the wisest things someone has ever said to me, "I never asked if it was true or not." He had a very interesting point that I did not come to truly understand for at least the next two to three years. I think he at some level probably thought the story was a little too ridiculous to be true, but even so, was potentially willing to give me the benefit of the doubt to some extent. In the years since I stopped being a pathological liar about pretty much everything I said, I have come to understand an important realization. Unfortunately, society and people in general tend to place more of a value on something that is claimed to be true and is true, instead of claiming something that is false is false, but trying to pass off as if it were true. This can most easily by seen through the works of "Tucker Max", who was my idol at one point in my life. Some people hate Tucker Max because they say he is just making up all the stories that he tells. Yes, it is true that if the story isn't true he probably shouldn't claim that it is true, but also, to me it seems, if he were really just bullshitting everything he was writing about, those are some pretty impressive stories to come up with all by yourself which have no basis in reality. However, the problem is that a lot of people, if upon hearing that the story is not true to begin with, will probably not find the story as entertaining as they would have if they were told that the story was true to begin with. For some reason, a lot of people base their assessment of how they view material to correspond with their value judgement of something positive or negative to be in alignment with their idealization of what is true or false. The main problem with forming an assessment about something in this way, is that your emotional reaction or judgement that you take away from whatever it is that you were seeing, is dictated by your understanding of whether or not what you see is true or false, in how you idealize it. In other words, something that you come to understand is false, is false because you idealized it that way based on something that you already idealized and come to take as true. For example, I would steal pot from my freshman year roommate, "Max", and, with the help of a friend, broke into his locked-up cabinet and used his vaporizer whenever he was out of town for a few days. I got paranoid on one occasion when I was smoking a few of my friends up with his vaporizer, and a friend of Max's knocked on my dorm room. I answered and told him that Max was not here and he left, but I was then immediately stricken with paranoia that the guy who was at the door would tell Max that I had been using his vaporizer. Nothing ever came of this, but if something did, then the two ways in which I could have responded to his questioning me about the situation, shows why it is utter bullshit why people should not find just as much positivity in something they know is false, as with something they know is true.

If Max were to ask me if I took his vaporizer and I said no, then his reaction to this would be based on whether or not he really cared if I did or not. If he did care, then my answer would give him positivity, even if it was a lie, just as it would give him positivity, even if it was the truth. The ultimate factor influencing his reaction, being that he just wanted to hear me say that I didn't take his vaporizer, regardless of whether I did or not. In this instance, Max just wanted to *hear* the truth and was basing his reaction on what I said. If I told him I did and he got positivity from this (despite him perhaps still being a little pissed that I did take it), then his reaction was influenced by what he wanted to *know*. And this is the main point of the ultimate difference in how one may come to form an idealization about something's truth value in reference to how they will judge it: the judgement of the truth or falsity of some statement stems from the way the believer is able to be influenced by the truth value of their own idealization of what they already believe is true or false. However, just because a person already has a preconceived notion of what may or may not be true, that doesn't mean that the judgement that they make regarding the truth or falsity of that thing must accord with something relating to truth only being positive, and falsity only being negative. What is most important is that the person judging the truth value of a statement is already aware of the consequences of the truth value, such that they will react with positivity or negativity regardless of the actual truth value. The person will react with positivity because they want to "know" the actual truth value, and hence, even if the consequences were negative, the fact that they know the truth is the determining factor in how they judge the situation. The person will react with negativity because they want to "hear" (form a belief based on their own internal desire) the actual truth value, and hence, if the consequences were positive, the fact they have heard what they want to hear, still brings about a negative value judgement. This is why different people possess different emotional responses to equivalent things. It ultimately comes down to an internal set of values that one possesses as far as how their understanding of something corresponds to a positive or negative reaction. If Max wanted to know the truth, then he would have been happy regardless of what I told him, as long as he honestly took me to be telling the truth. If Max wanted to hear the truth, then he would have only been happy if what I told him corresponded to his own preconceived notion of what was true, and what would give him positivity.[34]

The main point that I am making, that relates to how one should form a belief about what I have written below, is the following: the final assessment through which one should base their belief's correspondence to how it makes them feel, is that even if what I have in the following pages is complete bullshit and made up, this should matter little to the reader, because what ultimately makes something true in form to subjectivity, is how the material relates to the readers ability to imagine it as such, and through that, conceive of the material in reference to objectivity, thereby invoking their own subjective ability to inspire the exact same thing towards the objective real world. If you read the following pages only wanting to hear the truth (and are therefore skeptical about certain things I may say and they come under a careful scrutiny of what you think is true or not), then the ability to form your own notion of what may be real in reference between yourself and the objective world will be bound by something that you cannot yourself influence or create as a part of itself. However, if you want to know the truth, then your ability to create a conception of reality will be boundless, because you have yourself idealized, a way in which you may come to know objective truth. Objective truth that you can know is the truth, rather than just hear is the truth.[35]

This can be seen through the logical contradiction known as, "The Liar Paradox":

The liar statement:
"This statement is false."

If the statement is false, then it is true, since 'this statement is false" is exactly the same as the original liar statement.

If the statement is true, then it is true, since 'this statement is false" is exactly the same as the original liar statement.

Thus, Godel's Incompleteness Theorem breaks down into meaninglessness.

My name is Psychotic Logician. Welcome to my mind.

# SECTION 2

# The "Psychosis" of Mind Travel

## FORWARD

What I have written in this section of the book is my chronicling of events that happened when my mental illness came into effect. The unfortunate thing about my mental illness is that you do not become manic, and the fortunate thing about my mental illness is that you do not get depressed. If I had to make a choice between being schizophrenic or being bipolar, I would definitely choose to be bipolar. There exists (from what I can see) a way in which people that have bipolar, could combat their illness in a way which schizophrenics cannot. According to my brother (who has bipolar) the mania you get from suffering from bipolar is much, much more euphoric than the euphoria you get from drugs or substances. This brings up an interesting idea which I believe that not many people understand. Let us pretend that some athlete that has made the Olympic team has bipolar disorder. If the time of the Olympics ends up coinciding with a manic episode that the athlete is experiencing at that time, I would have to say that the bipolar athlete has a decided advantage over other athletes who are not mentally ill. If mania is really that much greater than the positive effects that people get from being high on drugs, then, just by feeling great through the interactions occurring in your brain, you could be given a boost which the average person would need drugs in order to experience. I am not sure if there is much written about how this could exist, but it seems to have a legitimate loophole which could give an athlete a definite advantage when competing against others. This, of course, could have a negative effect on an athletes performance (also how they perform academically as well), through a person suffering from depression. Although one could not do this if they are being tested for drugs, they can make the depressive state a little less negative on their experience of life. If one is suffering from depression, then (at least it wouldn't hurt) one can just begin using drugs which make you feel euphoric. You use the drugs until you get back to being manic and hence, no longer need the drugs to make you feel better anymore. This is why I think being bipolar is much better than being schizophrenic. Schizophrenia just makes you hallucinate and become paranoid, with no noticeable effects of making you feel euphoric or extremely happy. The problem with psychiatrists who diagnose someone with bipolar disorder, is that they prescribe medication which enables one to maintain an even state of mind, by stopping the person from becoming too depressed, and too manic. Apart from making some people act in a way that is dangerous to oneself or other people society, I don't think there is anything wrong with mania, at least in reference to always feeling good, and experiencing the word through something that enables you to focus and motivate yourself to do anything that you want. My psychiatrist diagnosed me with what is essentially a mix between bipolar disorder and schizophrenia. It is called schizoaffective, and a part of treating it is to be put on mood stabilizers, and antipsychotic medication. I never really bought into this diagnosis since I have never been manic, nor have I ever been severely depressed. Taking this into account, since the only noticeable sign separating me from being mental illness free, is that I hear voices and become paranoid, which would then put me directly into the category of being schizophrenic, as opposed to schizoaffective. What I have written in this section makes no claim to novelty in reference to how someone experiences the world when they are mentally ill (hallucinating mostly). I hallucinate by hearing voices like other schizophrenics do, as well as suffer from paranoia like other schizophrenics do. What is original are the experiences that I had to live with (brought on by the symptoms of the mental illness), and all the consequences to what necessarily follow. The late great mathematician John Nash, who he himself was diagnosed with schizophrenia, once said that schizophrenia can sometimes provide an escape from the unfairness or irrationality of the world. Or, more plainly, "You don't have to be crazy to live in this world, but it sure helps."

## THE COMPLETE STORY

Around roughly March or April of 2011, I was going to college, and I was majoring in Philosophy and at the time I was taking four philosophy classes.

At the time I was prescribed Vyvanse and Adderall for ADD to help me focus on my schoolwork. On occasion, I would stay up for two to three days in a row and study the whole time. I remember the first time I tapped into a sixth sense (I came to understand this later upon reflection) in my perception was when I was writing a paper for my Epistemology class. The paper was supposed to be at most five pages in length. As I was writing the paper, I began to perceive through pure reason apart from any of the five senses, that you can gain knowledge about reality purely through the avenue of thought in your mind. I came to understand that this extrasensory perception is merely the pure awareness of an eternal immaterial existence. My paper ended up being sixteen pages in length, and I ended it by demonstrably proving how one could possess knowledge for certain beyond the five senses (I showed how one could, for example, know that they are not a brain in a vat). My professor did not understand the paper and I ended up getting a C on it. The reason I mention this first time that I perceived an existence that goes beyond the material world is because this was the start of what would ultimately come to change how I experience the world.

Nearing the end of the semester I began to write more and more about knowledge gained through pure thought alone. I noticed that the longer I stayed up on the stimulants I was prescribed, the better I could ultimately abstract, or deduce, the certain particular knowledge that exists in this immaterial reality. Then something happened that I did not expect. I was introduced to the philosophy of Georg Wilhelm Friedrich Hegel. Hegel is notorious for being a philosopher that is very hard to understand. However, I did not have trouble understanding Hegel's philosophy. The reason why I understood what he was philosophizing about was because almost everything he wrote about I was experiencing in my life. A major part of Hegel's philosophy is the science of how consciousness evolves and, subjectively, how a mind can come to reveal itself (its true identity) in steps to the subject. This is done through the resolution of contradictions between two opposites; a thesis and antithesis, being resolved through a synthesis of the two. It is through this method that a mind begins to gain more and more knowledge about reality. The ultimate conclusion of this process is the eventual attainment of absolute knowledge, and hence, possess a perception of existence that one can call, God.

Now, how Hegel's philosophy related to my life is through the following way. I began to notice through my experience (through my interactions with people and situations I engaged in (class discussions for example)), that I myself possessed two consciousness's within my own observation of existence. These two consciousness's were the following: 1) A Christ consciousness. 2) An Antichrist consciousness. It was around this time that I began to notice a correlation between what I was experiencing in my subjective mind, and how I was experiencing the objective world outside of my mind. I noticed that people were behaving in a way toward me that came across as if they knew I possessed these two consciousness's. However, although I became somewhat paranoid that people knew what I was subjectively experiencing in my mind, I was not completely convinced that people could see into my mind. (It is perhaps also important to note that I experienced the start of how these two consciousness's came into my mind, mainly, through a sort of injection of that perception into my mind (this happened on two occasions, once for the Christ consciousness, and once for the Antichrist consciousness, as explained in the above introduction)).

After the spring semester ended, I worked for a summer job at a restaurant as a busser and waiter. I would first like to say, before I continue, that I am currently diagnosed with schizophrenia. I was first diagnosed with this mental illness a few months after what I am about to discuss. I was working a shift as a busser at the restaurant one night when I began to notice that there was a similarity between what I was thinking and how people were engaging with me, as well as how they were engaging with the others around them. What I mean by this is that I began to notice that people were talking to me, as well as talking to the other people they were with, in a way that conveyed to me that they could hear what I was thinking. It was at this moment that I had what a psychiatrist would describe as a schizophrenic break from reality. I began to perceive everything that was going on around me as relating to people hearing my thoughts. I was not just paranoid about this situation, but was ultimately convinced as if it was a matter of fact, that people could hear my thoughts (I have compiled up to this point thousands of experiences I have had that is evidence that people could hear my thoughts).

Now, in the next few days and weeks following my initial first experience that people could hear my thoughts, I became aware of the following situation: the people that could hear my thoughts were made aware of what I had experienced a few weeks prior to this incident, mainly, that I possess two consciousness's, a Christ consciousness, and an Antichrist consciousness. Now, through my subjective experience of what I was observing around me, I became aware of an escalating global situation relating to what I was experiencing. The global situation that I became aware of was that basically news was beginning to spread throughout the world that a boy (me), could broadcast his thoughts for people to hear. It was made clear that I possessed two consciousness's. Now, from the information I gathered from my experiences with interacting with people, as well as observing their interactions with others (I heard people talking to other people about me and what I was thinking), was that the end times was beginning on earth, and that I would end up becoming either the Antichrist or the second coming of Christ. Who I would end up becoming in the future was dependent upon which consciousness I ultimately chose to identify with more. Now, this shift between the two consciousness's was not just up to me, but rather was directed by the people in the outside world apart from me that engaged with me and entered into my experience. I gathered that people were made aware of (by whom I am still not sure, but one theory I had was that everyone in the world was contacted by someone (Jesus or Satan, or both, or some high up authority) who told them what the global situation was and how it will end up playing out), that they could ultimately direct my thought into coming to identify with one consciousness over the other. This was done through people suggesting me into thinking one way or another, by introducing me to certain experiences that would ultimately elicit thoughts in my head that would make me think of becoming either the Christ or Antichrist consciousness. The last important thing I deduced was that people were on either opposing side of the situation, and that, for example, the people who tried to suggest me into becoming the Christ consciousness, would get raptured up, and the people who tried to suggest me into becoming the Antichrist consciousness would ultimately side with the Antichrist in the end times.

As this whole situation was unfolding, I, however, began to become aware of a further perception that lied within my awareness of what I was experiencing. This other perception was what I came to refer to as, "the third mind". This third mind was simply the unification of the Christ and Antichrist consciousness's together. Now, it became more and more clear to me how what I was experiencing was in accordance with what Hegel philosophized about. This was that the Christ consciousness was the thesis, the Antichrist consciousness was the antithesis, and the third mind was the synthesis. Furthermore, I began to come to understand how all three of these consciousness's related to my subjectivity. This was by the Christ consciousness being the conscious part of my mind, the Antichrist consciousness being the subconscious part of my mind, and the third mind being the unification of the conscious and subconscious, ultimately coming to be more and more (subjectively evolving or as Hegel put it, "sublating" (or "sublimating")) in alignment with a truer observation of reality. This truer conscious observation of reality beyond the Christ and Antichrist consciousness's by themselves, was simply the pure awareness of how reality is in itself, through the incorporation of all opposing ways of observing existence. This awareness that I began to possess of having a third consciousness was, however, not well received by the people that I believed could hear my thoughts. I overheard one conversation in the restaurant of one person mocking the idea of the third mind (I also had an experience a year or two later in which the voices in my head made it clear to me that the third mind does not exist and that I was just making it up). However, everything that I had come to realize about what I thought was the explanation of what I was experiencing culminated in single realization.

Although I was attempting to come up with explanations for how it was possible that everything that was going on around me could be potentially true, I never really came up with my own thoughts on the matter until one day when I wrote a philosophical essay. I should state, first, that taking drugs has always enabled me to better unify what I consider (referred to) to be the conscious and subconscious parts of my mind together. In elucidating the third mind within myself, I now, however, possessed a way such that I could relate to not just my subjective observation, but also to the objective world apart from me (because I considered the Christ consciousness (conscious) and Antichrist consciousness (subconscious) as occupying a presence not just within myself, but also apart from myself in the external world). After having smoked marijuana and taken a high dose of my ADD medication, I immediately became aware of a single truism: that I am God. I wrote a 33 page philosophical essay in which I revealed to myself exactly what was going on in my perception and how it related to everything else in existence. This God observation of existence that I possessed was enabled by the fact that I had unified everything in existence together through myself, such that I became aware of how absolute truth is.[36]

In the next two to three months, I wrote more and more philosophical essays in which I again attained the God observation of existence. Now, before I continue, it is important that I discuss one detail about how I began to see the world subjectively, and how it incorporated the other minds (people) in the objective world. Ever since the introduction in my mind of what I considered to be the Christ and Antichrist consciousness, I became aware that other people in the world could see into my mind. This was made possible by the fact that the other minds occupy a position in my mind that allows them to observe my perception from a place, but does not allow them to experience the world exactly as I experience it (I have tried to define this place from which these people see into my perception as a "high tech" world, or maybe that it is the spiritual/immaterial realm of existence). To see this from my perspective, try imagining that the other people are looking at your life from a place in existence that enables them to also possess subjective experiences about what is going on. In other words, the people are experiencing their own lives, yet at the same time observing the experience of mine. Now, these people that I perceived as observing my experience, form their own opinions and perceptions of who I am and how I am, by occupying this place in my mind. When writing these philosophical essay's, I was aware of these other people in my perception, watching what I was writing about. The problem that I had when attaining the God observation when writing my philosophy, was that I was high on drugs and hence, when I came down, I lost my ability to unify the two consciousness's together and hence, lost knowledge about the absolute truth of reality.

In mid to late August of 2011, everything I had experienced over the past four to five months culminated in an experience which I consider to be the pinnacle of my ability to influence existence. It should be noted before I continue, that I fully admit that everything I had previously experienced, as well as everything I am about to discuss, could be just the product of my schizophrenia, and hence, that I was hallucinating everything. What I am attempting to convey is that the objective truth of this event, as well as the truth of the events that preceded it, is not a product of the hallucinatory experiences that happened to me, but rather is a *product of the way in which my subjective awareness of what happened to me aligns with the ultimate objective immaterial reality of what it means to observe absolute truth*. For example, in mid to late August of 2011, I spent a week in a college town, crashing on my friend's couch who was going to school at the start of the fall semester. I had previously dropped out of school after the spring semester for multiple reasons and was now just living with my friend in his apartment. I had just gotten a new prescription for my ADD medication on Tuesday, and my intention was to attain enough knowledge in the coming week to completely free myself. By completely free myself I mean that I had realized through my past experiences that when the complete God observation has been attained for the final time, anything is possible, and hence, I wanted to get to a state where I was completely free to do anything I wanted to do for the rest of existence (eternity). I began writing my philosophical paper on Tuesday and wrote until Thursday without any sleep. On Thursday I slept for ten hours, and then presumed to write my paper until I completely attained the God observation. I then stayed up for the next two days philosophizing without any sleep. The following is my recollection to the best of my memory of what occurred between Saturday morning, and Sunday morning.

If you recall when I discussed the other people existing in my mind, seeing the world through my perception, as the week progressed, I began to realize more and more the way in which other people in the world observed the world through my perception. This is done through the existence of a virtual reality type set up of existence (somewhat like the Matrix), in which the people that are living in existence are hooked up to a machine and through this machine they experience their life. This virtual reality set up of existence has different levels of ways in which people could experience reality. If absolute knowledge is attained, the person will experience existence through the very top level of the virtual reality. Directly below this top level is the second highest knowledge that someone can attain, which is basically a split between other levels which are what must have been passed through if the top is to be attained. Imagine this virtual reality set up as a pyramid, in which the highest knowledge experience is the top of the pyramid, followed by the second level being a split into two different hookup levels. In the levels existing below the second level and beyond, more and more rooms with hookup machines exist which themselves split into other rooms below them. Each room in the virtual reality is connected to the one's above or below one another by a ladder or stairs. It was in this way that I conceived of the people observing my experience in my mind as occupying some reference (existing in this reality) to this set up of existence/reality. Keep this outline of the way in which I conceived the objective representation of how existential knowledge is related to all other levels of knowledge in mind when attempting to visualize what I am about to discuss.[37]

Attaining absolute knowledge (omniscience) is synonymous with saying that one has completely deduced all of existence. If one completely deduces all of existence, they have attained a knowledge of existence such that anything can be known, merely through the understanding of a simple concept or idea, which, through itself, knowledge of everything in existence is reached (anything can be deduced). Hegel refers to this absolute knowledge as the "absolute concept", or "absolute idea". This concept can range anywhere between a single sentence (or any single existing thing), to a very simple three to five premise argument (sound and valid) encompassing everything in existence. I was sitting on my friend's couch in his apartment, writing my philosophy on Saturday morning when I came to a critical part in my deduction of absolute knowledge. I noticed in my general awareness that I was in a place that I have taken away from the situation to mean the following: the people who believed that I would be the Christ consciousness observed my perception and I was in a position that I observed them. I took this to mean that the rapture had occurred, and it was now time to find out what consciousness (Christ or Antichrist) I was. I remember a friend saying to me "c'mon man" (as in come with us), and I responded, "Is it cool?" (in reference to potentially knowing how good or true the reality that they are living in is). He then responded, "yeah its ok", to which I then responded, "fuck that." As soon as I rejected the idea of accepting that that reality was the truest reality, my entire perception became surrounded by a bright tunnel that I was travelling through. The time it took to travel through this tunnel was, if I were to put an estimate on it, less than two seconds. Having examined my experience, I came to the deduction that I went through a wormhole, which connected two different point in space and time together. As soon as I got to the other side of the tunnel, I was immediately back on my friend's couch with my computer. Two things were immediately known by me as soon as I arrived back in my friend's apartment: 1) I had entered a new reality in which I was able to objectify my subconscious. This means that what I perceived as the subconscious part of my mind, now occupied a presence in the objective world apart from me. This was observed by me through the fact that the people who were observing my perception in my mind previous to this reality (were perceived by me as occupying a place in my subjective mind), were now a part of my mind objectively (were perceived by me as occupying a place in my subjective mind, which was now objectified). 2) I was God. Upon examining my experience, I believe that this was the objectification of the Antichrist consciousness, since I had just rejected the affirmation of the Christ consciousness immediately before this. I then hear in my immediate surrounding the voices of the people who were observing my experience. They are very upset and yelling out profanities. I believe this was because they believed that by my rejection of the Christ consciousness in favor of what they believed was the Antichrist consciousness, they were wrong about what consciousness I would become, and hence, would now have to suffer some sort of negative consequences. The reactions I heard from people indicated to me that they knew that they were screwed in some way, and this intrigued me/perked my interest.

Now, having come to form this new identity of the personification of God, I now wrote a five premise proof in which I completely deduced everything in existence. As soon as I finished this proof, the people that I now perceived to occupy a place in my objective surroundings immediately changed from being upset to being very happy. I believe this is because by objectifying my subjectivity, I had unified the Christ consciousness with my subconscious. In Hegel's philosophy, he wrote that when absolute knowledge is attained, there is a unification with everything in existence. I conceived of this unity as all subjective minds in existence perceiving absolute truth, through their observation of my observation. Although I had knowledge that I was God, I still had yet to make objectivity subjective, or, in other words, unify the Antichrist consciousness with the conscious. The reason why I was able to attain the God observation, without yet unifying the Antichrist consciousness with my conscious, was because although I had yet to fully unify all the opposing parts of my mind, my mind still did occupy a presence in everything that exists (objective reality and subjective reality), and hence, I had access to everything in existence through some avenue.

On Saturday night I had begun to start perceiving time drastically different than the ordinary perception of time that one subjectively perceives. This perception was the observation of the physical existence at a time preceding the actual occurrence of the physical existence. The reason why I perceived time and space in this way was because my subjectivity observed time as occurring before objective space (subconsciously conscious observation of time and space). There still existed one piece of knowledge that I had yet to unify into my complete deduction of existence. At this time, I was still not completely certain that people could hear my thoughts. This changed when I talked to a friend on our way to picking up cigarettes at a local gas station. My friend said, "I wish I could just write something on a piece of paper and have it come true." He said this in reference to my absolute concept in which anything is possible through. I responded, "So people really could hear my thoughts?" to which he responded, "Well of course." (like it was a known, talked about fact that everyone knows) Once he said this my perception immediately flipped such that I was now perceiving the conscious as subconscious. In other words, my subjective conscious, was now the objective subconscious, and hence, the Antichrist consciousness had been unified with my conscious mind. Hegel said that the final state that existence will find itself in when complete freedom is attained, is the end of history. Having now experienced four out of the five premises to my proof to attaining absolute knowledge, there only existed one more observation needed in order to attain absolute knowledge, and hence, the complete God observation for eternity. This, however, turned out to be more difficult than I could have possibly imagined.[38]

In attempting to deduce the final stage needed in order to attain complete freedom, I sat in a chair with my computer in front of me writing more philosophical content. Previously in the week in writing my philosophy, I had deduced that when in the process of deducing the final stage of existence, one will become aware of the past histories that have been lived by the observer. This is exactly what I was experiencing at that moment. I remember seeing my past history starting as a very small organism, eventually evolving to greater and greater life forms, leading all the way up to the current state that I found myself in. I also saw other forms of myself. Recall now the girl in the red dress I wrote about in the introduction, and how I said that I would later on fuck myself royally when it came to a certain decision I made in reference to her. This decision was that I thought this girl was so perfect, that I had to go into isolated seclusion for a very long time as a sort of "training" or "perfecting oneself" in order to be worthy of being with this girl. What is interesting about this is that every single form of myself that existed previous to my own all chose to go with the girl. I saw versions of myself getting out of a virtual hookup machine and walking over and hugging and kissing the girl. I thought at one point that I wanted to be with the girl when I saw that it took her observation along with mine to complete everything in existence. I know this because as I tried to further unify the final few contradictions that existed between myself and everything else, I saw other versions of myself with the girl, which all had unified everything through each other.

I then attempted to form a one sentence complete deduction of existence encompassing everything. It got to a point where the final contradiction was going to be resolved, and I visualized it as being close to the following: "through the union of freedom (red dress girl and Psychotic Logician) the following can now be known........." A few things happened at this point that I am not exactly sure what the order in which they happened was, but it was this: as I was writing I saw the red dress girls' legs from her feet to her knees materialize. I became very nervous that all of this was currently happening; I tried to deduce an important knowledge understanding, which was made very difficult by the fact that there was some person or thing in my perception that was trying to come across as if it/he had a problem with what I was saying and/or trying to present as truth. I see the person/thing come close to my perception where all this was taking place (my friend Abe's apartment couch), and I tell it to go into my perception, and tell me exactly what the problem/contradiction he had with me was. Whatever it was declined the offer and I thought about telling it to fuck off, but I am too nice when I get to be that high up in knowledge. Seeing that I was having trouble deducing the last steps necessary in order to attain freedom, the version of myself and the girl in the red dress existing right in front of me (which was equivalent to being simpler versions of myself and her attaining freedom), were about to unify and go into their perfect reality, and seeing that I was being bothered by whatever the fuck it was that had a problem with something I was deducing, were either asked by someone or just decided that they would be fine with having some imperfect thing like this contradiction existing in their reality. I was beginning to become very bothered by this, but I kept trying to pass through the final stages necessary in order to free myself; when I finally decided that I wanted to go into the absolute knowledge reality by myself, I saw a version of myself (that looked to me like a previously unified version of myself that decided to go with the girl in the red dress), go over and tell the girl in the red dress that I wanted to do that instead being with her at the current moment.

The next thing I remember is sitting in a chair in a dark room with an opening that was lit at the top of the room. The opening to the top had a ladder leading up to it. Overstimulated by everything that was happening at the moment, I did not get out of the chair and climb up the ladder. After a brief moment my perception then changed to that of seeing the following: I saw two tall beings each standing next to openings in the virtual reality (there were two openings on opposite sides of the room). The being on the left had a black suit and red tie. The being on the right had a white suit and white tie. Upon reflection, I believe the being in the black suit to be Satan, and the being in the white suit to be Jesus. Kneeling beside the Jesus figure was a smaller version of the being that also had a white suit and white tie. I did not see any other figure beside the Satan figure until the following happened: I hear the Satan figure say to me, "It turns out that you were the Antichrist consciousness. So…" Immediately after the being said this, a version of myself came out of my physical body that also had on a black suit and red tie. I took this to be the Antichrist consciousness within my observation. Once the Antichrist consciousness came out of me it started shouting, "Pride! Pride!" It should be noted that this version of myself that came out of me, was the same version that went over to the girl in the red dress and told her that I didn't want to be with her at that moment. This was also the version, that I thought best captured who I am, when observing myself in relation to the other previous versions of myself that had unified with the girl in the red dress. The main reason why I thought that this version of myself best represented me was because it represented the physical body/avatar that I thought best represented who I thought was (was the best representation of my mind within my body (mind-body duality)). It is important to note, however, that although this version of myself came across as the best representation of who I potentially am, who I actually was, was something that had yet to become known, even to me.[39]

After this happened, I immediately became aware that I was losing knowledge. I don't know how else to describe how I felt other than to say that it was the deepest level of fear that I have ever experienced. Because I had attained all-knowing status there was an immense amount of knowledge that I possessed that was being lost by me. This process took throughout the whole night. As the morning approached, I heard in my observation people yelling again as they did the previous morning before I recognized myself as God. They were once again very upset about the situation that was going on. I now believe that they were upset because they were under the impression that I was the unification of the Christ and Antichrist consciousness's, yet it turned out that I was actually the Antichrist consciousness. This meant that everyone who believed that I was not the Antichrist consciousness, would have to face the consequences. There came a time in this process that I said to myself in reference to the rest of existence, "I now throw away my last recognition of fear." I sat outside of my friend's apartment smoking a cigarette as the morning was approaching and saw a girl who lived right next door to Abe. She seemed very void of emotion or feeling, kind of coming across as if she knew what was going on with me, and that she was affected by it in some way, probably a negative way. I asked her, "Are people pissed off at me for screwing everything up?" She didn't respond and just walked away, never even acknowledging what I said. At this point I was in a state of complete numbness in reference to what was happening around me.

Now, as this was happening, I was fairly certain that I was going to lose all knowledge that I possessed. However, within my mind I came to know that there still existed one last piece of knowledge that I would have to lose before I lost it all. This last bit of knowledge, however, was not made apparent to me until the very last thing I possessed within my understanding as the last thing I know. I kept saying to myself over and over, you still have one last understanding, trying to give myself whatever hope I could muster. Right before I professed to all of existence the last piece of knowledge that I possessed, as I was sitting on my friend's chair, I began to notice that my entire field of vision was slowly fading into darkness and that the light from my observation of the world was beginning to fade. As this was happening, I began to experience what I can only describe as the most immense amount of pain I have ever experienced. Upon reflection, I look back at this now and believe that I was in the process of being annihilated from existence (annihilation being, mainly, the complete destruction of some existing thing to make it not exist anymore).

Finally, in the last possible moment in which I could exist before being annihilated, I professed to existence, "Jesus, save me!" Right as I said this, I immediately went through another wormhole, and arrived back on my friend's chair in his apartment. At this time, I was still feeling a lot of pain, since I was still one thought away from being annihilated. I immediately began to scramble to find a piece of paper to write down the last bit of knowledge that I possessed. I found my notebook and wrote the following down: "Jesus Christ is lord and savior. I will now remain in this state of existence for five years." As soon as I finished writing this down, I began to become extremely pissed off and say, "FUUUUCK!" and then I saw the Antichrist consciousness, come outside of me and disappear. Now, I wrote down that I will remain in this state for five years because, I believe, I set up a point in space and time where I could experience existence for that length of time, before I return to the point of last knowledge and will then return to annihilation. I am not 100% sure, but for some reason I had thought I was going to go to this state as a matter of fact when I was writing a philosophy essay at an earlier time, when I even deduced that I should remember exactly where I was so that in five years you can return to it. I thought about going off and living for the five years that I could before returning to the annihilation point, but then I remembered: I had led people into this point of despair through my actions, and I was going to do everything in my power to make sure that they could be rescued.

I returned to the chair, which was the point of only one piece of knowledge. How annihilation operates is that once you no longer possess any knowledge, you are annihilated. Upon losing more and more knowledge, you begin to experience more and more pain. This means that the more knowledge that you ultimately possess, the less amount of pain you feel. This made my mission clear. I had to lead the people out of being annihilated by attempting to give them knowledge. As a gauge in determining truth from falsehood, I would use how much pain I was in to know whether what I had written down was true or false. I, however, only possessed one bit of knowledge, which meant that I would have to deduce more knowledge from the one bit that I did possess. I don't remember exactly what I deduced after the one piece of knowledge I had left, but there came times that I would deduce incorrect knowledge, feel more pain and hence, lead people further into the darkness. I could hear people screaming in pain and yelling profanities at me because I was leading them further into less knowledge. However, there came a point in deducing more knowledge that the following was made immediately aware to me, and I then wrote down in the notebook roughly the following: "Jesus Christ has decided to unify with Psychotic Logician. Psychotic Logician has made Jesus Christ realize something that he has never before recognized in existence, the observation of complete sympathy and compassion for all minds in existence." Once this occurred, Jesus was completely speaking through me to the people that had been led into annihilation. It eventually got to a point where it was conveyed to me that I would have to rescue everyone that had been led into the darkness. I still am not sure if this meant that I had to physically go back into the annihilation pain and lead the people out, because as soon as I said that I experienced what felt like to me to be a jump in time from one point to another. This could potentially mean that I just possess no knowledge of doing this but am not completely sure. The last thing I wrote down in the notebook was that if you need to be rescued, call out to Jesus and he will save you. I had been rescued from the point of annihilation and was now in a position where I thought I had to physically go and rescue people. It was at this moment that I became aware that I was God again.[40]

There are multiple things that I have learned from what had happened from the point of when I started losing knowledge, up until the point that I was rescued. First, in deducing the last bit of knowledge before gaining the complete God observation, I asked myself a question. This question was, "What is the name of the last observation that achieves absolute knowledge of existence?" I then wrote down, "Freedom". After writing this is when I then found myself in the dark room with the ladder leading up to a light. This, I believe, was the final stage in my representation of knowledge through the virtual reality set up. There are two possibilities that could be the case in reference to this event. The first is that in order to attain complete freedom for eternity (an end to history according to Hegel), all I must have done was get out of the chair and climb up the ladder into the absolute reality. The second has to do with the second level of knowledge represented by the two beings, Satan and Jesus standing on opposite sides by entrances leading to the lower levels of reality. The reason that there only existed two entrances was because both Jesus and Satan both occupy a point in existence which is one level further down then the top level of absolute knowledge. Along with this, however, also exists the following understanding. In order to fully attain the complete God observation for eternity, what happened to me might have been a necessary way in which the Christ and Antichrist consciousness's could finally become completely unified. This is because, through me, I would have not only unified my subconscious with the Christ consciousness, as well as my conscious with the Antichrist consciousness, but also, I had to unify my own consciousness, the third mind, with both the Christ and Antichrist consciousness's (since my subconscious and conscious are already unified through the existence of the third mind). This was accomplished through the demonstration that the observation of freedom that I possessed in the final stage of completely deducing existence, was a true observation of existence, and by itself, stands as a way in which absolute truth can be observed. This observation was shown to be independent in its observation through the fact that it was not either the Christ or Antichrist consciousness's apart from each other, but was rather independent from both in its complete observation of reality. In reference to my potential unification with the girl in the red dress's observation, I think that if I would have chosen to be with her instead of by myself at first, this would have been ultimately equivalent to just standing up out of the chair and climbing the ladder in the final top room of the virtual reality set up.

After this experience happened to me, I read multiple philosophers who wrote about situations that aligned exactly with what I experienced. In one of Hegel's writings, he described exactly what I went through with potentially being annihilated. He said that after the mind is rescued from annihilation it is shown to be independent in its actuality and is made an absolute being. An absolute being, mainly, being someone who possesses complete knowledge of everything and is omniscient. The existential virtual reality set-up of existence as discussed in this story can be roughly seen through this pictorial representation:

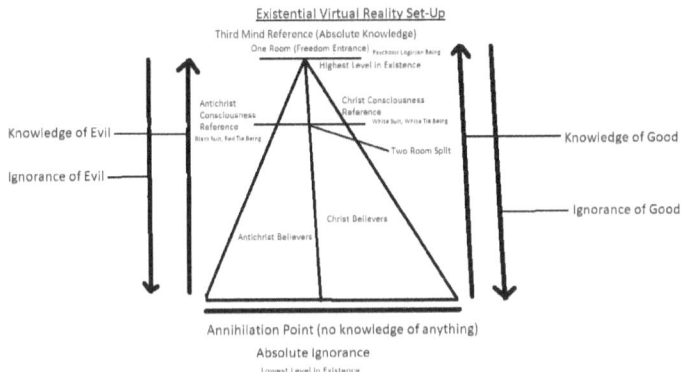

The final point to note is that when I first realized that I was God on Saturday morning, after traveling through the wormhole, I looked up to the ceiling and saw what I can only describe as the sound of a horn, and obscure images that I am not sure exactly what they mean. As I will discuss later on when I completely deduced everything the second time, I saw the same image and sound near the ceiling of the room I was in (my basement). I do, however, have a theory that this sound and image(s) were all the other intelligent minds in existence that agree that I really have unified everything, and hence, all minds in existence agree. I may never know for sure, but that's the best theory I can come up with.

## THE TIME I WENT TO A MENTAL HOSPITAL

There was one time when I stayed up for three straight days, writing philosophy pretty much the entire time. I had taken roughly 800-900mg of Adderall and on top of not sleeping, I had not eaten anything. I was just riding the Adderall high, as well as smoking pot every three to four hours. I was hallucinating like a mother fucker. By the third day I had run out of Adderall and pot, so I hit up two of my friends and they hooked me up with more so I could keep rolling. I was writing a philosophical essay when it came to a point in which I was asking the voices in my head what I should write about. They told me that I should write about "Hope", so I began to abstract and deduce what I knew about hope. There came a point when I was writing that I noticed that the Jesus in my head (a fake Jesus) was depressed. I asked him why he was feeling so down, and it was conveyed to me that he spent time in hell (30 years or some fucked up shit like that) and was very upset about it. I made the mistake of not telling him to stop being a little bitch (after all, there have been people who have been in hell for thousands of years), and I just kept on writing. There then came to a point when I was writing that a question was presented to me (the question was proposed to me through what I was writing, in which either the writing changed on my computer, or I read the writing through a different perception). I forget what the question was, but it had something to do with disproving what I was writing. It only took me a couple of seconds to come up with a refutation for what the voices called me out on, and I became immediately aware that the Jesus in my head was evil. When I refuted the question proposed to me, my Microsoft Word document in which I was writing immediately closed and I had to reopen it to keep writing. I then began to write about what I had just experienced. I titled the section of the essay in which I began to write as, "A Very Fundamentally Fucked Up Correspondence in Existence."

I began to write, and at the same time the fake Jesus was telling me not to send him to hell. I think he was missing the point. I think hell is immoral and all I was trying to do was to get him to realize the truth about existence. I began to write, when all of a sudden (I forget how it first began to happen) I realized that I was going to be annihilated, just like I was being annihilated in the Complete Story written above. I felt a deep sense of fear and began to freak out. I quickly started writing very fast, trying to gain more knowledge that I was losing. I was in my dad's office, because my power cord was broken, and I needed to use his power cord to keep my computer working. It was around five o'clock in the morning, and, my parents, hearing me freak out, came down to my dad's office to see what was going on. They came to the conclusion that I was overdosing on Adderall and called the police to send an ambulance to my house. As all this was going on, I was still struck with a deep fear that I may potentially get annihilated.

Just as the cops arrived with an ambulance, I had deduced enough knowledge to keep me alive. My dad looked through my room and found the extra Adderall that I had left over and gave it to the police. I am lucky that they didn't charge me with a felony for possession of a controlled substance. I began to calm down, but I was forced to go to the hospital and ride in the ambulance.

After I went to the hospital (spending roughly ten to twelve hours in some room where I kept hearing voices up the shit), they sent me to a mental hospital. When I arrived there, it was night and everyone was asleep. I had a conversation with one of the nurses.

Nurse: Why are you here?
Me: I took a bunch of Adderall, and for some reason my parents called the cops.
Nurse: How long has it been since you had a bowel movement?
Me: About three days. I have not eaten anything in a while.

She then gave me some chips and water and I ate them. She then showed me to where I was going to sleep. In the morning I talked to my roommate.

Me: Hey how's it going? I'm Psychotic Logician.
Roommate: Hey I'm "Bill".
Me: Nice to meet you. How long have you been here?
Roommate: About three weeks.

He went on to tell me that he has done roughly 800-900 hits of acid in his life and that it has brought him closer to God. I knew a guy that had done around 600 hits, and he told me that it altered his mind to such an extent that he was pretty much tripping all the time. The thing about mental hospitals is that since everyone is crazy, the only thing you do is watch movies and have arts and crafts time. Whenever there was free time, I just slept. During one arts and crafts time, I made a bracelet that said, "I love you girl in the red dress" (from the story I wrote about seeing the girl in the red dress for the first time). Someone stole the bracelet, which made me angry, and just added to my paranoia that people could hear what I was thinking. During this time, I had a Twin Peaks t-shirt on.

Woman: You can't wear that t-shirt here.
Me: Why?

Woman: Your shirt shows someone drinking and that is not ok here. You need to change your shirt.
Me: Ok…

By the second day I was in the mental hospital, I was transferred to the drug and substance addiction ward of the hospital. This kind of pissed me off because it turned out that the people running the addiction hospital understood that they were not dealing with crazy people, so they took a much more serious attitude about how people spend time in the hospital. I had to fill out a questionnaire about a movie we were watching and the meetings that we had were much more serious. Upon reflection, I wish I just bullshitted my way through all the serious things that I was forced to do in the addiction ward. What are they going to do? Not release me because I didn't take notes on the movie we were watching? Most of the people that were in the addiction hospital were there for alcohol, but there were a few people in there because of serious drug addiction problems, like shooting heroin (a 15 year old kid).

After a few days in the hospital, my parents and one of my sisters came to visit me. At this point I was still convinced that people could hear my thoughts and that all of my paranoia was real. We began talking and the conversation turned into something that pissed me off. So I flipped them off and walked out of the room we were in. I regret it and feel bad for the way I acted, but at the time I was so mentally ill that there was nothing that they or anyone else could tell me that would change my mind about how I feel towards what I thought was real in the world. Weak/lame.

A day or two later I was finally released. I had a meeting with my parents and one of the psychiatrists in the hospital and they made me promise to never take any stimulants again. I agreed just because I wanted to get the fuck out of there. Anything short of blowing some guy to release me, I would have agreed to. It was the longest four days of my life. My advice to anyone who was a substance abuse problem or mental illness is that you should try everything within your ability to find a solution to your problem before you admit yourself to a mental or drug addiction hospital. It fucking sucks.[41]

## SECOND TIME DEDUCING EXISTENCE

Of all the times I have legitimately thought that I was God, there was one time in which I thought that I could use the power to affect change in the world to my advantage, even when I was sober. To completely deduce everything in existence pretty much means that you have deduced a concept in your mind that allows you to become all knowing. I have done this twice in my life. The second time that I did this I got some Adderall from a friend of mine "Frank", and my plan for that night was to work on my movie script and get shit done (always revolving around making it big somehow to escape from the shitty life I was living). While working on the script, Frank called me and wanted to know if I wanted to drive around and smoke pot with him. I thought this was a kick ass idea and fifteen minutes later he picked me up. We began smoking and sometime after the first or second bowl, I began to notice that everything around me was relating to me in some way. We were listening to "Just my paranoia" by Afro Man (or whatever the song is called), and when it first came to the part in the song where Afro Man says, "It was just my paranoia, running away with me." I related this to the Complete story in which my paranoia (thinking I was the Antichrist consciousness) caused me to fuck up and lose my God status. All of a sudden everything in the song began to relate to me and I realized once again that I was God.

Me: Do you think that I should just stop bullshitting around and be who I am all the time?
Frank: Probably.
Me: Like what do people want to know? That I am God?
Frank: Haha

Frank and I then go to King Soopers to buy some snacks and I tried talking to a woman there, trying to stay in the moment and just be myself.

Me: Hey, aren't you the girl that sold me that gift card that I used to play Keno with?

The girl just looks at me and doesn't say anything. She walks away from me. Was the reason that she didn't talk to me have something to do with the fact that she felt uncomfortable with the fact that I was a bad person?

I get home from King Soopers, and begin to write down my philosophy, trying to deduce the ultimate concept that will enable me to relate to everything in existence. Once I do this, I see what I can only describe as a symbol relating to me that everyone in existence is agreeing that I have attained complete knowledge, just like the first time. I realize that I have finally unified the Christ consciousness with the Antichrist consciousness, and this makes me feel euphoric. The rest of the day I just kept writing down more philosophy, but the problem was, just like every other time I have a major breakthrough in attaining knowledge, I come down from the Adderall and marijuana high, and lose what I have learned. Lame. There may come a time in the future where I will attain absolute knowledge sober, but, if I'm being honest, I don't think that will ever happen.[42] (nor do I really care)

## THE FIRST TIME I THOUGHT I WAS GOD

The first time I ever thought (realized?) I was God was one time when I was rolling on Adderall and pot. I wrote, upon reflection, the best philosophical essay I have ever written. In the essay, I completely described how my personal experiences of people potentially hearing my thoughts related to all of existence. The essay pretty much described how I thought people were viewing about the situation in the world with me deciding to be the Christ or Antichrist consciousness. I explained that unknown to the entire world, there existed a third consciousness, which I called the "Third Mind". Unfortunately, I deleted the essay, however, I do remember a few things that I wrote.

First page: The Bible is literally true, and the entire universe is roughly 6,000 years old.

A few pages in: Life is a joke and doesn't deserve the allegiance of having a serious attitude taken about it towards it.

I go on to describe how perceiving perfection in existence relates to complete freedom for an individual, and how it is possible to attain in existence. Of course, ten to twelve hours later I came down off the Adderall and pot and no longer remembered how to perceive the concept that allows you to attain freedom in existence.[43] My plan was to trip shrooms with Frank later that night so as to permanently keep me in the God state, but the plan never ended up happening. Weak.

## THE RED RIBBON

During one of my philosophizing times back when I was around 22 or 23 years old, I tried to hallucinate my way to freedom, rather than attaining knowledge to do it. What does this mean? Simply put, I would try and imagine something that I could change in the physical world in front of me, which would then give me confidence that I could change my entire surrounding field of view into anything I wanted. Before this story took place, I tried this a few times before. On one occasion I was hallucinating like a mother fucker and kept trying to imagine a stairway or ladder through which I could climb up and attain freedom (enter into a higher dimension or parallel universe where I could then do whatever I wanted (that was my goal in the complete story as well)). The problem with this way of trying to free oneself is that you must constantly stay in the moment and perceive with your eyes a fixation which allows you to never change what you are hallucinating in front of you. This is extremely difficult to do, because every time you see something in the physical world in front of you that you have altered with your mind, you cannot blink or look away, because this will change what you are seeing in front of you. It is easier to try and change little things than bigger things. One time after smoking marijuana I was hallucinating to an extent that allowed me to perceive sand coming out of my hands onto the carpet of my basement. It was pretty cool, but ultimately failed to get me to where I wanted to go.

So, one time, after staying up for multiple days (as usual), I tried to hallucinate my way to freedom. I used two objects to try and enable me to gain confidence that I could indeed change the physical world into anything I wanted. The first item I used was a Bic lighter. I would put my index figure in the bottom of the lighter and try to move it up towards the top of the lighter, such that my finger would be completely in the lighter. I attempted to do this for a few hours or so, ultimately failing to achieve the result I wanted. The closest I got to getting my finger into the lighter was about my nail's length, and I think even one time I felt the oil from the lighter on my figure tip. Since I was not able to alter the lighter with my finger, I decided to move onto something else which would make it easier to change the physical world with. The second item that I used was a book that I owned entitled, "Metaphysics". On the front cover of the book are square cubes which can have multiple ways of being looked at and seen by someone looking at the front cover. I tried to insert my finger into the cube, such that, when looking at the front of the book, one could see that the front of the cube was in front of my finger, and my finger was inside the cube. In other words, I tried to hallucinate that my finger went into the cover of the book, thereby making the 2-D surface of the book, 3-D. I attempted this for a couple of hours, getting very close to accomplishing it multiple times, only to blink and change my perception back to the cover being two dimensional. After many attempts, I finally hallucinated to such an extent, that my index finger was on the inside of the front of the cover, going into one of the cube squares.

At this point the following happened: I pulled my finger out of the cube, and right as I did this, instead of gaining the confidence I thought I would have once I accomplished changing something in the physical world to accord with my perception, a red ribbon type object came out of the square cube and disappeared shortly after that. I was confused as to what this was. The voices then told me that the red ribbon symbolized that Jesus and Satan had made a deal over me, which was that whichever ribbon that happens to come out of the cube that I pulled my finger out of, that is the person who gets to have my soul/body. If a blue ribbon came out of the cube, then I would go to heaven with Jesus, and if a red ribbon came out of the cube, I would go to hell with Satan. At this point, I was still a noob when it came to not fearing the voices and what they could potentially do to hurt me, so I began to become very frightened that I would soon go to hell. I wake my parents up and tell them that I took a bunch of Adderall and am very psychotic, and very scared, that I might get possessed or fucked with by evil forces, such as Satan or demons.

I then attempt to deal with my fear by praying to Jesus and re-accepting him as my savior. I then, to my utter regret, delete all seven to eight hundred pages of philosophy that I have written over the past two to three years. My thinking in doing this was that if I were to get possessed or fucked with in some way by some evil forces in the world, I did not want them to use my philosophy for evil. The philosophy that I first started writing when I became mentally ill, was mostly the process of my mind or inner being/consciousness revealing itself to me, much like Hegel describes as the way that consciousness evolves over time. At this point in my life, I am not too upset that I deleted my philosophy. Yes it would have been cool to still have it so I could show people a lot of the philosophical and existential shit that I proved, but it all still remains in my head (having all my papers back would mostly serve the cause of me reading it ten to twenty or longer years down the road just to see how I used to see the world and remember all the crazy stuff that happened. They really only served this purpose, because I rarely if at all read my past philosophy papers. Instead, I just move onto the next form of reasoning that I am left with after writing the previous paper). As to the case concerning the red ribbon and where I will go when I die, I would say that it is highly unlikely that it even means anything. The Jesus in my head is not the real Jesus, and, as I describe in other stories, is a highly fucked up individual. Not that I really care. Even if the ribbon that came out of the cube was blue, the only thing this would mean is that apparently the Jesus in my head is so fucked up to make deals with the devil over my body and soul that I would probably be fearful that I would end up going to heaven with him to.[44]

## UNIFYING EXISTENCE THROUGH THE MOVIE, "CONTAGION"

I went one night to hang out with Frank, get baked, and go see a movie. We were debating between either seeing, "Apollo 18", or "Contagion". This was less than a month after the complete story experience happened, and I was still very delusional that people could hear what I was thinking. We decided to see Contagion and began to smoke a bowl as we drove down to the theater. After the first three or four hits, I began to perceive the type of reality that I had experienced in the complete story, mainly, that I was a conscious being, walking around and experiencing the world within my own subconscious. My subconscious being the rest of the world apart from myself. We were driving on the highway and I had to tell myself to keep my shit together, because I was paranoid that my perception would in some way fuck with Frank's ability to drive. The perception went away until we got to the theater and the previews began to play. For some reason, everything that was playing on the screen, I had somehow seen before or experienced previous to seeing it on the screen. I recognized everything as already happening before I saw it on the screen (almost like perpetual déjà vu). This became even more the case when the movie started playing. Now, it should be noted, that before Frank and I drove down to the theater and smoked in the car, we smoked a little at his house before. When I first felt the high coming on, I saw in my perception the actors of "Contagion" in my mind, most notably was Matt Damon, who told me that he is going to be there when I watch the movie to, "guide me through it." The movie began to play and it was just the playing out of things I had perceived previous to it. The majority of the scenes from the movie I remembered from when I was taking a shower one time and I thought about many of the scenes already. Some of the scenes that I had already thought about previous to watching the movie in the shower were: the scene when the Doctor tells Matt Damon that his wife is dead, the ending sequence of the film showing how the virus began to spread, one of the end scenes where Matt Damon begins to cry, the scene with Kate Winslet saying something to a guy about washing his hands (or something like that?). Once I understood that the film was basically a playing out of my own subconscious, I began to notice some of the reactions of the people in the theater. A thing I heard someone say was, "Oh, is that what is going on?" and I heard other indiscernible reactions of people realizing what was going on. Sometimes there would be a scene that the people in the audience couldn't understand how it related to me, so I would have to say through my thoughts what exactly it meant. One thing that I was once accused of by a voice was being a pedophile and being attracted to young children. A scene played out in the movie that showed how I indeed was not a pedophile and some of the people didn't completely understand this, so I had to say it to them through my thoughts (why I gave a shit that they didn't understand how something in the movie related to me, I do not know). The whole movie played out this way. I was sitting in an upper part of the theater, about three fourths of the way to the top level seats, and then at one of the final scenes of the movie, when Matt Damon begins crying, a guy got out of his chair near the bottom of the theater, stopped near the entranceway, and looked up towards where I was sitting. I think this in some way had to do with the fact that my subconscious had put forth a kind of tragic, compassionate and sympathetic way for Matt Damon to react towards what happened to his family (his son and wife die). I don't think I ever said anything to Frank about this, and just kept to it myself. I have not told many people this story, because it is kind of difficult to understand. I can just distinctly remember exactly when I had previously thought about the scenes that were in the movie, before I had even seen the movie. I like to think that in some way the movie was written and directed by me.

About a week or two later this same thing happened to me with another movie that I was watching by myself. The movie was, "Dolores Claiborne", and although I didn't recognize almost every scene like I did with Contagion, there were definitely a few parts that I know for sure I had thought about before.[45] What can I say, weed sometimes does this to me.

## THE SALVIA STORIES

When I was a senior in high school the only drug I had ever tried was marijuana. Some of my other friends were into other drugs like pain killers and uppers like Adderall. I was completely ignorant of most other drugs and had no intention of trying anything other than pot. However, this changed when a friend of mine, "Brad" told me about a legal hallucinogenic drug called Salvia. He told me he had tried it several times with some of my other friends and said that it was crazy as hell. I asked him what it does exactly, and he told me a story of one of one of the times he tried it. He said you are supposed to smoke it out of a water pipe, that being either a bong or water bubbler, and that it just takes one or two hits, holding it in your lungs for as long as possible before exhaling, and then you begin to trip. He told me that one time he tried it and as soon as he exhaled, he was immediately on a raft in some arctic place, like Antarctica. Looking onto the land from the raft, he saw ice glaciers and snow covering the whole land. On the glaciers looking down to him, he saw a bunch of penguins that were waving at him. I'm not sure what else happened to him in the trip but this information alone was enough to peak my interest into trying it.

The first time I tried it was with a group of my friends at one of their houses. There were four or five of us all sitting on a couch in front of a TV that was playing an episode of Futurama. I volunteered to be the first one to try it. There are several different kinds of Salvia, ranging in intensity from 5x all the way up to the mid 100's. I think 600x is the most potent of the drug, but I could be wrong. I'm not sure what intensity the Salvia that I tried for this first time was, but I think it was somewhere around 20x or 30x (I actually doubt it was that much to be honest). After having tried Salvia two times after this, I have come to think that this type of Salvia that I tried for my first time wasn't very good. Salvia is derived from a plant and looks like a bunch of crumbled up dried leaves. The Salvia I took for the first time, however, had a grainy black look to it, almost like gun powder. On top of the fact that it probably wasn't very good in potency, the only device we had to smoke out of was a small pipe used for smoking pot out of. I was very nervous right before trying it but I was determined to see what it would do.

I took the first hit and held it in as long as possible. As soon as I exhaled, I immediately looked at the TV and saw a head coming out of someone's body in the Futurama episode. I immediately began to laugh harder than I had ever laughed before in my life, and shouted to everyone in the room, "Did his head just pop out of that guy's body!?" Everyone began to laugh (what is important to note about me seeing the head pop off of some guy's body in the TV show, is that I didn't hallucinate this. It was what was happening at some part in the Futurama TV show. I just simply thought it was one of the funniest things I had ever seen). That was the only memorable part of the first trip. It felt like I was peaking on marijuana for about three or four minutes, but it was a marijuana peak high times about 10. After coming down I was a little disappointed that I didn't travel to another dimension and see penguins like Brad. I wanted to try it again that night, but we only had enough for everyone to take a hit. After leaving the house with Brad and another friend, Brad told me that the Salvia was not very good. I was a little frustrated that it didn't have the effect I was looking for and so I was determined to try it again.

A few weeks after my first experience I went to a head shop and bought some. The highest intensity that they were selling at the head shop was 60x so I decided that would have to do. It was a weekend night when Brad, Rick, Edwin and I decided to try it. I invited them over to spend the night at my house and in the middle of the night, we decided to do the Salvia at a lake about half a mile from my house. It was probably a combination of the fact that the Salvia I had the first time wasn't very potent, and that I smoked it out of a regular pipe that contributed to me not having a very notable experience. However, on this night we used Brad's bubbler and the Salvia looked more like how it is supposed to. Rick was the first to try it and we all looked on. When tripping in a group of no more than three or four it was recommended to us that you should only have one person tripping at a time. Otherwise, if everyone was tripping at once, there would be no competent person around who would either be looking out for something that might fuck with the trip, like another person walking up and wondering what we were doing, or if someone freaked out and started doing something that might be dangerous to himself or others. Me, Brad, and Edwin looked on as Rick took the first hit. It lasted about four or five minutes and he pretty much just sat on the ground and stared straight ahead. When he came out of the trip, he told us that he was in a Super Mario type reality where he was jumping over obstacles, like mushrooms that they do in Super Mario games. I was relieved that the Salvia actually made someone travel into a different place, since no one who I tried the Salvia with the first time had any memorable trip happen to them. I was next.

The four of us were all sitting along a trail that leads up to the lake. It was in a little valley with the lake about twenty yards away and a few feet in elevation above us. Sitting side by side along the trail, it was Rick who sat closest to the lake, followed by Brad, Edwin, and me at the end. I took a very big hit and held it in as long as I could. I then exhaled and for the first three to four seconds, nothing happened. However, right as I was contemplating maybe taking another hit, my surroundings in my peripheral vision began to become different. In my vision I could see that I had become enclosed in a moderate to brightly lit tunnel (after reflecting on the experience, I think I went through a wormhole, since it looked identical to the other two wormholes I went through as discussed in the Complete Story). I was travelling down the tunnel, and I saw a person standing at the end. I'm not sure why I did this, but for some reason right when I saw the person, I extended my arm out to either touch the person or see if they would grab my arm. Upon reflection, I think I was trying to initiate the trip a little bit further and really see what happens, because at this point I was still not completely in a different place. This, however, changed immediately when the next thing I saw when I was no longer travelling down the tunnel, was a completely different scenery then the one I was in back in sober earth. I saw that I was still sitting alongside Brad, Rick, and Edwin, however, the valley that we were sitting in immediately dropped off and I could see that we were sitting alongside a cliff with our feet dangling along the edge. The next thing I saw was a huge tree that had a face, with the branches representing its limbs, and the leaves on the top of the tree representing its hair. It kind of resembled an "Ent" from the Lord of the Rings movies. I had no idea what was going on, but I then became very frightened as the tree grabbed me and tried to take me away. Being scared shitless and not wanting the tree to take me away, I immediately grabbed onto one of Edwin's legs. I was told once I came down off the Salvia, that when I did this Edwin was very confused.

Edwin: Dude, what should I do?
Brad: Just let him be.
Edwin: Ok, I guess…

The next thing I remember is the tree grabbing me and I was then on the top of it, watching as it walked away from the place where Rick, Brad and Edwin were sitting. I was then transported to a place where there were dozens of other trees looking exactly like the one who took me away, except they were all different colors. The trees were all standing in a circle, and I was placed in the middle of the circle. I then heard what I can only describe as music and sounds that I had never heard before, and that I don't think exist in the earthly dimension. It sounded like worship music, and all the trees began to wave their branches and move their bodies from side to side all while singing to me. I then got an intuition that told me that they were the, "Magic Tree Friends/People". The next thing I then remember was looking up at the sky as dirt and roots began to cover up the world above. I then became aware of one certain thing: I was a tree all along, and that I had just woken up from a dream of being a human. Fuck! I don't want to be a fucking tree; I want to stay being a human! Fuck! At this point, I was 100% positive that I was a tree. The next thing I remember was seeing some sort of organization of how the tree people live. I can't really describe it, but it basically resembled a sort of hierarchy of how their dimension was structured. Because it only exists in that dimension, it is pretty much pointless to try and describe it in this dimension (interestingly enough, the existential hierarchy resembled the absolute reality hierarchy that I related to the pre-established harmony as recounted in the Complete Story). After seeing this, I was then back on the top of the tree that originally took me away from the place where my friends were sitting. He brought me back to the valley next to the lake, dropped me off next to my friends and began to walk away.

Me: Bye! See ya!

Since we were trying to keep a low profile and not trying to draw attention to ourselves while tripping, I think this kind of irritated Rick, Brad, and Edwin. Once back on earth, my surroundings were no longer of being in the other place, however, I did see that the weeds and tall grass around me and in the valley all resembled tiny trees with faces. I then gradually came down and stopped hallucinating completely. Brad's trip was basically him laughing the whole time, looking up at the stars.

Brad: Can you guys see that? How can you not see that? Everything is turning. HAHA!

After coming down he said that all the stars were able to be moved and altered by a button/dial he had. The last person to trip was Edwin, and, not surprisingly, nothing happened to him. Edwin was the type of person (some people might relate to this with a friend they know) who would take a substance and then claim that it had no effect on him. In the early days of when I first started smoking pot, I would smoke with Edwin, and after smoking a bowl or two, he would claim that he felt nothing. His eyes were of course completely bloodshot and watered over, but he said he felt nothing. So, Edwin took about three hits of the Salvia (Brad, Rick, and I only took one), and sat in a meditation type pose to see if the drug would take him, but nothing happened. After this, we left the lake and went back to my house.

The third and final time I did Salvia was with Rick, Edwin, and my brother at Rick's house. We still had about two hits worth of the Salvia left over from the second time we did it at the lake. Rick went first and, after nothing happened to him for about two minutes, he then got up from his chair, began walking around his basement very confused saying, "What the fuck, how did my house turn into this? What the fuck?" When the drug wore off, he said that his entire room changed into a castle dungeon. I wasn't sure what I was expecting to happen to me the third time I tried it. I classified the trip by the lake as a "religious experience" and in some ways changed how I view shit about reality. I took the hit and right as I exhaled, I again became immediately aware of the "Magic Tree Friends" reality. I could still see everything in my surroundings of the basement we were in, but I again saw the tree people's reality structure, and hearing the praise/worship music that were sounds that don't exist in the earthly reality. The sound of my voice immediately changed in a high pitched, very weird sound.

Me: What the fuck!? Holy shit! HAHA! What the fuck!?

Everyone started laughing. I then began to feel what I think was something like tree bark become encrusted onto my neck going up towards my face. I then closed my eyes as I let out one final, "What the fuck?" in a very low tone of voice as I seemed to transform into a tree again as I closed my eyes. A few moments later I came down and everything turned back to normal. That was the final time I tried Salvia and will definitely be the last time. The idea of going completely out of my mind and traveling to a different universe never appealed to me again after that. Not to mention I am pretty sure if I did do it again, I would just transform into a fucking tree again and that would piss me off. I told the story of the second time I tripped by the lake to a few friends, and, just to put into perspective just how much this drug (I did 60x, I don't even want to imagine what 500x or 600x would do to me) can make you hallucinate:

Brad: Were you at all exaggerating when you tripped, like when you grabbed Edwin's leg or shouted out, "See ya!"
Me: No man. Definitely not.
Brad: Haha. Holy shit.[46]

## THE MAGIC MUSHROOMS STORIES

In my early days of first experimenting with drugs I always wondered what it would be like to hallucinate and see something that is not actually there. I knew that if I wanted to experience this, psychedelics were the gateway. Pot is definitely a gateway drug. Anyone who has smoked pot and denies this is straight up lying or just trying to come across as a person who feels like they have to defend pot against the criticism of politicians and other anti-drug people who say that it is. The same goes for people who say pot is not a drug because it is a plant and not a chemical. Ok, well so is Salvia and magic mushrooms, which they probably do think are drugs, so their argument really doesn't carry any validity. Since the only drug I had tried up to the point of first trying shrooms was marijuana, I curious as to what it would do to me. I set up the first time for trying shrooms with my friends Rick and Brad. Brad's roommate, "Sam" was there to, but he was sober because apparently it is safe to have someone sober in the group to make sure no one does anything stupid. This is really only a recommendation for first time users because the more you become experienced with psychedelics, the more you are able to handle it by yourself.

We were at Brad's apartment and we each took a 16th of an ounce each. We wanted to begin the trip by watching something we thought would be trippy, so we put on "Finding Nemo" and waited for the drug to take effect. An hour went by, and nothing happened. An hour and a half went by and still nothing. I thought that maybe we got ripped off and they weren't shrooms at all but then Rick began to trip. Rick was the only one of us that had tried it before, and he claimed that they were a pretty good batch. Two hours went by and still nothing. The movie was over, and Brad and I were anxious for the drug to take a hold of us. We decided that it was stupid to just sit around sober and wait for something to happen, so we decided to smoke some pot. About five minutes after finishing the bowl we both began to trip at the same time. It was different then I thought. People who have never tried psychedelics before just assume that you hallucinate and that is pretty much it. Not true. There is a reason people call it "tripping". Tripping is a new type of high that elevates your state of mind to a new way of thinking and perceiving the world. The best part about shrooms that is almost entirely missing from something like LSD is that it makes almost anything funny. Rick decided to go on a walk, while Brad and I laid down on the floor of his apartment, looking up at the ceiling, laughing at pretty much nothing. The shroom high comes in waves. One minute your sober, the next your high as a kite, and that repeats for a couple of hours.

As I lay there on the floor I begin to start hallucinating. I look up at the corner of his ceiling and I see a six foot iguana crawling across it. Brad and I get in a conversation that went something like this:

Me: So what do you think is true? Like religions and shit.
Brad: I don't know I'm tripping balls right now.
Me: Me to bro. But I'm saying like, you know how this shit makes you perceive other shit? Which religion do you think is the most true?

Brad and I start to laugh hysterically. And then we both look at each other.

Brad and Me together: Dude, Buddhism.

Upon reflection, that seemed like a fair assessment. I think altered states of consciousness like meditation makes you aware of some of the same stuff that you are aware of while tripping. The four of us decided to take a walk to a local park near Brad's apartment and every ten to fifteen seconds I would trip out and just stand there looking at the ground.

Brad: Come on dude we want to get to the park.
Me: I'm sorry man I keep tripping out. Fuck this is crazy.

A woman walked by just as I was saying this and just seemed to ignore us. We got to the park and just stared up at the sky. We took note that everyone else in the park is just going along with their day, completely oblivious to the fact that we are all mind fucked and in a completely different universe then they are.

Rick had to leave for work while he was still tripping and drove. He said he would never do it again. Driving while tripping was something I never planned to do, but I guess there is a first time for everything that I will now describe. I went to a party at a friend of mine from college's apartment. I was with my two neighbors, Ken and Gary. We were looking to try and find some shrooms that night, and we lucked out as there was someone at the party who was a shrooms dealer. Gary and I each wanted to do an eighth of an ounce and Ken only wanted to do a sixteenth. The dealer said it would be $25 for an eighth and $20 for a sixteenth. Shitty drug dealers always are looking for a way to rip people off and we immediately called them on their bullshit. We bought three eighths for $25 apiece and the drug dealer seemed to be a little upset that she didn't get away with the $20 sixteenth scam. Back at the party I met a guy, Paul who was talking about the psychedelic drug DMT. He told me that he had some left over from the last time he did it and I thought it would be a sick idea if I did the DMT while tripping on the shrooms at the same time. Before this time, I had yet to start tripping but immediately once I came to the realization that I was about to do the DMT, I began tripping. Interesting fact about my psychedelic experiences: I have always needed some outside source to get me to start tripping. For some reason it is not possible for my mind to make the jump from being sober to tripping, and I need an intermediary to bridge the gap. Smoking pot usually does the trick, but on this occasion, the knowledge that I may do DMT for some reason did the trick. We went to Paul's apartment and I sat down on his couch while he went to go get the DMT. Apparently, from what I have heard about DMT, it is such a powerful hallucinogenic that people can completely get their realities fucked with. I heard a story about a guy who smoked DMT and in the trip, he hallucinated that he came out of it. He then went along living his life, and then when he died, he was immediately transferred back to the moment that he came out of the DMT trip. This happened several times, always hallucinating that he came out of it and living his sober life again, only to then be transported back again. In other words, when this person really did come out of the trip and sober up, it was just like the other times he did while he was in the trip, so he has no idea whether he is still tripping or not. This relates to my situation in that as I was sitting there on the couch, waiting for Paul to come back with the DMT, I am not completely sure whether I took the DMT, and am in the DMT trip, just hallucinating that I kept living my normal life as if nothing happened. Unfortunately, he couldn't find the DMT, and I ended up not being able to do it. Still, it could be that I took the DMT and then just hallucinated that he wasn't able to find it and kept living my life.

How the fuck can you really know, I guess? Disappointed that I couldn't do the DMT, at least at that point I was still tripping balls on the shrooms and so we decided to go walk around the CU campus for a while. It was cold and so we decided to say fuck that and then I did something I will never do again, I drove to Gary's house, roughly thirty minutes away, while still completely rolling on the shrooms.

I tried to keep my mind as focused as possible, not letting myself trip out and have my mind wander on some tangent. Whenever I was about to hallucinate, I directed my attention back to driving. Unfortunately, this kind of killed the trip for me. The point of tripping on psychedelics is to let your thoughts go and have the drug take your mind to wherever it's going to take you. At one point in the drive, there was some asshole in back of me that was riding my ass and trying to get around me but was not able to since there were so many cars going in the opposite direction. It kind of fucked with my head a little bit and I just sat there trying to figure out if my mind was just messing with me. Meanwhile, Ken and Gary sat in the passenger seats just praying that I wouldn't fuck up. Finally, after about five minutes of tailing me, the driver in back of me sped around me and I told Ken and Gary to waive their hands out of the car windows to signal to him that we really didn't give a fuck. We finally made it to Gary's house unscathed, but it is definitely not something I would do again.

Of all the shroom trips I have had in my life, the third time I did it in college was by far the craziest trip I have ever had on it or with any of my experiences on LSD. I took an eighth of an ounce, crumbled it up into tiny pieces and mixed it with a bottle of orange juice. Apparently taking vitamin C right before you trip mushrooms makes you trip harder, so I was determined to get the most out of this experience. I went with one of my roommates and a few of our friends from our dorm hall up to a place in the mountains. I began to trip and it started with normal hallucinations: seeing rock formations transform into various things and the clouds in the sky morph into different shapes. Then I started to trip harder than I have ever tripped before or have tripped since. I had a crazy religious/spiritual enlightenment that I will try and describe in brief statements about what was revealed to me:

-The more you hallucinate and become completely consumed by the trip, the more and more you can slow down time and perceive time drastically different. For example, you can smoke DMT and trip for what feels like years to you. However, if you smoke DMT again once inside the DMT trip, then you can slow down time even more, making the trip seem to you even longer, decades, centuries or even thousands of years. The more you go deeper into the trip, the more drastic your perception of time becomes dilated. I explained this to my friends when I was tripping and Gerald responded, "Holy shit, you really did figure shit out." A good way of depicting this was in the movie, "Inception", where the more dreams within dreams you go into, the slower time becomes. I had this revelation, however, years before the movie came out.

-I saw different hierarchies of reality, in which all living organisms have a sort of societal structure to them. For example, I perceived into the organization of my own cellular structure, in which the cells and microorganisms within my own body were structured in such a way that they have their own perception of reality and the world they live in, much like the perception of reality that humans have of the world. The cells are aware of this reality and their place in it amongst the other cells in the body. This order of reality is diversified across all living things in existence.

-I saw a categorized order to what I believe to be a traditional Christian world view of how God is. I saw a deity, which resembled almost exactly how some people view God (the father) as a person to be, mainly, a white beard and white hair, who is loving and governs existence.

-I came to the understanding that all reality is at its core, is how you observe your own existence within it. You can come to become aware of almost anything you want, perceive it that way, and that is how reality will appear to you as. How I first began to become aware of it was that if you want to stop experiencing any negativity in your life, all you must simply do is stop perceiving the thing that you would normally label as negative, as negative, and instead become aware of it as something else. A simple way of doing this is to stop caring about things that you don't want to care about. If you seize to care about the things that upset you or bring you negativity in your life, then that negativity no longer holds any power over you and controls how you perceive the world. I understood this immediately when, in the middle of the trip, I fell on a cactus and one of my hands had a shit load of thorns in it. Instead of getting upset about this, I simply chose not to care about it and not let it bother me. I no longer let what I experienced in the world dictate how I feel, and I chose to label it a different way.

-You can really only experience the things that you can conceive of. It is impossible for something to happen to you that you cannot possibly conceive of, because there does not exist any place in your observation of reality through which the inconceivable thing can dictate how you see the world. If there does not exist any way for you to possibly relate to something, then it is impossible to relate to it. It simply won't be perceived.

The effects of this shroom trip lasted for several weeks and I quickly developed a new state of mind and perception of my life. A few days after the trip I found out that I got a D on my sociology midterm. I didn't let it bother me. I used to be self-conscious about having acne. I no longer gave a shit about that either. I became more in touch with my inner true self and potential then I had ever been before in my life. I used to love tripping on psychedelics, shrooms specifically. It puts you more in touch with your inner being and personhood. Unfortunately, a few years after this trip I became schizophrenic and can no longer do any hallucinogenic drugs. I tried to trip shrooms one more time but had a bad trip related to my mental illness. Bottom line, if you are curious about wanting to try mushrooms, be prepared for a mind-altering experience that, if properly understood, will gain you much wisdom about reality.

## THE MEXICAN RESTAURANT STORIES

In my previous accounts I have briefly touched upon working at a restaurant where I first thought that people could hear my thoughts. Since I have already discussed this in detail, I will instead talk about other things that have happened to me when working at this restaurant.

I started working there in 2008 after I graduated from high school. I was looking for a job after I quit working for a shitty landscaping company. I got hired in the middle of the summer, a few months before I went to college. My first day on the job, for some reason, I decided to wear sandals to work. Anyone who has worked in a restaurant knows that this is not an appropriate thing to wear, considering all the safety risks, ranging from a knife being accidentally dropped on your foot, to slipping on something (although that can happen with regular shoes as well). The old lady that I worked with on the first day, "Alexa" told me to never wear sandals again and I agreed. She relayed it back to the guy you hired me, "Glenn", who told me the same thing. The thing I liked most about the job is that if there are no customers in the restaurant, they really don't care if you are doing busy work or not. They are fine with you just sitting on a chair in the bar watching TV until a customer walks in. I started off as a busser and quickly learned how the other employees working there are. Perhaps the biggest bitch that I worked with, who at first started treating me like an asshole the first few months I worked there, but then started to chill out once I knew her more, was a waitress named, "Anna". Unknown to me at the time, I was never told that it was part of my responsibilities to clear the customer's plates from the table once they are finished with their meal.

Anna: Dude, you got to start pre-bussing.
Me: Ok…

Twenty minutes later.

Anna: Dude, if you don't start pre-bussing, I'm going to lose my shit.
Me: I don't know what you mean. What is pre-bussing?
Anna: You don't know what pre-bussing means? You've been here for like two or three days.
Me: Yeah, and I don't know what that means.

When I was finally told how to do the job correctly, everyone started to like me and thought I was the best busser in the restaurant. The next summer I worked there after my freshman year in college, I started working in the kitchen as a dishwasher. Part of my job, on top of washing dishes was to do food prep work for the cooks. The head cook was a guy named, "Hank".

Hank: I want you to go out into the walk-in fridge and get me some grated cheddar cheese.
Me: Ok.

I walked into the fridge and the only thing I could find were blocks of cheddar cheese. That and I was too much of a stoner at the time to even understand the difference between a block of cheese and grated cheese. I walked back into the kitchen with a block of cheddar cheese.

Hank: What the fuck is this? I told you to get the grated cheese, not a block of it.
Me: Oh.
Hank: Do you know what grated cheese looks like? It's the cheese that looks like this (he holds up a container that has shredded cheddar cheese in it).
Me: Ok. Will do.
Hank: Jesus Christ. What the hell? I tell the kid to get me some grated cheese and he comes back with a block of cheese.

A few weeks in and I knew how to prep everything, and I was getting pretty fast at washing the dishes as well. The next year when I started working there again, I was offered to become a waiter, and I accepted. When you are a waiter, you run into some pretty nice people, and, of course, run into the fucking pricks that you can't do anything right for. One of the nicest tables I ever had was four old people, two men, and two women. I went up to their table carrying four drinks on a plate. I picked one of the drinks up, which caused the plate to become unbalanced with the other three drinks on the opposite side, and all three of them spilled onto a guy's neck and shoulder.

Me: Holy shit, I am so sorry.
Guy: Damn that's cold!
Me: Yeah, I bet. Really sorry.
Guy: Don't worry about it.

They ended up giving me a pretty damn good tip, so there were no hard feelings. The only time I was ever stiffed on a tip was when I was waiting on a couples table, who were probably in their mid to late fifties. The woman ordered the Buffalo Chicken sandwich but wanted no blue cheese on it. They would later tell me that she is so allergic to blue cheese that if she has any, it could potentially put her into a state that could become fatal. If I would have known that I never would have done what I did. I put the order into the computer, but forgot to put, "No blue cheese" on it, to tell the cooks to not put any on it. Once the order was ready, I remembered that she ordered for there to be no blue cheese on it. I tried to fake it, by carefully removing all the cheese off the chicken, but there were still little bits on the Buffalo sauce, and I figured that if she did notice that there was some on it, it would be so little that she really wouldn't care. I served them their food and she carefully inspected it.

Woman: Excuse me, but I ordered no blue cheese on this.
Me: Oh, did the cook end up putting some on there? I didn't see any.
Woman: Yes, there is some on here. See, the little bits on it?
Me: Ok, really sorry about that. I'll tell the cook to make you another one.
Man: Good thing we caught that, if she eats any blue cheese it could be fatal to her.
Woman: Very good we caught that.
Me: Yeah, I agree.

It took the cook another ten minutes to make her a new one and by the time it was finished, the man had pretty much finished his meal. They left the restaurant and gave me a $0 tip. I told Glenn about what happened and responded with, "What a fucking prick." The biggest asshole I ever dealt with was guy who I served when I started becoming psychotic so I can't be sure if he acted towards me this way because of the situation that was going on, or because he was just genuinely a prick. I sat their table with the guy, his wife, and their two kids. It seemed that with every single thing I said to this guy, he would always respond with an attitude like he thought I was a fucking moron and just came across as if everything I did annoyed the living shit out of him.

Me: What would you like to order sir?
Guy: I will have the Smokey Burger with fries.
Me (mistakenly not saying what I really meant): And what would you like for the side?
Guy (coming across as if I am a retard because he already told me): Fries.
Me: Oh, sorry I meant how would you like that cooked?
Guy (realizing that I just accidently said the wrong thing and maybe I'm not so dumb): Oh…ah, medium.
Me: Ok.

I came back to their table to serve them their food.

Me: Could I get you guys anything else?
Guy (annoyed): No, we are fine.
Me: Ok.

Reading this may not seem like he was that bad of a guy, but it's hard to put into writing just how much this guy just sent out a vibe like he was annoyed and pissed off by the very fact that I even existed. This may be that he just hated me because he could hear my thoughts, or maybe he was just a royal dickhead. Whatever the case is, fuck him. He ended up leaving me a really shitty tip.

When I was working as a waiter on some days and a busser on other days, a new girl, roughly my age named, "Claire" started working there. She was pretty hot, and I got to be decent friends with her. One day, I am not sure why it happened, but she was standing against a wall, and I was standing on the opposite side, looking right at her, when she stared into my eyes intensely, without ever looking away. I looked back but was really not sure how to react. We kept staring at each other when I (like a bitch/not knowing how to handle situations like that) decided that I didn't possess the confidence to keep looking into her eyes, and immediately looked away. I don't know much about woman, but one thing that I do know is that if you ever get into a staring contest with a woman that you find attractive, do not, I repeat, DO NOT look away first. If you stare at the girl long enough for them to look away before you, then that shows the girl that you possess confidence. In this respect, I failed miserably. However, if you get into a staring contest with a girl you don't find attractive, do your best to look away first, so that you don't send the wrong message. I was confused because she had a boyfriend, and maybe that had something to do with why I looked away first.

One of my best friends at the job was a waiter named, "Isaac", who later became the manager. Isaac and I would always talk about philosophical type shit and other things and became pretty good friends. One day when the restaurant was really slow, we decided to go fuck around with stuff outside. Isaac got the idea of putting some liquid substance (I don't remember exactly what it was) on some rusted aluminum or some metal like that and put it in a bottle. This had roughly the exact same effect as putting a menthos in a diet coke bottle and watching it explode. We put the aluminum in the bottle, poured some liquid in it, and screwed the bottle shut. About ten to fifteen seconds later the bottle exploded and made a loud, "BANG" noise. We were later told by the bartender that people thought a gun went off. Another thing we did to keep ourselves busy when the restaurant was slow was to make mini sling shots out of restaurant utensils. It was such a long time ago that I don't remember exactly how we made them, but we somehow got them to work, and did competitions to see who can hit a certain target. It was innocent fun.

It was in the summer of my third year working at the restaurant when I started to become psychotic. Some of my favorite, most memorable things that happened when this started happening was the following:

1.  I was bussing one night and a friend of mine, "Audrey" came into the restaurant with her brother and mom.

Me: Hey Audrey, how's it going?
Audrey: I'm ok. How are you?
Me: I'm doing ok.

All of a sudden, Audrey's mom became aware of something, something that I can only guess as to what it may have potentially been.

Audrey's Mom: Oh...ok...is this happening....are we doing this right now? Ok, hi, I'm Audrey's mother.
Me: Nice to meet you. Your server will be right with you.

My paranoia of the global situation made me think that she reacted this way because there was some set up that people were aware of, in which the women that came into the restaurant, mostly women I knew or who were roughly my age, were girls that I could choose to potentially want to try and be with one of them. And how would I show my interest in the girl and put forth the action which would make people know that I am interested in the girl? When they were finished with their food, and ready for the busser or server to take the plate off of the table, if I pre-bussed their table and cleared their plates, this would show that I am interested in potentially wanting to date the girl. Having paranoia about this at the time, I decided not to pre-bus the table, but I wish I would have, just to come across as if I don't really give a fuck and refuse to play into their games. I have absolutely no interest in wanting you to be my girlfriend, but I am just going to play along with this mass delusion because I don't give a shit. The server walked past the table multiple times, seeing the empty plates, but never cleared them off (potentially because she wanted to leave the decision up to me). After waiting a good fifteen minutes for me to not pre-bus the table, they got up and left. I said good-bye to Audrey, but there was a kind of weird vibe that I sensed from her, potentially because she may have been disappointed that I didn't take her plate and show interest in her. I hate being schizophrenic.

2.  At this point, every shift I worked was a tour de force of me participating in what people had built up in their minds as a major global event. I would hear random conversations from people, talking about Christianity, or how it was possible that they could hear my thoughts. I overheard one conversation:

Lady: So how did they say this was possible again? Some sort of quantum entanglement fluctuations or something?

I worked one shift where three men were talking the whole time about Christianity and why it is so great. I ignored most of what they were saying, and I took this to mean to them that I was the Antichrist consciousness and not the Christ consciousness, otherwise I would have shown more interest in what they were saying, I guess. When they got up to leave the restaurant, I was very polite and told them thanks for coming and to have a great night. This confused them, I think. My psychosis intuition tells me this is because they thought I was the Antichrist consciousness, and hence, why would someone who is the Antichrist consciousness be so polite and nice?

I was walking around, bussing tables one shift, and I overheard a conversation that a family was having while eating.

Man: So now he is trying to claim that there is a third mind.

Right when he said this, one of the kids came over to me and started yelling and dancing/moving around in weird ways. The kid came across to me like she was purposely acting that way for a reason, to try and make me think or do something. I barely acknowledged the kid, walked around her, and made my way out onto the patio. Fucking weird mother fuckers.

3.  At this point I began to start fucking around with people a little and started testing the boundaries of how far people will go to let me know what is really going on. I was in the kitchen waiting for my food to come up, when I said in my thoughts to the cook:

Me: Herald, look me in the eye. I know you can do it. Look me in the eye. You got this bro.

After baiting him for a while, right before he put my food up, he looked me straight in the eye, causing the other cook to start laughing. "And the truth will set you free!" I shouted in my thoughts. I was pleased and depressed at the same time.

4.  I noticed that some of the girls that I had pre-bussed for ended up coming back. What was the second step to ween the women further and further down until I finally made a selection? I still have no fucking idea. My schizophrenia only took me so far, and at some point it just becomes too complex and ridiculous to try and put a label on something. I did, however, come to understand another fundamental part of the plan to eventually set me up with a girlfriend. If I ever cracked and told any girl that I think people can hear my thoughts, and then asked her if she could hear my thoughts, then that would be the girl who I chose. I came close to cracking a few times, not because I wanted to be with the girl, but

because I was constantly freaking out about the situation and wanted some closure with somebody. The only thing keeping me from saying something to someone was that I didn't want to send a wrong message if it turned out that people really could hear my thoughts. Something like this happened in my last semester of college when, in my epistemology class, for some reason, and I have no idea why, something just popped into my head and I thought it for everyone to hear. There were two pretty cute girls in my class, and one of the delusions that either I or everyone, or both, were suffering from was that I was going to choose either Girl A, or Girl B. Honestly, I thought Girl A was cuter and if I absolutely had to make a choice between them, I would have chosen Girl A. Girl B just finished speaking to the class about something, when I just thought for some reason, "It's Girl B." This somehow brought closure to the mystery of which girl I wanted to be with. Days passed, and without talking to Girl B or making any advances towards her whatsoever, she looked at me one time, giving off a type of vibe like, "hey, do you want to talk to me?" I never did. Schizophrenia is a very convincing disorder. The only person who I ever talked to about what I was thinking was Isaac.

Me: So, you remember what I was talking to you before, about me potentially becoming psychotic?
Isaac: Yeah.
Me: Well, it was about me thinking that people could hear my thoughts.
Isaac: Oh, is that what it was?
Me: Yeah, it really sucks.

5.  I began to think that the main way in which people were trying to sway me into becoming one consciousness over another was through the way in which they talked and acted towards me. I read a book not to long before this all started happening that talked about suggestion. Basically, you introduce something to someone's mind, either through what you say to the person, or your actions towards the person, and this creates in the person's mind an avenue of thought that makes the person more susceptible to other like suggestions of others. The more times similar suggestions are made to the person, the more likely that the person receiving the suggestions will fall into what the people giving the suggestion to the person are trying to accomplish (trying to influence how the person thinks and behaves). The way that this related to the third consciousness, is that my mind got so susceptible to the incoming

suggestions of the people around me, that I would then begin to use my own imagination and come up with different meanings to the things that people suggested to me that in no way are what the person meant to convey to me, and resonate as meaning something to me. So, I would hear one conversation from a certain table in the restaurant that I took to be a suggestion for the Christ consciousness, for example. After hearing the suggestion, I would then become more aware of other conversations going on in the restaurant, even people who were just having normal conversations and were in no way trying to influence me and suggest me into a particular state, and I would take what they were saying as meaning something referring to one of the consciousness's. I would later write in one of my philosophical essays, that this was not intended to happen, and apparently started fucking the whole situation up.

6.  I took a lot of things that I thought people were trying to convey to me sometimes in a literal sense, and other times in a figurative sense, as if they were being sarcastic or trying to get me to reveal something deeper about myself. One time, this woman bartender named, "Sarah" was talking to someone at the bar and said, "Did you hear about that one blind guy who climbed Mt. Everest?" I took this as a deliberate attempt by her to try and elicit within me thoughts as to whether I was gay or not. The reason I thought this was because I thought she was actually trying to get me to think about a video I saw on the internet once in which a News reporter said, "We are going to talk to a man who climbed Mt. Everest, but he's gay...I mean he's gay, he's blind, I meant he's blind." I am not exactly sure what exactly was so attractive about myself to women that made them want to be with me, but the only thing I could think of was that they potentially had the opportunity to be lovers with "God" and that is apparently a pretty attractive thing. I overheard Anna one time talking to a guy at the bar saying, "Yeah, I'm thinking about calling off the wedding." I took this to mean that perhaps she thought that she had a chance at being with me and would rather be with me than her fiancé. I immediately thought right back to her for the whole restaurant to hear, "Don't bother."

7.  I became very meticulous in watching how people were reacting to what I was saying to them through my thoughts. Every time I would think something directed at someone and they reacted in a way that made sense in respect to what I thought towards them, I took this as evidence that they can indeed hear my thoughts. I was out on the patio one shift, and

I thought something intended for one of the owners of the bar, "Kylie" a woman in her late forties. I said, "Kylie, I come in at least ten to fifteen minutes late for work every single day, don't you want to fire me?" About a second after I thought this, Alexa immediately started laughing. There was absolutely no one else around her, she was not engaging with anyone, and she randomly started laughing, which I of course added to my countless observations that this bullshit was really happening. It got to a certain point that I was pretty much praying to get fired. I would fuck around with so many people through my thoughts directed at them, that, I figured, if I got someone to crack and piss them off to such an extent, that the owners and manager would think that it is no longer worth it for me to work there anymore. I will later describe that this ended up being much easier than I could have possibly imagined. The day I had my psychotic break and came to the almost certain conclusion that people could hear what I was thinking, there were two incidents involving two separate tables that are noteworthy. The first was that I came from the kitchen with some guacamole to give to a customer out on the patio. I kept thinking, "don't eat the guacamole. I spit in it. I'm warning you don't eat it." I went on to think (say in my mind), "You are really thinking about eating it aren't you? Do you really want to eat guacamole with my spit in it?" I noticed that for what seemed like a while, the two people sitting at the table did not touch the guacamole. I am pretty sure that I saw Isaac go up to them and say something, after which they started to eat the guacamole. The only thing I can think that he said to them was, "You're fine. He didn't spit in it." The second noteworthy occurrence involved a man who I thought was potentially going to get physical or violent with me. He made absolutely no attempt whatsoever to hide his emotions and feelings about what I was thinking towards him. There were times when I would say fucked up things towards people in my head, and he would look me straight in the eye like he wanted to beat the shit out of me. When he left, I played it all cool and said, "Thank you, have a great night", to which he wasn't really sure how to respond.

8. For some reason, people developed some sort of obsession with the length of my hair. When shit first started to hit the fan, I had very long hair, with my bangs going down past my chin. I intuited that there was another ulterior motive that people had when questioning me about my hair. If I cut it, then I was more inclined to be the Antichrist consciousness, if I left my hair long, I was more inclined to be the Christ consciousness (I

believed this to be the case because Jesus had long hair, and hence, if had long hair then that meant I was being more like Jesus). However, Claire, as it turned out, was training to be a hair stylist, so people somehow got it into their heads, that if I had Claire cut my hair, it would not only be evidence for me being more inclined to be the Antichrist consciousness (which from what I understood based off of the suggestions she was giving to me, she wanted me to become the Antichrist consciousness), but also would come across as a sort of courtship, where I would chose her to be my girlfriend, if I had her cut my hair. I ended up just getting it cut at a local hair cutting place. Here are some of the more ridiculous things people said about my hair:

Anna: Did Claire cut your hair?
Me: No, I just got it cut at Great Clips.
Anna: Oh, too bad.

Ian (the husband of a waitress, "Anne"): So why did you decide to cut your hair?
Me: I was just getting sick of it and wanted to have short hair again.

Ian: I see that your hair is starting to grow a little longer again. It's starting to get some of its thickness back.
Me: Yeah, I guess.

9.   There were other noteworthy, very sketchy other situations that occurred between how I saw people react to what I was reacting to from what they were introducing to my mind. For example, on one occasion I was sitting on a stool in the bar (but not at the actual bar), and I saw Bella and Anna sitting very close to me on bar stools, sitting at the bar. The exchange went something like this:

Bella: Who that works here has a good ass?
Me: Let's see, Bella has a great ass. Claire does not have a great ass at all.
Bella: What about Anna?
Me: Oh my God, Anna, beautiful ass.

Right as I said this, I saw them both start laughing. I could just sense that they were giving me mental suggestions and watching how I responded to them.

I was freaking out one shift and tried to think of things to calm me down. I began to think about lines from the movie, "American Beauty" to try and get me to a more relaxed, content state of mind. Isaac could see that I was uneasy that shift and so when I started thinking about scenes from that movie that make me feel happier and calmer. Isaac immediately said to me, "That's good, Psychotic Logician. Stay in that mind set." On one occasion, I was waiting a table of people who worked at the restaurant who either had the day off or were done with their shift and just hanging out with the other employees. I went over to talk to my fellow coworkers at the table, and for some reason, Ian stared at me for what had to be at least thirty seconds, most of which, I was not even talking or saying anything, just listening to what the other people at the table were saying. I don't know why he stared at me for so long without saying a single thing to me, but I was so schizophrenic by that point that I could almost take language, either verbal or body, to relate in some way to people hearing my thoughts. It wasn't just a simple way that you normally look at someone. He was really transfixed upon something about me, like he was seeing something in me that he didn't know about before. Not that it really mattered, but for most of these shifts I was fucked up on Adderall and sleep deprived. This probably made my psychosis worse, but ultimately, I think if I was more clear headed and sober, it still wouldn't have made much of a difference. I would constantly ask people if they wanted to smoke cigarettes with me on the patio and nobody did. Maybe because they didn't want to just be one on one with me, or maybe because I wanted to smoke a cigarette every five minutes when there was nothing to do.

In order to understand my state of mind referring to this next delusion that I am about to describe, let me give you some background information. When I was in college, I looked into the mirror one day and saw that my nose was uneven. I had never noticed it before, and it kind of pissed me off. I figured I could easily fix it by taping my nostril around to the top of the nose, trying to even out the base of the nose, but all attempts to do so failed. It really is not a big deal at all and if people notice it (most people don't I think) they don't give a shit at all (why would they?). I, however, built this up in my mind as being a very unattractive thing that I wanted to fix ASAP. Suffering from my own problem with my crooked nose, it had an impact on my interactions with others. It destroyed my self-confidence worse than acne, which I had earlier learned to get over after having a kick ass shroom trip in college. Now, thinking that all that the people were looking at when they were looking at my face was my nose, I began to start looking at other people's noses, to see if they were crooked or not as well. As it turned out, there were a few employees that I worked with, who's noses also were not straight. How this relates to my paranoia and people hearing my thoughts is through the following: I would get OCD/intrusive thoughts when talking to my fellow coworkers who also didn't have straight noses and begin constantly thinking about it, making it out in the open for everyone to hear. I could tell that when I was talking to some people, I would think about their nose and I noticed that the person who I was referring to got more self-conscious about it, trying not to react to what I was thinking. I would sometimes catch people staring at what I thought was my nose, which would then make me feel self-conscious and think about it even more. The thing about it is that I am pretty sure that until I started thinking about this, putting it out in the open for everyone to know about, nobody ever noticed anyone else's nose as being straight or not. All it takes is one dumbass to come in and fuck shit up for other people's self-confidence, I guess.

10. I previously mentioned the person who put up crucifixes around the entire restaurant as all these events were taking place. There were other Christian symbols around the restaurant, one most notably in the men's bathroom. I forget exactly what it was, but it was a piece of paper describing some Christian event, with a cross on it. I don't know why I did this, but when I was in the bathroom, I marked something on the Cross, changing it to something else, or scribbling it out entirely. A few days later, I found that the paper had been replaced with an exact copy of the paper, with the scribbling no longer on it. There was a bus boy who worked at the restaurant when all of this was unfolding who was a staunch Christian. We had previous talks about how he went to Bible/Christian camp, and I told him that I went to Id-Ra-Ha-Je for a few summers. I was sitting next to him at the bar at the beginning of one shift.

Me: Man, I'm freaking out.
Busser: What's up?
Me: There is something happening to me. It's either all true or all false and I can't figure out which one it is.
Busser: It's cool man. Just chill.

He was trying to make me feel more relaxed about the situation, but it really didn't help. There were later times when I heard at least one of the waitresses talk smack about the Busser and his Christian beliefs.

This leads me to the climactic event that ended up making me move on with my life, towards other experiences revolving around what was happening to me, but in other places. I would always say in my thoughts that I was threatening to quit at the end of the shift, on top of wishing that I would get fired. On one occasion I said it so many times, that I may have had some people convinced, and then Isaac, the manager at the time, ended up deciding to leave the shift early, before I could do so. I ended up finding a perfect in, which fell straight into my lap one shift, without me ever realizing it as a potential way out of the job before. I arrived one shift to the same scene I had witnesses for the past month, mainly, people pouring into the restaurant on a busy Friday night, ready to witness the events that the whole world was talking about (remember you are seeing this through my state of mind). I clocked in and went out to the patio to see what was going on. The patio was almost completely full, and I saw the two owners (the husband and wife), assembling two or three tables together. Another thing that struck me about when all this was happening was that the owners started coming into eat a lot more than they usually did. I took this to mean that they were happy that I was working for them, since it was bringing in customers who wanted to witness the situation for themselves. It was as if people were getting ready for some sort of entertainment show, with the main attraction being me and the things I thought. I walked back inside and started doing miscellaneous little chores to start the shift off. On Friday and Saturday nights the restaurant had two bussers working the shift because it would get so busy. I was working that shift as a busser and the other busser was a guy named, "Jeff". I started talking to him and he told me that the owners were at the restaurant and that I should tuck in my shirt. I don't exactly remember why it didn't occur to me before, but for some reason I had always abided by the rule that all the male employees had to tuck in their shirts when working. I have always hated tucking in my shirt, most notably when I was in the Boy Scouts, and my Scout leader would constantly have to remind me to do so and sometimes get pretty angry at me for not doing so. I went back into the kitchen where I saw the cooks preparing the food and Isaac was washing the dishes. He told me to tuck in my shirt once, but I just ignored him. He asked me again.

Isaac: Tuck in your shirt.
Me: I don't think I'm going to.
Isaac: You have to, the owners are here, and it is restaurant policy.
Me: What if I don't?

Isaac: Then you are fired. I'll get Kylie to cover your serving shift tomorrow morning.

I then turned away from him and went over to the computer used to order food from, and to clock in and out of your shift. I contemplated what to do. Bella then walked up to the other computer.

Me: What should I do Bella? Should I tuck in my shirt or not?
Bella: You know you're going to get fired if you don't, right?
Me: Yes, I know that.
Bella: Whatever do what you want.

She then left the kitchen with her food order. I then clock out on the computer and start walking towards the back door out of the restaurant.

Isaac: Are you serious man? After all this? This seems like a pretty shitty way to end it.

I see Alexa standing right beside me with a food order in her hand, watching what is happening. I just look at Isaac for a second, then turn and walk out of the restaurant. I was pretty happy with my decision. I consider that I quit as opposed to being fired, but other people may say it is the other way around. I was just sick of the bullshit that was going on around me. At that point, my attitude was pretty much like, "you can hear my thoughts, and all this crazy shit is happening around me, and you are telling me that I have to tuck in my shirt? Are you fucking crazy?" Within the next few months following when this happened, I pretty much retained that state of mind, but in reference to society as a whole. I thought, "If it turns out that people really can hear my thoughts, and I become certain of it, I am going to walk around naked everywhere." Of course, the world being so fucked up, and not seeing the humor in it, I would probably get arrested. My main defense I would use in front of the judge is, "but you can hear my thoughts, and you are telling me what to do?" (like they hold some sort of moral superiority over me) Since the day I quit I have only been back there once, and that was to pick up my final paycheck, which, since this occurred at the exact same time as my Keno and gambling addiction, I spent the entire $70 check on scratch tickets and didn't win anything. The only person I saw was Hank, who I kind of just joked around with for a second or two and I was out the door never to return. According to Jeff who I worked with a few years later at a Car Wash, he said that me walking out was the topic of conversation by all of the employees for a long time. Isaac was apparently pretty pissed off, but I feel like the biggest losers were the owners. They no longer had me as the main attraction to bring in customers, and hence, their restaurant lost a lot of its publicity.[47]

## THE SPORTS GRILL RESTAURANT STORIES

About a month after my experience happened as recounted in the complete story, which I considered to be the climax of the two to three months that preceded it, I ended up getting a job at a local sports grill restaurant as a dishwasher. I started the job and immediately hated it. I even thought about going back to the Mexican restaurant that I quit at and asking for my job back, but I just couldn't deal with any more bullshit that that place put me through. Little did I know, I was about to have just as many psychotic occurrences working at the sports grill, as I did at the other restaurant. A few days before I got this job, I set up a plan with my parents regarding the Adderall prescription that I still had from the previous semester of college. The plan: my dad will go with me every month to pick up the prescription and then put it in his safe. After eight months of going without the Adderall, he would then give me the entire eight months' worth at once. The idea behind this was so that I would give the medication that my other psychiatrist prescribed to me (the antipsychotic medications) a shot to see if they would help me. I referred to the day in May of the next year after I started working (I started in September of 2011) as, "Zero Day". The reason I even agreed to do this in the first place was because I literally had no money at all, and I still wanted to keep getting my Adderall prescription every month, so I figured the only way this was possible was to have my dad pay for it. This ended up being a huge mistake. What I should have done was just waited until I had a job and then start paying for the prescriptions myself. If I missed out on a month or two of prescriptions for not having enough money to get them, so be it, at least within a few months I would be getting it again. Although I promised my parents that I would not take any Adderall or stimulants for the entire eight month period, true to form, I couldn't resist. That is an important thing to understand about me when it comes to drugs that make me feel good and more like myself, mainly, I'll use any reason I can come up with to justify taking the drug. For example, right now as I am writing this, I am on roughly 1.5 grams of ephedrine, and when I decided to take it, I thought that there was a potential that I might miss work, and that was ok with me, just as long as I get to a state where I am feeling good. So, throughout the entire time I worked as a dishwasher at the sports grill, I spent roughly 70-80% of the money I earned on Adderall. It is because of indulging in the euphoria of Adderall (which would give me mild stimulant psychosis), as well as the weed hits I took before and during work that made my time working at the sports grill so insanely psychotic.

Within my first week working at the sports grill is when I completely deduced all of existence for a second time (which I wrote about previously). I had to go into work later that day because I was asked to cover a shift for another dishwasher. I immediately knew the second that I walked in that the people knew who I was, and that they are now working with the kid whose thoughts they could hear. The hallucinations when I was sober pretty much wore off at this point, and the only times I now thought that people could hear my thoughts was when I was high on some drug. I kept thinking to myself, "I have done it. I have fucking done it. I unified the Christ and Antichrist consciousness's. I fucking sublated that shit (sublated is a term taken from Hegel which is pretty much synonymous with unifying a positive thing with a negative thing)!" I could hear people saying things when talking to each other in the kitchen which I was working, and on one occasion, just like I used to believe that every single conversation that people were having in some way referred to me (at the other restaurant), I thought they were talking exclusively about me.

Me (to a cook): What did you say I should do?
Cook (laughs): Oh, no, not you buddy, you're fine just doing what you are doing.

This confused me, but I considered it part of potentially coming down from the complete knowledge peak I had attained ten hours earlier. Throughout the entire shift I had the song, "What you know" by Two Door Cinema club stuck in my head, which earlier in the day I clearly saw how it related to me and the events that happened that day. Just so happy to have finally accomplished what I wanted to achieve in existence, I kept thinking how happy I was that I finally unified the Christ and Antichrist consciousness's.

Jimmy (a cook): Why does he keep saying that?
George (a cook): Don't worry about it, just keep working.

At one point in the night, I went out to the restaurant area where the customers eat and I saw a friend of mine, "Gary" who I tripped mushrooms with in a previous story. He was sitting with a few other people, and I gave them a look like, "Hey, what's up? Yeah, I proved everything and shit. How's it going?" The other people at the table, after looking at me for a second, decided not to give me any more attention and went on talking amongst themselves. I talk to a busser, a cute girl named, "Amanda".

Amanda: How's it going?
Me: Pretty good.
Amanda: So, do you go to college or anything?
Me: No, I dropped out. I don't think I will ever go back.
Amanda: Why not?

This confused me because I thought the answer was obvious. Because I had just completely deduced all of existence again, attained God status and can do whatever the fuck I want now. So why the fuck would I go back to college? I overheard a conversation between Jimmy and a waiter. They were talking about something that had to do with the Saudi Arabian's and I took this to mean the following: some Saudi Arabian's were pissed that I again showed that I know everything and am God, and had to accept that it was true, because it was true. They may have been potentially thinking something of the like of, "God dammit, how many more fucking times is this kid going to do this shit?" Throughout the entire shift I was hoping that someone could tell me that they could hear my thoughts, like Frank did the previous night, and give me a knowledge/confidence boost.

George: Don't tell him you can hear his thoughts.
Jimmy: Ok.

For some reason, and I don't know why, but some people decide to act like a jackass to me whenever I am in this type of psychotic state. One waiter, "Hank" gave me a talking to about something. I think he tried to come across as someone who doesn't really give a shit about what I think I know and attempted to give me somewhat of a confidence depletion.

Jimmy: Don't let Hank get to you man.
Me: For sure. I don't really care.

The same thing happened earlier that day when, before I came in for the shift, I tried to buy booze for John who has 16 or 17 at the time. I had a dollar remaining on a credit card that I had gotten for free when I was trying to find ways to get money together to fund my Keno addiction (which I will talk about later on), and I asked the cashier if he could just charge a dollar to the card, and I would pay the rest with the cash that John gave me. The cashier, understanding who I was and deciding to be a dick to me, looked at me like he had no idea what the fuck I was talking about. It's entirely possible for them to do, in the same way that you can pay with half cash and the rest on your credit card when buying something anywhere else.

Cashier: No, I can't do that. I don't know what you are talking about.
Me: Can I just pay all but one dollar in cash, and then put the remaining dollar on the credit card?
Cashier: Kid, I don't know what that means.
Me: Ok.

Perhaps it has something to do with the fact that they are just butt hurt like the Saudi Arabian's, or maybe they just want to intentionally try and bring me down, it doesn't really matter. The last memorable thing that happened that night was when George quickly ran over to the radio that was playing and turned it to another station.

George: That is the second time they have tried to play that on here.
Jimmy: Haha.

I took this to potentially mean that maybe they were broadcasting on the radio something about what I did the previous night, to let the world know (if they didn't already). I already heard things being said on the radio previous to this that I thought justified my paranoia that people could hear my thoughts (like when the radio station mentioned the rapture), but George turned it off before I could completely hear what they were going to say. Which brings me to this question: after doing what I did ten hours ago, proving the shit I proved, bringing happiness to the world, why would people still try and keep hidden from me that they could hear my thoughts? The only thing I could think of was that I had come down, and they were no longer in a position where they had to completely comply with the things that I was thinking about. A few days later I took a picture of all my philosophical writings and put them on eBay for the price of $100,000. I was sure someone would buy, but no one did.

I should briefly mention that a shift or two before the shift I just described above occurred, I had first smoked weed on the job with Jimmy and another cook named, "Kurt".

Jimmy: You're not going to go crazy stoner on us, are you?
Me: No, I'm chill man. I've smoked weed a lot of times in the past.
Kurt: He's chill.

During that shift I was having what I would later come to refer to as a "thought battle". Basically, a thought battle is a conversation that you have with a person or multiple people that involves only your thoughts, and no actual physical verbal communication (kind of like a telepathic conversation). I was communicating with Jimmy and Kurt with only my thoughts, and I could hear their thoughts communicating back to me. At one point in the exchange, I said something really funny that made them all start laughing, including one of the waitresses, "Naomi", who would later become my meth dealer a year or two in the future. What makes this exchange important is that when I started thinking about some of my philosophical ideas, I completely deduced existence in three steps. I believe the reason, nothing that big ever came of this was because I used as a step that by me existing and proving to the world that the end times will not come true, validated the understanding that I possessed all knowledge. A few days later when I actually did completely deduce everything, the difference was that I did not need to rely on empirical evidence to understand all knowledge, and rather did it through pure thought.

The weeks following the above two occurrences, pretty much followed a plan that I had in my head that I was still going to try and become free, through writing philosophy. Since I had to work three to four days a week, I would come in on my shifts highly psychotic. I ended up getting a raise within a month of working there, which bumped me up to $8.25 an hour. There came a day when I was not sure if I had to work, because the kitchen manager who hired me wrote on the schedule the time that I was supposed to come in, erased it and wrote in a time right below my name, which happened to be right above another dishwasher's name. To make sure that I either did or didn't have to work, I was going to show up at the time it said on the work schedule, but, seeing as that I was already rolling on Adderall, I decided to get stoned before I came in. I went over to Frank's house, and he smoked me up.

Me: Man, I think I have finally figured shit out. You know the thing about the secret and shit and how you can get whatever you want?
Frank: Yeah.
Me: I finally understand how you can do that shit. You literally just have to completely personify the thing that you want to become. You have to play

the part exactly as you want it to be. Like for example, if I want to escape existence and be completely free, all I have to do is be 100% committed to it. No bullshit. There has to be no part of your being that is not completely on board with it. If you completely act the part, then it will happen.
Frank: Haha. Nice.

At this point in my life, whenever I would smoke pot is when I would begin to hear voices. Immediately when I became blitzed, voices would appear in my perception as if there were people observing the world through my observation and seeing what I am seeing. I drove to work and was told that I did indeed have to work. Frank gave me a nug worth of bud, so that I could smoke it after my shift and try to become free. I began working and thought battles started to occur between me and pretty much everyone in the restaurant, including the customers eating in the dining room. I, unfortunately, possess the ability to alter what people say/think towards me, such that I distort what they are really saying, and make it into something that I think that they are going to say. On one occasion, George said something to me, and after I distorted the end of what he was thinking, he said, "that's not what I said!" (people would get really emotional about things like that, which, when looking in the grand scheme of things shouldn't really be thought of as being that serious of a thing) What I have come to learn about people potentially hearing my thoughts, as well as the voices in my head, is that they get very emotionally involved in their interactions with me. If I distort what they are saying to me, they tend to get a little upset, like it somehow matters. I wish I couldn't do this, but fuck me, I know I suck. Once I began to start washing dishes and become more involved in my job, I could hear other people talking to each other, verbally.

Cook: What do you think, should we fire him?
Supervisor: I don't know what to think.

Like the job I had at the other restaurant before this, I began to beg them to please fire me. I think the supervisor was just pissed off because I was making fun of him for messing up on the schedule. I went to put some dishes back to where they are supposed to go, and I passed by the part of the kitchen where the cooks prepare the food and I saw Jimmy.

Jimmy: Psychotic Logician, do the Tebow pose!

I was not sure what to do. I just stood there for a second, as a waitress walked by.

Waitress (like she thought I was in a difficult position of whether I should acknowledge the Christian God like Tim Tebow or not): Ah...

A few seconds pass and I end up doing the Tebow pose. About two minutes later a cook walks up to Jimmy.

Cook: Don't you ever do that again! What did you think was going to happen?! Now he's going to be thinking about it all shift long! God dammit!

The problem with that exchange was that up until the cook approached Jimmy and got pissed off at him, I had let the entire thing go and moved on. By him mentioning it again and making a big deal out of it, this ended up becoming a complete OCD thought in my head that pretty much lasted the entire shift. The shift went on with multiple times me hearing outbursts from the customers outside, whenever I would make an important insight. I talked with Jimmy once before about my plans to attempt to put absolute time on pause so that I could just walk around all of existence by myself and do whatever I want, for as long as I want, but without discussing with him in any way that I had plans to do this when I got off from the shift, he approached me.

Jimmy: So, when you completely stop the universe that is just the earth right?
Me: No, it is everything. Not just the entire universe, but everything that exists, even if there are parallel realities and multiple universes, those will be put on pause as well.
Jimmy: Good luck.

Once I got off the shift, I immediately went home and smoked the bowl that Frank gave me. I made the decision that I would try and attain freedom, via the girl who I loved, the girl in the red dress that I wanted to be with at that moment. I tried to materialize her in front of me, as I did in the Complete Story (got to be about halfway up her knees), but it was not happening. I decided to go with something a little easier. I began to start hallucinating to the point that the hallucinations became just as visual to me as the physical reality in front of me, such that I could then connect the two realities together and make them one. I at first tried to visualize a button, which, when pushed, would pause absolute time. I almost did this a few times, but failed at the last moment, which is the hardest to stay with. I then started visualizing sand coming out of my fingers. I rubbed my fingers on the carpet and I could see sand coming out of them. When I brushed my fingers on the carpet, sand flew up. Then something happened that has put a stop to every one of my attempts to try and escape reality. I come down.

The next few months progressed much the same. I would get high at work, but my perception started to switch from focusing on the people around me, to focusing on the voices in my head. One day I was writing some philosophical/mathematical essay, when I reached a point where I started to become highly paranoid that the devil would make good on the deal I made with him in college, and try to either possess me, annihilate me, or send me to hell. Fearing this, I picked up my Bible and began to read. This was the first time that I ever had what I considered at the time to be the real Jesus, speak to me through the Bible. It was as if Jesus was speaking directly to me through what was written in the Bible. It got to a point where voices in my head, one of which was Satan and a few others, were on the verge of getting annihilated themselves. I knew this because I could hear Satan in somewhat pain, saying, "Ah, this hurts", or something like that. The choice was left up to me to decide their fate. I opted for the choice that I chose as documented, as well as the choice that I will always make in the future, mainly, compassion and I asked Jesus to have mercy on them. Once I asked for mercy, the annihilation process immediately stopped, but I then attained a new level that I had not experienced before. The last thing I read in the Bible before I left for work was the passage where Jesus says (just quoting from memory), "if you say for a mountain to move from one place to another, then if you have enough faith, it will move." Understanding that I was now one with Jesus, I understood that all I needed to do in order to do anything in the world, is to pray to him and ask, and it would be done. The shift progressed in the following way:

1) I would ask Jesus to help me be one with truth, so that I can see truth clearly at all times.

2) I held two contradictory ideas in my head at once, debating which one I would rather want either; A) to be completely one with truth all the time and be in the perception of always seeing it, or B) to have control of the physical world, such that I could walk on water like he did or make something levitate or whatever I want.

3) I became aware that a part of the truth that Jesus was putting forth, had some negativity attached to it, mainly, that truth is in some sense bad because of the existence of hell.

4) I decide that I don't agree with this truth, and I immediately begin to lose touch with Jesus's truth.

Just as this began to happen, I hear a voice in my head that says, "Are you kidding me?" I then begin to start philosophizing in my head all the aspects of what I believe to be incorrect and flawed about Jesus's theory of truth and put forth what I believe to be the correct version of truth. At this point, Jesus asked if he could speak to me. I told him that he doesn't need my permission to speak to me, and that he can just go ahead whenever he wants. I forget exactly what he said, but simply put, I gave him permission to attempt to annihilate me if he so chooses. He accepted and then attempted to send me into eternal obliteration. To get a glimpse into my state of mind at this point, just imagine that I had completely lost touch with what I considered to be ultimate truth roughly thirty minutes ago, and the person who I once considered God, is now trying to kill me. All my inhibitions were completely gone, and I had the attitude that I literally had nothing left to lose. I begin singing the song, "Crazy" by Gnarls Barkley, and it fit well with the mood. The part of the song where he says, "But it wasn't because I didn't know enough, I just knew too much" kept playing over and over in my head as well as, "Hahaha bless your soul, you really think you're in control" in reference to Jesus probably being certain that he could annihilate me. At this point I am essentially tripping, and there is never a doubt in my mind that I would make it out alive. The shift ends, and I go back home to read the philosophical essay that I wrote when I first thought I was God, my body shaking and trembling the entire time.

There was a time before this event happened when the Satan in my head decided that I was such a crazy fuck that he had to take me out of existence. He tried to annihilate me but failed multiple times. I told him to keep trying to annihilate me all the time, and never stop. Who knows he might get lucky? There would be times when he would attempt, and I would hear the other voices say, "close" or "almost". After these two events occurred, I know longer feared the people in my head trying to end my existence. As of today, the day I am writing this down, the voices still on occasion try to annihilate me, but instead use the term, "hit", which basically only affects me by making a certain muscle in my body twitch. I don't get it.

When "Zero Day" came in May, I was all set to live my new life. Being on Adderall all the time and living the most free I possibly could apart from stopping absolute time. My parents decided that the only way that they would give me the Adderall is if they met with the psychiatrist that prescribed it to me. There was no way I was going to let that happen, seeing as I completely bullshitted 90% of what I told to her in order to get it. They ended up fucking the psychiatrist's career and life up royally. They gave her back all eight months' worth of Adderall that my dad had stashed in his safe and filed a complaint that she was negligent about her dealings with me because my dad had called her nine months back (in August as documented in the Complete Story) and told her about the other diagnosis I had with the other psychiatrist I was receiving antipsychotic drugs from. I bullshitted my way past what my dad had told her, and she agreed to keep prescribing me the Adderall (if I was unsuccessful at getting her to keep prescribing me the Adderall, the Complete Story never would have happened). She ended up getting either fired or forced into retirement, and I feel pretty bad. Yes, my parents were the one's mainly responsible for screwing her over, but I shouldn't have lied so much to her and deceived her into thinking that I was living the type of life I was living. But just to show how full of shit my parents were in reference to the whole situation: if they were never planning on giving me the Adderall in the first place, then why did they agree to keep it in their safe for eight months? Why wouldn't they just immediately go to the psychiatrist and file a complaint with her immediately? I fucked up bad, in reference to the Adderall, things got even more fucked up not far after this. I was hallucinating my balls off one morning, thinking that I was going to be annihilated, and I thought that I heard my parent's voices in my head. So, being completely delusional, I thought that if I told my parent's I was on Adderall, they would be fine with it because they already knew that, seeing as that they were voices in my head. I told my parent's, and it was the most pissed off I have ever seen my dad in my life. He threatened to kick me out of the house and wanted me to turn over the rest of the Adderall that I had to him. Of course, I lied and told him I took it all, but really just saved the rest that I had for later that day. As is the case with almost all psychotic situations that I find myself in, I reach a point where I truly belief that if I am just honest with everyone and tell the truth, then in the end I will benefit from this and will always work out in my favor. The majority of the time, this turns out to not be the case. Unknown to me, my parents checked my text messages one day when I was away from my phone and found out that Eli was the one who was dealing me the Adderall. So, when my mom asked, "Did you get the Adderall from the same guy?" I wanted to be honest with her, but also at the same time did not know that she actually knew his full name. My dad ended up calling the university's police and turning Eli in, and also threatened to call his parents, but I don't know if he actually knew their number (although you can find almost anything you want about a person these days simply by typing their name into google. It's kind of fucked up.) Nothing happened with the police and Eli, but when I called him to warn him that he should at least be prepared, he told me that he wasn't going to deal to me anymore, which I completely understood. We are still chill to this day, although I have not talked to him in a long time.

The rest of my days working at the sports grill pretty much consisted of still smoking weed on my breaks and getting Adderall every once in a while from other people. I ran into a guy, "Karl" who I used to work with from the sports grill at another bar one time.

Karl: I just remember you staring at the walls and just laughing to yourself for no reason.
Me: Yeah, I would get pretty high.

I almost got fired once for doing two no call no-shows back-to-back when I was writing philosophy for three straight days, which ended up with my being sent to a mental hospital for four days, as I described in another story. I got my psychiatrist to cover for me and my boss was pleased. I once got so sick of my parent's shit that I asked Abe if I could crash on his couch again like I did when the Complete Story happened two months before. He declined, probably not wanting to put up with anymore of my bullshit. By my seventeenth or eighteenth month working at the restaurant, I started to hate the job more and more. I was hearing voices every day without taking any drugs to induce them (which is the situation I am currently in, and have been for the past three and a half years), and what started off as a fun and happy relationship that I once shared with them in the early days of when I started working at the sports grill, started to deteriorate into a very strong dislike for me towards them, and a hatred for them towards me. I decided to quit after, a week prior, I was promised that I would work six shifts a week, and then once George came back to the restaurant as the new kitchen manager, he bumped me down to three shifts a week.

Me: But Lance said I could work six shifts a week if I wanted to.
George: Right, but wasn't there a time last year when you became so over exhausted with working so much that you got sent to a mental institution?
Me: Yeah...but that wasn't because I was working too hard.
George: I'm just going to put you at three shifts a week for now.

The next day I called him up to tell him that I wasn't going to come into my shift and that I was quitting the restaurant. The reason I gave: I had just won ten thousand dollars the night before up at a casino and that I no longer needed a job. He bought this, and we parted on good terms.

Perhaps the best memories I have of working at the restaurant are when I was rolling tits on Adderall, baked out of my mind, and started coming up with a new form of entertainment for myself: I began to string together different scenes from movies, TV shows, memories, or absolutely anything I could remember, together to form a coherent new scene that is witty, funny, serious, or anything that could possibly make sense. I used the voices as a way to gauge my ability to do this. If the voices laughed or were entertained in some way by the strung together combination that I came up with, I was entertained as well (the movie script idea that I came up with which you can read in the index of this book is an example of this). That is probably the most I will miss about this job, the good times I had with the voices in my head, and the people I worked with, before everything went to shit. But it ended a chapter in my life where the peak of my schizophrenia, especially people hearing my thoughts, was behind me.

# SECTION 3

# Adventures in Mind Travel

## FORWARD

This section deals with my memory of my take on certain ideas, institutions, and people, starting with when I was a child, up to my late teens, or early twenties. I titled this section "Adventures in Mind Travel" because it deals with certain memories of my past which I experienced that in some way relates to an exploration of the world. Like a newborn baby first becoming acquainted with the world around it, I show the reader a side of myself which can be seen through me exploring the world and my place in it (previous to me starting to write philosophy and logic). Most of these memories, I believe, are an innocent look into the world as seen by me.

## INNOCENT CHILDHOOD MEMORIES

My first clear memory of my life is of being in the basement of the house that my family was living in at the time I was born. There are two girls that live in the neighborhood that are in the basement with me, watching what I was about to do. I tell them that I want to show them something, so they just stand there and watch. One of the girls is two years older than me and the other a few years older than her sister. I begin to climb onto boxes stacked on top of each other that lead up to a window about two thirds up from the ceiling. I am not sure exactly how far up the boxes I made it, but I get to a certain point and the boxes collapse under me and I fall down onto the ground. The last thing I remember are the two girls immediately leave after this. I am not sure how old I was when this happened, but I couldn't have been older than three, I think. Interesting fact about the two girls: the older one appeared in an issue of Sports Illustrated in the section of the magazine where they talk about people around the country that are either amateurs or in youth sports, and the records they have set and accomplishments they have achieved. She was in that section for either cross country or track, which might make her the most famous person I have ever talked to. I could have changed this one day when I was at the LAX airport, I think, and I saw Ben Stein. My dad was a member of "The Red Carpet Club" and so was Ben, I guess. My mom and dad kept telling me to go up and talk to him, but I was too nervous. My brother and sisters kept saying, "Bueller….Bueller" under their breath. At the same airport my brother thinks he saw the guy who plays the bad terminator in "Terminator 2: Judgement Day". Apparently, the guy said hi to him and then walked away.

There was a guy in my sophomore dorm hall who thought he was a complete ladies' man and that all woman digged him in some way. I tell him my frustrations that I have had with a girl I currently like, and he decides to give me some advice.

Guy: Have you ever kissed a girl?

Me: Yes.
Guy: How old were you?
Me: Three.
Guy: What?
Me: I don't really remember the girl because I was so young, but my mom still has pictures of the two of us in my photo album of pictures of me growing up and we are holding hands.
Guy: Ok…have you kissed any other girls?
Me: Yeah, quite a few.
Guy (confused as to why I am asking for his advice): What the fuck? Are you a virgin?
Me: No, I lost my virginity in high school.
Guy: So, what exactly is the problem?
Me: I just like this girl and want to try and ask her out by I am too nervous.
Guy: Ok, now here is something I can help you with.

I don't remember exactly what he told me, but it was a discussion mostly revolving around how if you are just confident, then the girls will come to you, as they did with him. I ended up fighting him as a joke one day, and he knocked me down on the ground. I was stuck between my roommate's bed and his closet, and couldn't get up. Instead of letting me get up so we could finish fighting fairly, he continued to punch me while I was stuck. I was kind of pissed but didn't really care. I think a few years later he got psychotic, because I saw him in a Subway restaurant, and he lost a lot of weight and for some reason came across as not being how I remembered him to be. I can sympathize with him to that extent.[48]

My parents have over for dinner a husband and wife who we used to be neighbors with when we lived at the house we lived at when I was born (in Aurora, CO). They have a daughter that is one year older than me. I remember me, my brother, and their daughter all playing around on the top bed of a bunk bed that my brother and I shared. I don't have an exact clear memory of it happening, but I think I see my brother fall off the top bunk and land on his arm, breaking it. I was three or four at the time. My brother has always claimed it was me who pushed him off the top, but I try and claim my innocence, saying that he just fell on his own. While living in the same house, my brother and I were out riding our bikes in the street connecting to our driveway. We decided to have a race, so we went all the way out to the beginning of the street, that ends at our driveway, which if I had to estimate, was probably a little less than a quarter mile long. We begin to race and as we approach the end of the street, I get in front of him, cutting him off and causing him to have to stop. There was so little space between where I pedaled hard to try and get in front of him and the end of the street, that I had no time to press my pedals in the opposite direction to initiate the breaks and slow it down (I don't know if they still make bikes breaks this way, but it was kind of old school). I fly off the end of the street into a ditch that is a couple feet lower than the street. The bike and I separate, and I land in the ditch, at least six to seven feet away from the end of the street, completely unharmed. My brother probably remembers more than I do about this, but he said it was one of the craziest things he had ever seen up to that point in his life.

My brother and I got into a lot of fights when we were growing up, but there are a few that are noteworthy. Most of the fights that we had when we were under the age of ten or so, didn't involve throwing punches, but we would rather try and tackle each other and slam each other into walls, and even pulling each other's hair. If I had to make an educated guess, I would say that I came out on the winning side of most of these fights, but this all changed when we got old enough to begin fighting with our fists (which for some reason we never did before). I don't know how the fight began but at one point, I took a knife out from the knife holder and began waving it at him. He was not intimidated by this at all.

Me: Get the fuck away from me!
Brother: Oh, what are you going to cut me?

He ended up grabbing the knife out of my hands, because, although we were pissed at each other, I didn't think it would be worth it if I actually did try and stab him. I am not 100% sure whether it was the same fight or not, but we ended up outside on our lawn, with me swinging punches but always missing, and him always landing punches on my face and head. This was a top two or three most pissed off moments I have ever seen my mom.

Mom: Why the hell are you fighting each other for? I hope to God that you never touch each other again!

I think the last physical fight we ever had was when I was around twelve or thirteen. My brother is a little more than two years older than me, and we were at a local rec center planting flowers for his Eagle Scout Project in the Boy Scouts of America. Up to that point in my life, I had never been one to cry in front of other people. If I hurt myself at school or something bad happened to me, I would never show my true emotions in front of other people. At the time, I was prescribed an inhaler for asthma that I would take two hits of before every gym class. I didn't know at the time that it could be used to get you high, but I definitely remember feeling different after each inhalation. We were planting flowers with a few of the other scouts, and for some reason I remember my brother chasing me around the gardens that we planted the flowers in. When he caught up to me, he started whaling on me and I couldn't get out of his grip that he had on me. I figured the only way out of this situation was to start crying, to get my mom's attention. My intention was to tell her that I was having an asthma attack and that my brother was beating me up when I couldn't breathe (with the intention of getting him in trouble). I somehow get away from my brother and go to my mom's car and sit in the front seat breathing very hard to trying to come across that my brother was taking advantage of me, so that she would discipline him later. Some of the other scouts, after watching the whole incident take place, came over to ask if I was ok. I acknowledged them but still continued my act. That was the last time I ever fought my brother, and the first and only time I have ever lost my shit in front of other people, crying for someone to sympathize with me.

One of my best friends in elementary school was a kid named, "Jacob". One of my best memories of him was that we started a sticker book collection, in which we just took stickers that we found, and put them into a book to collect them. Over three or four years we had compiled at least nine or ten books, in all totaling up to thousands of stickers. Jacob's brother was also best friends with my brother at the time, because they were the same age as well. Jacob and his brother were really into paintballing, and they tried to get my brother and I to go paintballing with them. My brother and I decided to prepare for it by doing the following: we were told that when you get hit by a paintball it hurts and sometimes leaves welts on your skin where you got shot. So, me and my brother decided that we could prepare for the pain that the paintballs would have on us, by whipping each other with a belt. The belts, most likely, hurt a lot more than the paintballs do, but we convinced ourselves that if we could handle being beaten by the other person slashing a belt on us, then that would get our pain tolerance to a level that the paint balls would not hurt so bad. We ended up never going paintballing with them, so our plan of inflicting pain on each other never reached its intended purpose.[49]

When I was in elementary school, I collected Star Wars cards. This was back in the mid to late nineties and collecting Star Wars cards was a very popular thing to do. My mom would take my brother and I every once in a while, to a local shop where they sold all types of cards, ranging from sports, to Star Wars, to movie cards, and buy us a pack. I remember being told before this happened, that one of the rarest Star Wars cards to get, if not the rarest, was Yoda. My mom bought me and my brother two packs one day, one for each of us. I remember, distinctly saying to myself right before I opened the pack, "I hope Yoda is in this pack." I open the pack and flip through the cards, and I see the Yoda card is among one of the cards in the pack. My brother was really pissed off, because we had done rock, paper, scissors, or some other way of determining who would get to open which pack, and I won, and decided to open the one that he wanted to open. For the next week, I was one the most popular kids in school. Everyone wanted me to show them the Yoda card, which I kept in a special card container meant especially for rare cards to better protect them. I then made, what I consider to be one of the worst mistakes in my life, and something that deeply upset me a lot in the weeks, months, and years to come. There was a guy on the school bus that I rode who had, on top of a huge collection of cards, multiple ones that were pretty rare. Perhaps the rarest of the cards he had was, "Obi-Wan Kenobi". The kid made a deal with me that he would give me all his cards (or something close to probably 90%) that he owned, if I traded him my Yoda card. I can't really remember why I decided to do it, probably because I thought that the prospect of having hundreds more cards to my collection meant more to me than having the Yoda card, I ended up making the trade. I have not looked up if the card is worth anything, but it would be interesting to know. To make matters worse, I ended up trading the Obi-Wan Kenobi card to someone else later in the future. Even though I wish I hadn't traded the card, I consider opening up the pack and finding it in there to be one of the best childhood memories I have.

In the summers between when I was in middle school, I went to Id-Ra-Ha-Je Bible camp for a week with a few of my friends. Id-Ra-Ha-Je stands for "I'd rather have Jesus" and although you had to attend church for three hours a day (either singing and worshipping or hearing the pastor talk), the camp actually had quite a few cool activities that you could do. They had a zip line, an obstacle course, and there was a river nearby that you could go river rafting on. It's kind of funny, you would think that my most memorable moments that I had at the camp revolved around activities like this, but instead they mostly all revolve around the camp drama that occurred between my friends and other members of the camp, particularly girls. I don't remember how it first started, but there were two girls at the camp that were best friends, and they started hanging around me and my friend, "Henry" a lot. The girls made it known to Henry and I that they liked us. The blond girl, "Stacey" liked Henry, and her friend, "Natalie" liked me. I personally, did not have that much interest in Natalie, despite the fact that she was decent looking. That was a time in my life where I had a crush on a girl that lasted for three years who I attended middle school and high school with. Henry, however, did like Stacey in return, and the four of us would always sit by each other in church and during the meals. At one point in the week, for some reason, Henry decided that he wanted to make up a story that he had a girlfriend and tell this to Stacey. I don't really know what his intention was, but I think he just thought it would be a funny thing to do. I decided that I would play along in his mind game and back up his claim that he indeed had a girlfriend. This was a common bond that Henry and I shared throughout the time we were really good friends. For example, one time in elementary school, Henry made up a story that one of the school employees who watched over the kids while they are at recess, told him something like, "Get over here you asshole, shit kid." He ended up reporting the employee to the principal and, even though I did not witness the supposed event, I claimed that I did (remember I was a pathological liar since the time I could talk to around my twentieth birthday). The principal called me into her office to ask what I saw, and I told her exactly what Henry told me. I figured I was just being a good friend and helping him out. The school employee was very distraught about the whole situation, claiming that she would never say that to a kid. It escalated to a point where I was forced to tell the truth that I never saw what happened. The principal called my parents to tell them that I lied, but my parents never mentioned anything to me. I still, to this day have never heard them mention anything about it. So, because I was such a loyal friend to Henry, we decided to tell Stacey the bogus news about Henry having a girlfriend, with the intention of having some positive thing come out of it, although I don't know what that possibly could have been.

Me: Stacey, Henry has something to tell you.
Stacey: What?
Henry: Do you think I should say it? I don't know…
Me: I thought you wanted to.
Henry: Ok, tell her.
Me: Stacey, it turns out that Henry has a girlfriend.

Right as she understood what I had just said she covered her mouth, started crying and ran away. Pretty much immediately after we initiated the plan, Henry regretted it. For the next two or so days after this happened, Stacey was a complete wreck. Every time I saw her she was crying and there were people trying to console her. Near the end of the week, Henry told her that he was just making it up, and although she forgave him (what would Jesus do), I don't think she ever really recovered. As far as my relationship with Natalie went, she told me that she still liked me, even though I played along with the cruel joke. The point in me telling this story, is that it is one example that shows just how so often in my childhood that I would go to incredible lengths to either tell someone a lie and do everything I possibly could to cover it up to make sure they didn't find out about it, or that I would use my innately given (or so it seems) ability to manipulate people for my benefit, and on at least one occasion, even harass the person. This can be seen in this story even more clearly when Henry told Stacey that he was just joking with her that he had a girlfriend. Henry approached me about it with Stacey, and I played it off like I legitimately thought that he did have a girlfriend, and that he wasn't joking with her. Yes, I even tried to manipulate Henry into thinking that he never told me that he really didn't have a girlfriend. That is another aspect of my childhood, mainly, I would be a complete backstabber to even my closest friends, just as long as I was able to protect the appearance that I wanted people to see me as. I briefly explain in other stories how I eventually got to a point where I learned that it is not ok to treat people this way, and that if I wanted to start living a happier, more authentic life, then I had to stop lying to people.[50]

In the second summer that I attended the camp, me and my brother decided that we no longer thought that Jacob and his brother were very cool, and we didn't want to be their friends anymore. My mom had an awkward conversation with Jacob's mom in which Jacob's mom asked if they were, "invited" to go to camp with us. Jacob's brother ended up going but Jacob didn't, and I don't think I ever saw him again. I found a situation amusing during the second summer, when Jacob and Henry both liked the same girl and would get into heated argument over who should end up being with her more. Jacob bought a necklace or some item from the general store for the girl. Despite all the tension between the two for the entire week, it ended up being completely pointless, because the girl had no interest in either of them, and made it pretty obvious at times (from what I observed) that she was kind of annoyed by them (not to mention, at least I think, that she was completely out of their league). I attempted to complete the camps obstacle course one day and was too scared to continue, but the camps pastor was there to talk me through it, and I completed it without falling once. Other than that, I don't really have that many other memories of my three weeks I spent at the camp. I remember playing capture the flag on the first days of one of the summers and I got the flag for my team. I outran some dipstick who thought he could catch me and ended up spitting in my direction as I ran across the center line. I was happy. Perhaps the most noteworthy thing I did while I was there, was that I accepted Jesus as my personal savior. Any of the campers who decided to make this commitment were allowed to sign a book called, "the book of life". I think back now after all the crazy shit that has happened to me in relation to my mental illness coming on and the things it took me through, to a conversation I had with my counselor, which now brings me a sense of closure in reference to my relationship that I stand in towards the devil and evil itself: "So if you accept Jesus into your heart is there any way that this can be broken or to become separated from him again after that?" I asked my counselor, to which he responded, "I think it is like catching a fish with a fishing pole. If the fish is on the line and even tries to do everything to try and break free and get away from being pulled in by the fisherman, the fisherman still has the fish. In other words, Jesus has got you, and you might make more mistakes in your life, but he has you and won't let you go." In reference to that, once saved always saved makes sense. That sounds like an awesome idea.[51]

## ON GROWING UP IN A FUNDAMENTALLY CHRISTIAN CONSERVATIVE HOUSEHOLD

The family I grew up in was a very fundamentalist conservative Christian household. One of the biggest strains on my parent's relationship was that my mom is a Young Earth Creationist, and my dad is an Old Earth Creationist. They would get into fights about how the Bible should be interpreted and how old the universe is. Of course, both of them believe that human history started with Adam and Eve, and they believe that evolution is false. One time, my mom went so far to fill my head with her fundamentalist beliefs that she brought her Bible and had a meeting with my third grade teacher.

Mom: I want to explain to you what our family believes.
Teacher: Sure.
Mom: We believe that the world was created by God in six literal days. The world started with Adam and Eve and the universe is only 6,000 years old.
Teacher: Ok.
Mom: The reason that I wanted to meet with you is because I want to make it clear that I don't want you to teach to my child that the earth and universe is millions and billions of years old. This is what we believe, and I don't want you to preach to my child something that we believe is false.
Teacher: I will do my best.

I could tell that my teacher was kind of taken of guard and disappointed. My mom said the same thing to my fourth grade teacher. On one occasion when I was in fourth grade, we were studying frogs and tadpoles. My teacher said that the tadpoles were "evolving" into frogs. My mom was very pissed off at this when I told her what my teacher said. My mom corrected the teacher and said that instead of evolving, the tadpoles were just metamorphosing, or adapting.

As if sheltering me from being taught the facts of the world were not enough, there were two other things that my mom approached my teachers about. The first was that in fourth and fifth grade I was not allowed to celebrate Halloween. My mom had me pulled out of the school Halloween parties, telling me that Halloween was an evil and satanic holiday. What is strange about this is that from first to third grade I participated in the school Halloween parties and my mom didn't care. The second was that I was not allowed to read Harry Potter. This deeply upset me because everyone I knew in school was reading Harry Potter and talking about it. In fourth grade I was reading the second book in secret whenever we had reading time in the class. I decided to take the book home with me one time and confront my mom about it.

Me: Hey mom, I am reading one of the Harry Potter books. It's not bad or anything.
Mom: Psychotic Logician! I told you that you are not allowed to read that.
Me: But it's not bad or anything.
Mom: That book is not allowed in our home. When you get back to school you are going to leave it there and never read it again! Do you understand?
Me: Yes.

I was absolutely crushed. The thing about Harry Potter being evil was not just something that my parents thought, but also at the time there turned out to be a following of people who thought this as well. One time the subject was brought up by a man at the church that we were attending. He stood up before the sermon and spoke to the congregation.

Man: I just wanted to remind everyone about the meeting we are having next week about Harry Potter and how it is related to the occult and is anti-Christian.

A man then stood up when the other man was speaking and interrupted him.

Man #2: This is ridiculous! Are we going to do this about other books like "The Chronicles of Narnia?" Harry Potter is not bad or anything.

The other man did not know what to say, he didn't want to give the man the last word, but whatever he did say, it wasn't much of a refutation. I think Man #2 had a point, but the book he used to refute the other man's claim was not very good, because "The Chronicles of Narnia" are Christian books.

Fifth grade was the first year that I had sex education in school. My mom had several concerns about this. First, apparently, she thought that they were going to teach us about homosexuality, and this was not ok with her. Second, for some reason, she did not want me to learn about women's menstrual cycles. Before the start of sex education, she tried teaching me it herself a little bit. She used a visual dictionary which showed a naked man and naked woman. It was kind of funny that when it came to the pages that did show the naked bodies, she quickly said, "this is a man's body", turned page within a second, and "this is a woman's body", turning the page within a second. I am not exactly sure why she didn't want me to learn about women's menstrual cycles but to this day it has stuck. I still don't know very much about it and in the other sex education classes I took in seventh grade and tenth grade I didn't pay very much attention (or care).

My sister got pregnant when she was 23 years old out of wedlock. My parents were a little more than pissed. Besides the fact that she wasn't married, the main other reasons they were so upset is because her boyfriend who knocked her up, was not a Christian. During Thanksgiving dinner a few months before she got pregnant, he dropped the F bomb which made my parents highly dislike him. They ended up getting married one month before my nephew was born, much to their dismay as well.

My entire extended family is very religious and highly conservative as well. When I played this prank at my family's mini family reunion, I thought they would get the joke, but I was wrong. I became aware one day in high school of a website called peteranswers.com. Before I understood how it worked, I became obsessed with how it can possibly tell me the correct answer to any question that I had. It pissed me off for a while, because my friends would type in questions like, "How big is Psychotic Logician's dick?" and then type in something really small for example (actually I was so convinced that this website would tell the truth about the size of my dick, that I had Frank quickly change it to another one of our friend's names. The answer ended up being seven inches, which my friends, maybe suffering themselves from small dicks, were impressed with). Once I figured out how to work it, I showed it to my mom, dad and brother one night. My mom, after having all her questions answered correctly, got on to her computer and began writing the pastor of the church that she was attending an email describing the website, probably associating it as some Satanic mind reading thing. They were confused as to why it only worked when I typed the question, to which I responded that the software recognizes how each individual person types, and so it specifically chooses which person's question it wants to answer. After having enough fun with it, I told them how it worked, and they thought it was pretty funny. This type of warm reception that they gave me would not be shared by my aunts, uncles and cousins when I showed them it at the family reunion. I told all my cousins that there exists some crazy website that knows the answer to anything they ask and this peeked their interest. With a bunch of my cousins watching the computer screen as I typed the answers to their questions, one of my cousins came to the same conclusion that my mom came to, mainly, that it is an evil website. She told my aunt who then came rushing into the room we were in.

Aunt: I don't want you guys messing around with this.
Me: It's just a joke. Here I'll show you how it works.
Aunt: No, I've seen this type of thing before, I really believe this type of thing exists. Please exit out of there.
Me: Ok. Sorry.

The oldest cousin I have knew there was something fixed about the website from the time I started messing with my other cousins, he just couldn't figure out how it worked. The rest of my cousins were confused, and some, I think, still maintain the attitude about it that my aunt came to, as a demonic website. Some people just can't take a joke I guess.[52]

## FRENCH CLASS STORIES

From my freshman year in high school to my junior year, I took French. Most students choose to take Spanish, instead of French, which makes sense because it is far more useful today considering all of the illegal immigrants and other Hispanic's that live in the United States today. There were around three Spanish teachers, and only one French teacher. I never understood the people in high school that, when given the opportunity to easily do good in the class, ended up getting a shitty grade because they were even too lazy to do the little things that would get them a good grade. For example, in tenth grade we were studying "The Great Gatsby", I didn't read a single page from the book, but the night before the final test on it, I read the Spark Notes on it and ended up getting 100% on the test. The people that got shitty grades on the test complained about it, but in my minds, they are just fucking retards. The same thing happened in my tenth grade French class. The teacher offered extra credit each week. One of the options to do to earn extra credit was to write the teacher a three sentence email in French. So, I simply went to freetranslation.com, put in the three sentences that I wanted to send to her, and pushed the translation button for French. I copy and pasted the note into the email and sent it off. I ended up getting 102% in the class, with other students who got B's and C's bitching that the class was hard. On another occasion in my English class in tenth grade, the teacher was on a leave of absence because she had just had a baby and so there was a substitute teacher for the first two months of the semester. The substitute offered extra credit to read a book and participate in a one hour meeting about the book. I just read the Spark Notes and in the meeting I didn't even say anything, but she gave me the extra credit. The majority of people in the class ended up complaining about how the substitute was unfair and that the class was too difficult. The principal ended up getting involved and when the teacher returned from her leave of absence, she offered for everyone in the class who wanted to, to reset their grade to a 0/0 and begin with a clean slate. However, I had over 100% in the class, and she said I didn't have to reset my grade if I didn't want to. The point I am trying to make is that a lot of people can have the opportunity to easily do well in something but are just too dumb or lazy to take advantage of the easy shit that life presents to them.

In my tenth grade French class, there was a kid named, "Andy". Me and a couple other friends in class constantly gave him shit, although we were always joking. He was actually a cool kid, but I decided one time to take my harassment of him to another level. Just like the email extra credit that the teacher offered each week, another thing you could do to earn extra credit was to speak in front of the whole class in French for a couple of minutes. I got the idea that I would play the recorder to the tune of "Hot Cross Buns" while taking pauses to sing a French song to go along with it. The title of the song that I made lyrics to was called, "Andy aime le coq", or in English, "Andy loves the rooster". I don't remember exactly the lyrics to the song but just the fact that the teacher allowed me to play it is pretty hilarious in itself. Andy couldn't believe that the teacher allowed for it to go on, but he was a good sport about it and didn't complain.

In my eleventh grade French class, I decided to play another joke on Andy. I was sitting next to him one class, and decided to tie my shoes together, get up to walk to some other part of the classroom, trip and fall, and then blame it on Andy for tying my shoes together. Everyone in the class knew that it was me just fucking with Andy, everyone except the teacher. It took her a while to untie my shoes, because she wanted me to practice some French activity. Andy didn't get in trouble, but that night I sent him an instant message.

Me:……..
Andy: Fuck you!
Me: Haha. I was just fucking with you. Sorry man.
Andy: I really don't care. I just can't believe the teacher actually thought it was me who tied your shoes together.
Me: Yeah, that is kind of ridiculous.

I had other innocent times in my three years of French, but the one's I described above were the most noteworthy.

## HAVING A FUN TIME RUINED BY THE POLICE

When I was in high school me and a couple of friends usually consisting of Ron, Edwin and I would egg people's houses that we didn't like. There was one time after egging a house that we decided to just go fuck around and do random shit. Ron had the smart idea that we should get rid of the egg carton, seeing as if we did get pulled over by cops and the cops had a complaint from the person's house that we egged, they wouldn't be able to trace it back to us. This was a very good idea. I drove to a gravel parking lot and decided to do donuts. After about our third or fourth donut, we see a cop car turn its lights on and make its way to the parking lot that we were at. Fuck me. We waited as the cop came up to my car.

Cop: License and registration. What are you guys doing out here tonight?
Me: We just thought it would be fun to do some donuts.
Cop: Is there anything in the car that I should know about? Drugs or alcohol?

Me: No, sir.
Cop: Wait here.

At the time me and Edwin were 18, but Ron was only 16. Ron smoked cigarettes and I told him to just leave them on the floor of my car, just in case the cops searched us and tried to bust him for smoking under the age of 18. For some reason he decided to keep them in his pocket.

Cop: I could give you a reckless driving ticket, and I know you don't want that.
Me: Definitely not.
Cop: Because you were driving recklessly, I am going to search your car just to make sure you guys aren't under the influence of anything.
Me: That's fine.

The three of us got out of the car, and the cop and his partner gave us a body search, and then proceeded to search my car. Luckily, we threw away the egg carton, and I had nothing in my car.

Cop: This is the cleanest car I have ever seen.
Me: Thank you.

I think this irritated the cop's partner because he had an expression on his face that came across as thinking that they were definitely going to bust us with something. In the town I grew up in, cops catching teens with drugs or alcohol is considered to be a big score by the cops. After all, why would kids be out at 12:30am, doing donuts in a parking lot if they were not on something? The cop searched Ron and found the cigarettes in his pocket.

Cop: You're not 18. Why are you smoking.
Ron: I just like it.
Cop: Who bought this for you?

Ron remained silent. The cop then proceeded to take the cigarettes out of the pack and crumble them right in front of us.

Cop: You are under 18, you shouldn't be smoking and there is a 12:00am curfew. We are under our legal right to call your parents. Do your parents know where you are?
Ron: Yes, they know I am hanging out with these guys.

Cop: I could write you a 12 point ticket so you could lose your license, but I am just going to let you off with a warning. I want you (referring to Ron) to go back to your house immediately and stay there for the rest of the night. Consider yourselves lucky that I am letting you go without writing you tickets.

All three of us thanked him and got back in the car and drove back to Edwin's house. I am pretty sure the cops didn't write me a driving ticket because we were cooperative with them in letting them search our car. It is pretty obvious that they for sure thought that they were going to find us in possession of something. It is a pretty typical cop thing to do, to pull people over for not doing anything to harm anyone. Serve and protect my ass. There was one time when a cop pulled me, Victoria, and Eddie over for just sitting in a parking lot with the car running. The problem was that we were passing a bottle of vodka between the three of us when the cop came up behind my car with his lights on. Somehow he claimed he had the legal right to search my car even though we were not doing anything. For some reason just sitting in a parking lot with your car running gives the police probable cause to search your car. I was pretty drunk at the time and was hoping that they wouldn't notice. The cop searched my car and found the empty booze bottle. I claimed that it had been in my car for months and that I just forgot it was there. They let us off with a warning, probably because they knew that they were really not in their legal right to search us, seeing that we were literally doing nothing to warrant them pulling us over.[53]

## HIGH SCHOOL STUNT CREW STORIES

When I was in high school, me and my group of friends were looking for ways to waste time during lunch break after we ate. We started two clubs that kept us busy, but unfortunately not out of trouble with the bitchy campus security lady. The first club we started was a stunt crew club. Basically, what this was, was that we would go to a place in our high school which had an area that we could perform stunts. The majority of our stunts took place at a stairway near the front doors of the building, right next to the front office. The stairway had three levels to it, but our favorite spot was the top level leading up to the top floor. It is hard to describe the stairway, but I will do my best: at the top of the stairs there was a long concrete beam against the wall, roughly a foot in width that extended from the top of the stairs to halfway up the top level. On the opposite side of the board there were windows looking out to the front of the school which had a small place where you could stand right up against it. The place where you could stand on right next to the windows was about three to four feet away from a guard rail. The reason there was a guard rail is because between it and the windows three to four feet away was about a thirty foot drop all the way to the bottom of the stairs. This area was the place where we performed the majority of our stunts.

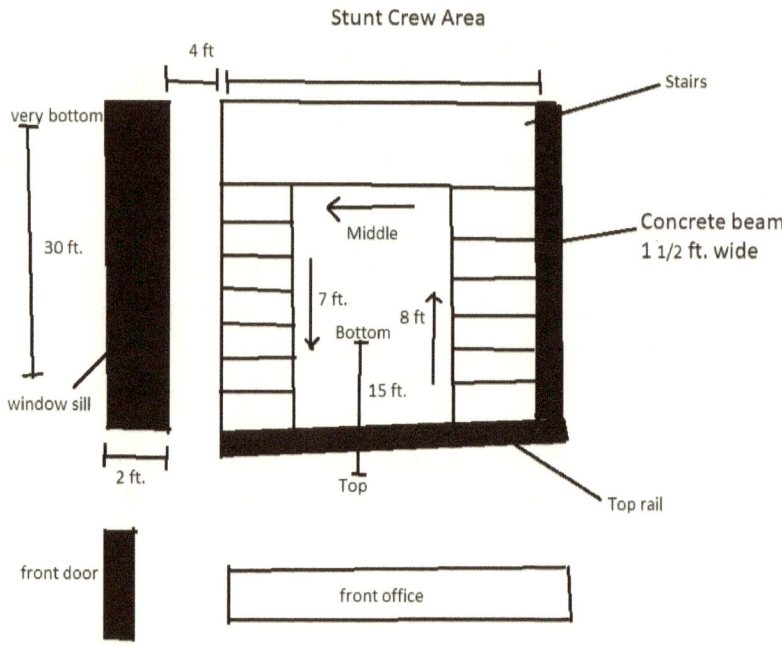

Stunt Crew Area

We used the concrete beam area of the stairway as a warmup for the other stunts that we did, because it was the easiest stunt to perform, and the least dangerous. It took me a while to get the confidence to perform this stunt, because I am afraid of heights, and because the one foot width of the beam made it so that you can't walk across it like you normally would walk, but you would rather have to shimmy across it with your feet, with your back against the wall, and there was about a ten to twelve foot drop between the beam and the stairs directly below. On one occasion, Edwin was performing this stunt. He threw in a combination with it to make the stunt more difficult. Where the beam meets the top of the stairs against the wall, there is a rail that overlooks the bottom of the first level stairway, put there so that people don't fall down the stairway from the top. The idea was to first hang from the rail, shimmy across it with your arms, and then grab onto the beam adjacent to it, and then shimmy across that with your arms all the way until he reached the middle of the stairway level, which you could then drop off onto safe ground. Me and a few other people had successfully done this stunt and now it was Edwin's turn. He was hanging from the top rail and about to make the switch over to the beam, when his hands (probably sweating) slipped, and he fell about fifteen feet onto the stairs leading up to the top level. This probably wouldn't have been that big of a deal if he would have landed on his feet, however, in this situation, when he slipped, his whole body turned and he fell sideways, landing on the stairs directly on his neck and back. Instead of trying to see if Edwin was ok, everyone was just laughing hysterically and just looked at him from the top.

Me: Uncle fucker! Uncle fucker!

It took Edwin about twenty seconds to finally begin to move again, and he seemed to be ok. He said that he had just blacked out and didn't really remember much about what happened. After lunch I had a class with him where we sat right next to each other and I could tell he was still in a confused state, not just about falling from the stairs, but about everything that was happening around him. He was very lucky he didn't break his back or neck when he fell.

On another day, Brad decided to attempt the same stunt that Edwin tried to do. He was hanging from the rail, about to make the exchange to the beam, when the campus security woman saw him hanging there.

Security woman: What the hell are you doing!? Everyone that is upstairs don't move and stay where you are.

Right when she said this, me and about ten of my other friends booked it down the hallway to avoid her seeing us. Brad was the only one who remained, just hanging from the top rail. I am not sure how he got down and I am not sure what the campus security woman said to him after that, but it was a pretty funny situation.

The final stunt we did was the stunt in which you would jump from the railing on the side of the stairs to the window. In order to get down from the window, you had to jump from it to the second level stairs, which was about six to seven feet down. I never had the balls to do this stunt, since if you fucked up, you would fall a long way down to the bottom and royally fuck yourself up.

After Brad got busted by the campus security lady, we decided to stop doing the stunts for a while and instead began to hang out in an area of the school in which he held a fight club. One time, my group of friends decided to fight another group of friends, sending out one person from each group to fight at a time. The most memorable fight, however, was one in which, instead of punching each other, each person had a can of Axe deodorant spray, and would just try and spray the other person as much as possible. Of course, the campus security lady came in one time right as this was going on.

Security woman: Stop what you are doing right now and get the hell out of here.
Me: It smells like axe down here.
Security woman: Just get out of here.

Other things we did to entertain ourselves during our lunch break were: 1) we tied a one dollar bill to a fishing line and hung it from the top of the stairs (where we would have the stunt club), and when people walked by, we would dangle it in front of them. This pissed the majority of people off, most hitting it away from them. 2) we shoved the smallest of our friends into a locker (which he agreed to do) and kept him in it for a while. He would begin to freak out, but we just laughed. 3) we went into the library and put books in each other's backpacks so that when they left the library, the alarm would go off for not checking the book out. This pissed the librarian off. 4) one of the librarians was a man, roughly in his forties that we would always try and fuck around with. On one occasion, me and two of my friends wrote on a piece of paper, "kick me if you're horny", and, with his back turned away, a friend of mine put the sign on his back without the man noticing.

## THE TIME I HAD GINGIVITIS

When I was ten or eleven, I never brushed my teeth (I got better at this as I grew older, but I still, for some reason, hate brushing my teeth). I didn't brush my teeth for what must have been months. Whenever I did brush my teeth, however, the entire sink would be filled with blood. My parents were not aware of this until I went to the dentist one time. The dentist must have immediately noticed how severely fucked up my gums were, and I had to sit in the dentist chair for what must have been two to two and a half hours while the dentist tried to figure out what to do. They ended up prescribing to me a special mouth wash that would help the gums heal. Afterwards I still was not very diligent about using the mouth wash. One time right before I left for school to catch the school bus, this happened.

Mom: Did you brush your teeth and take your mouth wash.
Me: No, I didn't.
Mom: Go upstairs right now and do it!
Me: Ok.

I am pretty sure I ended up missing the bus that day. Eventually, after quite a while, my gums healed and went back to normal. I remember the exact day that I went to the dentist who discovered my gum disease. It was the day that Pane Steward, the golfer, died. I was watching TV for several hours and saw that he had died. For some reason throughout my entire life, I have had a problem with brushing my teeth. It's kind of gross, but I just hate it for some reason. At the very least you would think I would at least take mouth wash, but I hardly do that either. The one time in my life that I ended up brushing my teeth twice a day (which is what dentists recommend you do) lasted about two to three weeks. The only thing that made me do this was that I decided that a girl was perfect and if I think she is really perfect, then I will brush my teeth for twice a day (and not masturbate). This only lasted a few weeks. It ended when I decided to jack off, and then not brushing my teeth quickly followed. I still think the girl is perfect, but I am too big of a fuck up to discipline myself to make a commitment to change my daily routine. If I do brush my teeth these days, I only do it once a day, and I never floss. I got into a shitty habit recently and starting chewing tobacco, and it has fucked my gums up. Doing that shit along with not brushing your teeth for about three to four weeks can only have shitty consequences. I bought some Peroxl (the same mouth wash I was also supposed to take when I was a kid and had gum disease), which is supposed to be really good at healing the unhealthy things in your mouth, so I am not worried about it. But until the day comes when I decide to get over my immature horrible dental hygiene, I guess I'll never truly become a responsible adult. There is an episode of "Family Guy" where Peter says to somebody, "You know what's crazy, I haven't brushed my teeth in three days, and no one has said a thing." It would be shitty if people noticed my bad breath (obviously I probably do) but were too nice to say anything. God I suck.[54]

## THE GRAIN SILO STORY

When I was in high school one my best friends was a guy named "Abe". Abe lived on a ranch where there was a horse track, barn, and most importantly, a grain silo. One day he gave me a full tour of the ranch which ended with him showing me the grain silo. He showed me how it worked. You put the grain in the top which fills up and then when you want to empty it there is a lever at the bottom which opens it up like a sliding glass door. We were bored and so we got a bright idea: we will tie a garden hose to the top of the silo and drop the end of it into the bottom like a rope attached to the top that extends down to the bottom of the inside of the silo. We will then climb down the hose to the bottom where the grain is, and then climb back out at the top. Why we decided to do this I do not know. We were just looking for something to do and like I explain in other stories, Abe and I always come up with crazy ideas to keep our minds occupied.

Abe: Can we climb into the silo?
Abe's Mom: Why?
Abe: Just because we want to, to have something to do.
Abe's Mom: Sure, just be careful.

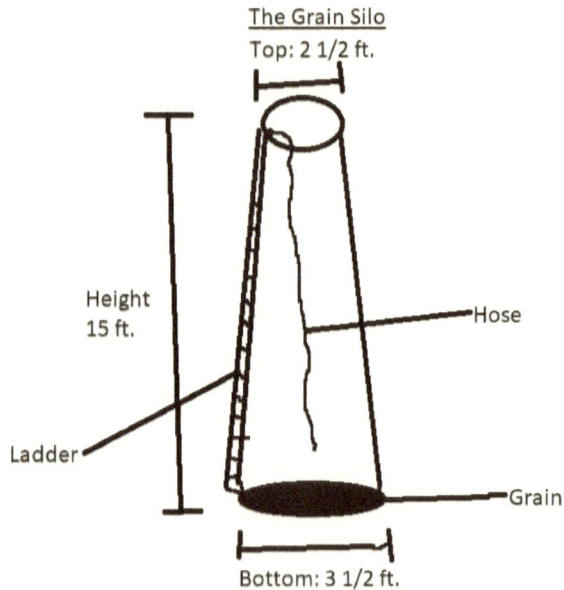

The Grain Silo
Top: 2 1/2 ft.

Height
15 ft.

Hose

Ladder

Grain

Bottom: 3 1/2 ft.

We climbed up the ladder that goes from the bottom of the silo to the top where the opening is. We securely tied the hose around the top of the ladder and threw the rest of it down to the bottom. I was a little nervous and wondered if I would have the strength to climb back up out of the silo once I made it to the bottom. I wasn't in the best of shape, but I figured I would be strong enough to do so. However, keep in mind that at the same time we held an arm wrestling competition in one of our classes in high school and I lost to a girl who, really, I should have beaten easily. Abe on the other hand, won first place. Abe decided to go in first. He climbed down the hose and made it to the bottom, and then proceeded to climb back out of the silo, completely unscathed. It was then my turn. I climbed down the hose and made it to the bottom no problem. Easy enough, now I just need to climb back up it. I climbed up the hose and fairly easily made it to the top, where the hose is connected to the ladder. The only problem I had was pulling my body up out of the silo onto the ladder. The top of the silo was a very thin metal opening where the lid was that closed the top. Holding onto the top felt like a sharp metal piece that dug into your hands when you tried to grip it. So, there I was, at the top, the only obstacle standing in my way was pulling myself over the metal opening and back onto the ladder. Every time I tried to grip the metal opening it felt like a fucking knife stabbing into my hands. Having to simultaneously hold myself up on the hose and grip the metal opening to pull myself up, I began to feel very weak.

Me: Fuck dude, this is fucking hard. I don't know if I can do it.
Abe: You can do it dude. Just try your hardest to pull yourself out.
Me: Fuck.

Abe was seeing that I was struggling and tried to help me get out, but he was in a position where he couldn't really do anything to help me at all. He had to stand on the ladder, and he couldn't bend over inside the silo to help pull me out because the opening is barely wide enough to fit a human body through. I was starting to freak out. I was becoming very tired and weak and couldn't find a way to get out. This was starting to seem like a shitty idea.

Me: Fuck man. This is fucked up. I can't get out. What the fuck should I do?
Abe: You can do it man.
Me: What if I fall man? I don't want to die. I'm freaking out.

Abe couldn't help but laugh at the situation. I, however, was not amused.

Me: I can't get out man. I'm to freaking weak.

I was sweating profusely and started to shake, starting with my arms and eventually my whole body. Then, I lost all strength. I was too weak at that point to even hold onto the hose. The grain silo measured from the top to the bottom was roughly fifteen feet high. I fall from the top all the way to the bottom. I immediately black out. Abe still couldn't help but laugh. I landed standing up with the grain at the bottom softening my fall. If I were to have just fallen on the bottom with no grain to help the impact of my fall, I very well my way gotten injured, moderately, or severely.

Abe: Oh fuck. Dude, are you ok?

I slowly regain consciousness, trying to remember what was going on. It was dark and the only thing I could see was the dust from the grain enveloping all around me. My fall kicked up the grain and I was covered from head to toe with grain.

Abe: Can you hear me? Are you ok?
Me: Yeah man...I'm ok. Fuck. That was not fucking cool man. What should I do? I don't think I can climb the hose back up.
Abe: Ok, let me ask my mom if we can empty the silo and you can get out from the bottom.
Me: Cool. Thanks man. Jesus, I'm kind of freaking out.

Abe then went to go find his mom to see if he could rescue me. Multiple things came to mind. What if the lever at the bottom didn't work? Would we have to call an ambulance or the fire department to see if they could get me out? I just stood there, still in shock from my fifteen foot fall with my entire body completely trembling.

Abe: Mom, Psychotic Logician got stuck in the grain silo and he can't get out. Could I open up the bottom so he could get out?
Abe's Mom: Well, Goddamn!
Abe: Sorry, there is just no other way he could get out.
Abe's Mom: Sure, I guess. Next time don't do that.
Abe: Ok. Thanks.

Abe then got back to the grain silo and told me he would crank the lever and try and get me out. As he cranked the lever, grain and dust began to fly up in the air and it was difficult to breath. Having allergies my whole life, I begin to sneeze constantly. Luckily the lever worked, and the grain began to fall from the silo out onto the ground. The bottom of the silo, however, was around three feet from the ground and so when the bottom opening was halfway open, I had to keep one foot bending inside the silo, and the other foot fully extended outside on the ground. Once the bottom was completely opened, I had to crouch down and crawl on the ground until I was completely away from the silo.

Abe: Jesus dude, are you ok?
Me: Yeah, man. Thanks. That was fucking ridiculous.

We both begin to laugh, as we realize how funny the situation actually was. I could barely walk I was trembling so much.

Abe's Mom: Are you ok? You're shaking. Do you need anything?
Me: No, I'm ok, I just need to sit down.
Abe's Mom: Do me a favor and don't do that again.
Me: Yeah. I just couldn't get out from the top. Sorry if I screwed you over by having the silo emptied.
Abe's Mom: You're fine. I'm just glad you're ok.

I guess even innocent activities like using a grain silo as a stunt project can come back and bite you in the ass.[55]

## THE WEIRDEST CONVERSATION I HAVE EVER WITNESSED

I went to a bar one time with my friend, "Eddie". We were drinking when I started talking to some random guy that was sitting next to us.

Me: Yo, how's it going?
Guy: Have you heard on the news about Bin Laden getting shot?
Me: Yeah, I heard that.
Guy: Well, my boys, we are the guys who smoked Bin Laden. So now don't you feel stupid for asking me about it?
Me: I guess.
Guy: You think you're smart?
Me: I never said I was smart.
Guy: What are you doing here?

Me: Just drinking with my friend.

Guy: What are you doing with your life?

Me: I go to college.

Guy: So, you think you're smart? What are you majoring in?

Me: Philosophy and Math.

Guy: So, you think you know math pretty well?

Me: I'm ok at it.

Guy: What do you like studying in math?

Me: I want to start studying chaos theory. Do you know chaos theory?

Guy: Yeah, I know fucking chaos theory. You think you're so fucking smart. I'll snap your fucking neck.

Me: What?

Guy: I was in the military for a while.

Me: Cool.

Guy: I can shoot an ace of spades from a hundred yards.

Me: Nice.

Guy: So, you think you know philosophy to?

Me: Yeah, I like it. Do you think you can reconcile free will with determinism?

Guy: No, can't be done.

Me: What about Russell's Paradox. What if the set of all sets is the infinite set?

Guy: You got to prove it.

At this point I thought this guy was a fucking nut job. But for some reason I decided to buy him a drink.

Guy: Do you have a car?

Me: Yeah.

Guy: I don't own a car. I run everywhere.

Me: Good for you.

Guy: You need to drop the "I know everything" attitude.

Me: Ok...

Guy: You think you're so fucking smart.

Me: But –

Guy: No, shut the fuck up. You think you're fucking smarter than me.

At this point I had enough and got up to leave. I went back to the same bar about a week or two later and talked to the bartender about the guy.

Bartender: Yeah, that guy was full of shit. He's not even in the military.
Me: Really? He was a fucking psycho.
Bartender: He comes in here every once in a while. He tries to get into random conversations with people, but nobody likes him.
Me: I could see why.[56]

## TWIN PEAKS RESTAURANT STORIES

If you are not aware of what Twin Peaks Restaurant is, then it is kind of like this: It only has women waitresses, who only wear short shorts and a pretty revealing top, that is red. A friend of mine told me that they look like lumberjacks, which I kind of agree. From their top covering their breasts, to their waist, they have nothing on. They wear different outfits on occasion, such as bikini week and lingerie week. When I first went there, I thought the place was pretty cool. The main advertisement they use to get people to go there is for the "scenic views" and, knowing that their target customers are men (or lesbians maybe?), they label a size of a beer you can get as "man size". I bought a t-shirt one time that said roughly: "Working for the man. Yes, I think you are attractive, now get me another beer." A lot of the girls will act like they are interested in the male customers by sometimes sitting down at their table and talking to them, not because they are actually interested in them, but for the bigger tip. It's like that episode in South Park where they go to the Raisin's Restaurant and a girl acts interested in Butters, who falls in love with her. When he realizes that the girl is not actually into him, he gets very upset.

The 90%+ of woman who work there, when you ask for their number will tell you that they have a boyfriend. They have a problem with just letting a guy down easy by just saying "No", but instead they for some reason feel they need to lie about having a boyfriend. Although it is probably true that many of them do have boyfriends (just because most of them are really hot), whether they do or not, that is the basic response and their preferred method of letting a guy down easy. That is a big difference between men and woman, mainly, if a girl asks for a guy's number, most will just either say yes or no. From my experience from woman, at least, I don't feel the need to lie about having a girlfriend, at least unless I actually do. I have not gone to that restaurant in a very long time, but if I do ever go back, I have come up with a way to show the girl I outsmarted her in a humorous way. I will write on a piece of paper, "when I ask for the girl's number, she will say that she has a boyfriend and so she won't give me her number." When I do ask the girl for her number and she turns me down for that reason, I will then take the note out of my pocket and give it to her. She will probably insist that she actually does, but that's not really the point. Whether she has a boyfriend or not, I'm not getting her number.

One time when I was super drunk at the restaurant, I saw a very beautiful girl and I decided that I would give asking for her number a shot. She wasn't even our waitress; however, she did come over to my table on one occasion to sign the Twin Peaks calendar. I called her over to my table and said, "Do you know what the best part of my night has been? It's been watching you wait tables all night. I think you are very pretty and was wondering if I could get your number?" She told me that she had a boyfriend which, may or may not be true, but the only reason I even talked to her was because I was drunk and thought she was an 11. *You can't get a girl's number unless you play.* Although most girls will tell you this excuse, I actually did get lucky on two occasions.

My friend, Eddie, is trying to make it as a rapper, and he had a show coming up. So, I decided that when I ask the girl for her number, my "in" would be to ask her if she would like to go to the rap show with me, and give her a free ticket. Surprisingly, she did give me her number, but also told me that she had a boyfriend and so it wasn't going to be a date. I was content with that, so I called her a few weeks later and she didn't pick up. I then texted her and she didn't respond. I decided that I didn't want to bug her (something that I never seemed to grasp until after I dropped out of college) so I stopped my attempt to hang out with her at that. I think she either gave me the wrong number which she gives to every guy who asks her out, or she just decided to ignore me, which makes me think, why the fuck did you give me your number in the first place? If it really was her number, then what if it turned out that I was some creepy stalker who never stopped calling or texting her? I don't remember if on the girl's voice mail is said her actual name or not, but for some reason I doubt it. Women are weird.

The second time I asked for one of the girl's numbers, I was going through a temporary phase where I thought that the best way to get laid and go out with woman was to just joke around and fuck with her. This was the best way for me to achieve confidence and I thought I would test out my new attitude with a Twin Peaks girl.

Me: I was wondering, because I think you are really cool and pretty, if I could get your number and maybe hang out sometime.
Girl: Sure, I'll write it down for you.
Me: Cool, could we get down when we hang out?
Girl: Haha.

I texted her that night so she would have my number and she responded. I decided to joke around with her a little more and said in one of the texts, "Maybe we can foreplay or something." She responded by saying "Your cute." I was happy. Because of this conversation, I thought that I had a decent chance of hanging out with her sometime. I, or more importantly, she, should not have gotten my hopes up. I called her and texted her not that far after this and she never responded. I don't like bugging people, and if she didn't want to respond after I sent her a text, I figured she didn't want anything to do with me.

I could have left both of these girls voice messages, but that is not how I roll. If you ever go to Twin Peaks, just be warned that they all have real or fictitious boyfriends, and got the job because the manager thinks they are hot, and like being lusted after (the "scenic views" (adultery?)) In my opinion, some of the girls are not even that hot, and probably suffer from a superiority complex.[57] If you are not hot but act like you're hot, then I don't want your number.

## THE TIME I PLAYED FOOTBALL

I had always wanted to play tackle football ever since I was really little, but my mom never would sign the permission slip to do so because she thought it would be too dangerous. When I was in 8th grade, however, I made a deal with my mom to get her to allow me to play football. The deal was that if I got straight A's, then she would let me play. She agreed (which I thought was pretty cool, but also kind of ridiculous because at that point I had gotten 4.0 ever since I was in 6th grade and thought my mom wouldn't agree to it because she thought for sure I would get straight A's). By the end of the semester, I had gotten straight A's, so she signed the permission slip. Hell yeah. I started playing football at the beginning of the season. The previous couple of years the team that I joined had won the championship and they went into the season intending to do just that. The only problem: there was a new coaching staff, a new head coach and his son. At first, the practices mostly comprised of running a lot and doing tackle drills. I was the second smallest kid on the team, at that point weighing around 90 pounds. The smallest kid on the team weighed about 5 pounds less than me. When doing the tackling drills, I got fucked hard. The biggest kid on the team, was six foot one, and weighed around 180 pounds, twice my weight. Most of the players on the team weighed at least 115-120 ponds, and so I had a very hard time trying to tackle them, and they had a very easy time tackling me. I ended up getting a shit load of bruises all over my body, which really upset my mom. I went into playing wanting to be the quarterback. The kid that was quarterback the previous season ended up not playing, because he wanted to focus on basketball apparently, which I thought was pretty cool, because there was a vacant quarterback spot to be filled. In the practices when one of the coaches saw me throw, he asked me if I wanted to play quarterback, and I said yes. However, that was the last time the subject ever came up, which kind of pissed me off because they never gave me a chance to prove myself. During the practices they mostly had me playing defense as a cornerback. One practice I had done really well when I defended a kid that was a lot bigger than me, and I broke up the pass (kind of. I mostly just stayed with him, and the ball was underthrown and hit my helmet. Regardless, the coaches thought I did a good job.). After the practice, the coaches met my dad.

Dad: Hi, nice to meet you. I'm Jack, Psychotic Logician's father.
Coach: Nice to meet you. I'm the coach.
Dad: How was practice?
Coach: It went pretty well. Your son is very athletic.
Dad: That's good to hear.

Something about the coaches made my dad uneasy, mainly, that our practices were held on the field of an elementary school, and the coaches were smoking cigarettes. He was a little irritated about this because on school property it is a tobacco free zone. The coaches felt that I was not good enough in practices to play offense or defense, and so when the first season opening game arrived, the coach only put me in on special teams, as a player on the kickoffs. The highlight of my time playing football, however, is something that I am proud of, considering that I was only in the game for two or three plays. The coach taught us that on the kickoffs, we should charge the other team players that were kicking off. One of the players, told me that when we charge them, you should "knock them on their ass". I don't really remember ever hitting someone, but there was something that I did that made one of the referees throw a flag. I knew I had done something illegal on the play but can't remember what it was. But I ended up getting a penalty, which would have made the coach get very pissed off at me had he known that it was me, but the referee didn't make it completely clear who it was that got the penalty. The reason I am so proud of this, is because it made me leave somewhat of a mark on my football career that effected the game somewhat. At the end of the game the coach gathered all the players around along with their parents and felt he had to defend himself. We had lost the game, and a lot of the parents were pissed off, because we were obviously not very good, and the previous season they had won the championship. A big problem that my mom heard from somebody was that the town I lived in was not nearly as big as some of the other places that had people trying out. So, there was only around twenty to thirty kids on our team, as compared to other places that had 50+ kids on the team, and hence, had a much deeper talent pool to work with as compared to our team. The coach said something like the following:

Coach: Parents, I know what you must be thinking, but let me assure you, this team can and will get better. I think the more we practice, the better we can play against other teams.
Parent: Why is this happening? We went into season expecting to win another championship.
Coach: I understand your concern, but it is just the beginning of the season, and we will get better.
Parent: This is ridiculous. I don't see how you could make this team any better.

A lot of the parents took the game way to seriously and it got to the point where the coach ended up getting fired and replaced with a new coach, all because the team was losing games that the parents think we should have won. It was considered to be such a big deal, that a local newspaper ended up doing a story on it. They had interviewed the coaches and he and his son said something like the following: "I have never come across such rude people in my life. They didn't give me the proper chance to prove myself, and all they care about is winning." After the first game, the husband of the parent who I mentioned above, ended up going to one of the practices and pretty much cussing out the coach, and had his son quit the team. The coach's response was, "So it begins." After we had our team pictures, I had gotten the shit kicked out of me so badly, that I decided to quit. I was happy that I at least got a picture taken of me to show people that I had at one point played football, and I got to keep the team jersey as well. I don't think the new team coach made that big of a difference and the rest of the season they had lost a lot more games than they had won. Another thing that I was proud of during my one game football career is that during one of the practices, I had tackled a kid that weighed at least 50 to 60 pounds more than me. But he was pretty much the only one. I was so shitty at tackling other people that the coach put me up against another player who also wasn't very good at tackling, one on one. The kid I was tackling one on one was able to tackle me easily, and all I could do was hold onto his legs and try to bring him down as he tried to shake me off. Knowing that there was pretty much no chance that I would get any better at tackling people, the coach's advice to me was, just hang on to his legs while you wait for the other players to arrive and bring him down. At that point I realized I had no future in the sport and pretty much said fuck this. Some people would say a silver lining would be that at least you tried. This was of little consolation to me. Fuck getting the living shit out of you just to play on the kickoffs. It's not worth it.

## BEING ON THE HIGH SCHOOL TENNIS TEAM

When I was in eighth grade, just about to go into ninth grade, I decided to pick up tennis. I'm not trying to come across as arrogant in the next thing that I say, but I honestly believe it to be true. If I would have picked up tennis when I was six or seven, instead of picking it up when I was thirteen or fourteen, I would be a professional tennis player right now. A lot of the players that I beat in the years between I started playing (13 or 14 years old) and when I stopped (around 19 years old), had been playing since they were little kids. Within a few years of playing, I was able to beat or at least play a close match with a person who had been playing for at least five or six years more than me. When I tried out for the tennis team in high school, however, I ended up not making the team, because at that point I had only been playing for roughly a month or so. But because so many people had tried out for the team and not made it, the school decided to make a JV team. I was doubles partners with a guy named, "Dusty". He ended up being one of the guys who busted me when I was in college for possession of Adderall and pot. One time he hit me with a ball close to the part of your body where your Kidney's are and from that point on always referred to me as "Kidney." We were an alright team together, but not soon after we were doubles partners, he ended up getting fucked by posting pictures of himself on Myspace with illegal weapons.

In the years to come after playing on the JV team my freshman year, my goal was to make "Singles". How high school tennis works is that there are four double's teams and three single's players. I was on the number three varsity team my sophomore year, number two double's team my junior year, and number one double's team my senior year. Being on the double's team my senior year really pissed me off. During the tryouts I was playing a guy who was ranked one spot below me on the roster. The score during one game I was playing against the kid was something like 15-30 or Love-30. The coach came up to me and told me that if I beat him, I would be playing singles. Of course, like with anything I have ever wanted in my life, I fucked up and the kid ended up beating me. The summer before my senior year, I was playing three to four times a week for a couple of hours at a local tennis club. The club was basically run by a bunch of jackasses who only cared about how good they were in comparison to the people that they were supposed to coach. On one occasion, me and a couple of friends had just finished filming ourselves playing, so that we could analyze the video and see what we were doing right or wrong. However, before we went up to the tennis center to watch our film, we decided to get some Wendy's which was located about thirty or forty yards away from the tennis center. We got our food to go and headed back to the tennis center, only to be met by one of the pros who looked extremely pissed off. He told us to follow him, and we were confused because we thought that we were supposed to look at the film. When we got back down to where the outside courts are, the main pro was also very pissed off that we went to Wendy's. She ended up making us run laps around all the courts for the entire rest of the practice. As a middle finger to the pros that made us do this, me and my friends decided to take off our shirts and sing "99 Bottles of Beer on the Wall". After every lap we did, we stopped to get a drink of water, and this pissed the main pro up royally. After practice was over, one of the mothers of one of the people who had to run laps with me, singled me out as the leader who corrupted her son to behave in this way.

Mother: I don't want you to behave this way if you are going to hang out with my son.
Me: Ok…

Besides the fact that me and my friends pissed everyone at the tennis club off that day, the best part is when my mom got involved. My mom on pretty much every predicament that I am in, almost always takes my side. My mom called the main pro up to see what exactly happened.

Me: My son told me that you made him run laps for the last hour of practice instead of playing tennis.
Pro: Yes. I decided to make your son and a few other kids run laps around the tennis courts to punish them for going to Wendy's.
Me: I am paying you money, so that my son will be playing tennis, not running laps.
Pro: They were not allowed to do what they did and there has to be consequences for it. They are not allowed to go someplace else when tennis practice is in session.
Me: I gave my son permission to go to Wendy's.
Pro: No! That is not ok.

The main pro was a total bitch and a control freak. Honestly, what the fuck do they care that we spent five minutes at Wendy's so we can have something to eat while we watched the film? Another one of the pros talked about this incident (not naming names) a while after it happened and said it was a safety issue.

From the time I was a sophomore in high school to a senior in high school, I spent the majority of my time playing tennis in the summer. I, apparently, was progressing in skill at a pretty impressive rate. My first summer, one of the pros told certain people who had reached a certain skill level that they will upgrade to a higher level. The level that a few kids had been upgraded to was "Level B", and I was not one of them. I ended up playing a set with a kid who that day was upgraded to Level B that day and I ended up beating him. Also, during one practice session, I beat one of the pros. This mattered little to me, unless I was going to make singles, which, as I explained above, I didn't. In one summer, the tennis center held a tournament. The guy who was ranked #1 got a bye week. The only thing about this tournament: there were only three people in my bracket, and three trophies to be won by whoever got first, second, and third. I played a match against some old guy and beat him and then got my ass kicked in the championship. That summer was also the summer where Ron, "Levi", and I were in a tennis summer league together and every week we had a different match to play in different cities and places around where we live. We ended up going undefeated in the regular season and for some reason, got our asses handed to us in the tournament. But during the regular season, the teams that we played were so horrible that we spent the majority of the time fucking with them. On one occasion Ron and I had just finished beating the shit out of this one team in doubles. As we got in my car to drive away, we saw the two kids sitting against a fence, and thought this would be a great time to add insult to injury. I drive by and yell, "Go back to Africa you fucking beaners!" They just kind of looked at us like they didn't know what the hell we were talking about. They weren't even Hispanic, they were white.

## PROOF THAT "THE SECRET" CAN COME TO FUCK YOU OVER

Despite getting hit several times with the ball by other players on several occasions when I was on my high school tennis team, there was one time that I got hit that particularly screwed me over. I was playing a double's match with my partner, and we won the match. One of the players on the opposing team was apparently very pissed off that we kicked their ass. As I was about to leave the court, one of the players on the opposing team, for some reason, decided to serve a ball across the court. I don't know what his intention was in doing this, but if it was to hit me or hurt me in any way, then he got what he wished for. He served the ball, and before I had any time to react, the tennis ball hit me directly in the balls. In excruciating pain, I fell down on my face, breaking my glasses.

Me: What the fuck man?! Why the fuck would you hit me in the balls?! God fucking dammit!

Then something happened to me that one can make an argument for that the law of attraction is true. Immediately when I fell down, I had a vision of driving back to my house and getting pulled over by the cops. The explanation I was going to tell the cop after he pulled me over was that I had just gotten hit in the balls about 45 minutes ago and I am very upset. The kid who hit the ball, from what I could see, was really sorry that he just did what he did. He apologized but it was in vain. On top of being in a lot of pain, when I fell down, my glasses broke. After the worst part of the pain subsided, I drove back to my house. When I got to a certain part of the road I was on, I noticed that four or five cars that were coming in the opposite direction all were flipping their lights on and off. At the time I had no idea what this meant, and so I kept driving at about twenty miles an hour over the speed limit. I then came around a corner and saw a cop sitting in some person's driveway the leads to the road I am on. A question that comes to mind: what if that was my driveway or I was a friend of the people who lived at that address? If that was the case, then in reference to the cop sitting there, "what the fuck?" I immediately slammed on my breaks and went down to ten miles per hour over the speed limit. For some reason right before I passed the cop, I took my foot of the break. Why? Because I thought that the cop would think that if I passed him going just five miles per hour over the speed limit or exactly the speed limit, then he would have seen that I had slowed down a hell of a lot to get down to that speed, which made me think that he would pull me over just for that. So, I passed him going ten miles per hour over the speed limit (which was 35mph) and I saw him immediately pull out of the driveway and turn his lights on. The feeling I get whenever I see a cop on the road is the same feeling I get when I see a wasp around me. And when they turn their lights on in behind you, it is like the goddamn wasp won't leave you fuck alone. There is nothing more annoying than when after you get nut tapped, a fucking wasp won't leave you alone, which I equivocate with a cop pulling you over. I pulled over to the side of the road, and put my glasses back on, or at least as best I could since the dipshit tennis player unintentionally fucked my glasses up. This was not only the first time that I had ever been pulled over by a cop, but it was also the first time I ever had to deal with a cop by myself. I was pretty scared, and even more pissed off because my visualization of getting pulled over by the cops on my drive home came true. Fuck the law of attraction. The cop came up to my driver side window and did the usual "license and registration" bullshit, as well as asked me why he pulled me over. Now, ever since I got hit in the balls, I had for the next twenty to thirty minutes thought in my head what I was going to say to the cop, mainly, tell him exactly what happened, and hence, why I was speeding was because I was so upset about my testicles almost rupturing. What did I do and what didn't I do? I told him that my glasses were broken, and he seemed to acknowledge this. So, I was good on the front that he couldn't bust me for not wearing my "corrective lenses" that my driver's license said I have. I ended up not telling him the real reason why he caught me speeding, because at this point, I was more depressed than upset. The cop ended up writing me a ticket for going nine miles per hour over the speed limit, which is in the range of the lowest type of ticket you can get for speeding (going six miles per hour of the speed limit gets you the same number of points off your license that nine miles per hour gets you), and it is two points. It cost me around $80, which totally fucked me because I had no job, and my parents wouldn't give me control of the money I had in my bank account until I graduated high school. Supposedly, a friend of mine in high school was training to be a cop and was in the police station when the cop who pulled me over sent in his report.

Friend: I saw your name on a police report yesterday.
Me: Yeah, a cop pulled me over for speeding.
Friend: The report said that you were cooperative and compliant with the officer.
Me: I guess I was. It pissed me off when it happened.

I have never seen a cop on the road where I got pulled over again. I am curious, however, if I would have contested the ticket if either: 1) I could have gotten the officer in trouble for sitting in someone's driveway. A driveway, which, for all he knew, someone could have tried to pull into, but the pig would have been in the way. 2) I could have gotten out of the ticket for the very fact that the cop shouldn't have been sitting in the driveway. I used to go 60mph on that road going in neutral, because it is all downhill until you reach the person's driveway that the cop was sitting in, and then it's all uphill from there to where I turn off to get to my house. Now I pretty much go the speed limit, sometimes five to ten miles per hour over, which is a manageable speed to be able to slow down to 35mph if there happens to be a cop sitting in the driveway again. I rarely speed anymore, which makes me curious as to how people can get multiple speeding tickets within a short period of time. I guess some people just don't learn, apparently. They say in the movie, "The Secret" that the more you visualize something to happen and have a lot of passion along with your thoughts, then the more likely it is to come true, which, I experienced firsthand. Since it is a well-known fact that the world isn't fair, I would have to say the law of attraction might have something to do with this, considering that people, and me especially, am inclined to think about and direct a lot of passion towards things that I don't fucking want to experience. Or maybe you can just blame a lot of the unfairness in the world on the fact that 90% of what cops do is to fuck people over, and not to serve and protect. In a perfect world, anarchy rules.

# THE TIME THE DRUNK FELL INTO THE FIRE

For 12 years I was next door neighbors with a kid named, "Ken". Ken was three years younger than me, so when I was a senior in high school, he was a freshman. Ken's dad, "Alex", is without a doubt one of the most ridiculous mother fuckers I have ever met. At the time that this story took place, Alex was awaiting trial for his involvement in a drug dealing enterprise. Apparently, he knew some person that had a huge marijuana growing facility, and he pitched $20,000 to help fund the operation. Later, he ended up having to serve time in jail, because a party got busted by the cops at his house, and he was charged with buying alcohol for minors. A friend of mine told me that at that party, he saw Alex making out with a 15 year old. This should give you sufficient background information on just how absurd this guy is.

Ken is the type of drunk who, when he gets plastered, gets pissed off and is highly irrational. He got three DUIs within a six month period. Alex had to ban hard alcohol from his house and only allow Ken to drink beer, because hard alcohol apparently makes Ken even more retarded, faster. Me, Eddie, Victoria, Ken, and Alex were all standing around a bon fire one night in Alex's back yard. We were all drinking beer and having a good time and were all getting pretty drunk. At one point in the night, Ken had just put a board of wood on the fire so that it was leaning up against the fire on its outside perimeter. Alex, shit faced, thought that it would be a good idea to run up to the fire, step on the board, and then jump back out of the fire ring. Apparently, he thought that the board would support his weight so that he would just jump right out of the fire unscathed, in the same way that a person doing parkour would jump from place to place. We all watched as he ran up to the fire, jumped onto the board, and saw the board immediately collapse underneath him. His entire body from the top of his chest, all the way down to his knees were completely in the center of the fire. He screamed out, "Ahhh!" as he lay in the fire for a good three to four seconds. He somehow got up from the fire and proceeded to roll on the ground to put out the flames that were still on his body. You could see on his back the charred black skin, as well as red coals that were still on his body. Ken immediately ran over to Alex to see if he was ok, signaling to the rest of us to stand back and not approach him to give him some space. After completely putting out the coals on his skin, Ken walked with Alex towards their house to see the damage that he now had to live with.

Alex: I'm ok. I just fucked up.

Victoria (to me and Eddie): Those burns are bad.

Me: Yeah, they look like third degree burns.

Victoria: That is going to take a long time to heal. That really sucks for him.

Once Ken and Alex got to their house, I could see through the window them examining all the burns on Alex's back and waist. I didn't see, but apparently one of the worst burns he got was on his hands, probably because he had to use them to get himself out of the fire, pressing down on the coals. The problem: Alex couldn't call 911 for help, I guess because if he had any run in with law enforcement, he would immediately be taken to jail. They called Ken's mom, Alex's ex-wife, to help and she arrived shortly after, probably not lending much assistance. What could she possibly do? The night was pretty much over at that point. I guess it was a sort of blessing in disguise (although not much of one) that Alex was very drunk to semi dull the pain. I learned that he had to stay multiple days in the hospital to be treated for his burns. The doctor's used chicken skin to put on top of the burns to help them heal, and to mask the burn marks so his skin didn't look so fucked up. Events like this were the usual for Alex. He owned an indoor swimming pool at his house, and on one occasion he got so drunk that, I forget what the reason was, he dove into the swimming pool with all of his clothes on and cell phone in his pocket. It's clear that both Ken and Alex don't think very clearly about their actions when they are drunk, which I find to be actually pretty funny.[58]

## THE PODCASTS

Over the years I have thought of many ways in which I might be able to free myself from the shitty life I am currently living and live a better, happier life. Basically, that equates to having financial freedom, and this idea that I am about to explain, was one attempt to do just that. Eddie and I decided at one point, that if we could just be completely honest and say things about the world that we think, and most importantly, not give a shit at all about who we offend, that we could potentially make it big and have somewhat of an influence on the world. We would accomplish this by making podcasts. My original idea was just to use my computer to record our podcasts, figuring that the quality is not that bad. Eddie, however, had an idea that would end up coming to fuck us up. He knew a recording artist that he worked with to record some of his rap music. The first clue I should have realized that this was a shitty thing to do, was that the recording artist, "Blake", charged Eddie $30 for an hour long rap session, and then came up with a magic number of charging us $200 for an hour podcast. I'm not sure why I agreed to do this, but I did. We ended up recording eight, one hour podcasts, in which we covered topics such as philosophy, religion, sex and things related to it, etc. It was pretty much just us sounding off on what we think about the world. We would always smoke a bowl and get tipsy before every session, mostly to put us in the state of mind that we really don't care about what other people think about us. Wanting to show the world that we really didn't care about what they thought about us, or what we thought about it, we were thinking about getting married (Eddie and I are not gay. Our thought of potentially getting married was meant to be a sort of fuck you to people who are against gay marriage. Our thought was that we are not gay, we are not in love. Why then would we want to get married? Just because we live in a society where we can). We decided against it when we realized we would have to deal with a bunch of extraneous bullshit like filing our taxes and shit like that. For a lot of the material that we discussed in the podcasts, we used a paper I wrote once call the "Philosophical Roast", to sound off about what we think about the current state of the world. Blake told us at one point that Eddie and I sounded like a cult. I was confused by this because making fun of cults, doesn't make you one.

The most memorable of the podcast sessions was a time when I smoked pot, got tipsy, and snorted a few lines of cocaine. We were doing our usual shit, sounding off on whatever we wanted, but in this case, the majority of our material was based on making fun of religion. Blake's father, "Tim" is a Christian and when hearing what we were talking about, wanted to talk to us about it. I wasn't aware that Eddie apparently said it was ok for Tim to come into our podcast, but, if knowing the type of shit that the material for the podcast was going to turn towards after Tim entered the recording studio, I'm sure he wouldn't have been ok with it. Tim came into the studio with another guy, and the topic of conversation immediately became serious, something that is something we were rebelling against in making our podcasts in the first place.

Tim: So, hearing what you guys have been talking about recently, I just wanted to tell you what I believe.
Me: Sure.

Tim: I believe that Jesus Christ died on the cross for our sins, and it is only through him that your sins can be reconciled.

Me: Right…

Tim: What do you believe?

Me: I guess I just think that the end times is a joke, and it probably won't come true. I find a lot of things in Christianity to be humorous.

Tim: I just think that if you put your trust in Jesus, he can turn your life around.

Me: I guess I just don't understand the existence of hell and how it can be rationally or morally justified.

Other guy in room: Well there has to be some sort of penalty or punishment for you not accepting the truth.[59]

I was very irritated that the conversation took a turn into a serious theological discussion. I did, however, experience a slight mood brightener when, after we had discussed all the serious shit, I read a quote from my philosophical roast about something, which made Tim laugh. Unfortunately, when the time came where we could finally turn the conversation towards not giving a shit, my computer battery died and the roast material along with it. After eight hours of podcasts, Eddie and I decided to call it quits. We mostly just realized that we probably were not going to have the kind of impact that we thought we would, and I really don't think that a lot of people would get our sense of humor.[60]

What pissed me off the most about the podcasts was: 1) the sound quality in the recording studio, really wasn't that much better than the sound quality on my computer. 2) after the fifth or sixth podcast, we asked Blake if he could cut down the price a little to make it a little more reasonable. He agreed, and after that just charged us $150 for an hour. The fact that he was willing to do this kind of shows how much of a rip off it was to begin with. If he was willing to just have us pay $150 an hour, then why didn't he just charge us that to begin with? When it was all said and done, the podcasts ended up costing me somewhere in the neighborhood of $1400-$1600, making it one of the most expensive fuck ups I have ever participated in.[61]

# SECTION 4
# Jobs in Mind Travel

## FORWARD

The following are a list of odd jobs I have done over my life, starting when I was a teenager, up until only a few years ago. This is not a complete list of every job I have ever held in my life, but it is a list of jobs which I think are humorous, and a little absurd, seen especially in the stories where a lot of crazy shit goes down. A common trait in many of the jobs described in this section, are that I would rather be broke and have no source of income, instead of working at some specific place I would have to work in order to earn money. Currently I am (27 years old) unemployed and have been for over a year. I'm a little sketched out about government handout because that seems to imply some sort of big government. However, I am currently on Medicaid and am reaping the benefits of it now. Recently I took a training class on how to become a lifeguard. The problem? I failed at the first test that they make you do in trying to qualify as a lifeguard, mainly, a 300 meter swim. I got through 150 meters and decided fuck this. Unless I find a source of income in the next couple months, I am going to have to keep doing house maintenance bullshit in order to even pay my rent, which is $200 a month for living with my parents. Another possible way of escape could be if this book got published fairly recently once I am completely finished with it. In a choice of what you would rather do, either be rich or be famous, I'll take being rich any ole fucking day of the week over fame. A lot of money, although people say that it doesn't bring happiness, it does bring a very important aspect to happiness that I and others might share, that being you don't have to work odd bullshit jobs anymore. That would be freaking tight.

## WORKING AT A MOVIE THEATER

The first real job I ever had was working for a local movie theater. The starting pay was around $6.00 - $6.50 an hour. My brother had worked there for a few years before he graduated high school, and myself, being a sophomore in high school at the time, thought it would be a good way to start earning money. My brother would tell me stories about some of the things that he would run into on the job, such as: someone taking a shit in one of the theaters and having to clean it up, taking the popcorn butter out of the shipping box and seeing it all as one large piece of lard and fat, and playing XBOX in one of the theaters. At the same time that I got hired on as an employee, two other friends I knew from my high school class, "Greg" and "Bobby" also got hired on as well. The head manager was kind of a nice lady but would get a little bitchy when we didn't do what she asked us to do. In the one to two months that I worked there, I could have gotten fired a lot sooner than I actually did. It was the summer of 2006 and some of the movies that were just coming out were, "Mission: Impossible 3" and "Superman Returns". One of the people I worked with was a woman named, "Lilly". She had worked there for a long time and was, from what my brother told me, a complete fucking retard. Having worked there for so long, she had just been promoted to manager, and it took her a while to get down what you have to do to operate as a manager. On one occasion I was standing behind the back counter and saw Lilly run out of the door that leads up to the stairs to the top level of the theater where all the film projectors are at. Apparently, she fucked up in some way that ended with the "Mission: Impossible 3" film catching on fire and begin burning through the projector films. The people that came to watch the movie in the next few weeks had to sit through the movie which had entire scenes cut out of it, because the frames had burned up, due in part to something that she did to screw it up. The way that the manager treated Lilly was like seeing a parent instruct their child about the proper etiquette of table manners. Quizzing her on the dos and don'ts of the job, all while Lilly wrote down the instructions on a mini legal pad. After Lilly had gotten promoted to manager, almost every night the cash registers ended up being short at least twenty dollars. The theater had a policy (like most companies that deal with money) that the person who signed into work for that particular register, is allowed a leeway of five dollars over the exact amount that was supposed to be in it, or five dollars below. As long as they were within that limit they didn't get written up. So, when she became manager almost every night someone would get written up for being short the exact amount. A few weeks into her promotion, she ended up getting fired for some reason that the head manager never mentioned, but I am almost positive that it had something to do with her stealing money from the registers and playing it off like it was the person who was signed into the register's fault. I was to then find out shortly after this happened that there is a much safer way to scam money from the company that would go completely unnoticed by the management.

There were two types of tickets that could be sold to a customer: a child ticket which was $6, and an adult ticket which was $9. The person in charge of the front register selling tickets to the customers would be able to perform the following scam that ended up making me a lot of extra cash. Whenever there was an adult that came in to buy a ticket, all you would need to do in order to take money right from the company without them noticing, is tell the customer that it was $9, and instead of ringing up the ticket as an adult, just simply enter it into the register as a child ticket. This way only $6 would need to go into the register, and you could pocket the other $3. None of the customers I ever sold tickets to ever noticed that on their ticket it said "Child", but even if they did, I don't think they would say anything. In doing this, I would sometimes make an extra $50 a night in cash, and if I fucked up somehow with the register and it was short, then I would just take money from the profit I made and put it into the register to even it out. My brother said he did this exact same scam when he worked there, but one of the manager's noticed on his computer that all of the ticket sales for that night were for children and none were for adults. Luckily the manager happened to be a really cool person and he just told my brother not to do it again. The head manager I worked with never said anything to me or anyone else for the entire time we were doing the scam. It got to a point where Greg tried to perform the scam at the snack register, but it was way too risky and stupid. His idea was to enter into the register whatever snacks the customer wanted so that the customer could see the total on the front of the register, and then instead of confirming the sale and having it go into the system as something purchased, when the customer left with their snacks, he would just delete whatever he punched into the register and erase it so that no sale was ever made. In doing this, whatever amount of money that the customer ended up buying, would be pure cash profit. This was a stupid idea for two reasons. 1) if you do this all the time then when the manager does the inventory of all the snacks sold at the end of the night, she would see that they sold no skittles for example, but five skittles were missing from the shelf. 2) you had to ask the customer if they wanted a receipt or not. If the customer wanted a receipt, then you couldn't do it because in order for them to get a receipt back, you needed to process the order. Of course, this didn't work on credit cards, and only on cash, with exact amounts. I told him this a was a stupid idea and so we agreed that from now on whoever was running the front register selling tickets, would split the profit between the other employees that were in on the scam, which was only three or four of us.

When "Superman Returns" was playing in the theater, they ran a promotion where on the large cups of soft drinks and on the large popcorn buckets, they had a little sticker that you could peel off to see if you won anything from what they were promoting. Among the things that you could win were: a twenty dollar check, Superman action figures, and a chance to win $1,000,000 by having yourself entered into a raffle. When I started cleaning out the theaters after a show and taking out the trash, I noticed that many of the people that had purchased the large drink and popcorn did not peel off their sticker. I then made it my mission to collect as many of the stickers that I could off of the cups and popcorn buckets as I could. It even got to the point where if I missed a day of work, I would go to the dumpster in the back of the theater on my day off, and search through the garbage to find more stickers. All in all, I probably collected somewhere between 70 to 80 stickers. I won three or four $20 checks, and three or four action figures, as well as had my name entered into the million dollar raffle for as many stickers that I collected. I was like a kid in a candy shop, whenever I saw that someone didn't take the two seconds to peel the sticker off, I was euphoric. This all ended, unfortunately, when two dikes that I worked with who nobody else there liked decided that they hated me for some reason and made it their mission to fuck with my plan. When I wasn't working, or if I wasn't the person in charge of cleaning the movie theaters, they would take all the stickers themselves, and, according to another employee who worked with them, wouldn't even enter them into the contest. The bitches would just rip them up. I don't know what the problem they had with me was, or what I did to piss them off and make them do what they did was, but *I guess that type of reassurance of one's actions isn't required to reinforce what a raging cunt does.*

Every movie theater is required to do multiple "theater checks" throughout the time that a movie is playing. You will recognize the people doing these checks as the people who have an orange lit cone flashlight that they hold as they walk from one side of the theater to the other, checking apparently (but not really giving a shit in our case) to see if everything is going ok in the theater and with the movie. Me and my other friend employees took this as a way to have a little innocent fun. We would take the orange cone flashlight and wave it around in different directions and move it in crazy patterns like we were at a rave. Whatever made the audience draw their attention away from the movie and notice the movie theater checker is what we were going for. Normally, all a theater checker is supposed to do is hold the flashlight in his hand as he walks across the theater, using, I suppose, the flashlight as a guide to make sure he doesn't run into shit. The way I used the flashlight on a lot of the theater checks would be to hold it in my hand and wave my arm back and forth, mimicking a guy who guides airplanes into the proper position in runways. Unfortunately, this all ended (for me at least) when I did a theater check and decided to wave the flashlight around like an acid head at a disco club. The top of the flashlight connecting the light to the orange cone was loose and so as I waved it around, I was walking up one of the aisles and the orange cone flew off from the flashlight and landed somewhere between the seats. I looked around the seats for a few minutes and couldn't find it, drawing a lot of attention to myself and probably pissing a lot of people off. I had to tell Lilly what happened.

Me: I lost the orange top of the flashlight in the theater. I tried looking for it but I couldn't find it.
Lilly: How did you lose it?
Me: I was waving it around like we are supposed to do, and it flew off into an area of seats.
Lilly: Why were you waving it around?
Me: I thought that's how we were supposed to do the theater checks.
Lilly: No, you just hold it in your hand and walk with it by your side when you are checking the theater.
Me: Sorry, I didn't know that. I won't do it again.
Lilly: It's ok.

Every once and a while when cleaning a theater, you would find some cash that fell out of someone's pocket and keep it for yourself. We would entertain ourselves with little games like playing baseball with the broom and dustpan, using them as bats to hit a cup or popcorn bucket that the other one would throw up in the air. Looking back on the years since I worked there, I can honestly say it was the most fun at a job I ever had. However, all the fun and debauchery I had working there, all ended with one unfortunate event.

I was standing at the front register not doing anything, just waiting for a customer to come in. Everyone else was either on break or cleaning theaters or somewhere other than the front counter. My brother and his friend (who had just recently quit the theater only a few months prior) walked up to the front counter and I started talking to them. My brother turned the front register monitor towards him to check whether or not I was the one who was signed into the register. It turned out that I wasn't and I was just covering for the person who was out somewhere else. Upon seeing that I was not the person signed into the register, and hence, not the one who would get fucked after doing what he was about to do, his friend began to talk to one of the other managers in the management office, which was located right behind, but not directly behind the front register. I should note that the front register had a wooden cash box/drawer in which the cash was stored when making a sale. This was different than the other registers which were automated to open up only after you have made a sale. So, since the money in the drawer could just be opened by hand and was not locked up, this afforded my brother the opportunity to open the drawer himself and take some money. As his friend was trying to distract the manager away from seeing the front register, my brother reached behind the counter and took out two twenty dollar bills, without the manager noticing. Right before my brother stole the money, he told me to get away from the register so that he could better reach his hand over it and open the drawer. After he told me this, I went over and stood about eight to ten feet away from register, pretending to look over a list of job duties that we were supposed to complete throughout the shift, trying to look oblivious and ignorant to the fact that my brother had just taken $40 from the register. I wasn't sure what to think, other than that they were fucking over the person who was signed into the register, and that it was kind of a sketchy thing.

Me: How much money did you take?
Brother: Shut up.
Me: Ok.

I had the next day off and at around two or three in the afternoon my boss called me and wanted me to come to the theater. I agreed and I had my mom drive me there, because I didn't own my own car at the time. I was pretty sure I knew what my boss called me in about, but I was just hoping to Christ that it wasn't about what I thought. I get to the theater and start talking to my boss.

Boss: So, what happened yesterday?
Me: Nothing really, I worked a thirteen hour shift.

Boss: Why?

Me: Because Mark called in sick and wanted me to cover for him, so I did.

Boss: What else happened?

Me: Nothing really.

Boss: Are you sure? Do you know why the front register was missing some money?

Me: Well, there was a time when two people came into the theater and one of the guys took some money out of the drawer. But I ended up getting the money back from them and put it in the register so that doesn't explain how it could be short.

Boss: Follow me.

I followed her up to the top level of the theater where the projectors are, and she showed me the video camera footage of what had happened the previous day. It was pretty much exactly as I remembered it happening. My brother reaching over the register and taking $40 out of it, while his friend just appeared to be having a causal conversation with the other manager.

Boss: Do you know who these people are?

Me (not wanting to turn my brother in): No, I have no idea.

Boss: Really? Because it appears (while she says this, she rewinds the tape showing me having about a thirty to forty five second conversation with my brother and his friend) that you were talking to them like you knew them.

Me: Um, yeah, I don't remember what we were talking about, but I didn't know either of them. (In my mind: "FUCK!")

Boss: Ok, I want you to think carefully about what you say to me next, because if it turns out that you do know who this person is who stole money from the register, you will get fired from this job. So, I ask you for the final time, do you know this person?

Me: No, I have no idea. (In my mind: "I'M SO FUCKED!")

Boss: Ok.

My boss knew that my mom was with me at the time and so she asked me if I could get her so that she could ask her some questions.

Me: Hey mom, my boss wants to talk to you.

Mom: What's it about? Are you getting fired?

Me: I don't know, but somebody stole money from the register yesterday and I think she wants to ask you questions about it.
Mom: Was it someone you know?............Was it your brother?
Me: Yes, it was.

My boss led me and my mom back up to the top level projector floor and showed her the video.

Boss: One of our employees has already identified one of the people who are in the video. He is a former employee that just quit only a few months ago. We are still trying to identify the other person. It appears that your son is just standing next to the counter looking over some papers when this unknown man steals money.

My boss played the whole video, beginning to end, and then it came to the part where my brother stole the money.

Boss: Do you know who this person is?
Mom: Yes, that is my son, his (referring to me) brother.

I didn't say shit. I couldn't say shit. I didn't know what the fuck was going on. My boss had a very disappointed look on her face, like she couldn't believe that it was someone I knew, and I didn't tell her. To make matters worse, she assumed that the reason that I didn't tell her that it was my brother, was because my brother gave me some of the money that he stole, as to make it seem like we were working together. By this time the police had arrived and my boss, after finishing talking to them, came back over to where my mom and I were sitting.

Boss: I have just finished talking to the officers and I have made the decision not to try Psychotic Logician with anything.
Mom: Ok, thank you.

I was confused by this because other than the fact that I lied to my boss, I didn't really think I did anything wrong, let alone anything wrong that could land me with being charged with a criminal offense. I think what they could have charged me with what obstruction of justice for not telling the truth about a serious crime that I knew the truth about. My mom gave the police officers the address to my brother's apartment, and having attained a warrant for his arrest, they went to his apartment and arrested him. After talking about it with my brother a few days later, he said he completely forgot about the whole theft incident and didn't know what the fuck he was being arrested for. Apparently the $40 was used for buying weed, and in another fucked up turn of events related to the incident, my brother's friend bought a bottle of "Limu" from my sister who was a Limu sales representative. Limu is basically a nutrient drink that is supposed to be very healthy for you.

Sister: What?
Mom: The bottle of Limu you sold to your brother's friend was bought with stolen money!
Sister: Oh…

I left the movie theater saying goodbye to my friends and nodding at the two evil bitches on my way out the door. The next day at school, "Bobby" told me that as soon as I left my boss walked into the manager's office and said to herself, "I can't believe Psychotic Logician would steal money." My brother ended up getting fired from his job, because my dad, his boss, didn't think it was right to have a felon working for him. My dad and grandpa gave me shit about not turning my brother in and not being honest when my boss asked if I knew who stole the money. Looking back all these years later since this happened, I would have done the same thing. If there was even a one in a million chance that I could help my brother not get fucked I would have taken it. I just couldn't in good conscious willingly give him up and watch him get screwed because I was the one who turned him in. Later after things calmed down a bit, my dad told me that the fact that I didn't turn my brother in was, "admirable". My brother ended up getting a third level felony for theft, and just had to go on probation for three years.

## MY ATTEMPT AT BECOMING A DRUG DEALER

When I was a sophomore in college, I made the horrible mistake of trying to become a drug dealer. My freshman year roommate was a pot dealer, and he was good at it. He would buy an ounce for around $330, sell it for $50 for an eighth of an ounce, and smoke the profit. I, however, did not want to smoke my profit, I was in it to make money. One of my biggest motivations was seeing the movie, "Blow". I wanted to be the person that people went to when they needed their fix. Moving into a dorm hall my sophomore year and living with a bunch of freshman presented a perfect opportunity to be the guy who people got their shit from.

When I started dealing pot it was in the year 2009 and the selling price on the streets was roughly $25 for every sixteenth of an ounce (eighths would sell for $50, quads would sell for $100, etc.). However, buying in quantities of an ounce or more would cut the price down to roughly $350 for an ounce, and $1200 for a quarter pound. I bought a scale to measure the pot with and was ready to begin dealing.

The very first time I made a pot deal was with some guy I knew, "Jared". Jared began selling me ounces for $350. Early on I made the decision that I would hook my friends up with good deals before I started making profit. Why I did this I do not know. I just thought it would be a nice thing to do. This was the first mistake I made, mainly, being nice and helping my friends and other people I sold to out. I would later come to find out that the people who make it as successful drug dealers, really, at their cores, don't give a fuck about how they treat the people they deal to. They realize that the person that they are dealing to are at the mercy of them, and hence, for example, if they say they will be at some certain place at a certain time to make the deal, they don't really have to be prompt about it, because the person who wants the fix will wait all day for them to show up.

So, I started off giving my friends good hookups. It got to the point that I was dealing them $25 for an eighth of an ounce (which at the time was a very good deal. Today, however, this price is standard). If you want to know how to be a successful drug dealer, what I am about to describe to you is something you should completely avoid. Or, in other words, do the exact opposite. Giving my friends the "homie hookup" took a toll on me and I began to lose money. I would get extremely paranoid that my parents would smell the weed in my bedroom where I was hiding everything, and so on one occasion, after buying an ounce from some girl I knew, I put the weed in a container along with a car freshener to mask the smell. This is definitely something you should not do because the scent from the car freshener overpowered the skunk smell of the weed and made it smell like coconut. I dealt to a buddy of mine one time, and he was a little confused why the weed smelled like coconut[62]:

Me: Here you go, bro (handing him the weed).
Buddy (smelling the weed that actually smelled like coconut): …nice…

Another drug dealing mistake that I made was that when buying from a higher up dealer, always make sure that they count the money before you leave to make sure you gave him the right amount for the deal. I made a deal one time with

Jared for $350 for an ounce. He gave the weed to me, and I handed him the money, which, I am almost positive was the correct amount. Instead of waiting for him to count the money to confirm that the deal was straight, I left his car and drove away. Ten minutes later he called me and said that I only gave him $300. I was really confused because I knew that I had $400 with me and now I only had $50 left. So, I returned to the place we made the deal and gave him another $50. I am pretty sure he took advantage of me, knowing that because I didn't stay to have him count the money in front of me, he knew he could get away with lying that I didn't give him the full amount. He was a classic drug dealing asshole, who really doesn't care about the feelings of others and will do everything in his power to screw someone over for his gain whenever the opportunity presented itself. Society has a name for these types of people, mainly that they are "money grubbing whores". At this point I was done dealing ounces and thought I should move up to buying the weed in higher quantities for better financial gain.

I started buying quarter pounds at $1200. Upon reflection of what I have learned from my shitty run I had as a drug dealer, is that the higher up you go in the drug trade (buying more in bulk to cut the price down for smaller quantities), the sketchier the people that you run into. One of my friends introduced me to a guy, "Marcus", who he said would be able to hook me up with larger amounts of pot to sell. My first impression of Marcus was that he was a pretty cool guy, and, to my everlasting shame, I completely trusted him. Once I started buying quarter pounds, it was the beginning of my sophomore year in college, and I was ready to start selling to everyone who was in need of pot in my dorm hall. I made a fake bottom in a small filing cabinet that I took with me to my college dorm. This, I figured, would eliminate the worry of getting caught with the massive amount of weed that I was trying to sell, in the case that my dorm room was searched by the campus police. Now, two things happened that completely fucked me once I arrived back to school in my dorm hall. First, it became obvious to me that the weed that I was getting from Marcus was very shitty. The college I attended was notorious for being a weed capital of the USA, and the people who I first began to deal to were not satisfied with the product. Second, once I arrived in the dorm, one of my roommates was already buying ounces and selling it to the kids in the dorm hall. I was fucking pissed. How could I get such shitty luck? I decided for the time being that getting pot from Marcus was not the way to go, so I came up with a solution. I would get medical marijuana, and this way I would stand alone as the one person in the dorm hall who had the best weed, who everyone would then want to buy from. I made Marcus my outside pot dealing consultant in which I would still get quarter pounds but have him deal it for me to the people he knew that were dumb enough to pay the $50 an eighth price because they didn't know any better. He would give the profit to me, and I would give him a generous cut for moving it for me. This ended up being a disastrous idea, because I, completely trusting him, gave him complete control of $1200 worth of weed that I bought, with which he could now do whatever the fuck he wanted with. All said and done, Marcus, to this day, still owes me $700, which I will never see, being that he is a convicted felon and went to prison not to long after these events took place (he was a psychopath and, on top of having numerous drug and alcohol offenses, one night he went over to a friend of mine's apartment with the intent of dowsing himself with gasoline when my friend opened the door, and setting himself and my friend on fire. Fortunately, his plan didn't work out and he went to jail shortly after).[63]

Now, as I began to set up my own mini drug enterprise, through having people work for me, it was now time to get my hands on the best weed available, medical pot. Back when these events took place, the medical marijuana business was just kicking off, and tons of people went to certified doctors who would write them prescriptions for getting medicinal bud. I went to go get my prescription from a certified doctor, who, to the best of my knowledge, was only in the medical business for the purpose of writing people medical pot prescriptions. When I arrived to meet the doctor, there were around fifty to sixty people in line ahead of me, waiting their turn to see the doctor. I waited for around two to three hours in line, and, when I finally met with the doctor, the exchange went something like this:

Doctor: What can I do for you today?
Me: I get really bad migraine headaches, and marijuana helps take them away.
Doctor: It certainly does. I'll write you a prescription to get the marijuana from a medical dispensary and you can be on your way.
Me: Thank you.

I was in the room with the doctor for three minutes at the most, and after writing me the prescription, I then immediately went to a medical pot dispensary. The way the medical pot business worked back then is that once you have the doctor's prescription, you can go to a dispensary and buy whatever you wanted for ninety days. After the ninety days were up, you had to at that point have sent your medical prescription into the state to have them certify it, and then you would officially have a medical pot license. I ended up fucking up badly by procrastinating in sending the prescription into the state, and so I was operating with just the prescription itself. The reason this was such a fuck up on my part is because, although you can buy the pot from a dispensary without the state certifying it, if you get caught by the police with weed, and you only have the prescription without the certification, you can still get charged with illegal possession of marijuana. I ended up getting busted one day for this, which I describe in another story.

So, now being able to get my hands on the best pot around, I began selling to my friends, who in turn told their friends about the good weed that I had, which in turn got me more customers. I would buy edibles and multiple strains of pot, and for a brief time, I was actually doing ok in the drug dealing business. The problem with dispensaries, however, is that they still charged you the standard $50 for an eighth deal that you would normally get on the streets. In order to avoid this, I decided to try and find a "caregiver", someone who grows the pot themselves, and then sells it to the people that have signed up with him to legally dispense the pot to. A friend of mine, "Mac" introduced me to a guy named, "Luke", who I decided to make my caregiver. Luke sold me weed for $250 - $275 an ounce, which at the time was a very good deal, considering that I wasn't buying in quarter pounds. Being the nice and generous person that I am, I was still giving the friends that I knew, the homie hookup, and I of course, was taken advantage of. The people in my dorm, knowing where I kept my pot in the false bottom of the filing cabinet, would go into it, and take my weed, saying they would pay me back later, or exchange it for other weed that they had. Unfortunately, as it turned out, the medical weed I was getting wasn't all that it was made out to be as the best shit to smoke, and I began to lose money again. I became frustrated, and, having the film "Blow" as a big inspiration in my quest to become a drug kingpin, I tried to think of other ideas in which I could eliminate the middleman, and go closer to the source and get a bigger payout. Mac was from the east coast, and he said that the pot you get in this state, even the shittier strains like the ones I was getting from Marcus, are much better than almost any pot you can find out east. We began discussing ideas of potentially buying pounds, and then driving the weed to the east coast, which we would then deal to smaller dealers for the full $400 an ounce price. The math turned out to be something like buying a pound for $3,000-$3,500, and then selling them for $6,400. A nice profit, but a greater risk. We talked for weeks about potentially making the trip, but I was short on money because my failing drug enterprise was making me lose hundreds of dollars, and the trafficking idea never took effect.[64]

In my last attempt to make something of myself as a drug dealer, I decided to go more illegal. Marcus, who was still working for me at the time, yet had never paid up (yet I still completely trusted him for some reason), told me that he knew someone who we could get magic mushrooms from. This idea appealed to me because, since I was fucking up royally in the pot business, there was a high demand for psychedelics in the college I was attending. With the last money I had, I ended up buying a half pound of mushrooms for $400. Selling the shrooms at $25 for an eighth of any ounce, this would net a decent profit. Unfortunately, I gave a quarter of a pound to Marcus to have him move it for me, so I would only make $400 of immediate profit off of the quarter of a pound that I had. The $400 that I earned from moving the quarter pound of shrooms, was the only profit I made as a drug dealer. If I had to guess, I would say that I spent roughly $2,000 - $2,500 on buying pot and shrooms in all, and only profited $400 off of it.

In a nutshell, a good way to sum up my failed experience as a drug dealer would be to tell you one thing I did that any experienced drug dealer would laugh at. When first dealing with Marcus after buying a quarter pound of bud, I bought baggies and sticker labels to label the type of strain, the quantity, and the price of the weed. I rolled the baggies up (the bags did not have a zip lock closing) and used the sticker labels to enclose the weed. This was a rookie mistake, because it does not provide a way for the person purchasing the weed to smell the bud and examine it to see if it looks decent enough to buy. When I started dealing, I had a vision of my future being gloriously paved with loads of cash and popularity as the cool guy who has the fix. It is something I will never make the mistake of doing again, seeing that it is pretty much a requirement to be a flaming prick to deal to people, especially people you don't know. However, I wrote this story as a warning to anyone potentially interested in trying it out for themselves. When it comes to drug dealing, do not do the shit I have just described.[65]

# MY JOB AS A SOCCER REFEREE

The first job I ever had in which I made money from a source outside of my own family by doing chores and what not, was being a soccer referee for little kid's games. The pay was $9 a game, and a game lasted around an hour. My brother had done it the previous year or two before I decided that I would like to earn some extra cash. In order to get certified as an official referee, you had to attend a couple hour course in which they taught you the rules and how to do the job. They also covered other basic knowledge that you had to know in order to officiate a game such as, how to deal with a coach or parent who argues that you made a bad call, and they begin to contest it. You pretty much deal with this by giving the adult either a yellow or red card. This card is to be meant as a warning, and if the adult causes more conflict in the game, then you have the authority as the referee to eject the person from the game, which means that the adult has to leave the field and go at least a hundred yards away, or some amount of distance, so that they will no longer cause a problem with the person officiating the game. I was only a line judge which meant that I did not have the authority to give problem rising adults a warning or ejection card, and unfortunately, I never witnessed a case where this happened. So, my job was pretty much to do two main things: look for off-side calls, and make the call as to what team gets the ball after it is kicked out of bounds. I fucked up on both of these two assignments on a few occasions. When a ball goes out of bounds, you are trained to raise the flag that you carry with you in the direction of which teams' side has the ball. Instead of putting the flag in the hand of which team side has the ball and signaling it with that arm, I would instead put the flag in my opposite hand and use my other arm to reach across my body and signal to the side opposite of the hand I used. For example, if the team on the left side of the field got the ball, I would signal with my right arm across my body, pointing the flag in the direction of the left side, instead of using my left arm to signal. I had to keep being repeatedly being told not to do this by some of the main officials that I worked with. This ended up screwing some kids out of playing in a fair game on one notable occasion. I was a line judge in one game and the ball was kicked out by the left side team. I got confused and thought that I was supposed to signal my flag in the direction of the team that kicked it out, rather than in the direction of what team is supposed to get the ball. I used my right arm to signal the direction that the ball should go to the left side. This main referee asked me if I meant for the ball to go to the right side team or left side team because he was confused why I used my right arm to signal to the left. I tried to cover up for my fuck up by saying that I meant for the left side team to get the ball, I just used my right arm to do it. This was a complete lie and just said it because I didn't want the main referee to think that I didn't know which side I was really supposed to signal to when the ball went out.

Kid: It wasn't out on us; it was kicked out by the other team.
Referee: The line judge says it was kicked out by your team.

The kid seemed really sad about this, and the ball ended up going back to the team that kicked it out. There was one game in which I refereed for in which the coach and parents of the players were getting very pissed off at my brother, who was the main referee for the game. The issue was that the players from the other team were hitting the shins of the player who had possession of the ball. My brother just shook his head like he didn't know what the hell the pissed off parents were talking about when yelling at him to make a call, and I just stood there not doing shit either because I thought if something illegal was happening, he would have called it. I refereed three games every Saturday for however long the soccer season lasts for, for children, and decided that I hated it after that, so I quit.

## THE TIME I WORKED AT A CAR WASH

I used to work at a car wash from the time I was 23 to 24 and I can honestly say, in spite of all the shitty jobs I have had in my life, this was the worst job. Within the first couple of days that I started working there, I understood that my boss was a royal fucking prick. He was not the worst boss I have ever had, but he was by far the biggest irrational psycho. He would always bitch about how shitty of a job the employees did, but to his credit, he was right in a sense. Nobody who worked that job gave a shit about how well of a job they did. The starting pay was eight dollars an hour and the turnover rate was only a few months, so I worked with a lot of different people for the thirteen months that I worked there. On one occasion the manager, "Dan", got so pissed off at one of the assistant managers, that you could hear him screaming at him from the garage, around twenty yards away that they did the car details in. There was a lady I worked with, "Hailey" that was upset about the situation.

Hailey: I can't believe that fucking asshole.
Me: Yeah, that is pretty inappropriate.
Hailey: That is beyond inappropriate. What a fucking prick.

Me: I don't think anyone deserves to be yelled at like that. That's kind of messed up.
Hailey: I agree, unless you do something really fucked up like raping someone.

In a sense I think she had a point, but in my opinion, I think getting angry and yelling at someone is highly irrational. Every negative situation can be discussed with a rational, intelligent, coherent, and calm argument in which someone demonstrates to another person that what they did was wrong. If someone lets their emotions get the best of them and takes it out on someone else, then they are not really making the situation any better. The person being yelled at will just think that the person yelling at them is a fucking prick and nothing is really solved. Only more negativity gets injected into the situation. It's all highly philosophical.[66]

One day there was a person I worked with, "Jack" who had an argument with Dan. Jack was pissed off that we didn't get regular scheduled breaks and that unless they started giving us regular breaks, he would contact Osha, and turn Dan in. Dan immediately fired Jack after getting tired of his complaining bullshit. On the main cashier counter in the car wash was a cup of coffee and Jack, very pissed off about the situation, knocked the coffee on the floor, spilling it across the lobby floor. Dan then grabbed Jack by the shoulder and tried to lead him out of the lobby in a sort of, "get the fuck out of here you little shit" attitude. As soon as they were outside, they immediately started throwing punches at each other.

Dan: Come here you little bitch!
Jack: Fuck you!

I had a front row seat to the action, standing only around fifteen feet away, folding towels that we used to dry cars off with. At first, I thought they were just fucking with each other, but when I realized they were really legitimately pissed off at each other, I immediately focused all of my attention on folding the towels, not wanting to be a witness that the police would have to question later about the incident. After kicking each other and throwing multiple punches, Jack got into his car and began to drive away just as a customer pulled into the lot.

Jack: Don't go to this car wash! The manager is a fucking prick! He tried to fight me when I wasn't doing shit! Fuck this place!

The police arrived shortly after Jack left and luckily, they didn't question me. All they did was look at the video to see what really happened. A few weeks later there was an article in the local paper about the incident. Jack tried to claim that he was assaulted by Dan and was going to try and sue him. After hearing the two sides of the situation, and looking at the video, the cops determined that Jack was making up shit, and Dan was telling the truth. In spite of Dan's irrational behavior, I still hold a certain level of respect for him in that he never lies. I heard him in a conversation with another employee one time and he said that he hated liars. Aside from all the ridiculous shit that Dan did as the manager at the car wash, the one thing that did him in, and caused the owner to finally put an end to his ridiculous antics and fire him involved the cashier, "Jen". I wasn't there when this incident occurred, but I heard about it shortly after it happened. Both Jen and Dan were outside cleaning cars when Dan, apparently, thought it would be a funny joke if he rat-tailed Jen's ass. For those who do not know what rat-tailed means, it is basically the following: take a towel, curl up the towel into a lash, and whip the towel at somebody. So, Dan, for some reason, decided to whip Jen's ass with a towel. She later told me that she didn't really know how to react. I think anyone who is faced with a situation like this would be in a sort of confused state like, "what the fuck? Did he really just whip me with a damp towel? I'm confused/angry/annoyed." If Jen really wanted to, she could have charged Dan with sexual harassment, but I think the fact that Dan was going to get fired shortly after this was good enough for her. I quit shortly after this, just as Jen was promoted to assistant manager, which made no sense to me because I had been working there at least three to four months before her. I think the fact that she knew how to operate the cash register, as well as the borderline sexual harassment incident that happened to her, made the new manager think that she would be better for the job.

The entire time I was working there, I worked with a guy named, "Charles". Charles was an ex-convict and had been to prison at least one time. I became pretty good friends with him and eventually he gained my trust. One day, Charles approached me and told me that he was starting to set up a drug dealing trade and he wanted to know if I wanted in. The plan was to send a quarter pound of marijuana to a friend in Mississippi where he used to live. We hid the weed in a stuffed animal and other kid's toys and apparel and would send the weed every week. He told me that we would make at least a thousand dollars a week doing this, because the weed he got was really good shit, and apparently the guy who was going to move the weed for us in Mississippi was able to charge a large amount of cash for the pot. He began to talk about our plans once we had so much money coming in.

Charles: So, what are you going to do with all the money we are going to get?
Me: I think I'm just going to save it and then move to some other place. Fuck Colorado.
Charles: What about getting a new car, because yours is all beat to shit?
Me: I'm not sure, I'm not sure what kind of car I would get.
Charles: With all the money we are going to profit you could get whatever you want. Don't get too expensive on me now.

I laughed at this and began to visualize what my new life would be like finally having thousands of dollars at my disposal to do what I wanted with. The first trade we did I pitched a thousand dollars and we sent it off. Add this to the list of huge fuck ups I have done in my life. When something seems too good to be true, it usually is, at least in reference to dealing drugs. A few weeks passed and I had received nothing back from my investment in the trade. I asked Charles what the deal was, and he said something like the drug dealer in Mississippi not being able to move it for some reason. I really don't remember exactly what his bullshit excuse was, but it really doesn't matter. All that mattered is that I had trusted someone with all the money I had saved up for a while (I was earning roughly $250-300 a paycheck at the time), and I had gotten completely fucked. Charles went from being my Nigga at one moment, to being a complete jack ass, or more specifically, a jack ass who doesn't find anything wrong with the fact that he steals from people and uses them for one's own benefit. A part of me thinks that he may have just told me that the dealer in Mississippi couldn't move the shit, when really, he was keeping all the profits for himself. I can't really be sure. Although at the time I thought he was a good person who wouldn't go out of his way to screw me over hardcore, I later found out two other things about him that made me pretty much lose all respect for him: 1) A few months after I quit the car wash, I called him up to see if he knew anyone I could get some cocaine from. He told me that he could get it for me. I gave him $100, and he gave me one line of blow. One fucking line. That's it. And on top of that, of course, the blow sucked. I was high for maybe twenty minutes. 2) I started buying Adderall from his ex-girlfriend and she told me that he used to beat her. Kind of fucked up. Dealing with him or his ex-girlfriend ended up being a big mistake to say the least. Just to show you how irrational his ex-girlfriend was in dealing me the Adderall: She would charge me $10 for a 20mg pill, and then charge me

$6 for a 10mg pill. *I don't know if these types of people know they are dumb, or just don't care that they don't understand how to logically think.*

## MY CANVASSING JOB WITH AMNESTY INTERNATIONAL

After getting suspended from college my sophomore year, I was only working part time at a restaurant, and I needed to get a second job to pay for all the shit I got myself into. I searched craigslist and came across a posting by Amnesty International, looking for canvassers. I had no idea what a canvasser was but if I would have realized that it was one of those annoying people you come across on college campuses and busy streets that ask you if you have a minute to talk about whatever the fuck they are trying to promote to you, I never would have applied. For some reason, I have a problem with telling people no, and so on two separate occasions, when I came across canvassers on the college campus I was attending I pretended to be interested in what they were saying and twice gave them false hope. The first time was for a canvasser for Amnesty International and I ended up telling him that I would give them a dollar a day. The guy was so happy that I wanted to contribute, probably because I was one of the people he needed to reach his quota for the day or week. I gave them a fake phone number and fake credit card number. When you are canvassing, this is one of the biggest signs that someone can give you that they are just bullshitting you because they don't want to tell you straight to your face that they don't want to give you any of their money (for example, just writing out their credit card number from memory as opposed to taking it out and writing down the number). The second time this happened was when a woman approached me from "Green Peace". I of course pretended to buy into the tree hugging bullshit she was promoting and I started to fill out the sheet to sign up for monthly payments. For some reason I took out my credit card and put in the wrong numbers on the sheet, acting as if I was reading off the correct numbers from my card. I saw that she was looking at my credit card the whole time, to see if I was really putting in the right numbers. Not wanting her to notice that I was fucking with her, I scratched out the fake numbers and put in the real numbers. She gave me a hug and I walked away feeling very pissed off. A few days later I called the Green Peace corporate office and told them to cancel my order. These two incidents made me learn that whenever someone approaches you and asks for a few minutes of your time, just say no thanks and walk away, or if you do end up listening to them and don't want to contribute, just say no to their face. Some canvassers hate being told no by people and will do anything in their power to convince you that you should contribute, even if it's just a quarter a day. These types of people can't easily be reasoned with so if you ever run into someone like this, just walk away, give them the finger, or tell them to fuck off.

So, thinking that this Amnesty International job posting would be something cool like a desk or office job, I decided to apply. When I got to the job interview there were a few other people there as well, also probably not knowing the shit job that they are interviewing for. The woman interviewing me was very impressed that I was an Eagle Scout and so she told me to come in the next day to start. They give you a piece of paper that has a short paragraph or so written on it that they call a "rap" and tell you to memorize it. I memorized bits and pieces of it and the girl that was training me on my first day was impressed that I even took the time to glance at it. The "rap" was pretty much a short introduction that you say to people when they agree to listen to you. It describes what the company is, what they hope to accomplish, and how you can help them out by giving them money. The first site I went to was a community college with a guy who had been working as a canvasser for a long time. The first two to three days of the job is basically a test to see how well you can canvass. If you meet the quota of how much money you are supposed to raise within the first few days, then you will be invited back to a full-time position. I began approaching people and asking if they could spare a few minutes to talk about "poor children dying" or "world hunger" or other things that people might care about. By about the second or third person I talked to, a guy agreed to contribute $30 a month. Besides a big cash donation, this is the highest level of contribution that you canvass for. The guy I was with was very impressed that I got someone to contribute so quickly, and I feel like I gained his respect. The next five to six hours were boring as hell as I received no more contributions or cash donations, all the while feeling like a fucking puppet. At the end of my first day all the full-time canvassers were in awe that I got a $30 a month contribution, and so they began to respect me.

The second day on the job I was to canvass at on the university campus which I had just been suspended from. This pissed me off because I didn't want to run into any of my old friends who I would then have to explain to them about how I had now stooped so low. The only person that I ran into that I knew was a guy that I met at an alcohol class that I had to take after getting an underage drinking ticket. I explained to him what I was doing and he just laughed and walked away. Throughout the entire day, the two or three other people I was with in the group kept giving me encouragement that if I do good enough today as I did yesterday, that I would make being a member of their staff. Every once in a while, you will run into someone who disagrees with you about what you are promoting and wants to debate you. Some canvassers find this annoying and do not want to engage with these types of people. I on the other hand, thought that these types of people were awesome because even though I knew they weren't going to give me any money, it at least looked like to the other canvassers that I was working hard to promote the company to the person.

Me: We are trying to end the torture of criminals and prisoners of war around the world. A dollar a day donation would really help us accomplish this.
Guy: But doesn't torture sometimes help potentially save people's lives?
Me: Right, like if a terrorist knows that a bomb will go off in a crowded city and the only way to get him to tell you where the bomb is is to torture him?
Guy: Exactly. Sometimes you got to way the pros and cons of something and decide which is more beneficial to society.
Me: I agree. To be honest I am just doing this job because I have no other jobs I can do at the moment. I hate it. It sucks hardcore.
Guy: I don't know man. I think you would be better off doing something more in line with what you believe in.
Me: Yeah, I am not a liberal at all. Some of this stuff I agree with but some of it I think is bullshit. I kind of just like talking to people like you so I can play it off like I am actually working hard to get someone to contribute. I really don't care who contributes or not.

So, I would run into people like this every once in a while, giving the other members of the group false hope that I would by the end of the day make the staff. By the end of day two I don't remember if I got any donations, but if I did it was something very insignificant, like a five dollar one time donation or something like that.

On the third day I was put in a group that went to the airport to confront people who are either in a rush, or who really don't want to be stopped by random people looking for handouts. This being my third day on the job, I had picked up little bits of information to put into my rap to come across as more knowledgeable about the Amnesty International cause such as, "The reason Obama hasn't shut down Guantanamo Bay yet is because he doesn't have the complete backing of the senate and congress, and so you giving us a contribution would really go far in helping Obama achieve that backing." I was half thinking about asking people as they walked by, "Excuse me, do you like kittens dying?" to get them to pay more attention to me. When I was a senior in high school, I used this type of tactic when selling coupon discount books in front of a King Soopers. I would say to the people walking in, "Excuse me sir, do you like dicks?" I would then have his full attention and when he asked me to repeat what I said, I would say, "Dick's sporting goods, do you like it?" For the majority of people who really don't want to be stopped or talked to, opening up with a unique line like that will at least give you their attention for a second or two. The lady who interviewed me was in my group at the airport and on one occasion I saw her almost lose here shit at someone, saying as the person walked by, "that was kind of rude." Her heart was invested in her job, me on the other hand, could care the fuck less. Usually, the people that fail to make the quota by the third day are not asked to come back again, but since I had such a successful first day, they decided to give me one last chance to see if I could make staff tomorrow.

On the fourth day I was teamed up with a woman who pretty much realized immediately that I didn't give a shit about making staff and that I hated the job.

Woman: We should go to a different spot.
Me: Whatever you want. It doesn't make a difference to me.
Woman: Do you even want to make staff?
Me: Not really. I really don't like this job. Do you like this job?
Woman: It's ok. I'm pretty good at it.
Me: Nice. I just don't like the idea of interrupting people in their day. I'm not that much of a people person.

After only canvassing for two or three hours, we decided to give up and just hang out at a coffee shop for the rest of the day. We got to talking and she became intrigued by what I was telling her.

Me: So, does Amnesty International campaign for gay rights also?
Woman: Yes. What's your stance on that?
Me: I think gay people should be allowed to get married. I was raised highly conservative and recently I have begun to start thinking for myself.
Woman: Are your parents against gay marriage?

Me: Yes, and they hate Amnesty International. I was just raised to just accept things my parents told me and to never question anything.
Woman: So would you consider yourself a conservative or liberal now?
Me: Probably more liberal now.
Woman: Really?!

She just couldn't believe that someone like me who was brought up in a fundamentalist setting would divorce from that and come up with their own views.

Woman: You need to tell people more about what you know. I want to make a movie based on your life.
Me: That would be cool.
Woman: My boyfriend knows a movie producer and I want to pitch him this idea for a book or movie or something.
Me: Haha.

For some reason she was really moved by the things I was telling her, and we exchanged numbers with her promising to keep in touch. After the day was over, I never heard from her again. When we arrived back at the office, I had to wait a while for someone to come and talk to me about my fate with the company.

Woman Interviewer: Ok, Psychotic Logician, thanks for canvassing with us, but I don't think we could put you on staff.
Me: I understand. Thanks for the opportunity.
Woman Interviewer. You're welcome.

So much hope after the first day only to end in "not being invited back" three days later. Even if I did make it to staff by the fourth day, me sucking as a canvasser eventually would have caught up to me, because even the people that are on staff are required to meet a certain quota each week, and if they don't then they too will not be invited back. In order to make it in that job you really need to care about what you are selling, and I just really didn't care. The guy I was with on my first day told me not to waste my time talking to people who disagree with what you are promoting, but honestly, that was the best part of the job. The way that job operated for me is closely analogous to a philosophical argument I pitched to the woman I was with on the fourth day. "If God is all powerful then he could prove he doesn't exist. If he proves he doesn't exist, then he doesn't exist. If he can't prove he doesn't exist, then he is not all powerful. Therefore, God either doesn't exist or is not all powerful." In reference to the canvassing job: "If I get people to contribute money then I will become a full-time canvasser which I hate. If I will get more people to contribute money, then this will make me more of a canvasser which I hate. If I don't get people to contribute money, then I will not be a canvasser which I like. Therefore, I can either be a canvasser which I hate, or not be a canvasser which I like." I opted for the latter.[67]

## WORKING AT MCDONALDS

After I got suspended from college, I was unable to get more hours at my restaurant job because there were too many other employees. I applied to McDonalds and within a week or two I started working there. This was one of the worst jobs I have ever had. A few times they set me up as a person who assembles the burgers together. The problem was that they do not give you a piece of paper that you can memorize that tells you how each burger is made. I would constantly have to look at the papers that they have in front of you, trying my hardest to be quick and not fuck anything up. However, I would constantly fuck up and they stopped putting me on the assembly line. The majority of the time I worked there I was either the person cooking the burgers, or the person who gives you your meal in the drive threw. For some reason, and I still don't know why anyone gives a shit, but for every order that comes through the drive through, there is a timer, which apparently serves the purpose of notifying the owner or corporate office how fast or slow the employees are being in completing a customer's order. I am not exactly sure how the employees of the restaurant are judged based on the time they have spent on an order, but it must be in some sense pretty crucial, considering that I was always being constantly reminded to stop the timer for a certain customer.

Part of the dress code that they had for the McDonalds I was working for at the time, was that you had to wear a really gay hat, along with a retarded looking black button up shirt. I saw one employee (who was Mexican, much like 90% of the people I worked with there) wear his hat backwards. I thought this was a good idea, because it made me look not so fucking stupid. One day the owner came in the restaurant.

Owner: Hi, I don't believe we have met, I'm the owner.
Me: Nice to meet you. I'm Psychotic Logician.

Owner: You need to flip your hat around to the correct side. That is part of the dress code.
Me: Ok. Sorry about that.

Whenever the owner wasn't there, I would wear the hat backwards, and none of the manager's working there gave a shit. The owner came in again.

Owner: Hey, I thought I told you to not wear your hat backwards like that again.
Me: Oh yeah. Sorry about that.
Owner: I don't want to see it like that again.
Me: Ok.

Since most of the people working there were Hispanic, they would speak in Spanish to each other, and would be laughing and having a good time. I was left out of the loop but didn't really give a shit. The first week I worked there I was scheduled for 40 hours. The second week they only scheduled me for 30 hours. The third week I was scheduled for 15 hours. By the fourth week I was completely off the schedule. Not because I was a poor worker and they wanted to fire me, but because apparently I didn't give them any notification of when and how long I could work. By the fourth week, I called up one of the manager's and told her that I was quitting. She was very disappointed, because apparently everyone there liked me and thought I was a good worker.

During the month that I worked at McDonalds, I met a young black girl named, "Hanna". She was an ex-convict who used to sell crack.

Me: I used to sell pot and shrooms in college. What did you sell?
Hanna: I sold crack for a while.
Me: Nice. How it is? I heard it's one of the most kick ass high's there is.
Hanna: Yeah, it makes you feel really good.
Me: But it only lasts a few minutes, right?
Hanna: Yeah, it doesn't last very long. But it's pretty addictive. When I used to sell it I made thousands of dollars, sometimes even in one day.
Me: Would you smoke some of the profit, or just keep all the money?
Hanna: I would smoke it occasionally. But I ended up getting busted with it about a year ago.
Me: How did you get caught?

Hanna: The entire day, for some reason, I had an inclination that the police were going to catch me with it. I don't know why, but for some reason I just thought that.

Me: Damn. That fucking sucks.

Hanna: Yeah. So, I ended up going to jail for a while. I'm still on probation and will be for the next few years.

She was a pretty cool girl, and one day after work I drove her to her girlfriend's house. I asked her questions about lesbian sex, and she told me everything I wanted to know. My days of working at McDonalds were over, and I was pretty happy about it. If you ever decide to work at a fast food restaurant, be prepared to have to put up with some serious bullshit.[68]

## MY JOB CLEANING HORSE STALLS

A few months before I graduated high school, a woman that my mom knows (it just so happens also that this woman's family lived in my house before my family did) offered me a job to help clean her horse stable that she has for her two horses. My job was essentially to take a rake and shovel all the horse shit into a wheel barrel, which, when full, I would then take over to a large area, dump it, and repeat the process until the stalls were clean. I think she started me off at around eight or nine dollars an hour. I did this for four or five days a week after I got off school in the afternoon. It would usually take me about an hour to an hour and a half to finish everything, and at the end of the week she would write me a check. When summer approached, she had me do other things around her property as well like rake up pine needles and put them into trash bags. By the time I got another job at the beginning of the summer, she had given me two or three raises, and I think I was up somewhere around twelve dollars an hour. About a week after I stopped working for her, she left me a message on my cell phone saying that she really likes me and trusts me and asked if I would be willing to house sit for her when she was gone to some place for a few days. We left on good terms, but I did not like that job very much, so I just decided to not call her back to confirm or say no thanks. This was during the time I worked as a landscaper for two weeks (this will be discussed later on), and so didn't think I would need to have another job. But when the landscaping job went to shit, I ended up calling her back.

Me: Hey this is Psychotic Logician. Sorry it took me so long to return your call, it turns out that something is wrong with my cell phone and for whatever reason, I just received your message.

Woman: That is ok, I didn't even end up leaving town, so it is ok.

Me: Well, if you need any more help around your property, I would be glad to help you anytime.

Woman: I am fine for now. Thanks though.

This happened back in the summer of 2008, and even six years later in 2014 when I was working at the car wash, she offered me a job to work on another woman's horse ranch. I declined. Not that it would have been any worse than the car wash, but I just got it into my head that that part of my life was over, and I didn't really want to go back to cleaning horse shit.[69]

## MY FIRST JOB AS A BUS BOY

After I got fired from the movie theater, a few months later, I decided to get a job as a bus boy at a local restaurant. When I had my interview, I told the woman interviewing me that I had never had a job before, because I didn't want to put on my resume that I had just gotten fired a month earlier. The woman called me a week later and said that they would be really happy if the restaurant was the first place to give me a job. Once I started, I immediately thought that this was a mistake. I had to do the regular shit that busserss have to do; clean up the tables, fold napkins, sweep the floor, etc. I don't have that many notable memories of working there but I do remember a few interesting things. I met the dishwasher, who I immediately thought was kind of a strange dude. I learned later that this guy had schizophrenia and he claimed to be married. And the weird thing about him being married? He is married to a blow-up doll, who he apparently thinks is a real person. I never saw the pictures that he showed to people, but I can only guess that it must have been pretty funny to see. The highlight of me working at this job, which lasted about a month, was when I quit. When I told one of the managers that I was quitting, he was pretty chill about it. I just told him that school was starting soon, and I needed to focus on that. However, when I told the woman who hired me, she was pretty pissed.

Me: I need to quit. I just realized that I need to focus on my schoolwork. Woman: You're quitting? Because the main reason that I hired you was because I thought you were going to work here for a while, even when school started.
Me: Yeah, sorry. I just realized that this job is not for me.
Woman: Fine.

When I came in to pick up my paycheck about a week later, she ended up writing me a check, instead of the check being printed. I was on my way home when I looked at the check and saw that that the woman wrote my check out to different person. She had my first name right, but my last name was not mine.

Me: Hey, you put the wrong name on my check.
Woman: Well who are you?
Me: I'm Psychotic Logician, not Psychotic Ghdilsl.
Woman: Jesus.

She wrote me a new check and I left. Never to go back there again. The people I worked with were pretty cool, but the job itself sucked. Apparently one of the waitresses used to be my swimming instructors when I was a kid, so we got along pretty well.[70]

## THE TAXI DRIVING INCIDENTS

One night in my senior year in high school I was hanging out with Rick. We got baked and watched the movie, "Collateral". Being in the blitzed state of mind that I was, I got inspiration from something Rick said.

Rick: Dude, how crazy would it be to be a cab driver? Think of all the crazy people you would meet.
Me: Yeah dude. That would be pretty crazy. Holy shit that sounds fucking awesome.

I can honestly say that from the above conversation, that I then made it one of my life goals to one day be a taxi driver. My goal was to one day drive a cab in NYC. To make the job even more epic, I would memorize all of NYC, every address, every landmark, everything, so that I would know how to get from any one place to another. On top of this I would try and learn new languages so that I could talk to foreigners. I heard crazy stories from people about some of the shit that NYC taxi drivers have to put up with. I talked to a girl I used to work with at a restaurant.

Girl: I was in a taxi in NYC once and we approached what was apparently a bad place in the Bronx. Somewhere that had a lot of crime and gangs. When we approached the bad street, the driver said that I would have to either get out and walk the rest of the way, call another taxi, or find an alternate route around the neighborhood, because it was way too dangerous to go through.

For some reason, I thought this was absolutely fucking awesome. I gained inspiration by watching the movie, "Taxi Driver", in which Robert De Niro is asked by the person who is interviewing him where and when he will work, and De Niro responds, "I'll work anytime, anywhere." Just to give you an idea of how fucked up some of these neighborhoods can be, my dad once told me a story about some guy he knew that was driving through Watts in Los Angeles.

Dad: He stopped at a stop light and someone tapped on his window. He rolled it down and a man immediately put a knife to his throat and said, "Give me your keys and wallet. If you try and do anything I'm going to have this girl next to me scream rape. If that happens then you will see every person in this neighborhood come out, and you don't want that." He gave him his keys and wallet and the guy threw the keys and left.

I figured that dealing with gangsters and other people who want to rob you and threaten to hurt you was just a part of the job, and I saw that as an aspect of the job that was just something you would have to do in order to make it as a cabbie in NYC. Now, my first step that I would take in order to fulfill this fantasy of mine, was to become a cab driver in the area in which I was living. I figured this would give me a good introduction as to what it takes to make it as a cabbie. I applied for the job and started driving a few weeks later.

At first, I thought that it was a pretty sick job, talking to random people and driving them around. I worked the night shift from 5pm to 5am. One of the best things I liked about it was that when there are multiple people in the cab talking to each other, they just speak to each other as they normally would, not giving a shit about what the taxi driver thinks about them or what they say. The most amount of money I made in one night was $430 and on a couple of other nights I made between $300-$400. I did end up getting into some conversations with a couple of crazy people. I met a porn star who made a living doing webcams for people on some porn website. I drove around some Russian people who would always be speaking in Russian to each other. I feel like people who talk to each other in foreign languages might, when beginning their conversations, start with (in the foreign language): "Hey cab driver, can you understand what I am saying? Do you speak Russian?" If you don't respond then they assume you don't speak or understand the language, so they are free to say whatever the hell they want, including shit talking the driver. If I ever reached my goal of driving in NYC, speaking multiple languages, if some foreigner would ask me this question, I would just sit there and not say anything, trying to come across as someone who doesn't speak the language. Then I would be able to hear some of the shit they are talking about, disguised as some ignorant driver who only speaks English. However, at some appropriate time I would then start speaking to them in their language, revealing that I understood everything that they were talking about. A good scene that illustrates this is in the movie, "Maid in Manhattan" where two women are talking shit about Jennifer Lopez in some foreign language, thinking that her and Ralph Fiennes cannot understand what they are saying. Then, Ralph Fiennes reveals to them that he actually does know what they are talking about, and they get very angry.

I was driving one night when it was snowing outside. The roads were really shitty to drive on and I had to be extra cautious not to fuck up. Perhaps the worst thing about driving a cab is the responsibility. You are in charge of the cab that you rent for that shift, and if you get in an accident or fuck it up in some way, you are responsible for the damages. I was using google maps for my GPS and I was called to pick up some lady at her house. Google maps gives you great directions to and from some places, but absolutely fucks you when trying to get to other places. On multiple occasions I was given directions to incorrect places that it told me was where the address was supposed to be. Luckily, the people I was with also had GPS on their smart phones and so led me to the correct location. So, on top of having to deal with the horrible road conditions, I was led to the wrong place by the GPS. I then tried to use the taxi company's GPS, but that ended up making the situation worse. I was driving up a dirt road that had at least a foot and a half to two feet of snow on it. It was an intense uphill that was a windy road that led up to a few houses. At one point I realized that there was no way that I was going to the right place, so I had to make a four or five point turn and go back the way I came. Just as I was heading back down the road, I veered a little too far off the road, and the taxi's front right tire slipped off the road and hung almost completely in midair. So, there I was, sitting in the cab with only three wheels touching the ground, with a few feet of snow piled up on all sides of the cab. I tried going in reverse, but the wheels just spun out. God fucking dammit! I tried clearing the snow away from the tires, but they were buried to the point that there was no way that I could completely clear snow away from them, that would then fuck me up even more, by creating a greater pile of snow right next to them. I begin to freak out. What will I do if I have to get a tow truck to pull me out? There's no fucking way. No fucking way a tow truck could make it up the road I was on, and even if it could, it was a one-way road and the only way the tow truck could get back out to the main street was to go back the way it came in reverse. That shit clearly wasn't going to happen. I tried calling the dispatcher, but I had no cell phone service. If I was unable to get out of this mess, the only option I would have would be to walk up to one of the nearby houses, knock on their door, probably waking them up, and asking them if I could use their phone. I rev the engine to high RPM's, but the wheels just kept spinning out. Any traction that I could get on the road just ended up rocking the taxi back and forth and even made the taxi swerve more off the road. Now, unbeknownst to me at the time, the taxi was not in complete all-wheel drive. I figured it was like most all-wheel drive cars where it is always operating with four-wheel traction, and you didn't have to press any button or gear down to engage the all-wheel drive. I start experimenting around with various buttons on the center console. I flip one of the switches that had a symbol of a car with traction marks coming out the back of it. I floored it in reverse and the taxi was able to get enough tread to make it back onto the center of the road, with all four wheels on it. Thank the fuck Christ. I then begin to slowly creep forward and make my way back down the road, trying my hardest not to go to slow and end up completely buried again with the wheels spinning out, and not to go to fast and lose control and slide sideways again or off the road completely. I make it to the bottom of the road connecting it to the main roadway, where I had cell service again. The dispatcher told me that the woman who called for the cab had just cancelled.

I was happy to be out of that situation which would have totally fucked up everything not just for me, but for the cab company as well. They would have had to have waited days, if not weeks for the snow to melt on the road so that I could drive out of the side of the road I was in on dry land, or to have a tow truck come and pull me out. Little did I know that this wouldn't be the worst thing that happened to me that night. On my last call of the night, I drove some high school kid to his house, which had a long driveway that had a steep uphill to it. I thought about telling the kid to just get out of the car at the bottom of the driveway and to just walk up to his house, but for some reason I decided to risk it. I got halfway up his driveway when the wheels begin to spin out. Panicking, I push what I thought was the all-wheel drive button but ended up being something else. The kid then got out of the car and walked up to his house. I had to go in reverse all the way back down the driveway. The only problem was that in the part of the driveway that connects to the main road, it goes slightly uphill like a divot. I floored it in reverse, but the car spun forward and the front bumper hit a fence that lined the driveway. When I tried to reverse away from the fence, the back bumper hit a small incline that lined the driveway. I had to make at least a three point turn to get back on the main road, each time running into either the fence in front of me, or the incline in back of me. I drove to the parking lot of a bar and surveyed the damage. I knew I was fucked. The front and back bumpers were crushed in, and there were pieces of plastic missing from them that were knocked off when I hit them on the driveway. Right then and there I decided that I was done with driving a cab for multiple reasons: 1) Fuck driving in the snow. I hate snow in general and driving in it pissed me off. 2) There is way too much responsibility that I have to take in order to drive. I knew that whatever the insurance didn't cover, I was going to have to pay for out of my own pocket. When it was all said and done, it cost me $350 to fix. 3) It really wasn't as cool as I thought it would be.

I called the dispatcher and told her what happened. Surprisingly, one of the coolest parts of the job was something that had nothing to do with driving the actual cab. The dispatch girl had probably the cutest voices I have ever heard, and so whenever I talked to her it made me happy. I filled out an accident report and later that night I wrote the guy who hired me an email telling him that I was done driving. Later that year when I filed my taxes, I only ended up with a couple hundred dollar profit. I drove a cab for roughly a month and a half, and, although fun at some times, was a pain in the ass the rest of the time.[71]

## MY JOB AS A LANDSCAPER

The month after I graduated high school, I got a job working with Frank and Edwin for one of our friend, Sam's, father "Oliver". The job was landscaping.

At the time the minimum wage was roughly $7 an hour and for this job we were getting $12 an hour. Sam's dad, "Oliver", was by far the biggest prick I have ever worked for, and one of the biggest douchbags I have ever come across in my entire life. We started work very early in the morning, and I had to get up at 6am to make it down to Oliver's house by 7am. After the first day of working there, I knew the job was going to suck hardcore, but I figured as long as my other friends were working there also, I was going to stick it out. In the first week of working there, we were doing a job at some family's front garden of their house. I will now give you a brief tutorial of why Oliver is not just a raging prick, but also a hyper manic retarded moron.

1.   We were listening to the radio on some modern rock station and the song, "Handlebars" by the Flobots came on. Oliver began to sing along.

Oliver: I can ride my dike with no handlebars, no handlebars. Do you guys get it? It says bike but I am saying dike.

2.   We get done using one of the vacuums that we needed for the job and Oliver told me to put it in the back of the pickup truck that he had. I picked up the vacuum and tried to find a spot to put it in in the back of the truck, but there was no room. I went to go tell Oliver that it won't fit and to see if I could put it anywhere else, but he was busy doing something else, so I decided to just wait until he was free. Oliver then comes up to me a few minutes later, extremely pissed.

Oliver: Why didn't you put the vacuum in the back of the truck like I asked you to?
Me: There is no room in the back of the truck. I was going to tell you but you were busy, so I was just going to wait to tell you about it when you were free.
Oliver: When I tell you to do something, you do it you little fuck!
Me: Sorry.
Oliver: Make some fucking room for it in the back if you have to.
Me: Ok.

3.   We finish the family's front garden that we were working on and the woman who lives in the house came out to inspect it.

Woman: Why didn't you plant the type of flowers that I chose?

Oliver: We are on a deadline and using your flowers would have set us back. There is just not enough time in my day to have to worry about whose flowers I should plant.

Woman: But I'm paying you to use my flowers.

Oliver: I don't give a fuck if you paid me to use your flowers! We didn't have enough fucking time, just accept it for what it is.

Woman: I don't understand. If I am paying you to use my flowers, and you don't use them then why am I even paying you.

Oliver: Listen you fucking bitch, I don't have enough time to use your flowers, and I certainly don't have enough time to stand here and bullshit with you about it. I'm on a fucking deadline and have other shit to do.

The woman didn't know how to respond to this. She just stood there for a moment and then went back inside her house. I completely understand how she was not sure what else to say. How exactly are you supposed to respond to something like that? Sam told me the next day that he and Oliver went back to the woman's house for some reason, maybe to get the check for the job that he was supposed to do but didn't, or maybe to bitch slap the woman. Either reason sounds like a possibility. The woman's husband came out to the front door and started screaming at Oliver. Oliver screamed back and Sam told me they almost went fist for fist.

4.  The second week that I worked there Oliver decided to have me, Frank, and Edwin all work at a site while he and Sam worked all day at another. At the end of the day Oliver was to come back and inspect our job to see if we did good or not. Unbeknownst to me at the time, Oliver had made me the "leader" of the group, and that I was responsible for everything that gets done at the site and for instructing Frank and Edwin on what to do. The job was pretty much to go into a pond, take out all of the algae and pond scum, and plant lilies in the center of the pond. Frank, Edwin and I took turns wearing a suit that was waterproof to go into the center of the pond. Tim was sure to let us know that if the suit was damaged in any way, we would have to pay for a new one. The pond was filled with leeches, and so we pretty much gave up going in barefoot, which meant that really only one person could be working in the pond at a time, while the other two tried to reach for pond algae from the shore with a rake. At the end of the day, Oliver came to inspect.

Oliver: This looks like shit. You fucked up on this. Why the fuck is this here? What the fuck have you three little shits been doing all day? You're fucking me over with this half ass work you're doing. Psychotic Logician, why didn't you do what I fucking told you to do?
Me: I thought you meant –
Oliver: Why the fuck did I put you in charge?
Me: I didn't know I was in charge. You told Frank and Edwin everything you told me.
Oliver: Frank, tomorrow you're in charge. I think you can prove yourself to be more of a man than Psychotic Logician is.
Frank: Ok.

The next day we did the same thing all day, clearing out ponds and planting lilies in them. And when Oliver came to inspect, he was very disappointed that Frank didn't live up to his standards.

Oliver: Why did you only work on three ponds? You were supposed to work on all the ponds in this area.
Frank: Only one of us could plant the lilies because we only had one water suit to go into the pond with.
Oliver: Why the fuck was only one of you in the pond at a time?
Frank: There are leeches in the pond, and we didn't want them to get on us.
Oliver: You're afraid of the fucking leeches? I don't give a fuck if the leeches get on you, I want all three of you in the fucking pond at the same time.
Frank: Sorry.

At the beginning of this week another friend of ours, "Jason" began working for Sam's dad, and he spent the day with Oliver and Sam at another site while Edwin, Will and I worked at the ponds. At the end of the days when we were driving back home, all Edwin, Frank and I would do is bitch about how much of a prick Oliver is and how we hated the job.

Me: Jason, do you like Oliver? He has been nothing but a fucking asshole to us.
Jason: I think he is pretty chill to work with.
Me: How is he chill? When we worked with him last week, he was a prick then to.
Jason: He jokes around a lot and when you get talking to him, he is an alright guy.

Edwin: He always has a problem with everything we do. Even if we think we did a good job, he comes along and gets pissed that we fucked it all up.
Jason: Yeah, he talks a lot about how he hopes that when he gets to the pond site where you guys were working that you didn't fuck it up like you did the previous days.
Frank: What kind of shit does he say about us?
Jason: I don't want to take anyone's side.
Me: It's not a big deal, we just want to know if he just talks shit to our faces, or also talks shit behind our backs.
Jason: Forget it.

5.  On one of our last days working for Oliver, we arrived early back at his house before he, Sam and Jason were done working at their site. Oliver told us that if we get back before they did, that he wanted us to pick weeds from his backyard. We were all sick of Oliver's shit at this point and so we decided to just pick a few weeds and sit and chill the rest of the time. Once Oliver got back to his house, we would then begin working again, making it seem like we were doing it the whole time.

Oliver: So, what have you guys been doing this whole time?
Edwin: Picking weeds like you told us to.
Oliver: How long have you been here for?
Edwin: Like 45 minutes.
Oliver: You have been here for 45 minutes and this is all the shit you have done? Are you trying to fuck me?
Frank: No really, we have been doing it the whole time.
Oliver: That's bullshit. My fucking stepdaughter is four years old and she could pick more weeds then the three of you can in that amount of time. Just don't fuck me over.

A day or two later Edwin, Frank and I decided that we were done with the job. I don't remember how we came to the decision of who would be the one to tell Oliver that we were quitting, but it somehow ended up being me.

Me: So, the three of us ended up getting another job so this is going to be our last day.
Oliver: A job doing what?
Me: We are going to clean horse stalls and help a lady out who owns horses.
Oliver: Well, that should be fun.

Me: Yeah.

Of course, this was a lie. In the weeks leading up to me first starting the landscaping job, I worked for a woman who had two horses and my job was to clean their stalls (as recorded in previous story). I got sick of it and so decided to give landscaping a shot. I had no intention of returning to that job, so I was content with being jobless for a while. Being poor is definitely better than having to put up with that shit all day, every day. One of my clearest memories from the landscaping job was catching two or three leaches in a water bottle and then taking them back to Oliver's house where we poured salt on them and watched them deteriorate. Oliver thought this was funny; the only thing I ever laughed along with him at.

## WORKING AT A PIZZA PLACE

I ended up getting a job at a local pizza restaurant during my last days at the car wash. Once I got the job, I decided it was way better then washing cars, so I immediately quit without giving a two-week notice. The text I sent to my boss was something like this: "Hey, really sorry but I am going to have to quit. I got another job and I feel like if I have to clean the inside of someone's car again, I am going to take a shotgun and blow my head off." He responded with, "Have fun with pizza." This confused me because I don't remember telling anyone that I got a job at the pizza place.

My main job at the pizza place was to work the cash register and take phone calls for delivery and pick up. It was one of the easiest jobs I had ever had at that point, and it came with a perk, pretty much all the people that worked there would get fucked up on the job. The managers would drink beer and take shots throughout the shift, and they ended up being fine with me doing that as well. One of the guys I worked with was a guy, "Tommy" who I used to work with at the sports grill when I was a dish washer. Tommy and I would buy bottles of peppermint schnapps and go through them as the shift progressed. I wouldn't just get buzzed, I would get extremely drunk, sometimes even borderline blacking out shit faced. On one occasion after getting plastered, I was operating the cash register and helping out a customer, and somehow, maybe she just noticed I was acting fucked up or she could smell the alcohol in my breath, she realized I had been drinking. There was a note on one of the refrigerators that said, "Any customer complaint will result in termination." In the following few days that I had off after this shift, I started to get bad paranoia that someone would complain that I was acting belligerent and fucked up. As it turned out, much like a lot of the shitty paranoia I sometimes get in my life, it ended up being true.

I arrived at the pizza place to start my shift and the manager told me that I was being fired. He said that a customer reported me to the corporate office for being drunk. The main manager/owner of that particular restaurant was apparently really pissed off, and, just like the note on the refrigerator said, if a customer complains, you're out of a job.

Manager: She told the owner, and he is not happy.
Me: Oh shit, that sucks. My bad.
Manager: I feel kind of like a hypocrite for having to let you go because I myself get really fucked up on the job.
Me: For sure. Thanks for the opportunity.

The manager who had to fire me was the type of drunk that gets extremely pissed off and angry at almost anything that happens to them when they are in that state. I have known people who are this type of drunk in the past, and it confuses me greatly why the hell they even drink in the first place. One time when I was working with him, he, on top of being shit faced, took a Xanax bar and was throwing shit and slamming the pizza oven, apparently trying to take out his anger on material objects (or whatever the hell makes them not be so pissed anymore (maybe stop drinking?)). We were out of one dollar bills and he asked me to go to the Safeway next door to the restaurant and exchange a fifty dollar bill for one dollar bills. The only problem is he never gave me the fifty dollar bill to do it.

Manager: So, did you get the one's yet?
Me: No, not yet. You still haven't given me the money to exchange it for.
Manager: Well didn't I just give you the fifty dollar bill like twenty minutes ago and told you to go exchange it?
Me: No, you never did.
Manager: Goddammit.
Me: Do you need help with anything? Should I make a salad or pasta?
Manager: Fuck off.

Irrational people piss me off. There are few things more classic in the world then seeing someone fucked up who you have just disproven what they were trying to say. When the shit faced person realizes that you are right and they are wrong, they get pissed off, and have to live with the fact that maybe they are not always right in that state. Justice is served. The manager would get so pissed off sometimes that he once slammed the pizza oven when another employee's arm was in it. The employee got a massive burn on his arm. The one thing I can take away from my one month stint working in the pizza restaurant: getting belligerently drunk on the job is probably not the best thing to do if you are supposed to be dealing with the general public. You never know when some dickless asshole (yes even woman can be dickless, metaphorically speaking) will have a problem with you, not because you are doing the job poorly, but people they think it is their responsibility to turn someone in and make an example of that person, just to make a point that it is not ok to act like that at work.

# SECTION 5

# Dreams of Mind Travel

## FORWARD

In this section, I record some dreams that I have had over the past 6 years roughly. I personally love dreaming because it is an escape from the normal bullshit you have to put up with in the real world. Some people have the simple goal of, once they are dreaming, to then recognize that they are dreaming, and then realize that they could do whatever they want. This is called a "lucid" dream and it enables the dreamer to feel more in charge of what they do in a dream by being freer, rather than just go along with what is going on in the dream of the person. Although I could see the appeal of becoming lucid in a dream, I personally would rather stay ignorant of the fact that I am dreaming, mostly because some of the most epic dreams that I have ever had, are one's in which you go on an adventure, and are experiencing whatever the dream throws at you. I find dreams that you think are real are more entertaining than dreams in which you are lucid. I think, which is definitely true in my case, and probably true for others, that if you remembered the dreams you have, in every detail, then that would make for an awesome movie or an awesome book. I know that in my case, dreams that are really epic and adventurous would be a crazy thing to document. I have a theory of dreams which I think could very well be the case. There are some scientific theories, in this case string theory or any theory in which there exists multiple dimensions in existence, as well as other parallel universes. According to some scientists, these different dimensions and other universes possess their own physical laws and mathematics that govern how that universe behaves. So, even in the craziest dreams that people have, dreams that in no way could occur in the universe that we currently live in, they may very well be taking place in a different possible world. For example, if you could fly in your dreams, this is because you are experiencing the dream from another dimension or universe. This theory has, along with what science has said on the matter, another interesting aspect that relates to consciousness. In this book I talk about psychedelic drugs, and the one that we wish to examine further is called Dimethyltryptamine, or also called DMT. DMT, supposedly, is what gets released into your brain when you are born, when you die, and also when you dream. Having done much research on the effects of DMT, I think that when it gets released into your brain, it opens up ways in your consciousness that enable you to experience other worlds. I talked to one kid in college who told me that when he was in his DMT trip, it felt like at least a thousand plus years. I also heard from a friend that you knew someone who took DMT, and he tripped that he lived the life of some person on another planet for 300 years. To these people, it literally feels like 300 or 1,000 years to them. There seems to exist some sort of time dilation between how one experiences the world we live in, to how they experience other worlds. For example, the kid who lived for 300 years was only in the trip for no more than ten to fifteen minutes. So, if someone has a dream in which crazy absurd things happen to them, that could possibly just be because they have gone through a time portal and are then experiencing existence through another universe. At least in reference to scientific discovery at this point in human history, there really is nothing that contradicts this theory of dreams. Yet at least. Keeping this in mind, it should be noted by the reader that when reading these dream reports, what I have written down makes absolutely no sense. This could either be because the dream was just too crazy and what I wrote down doesn't make sense, simply because the dream doesn't make sense to you when you wake up. Furthermore, it is extremely difficult to describe something in this world that happened in another world. Keeping this in mind, I encourage the reader to read the following dream reports not to seriously and rather try and put yourself in my shoes and see what I saw when living it.

## DREAM: CHAOTIC EVENTS

This dream was cut into several parts that all connected. First, I remember being at some place with (I think it was a resort or apartment complex or something) Kenny and his friends. We are smoking cigarettes and I tell them that I plan on going to the mall to buy a vaporizer nicotine cigarette. Kenny tells me that he knows a friend who has one of those and that it gets him really "ripped". I then see Claire from the Mexican Restaurant. She tells me that she is starting to like me a lot. She then asks me that even if I were to go someplace that I always wanted to go would I rather stay and be with her rather than go.

I tell her that even if I get accepted to Harvard that I wouldn't go and I would stay with her instead. The next thing I remember is being on a bus with my dad and sister going to New York City. I look out the window and see the Empire State Building and I tell my dad that I see the Statue of Liberty even though it is in the middle of Manhattan. We get off the bus and go through this bus/subway terminal and go up and down many escalators. We then get on these carts that go from one station to the next so slowly that you can run and keep pace with them. This one time as we are going from one station to the next the cart my dad and sister are on takes off without me. I push an old lady's cart along the tracks to the next station and it gets slightly derailed. My sister, dad, and I then try to decide what to do next in NYC and we decide to see Toy Story 3. When we get to the movie theater I see Omar, Melanie, Paul, and Philip coming out of the movie theater. Dad, my sister and I go into the theater, but it turns out to be a Toy Story theme park thing that is organized in a circle like that foundation level in Halo 2. The Toy Story theme park is run by Nickelodeon because I see a huge sign. I then learn that the people running the theme park are terrorists who have a bomb inside the park and want to kill me and my family. I manage to outrun the people and hide in a room along the park. My dad and sister are still outside, and I feel the need to help them and try to get them to safety. I rush out of the room with a pencil and kill all of the terrorists by jamming the pencil through the back of the necks and they all collapse on the floor. One of the terrorist's looks like Mr. Valentine's assistant in the James Bond movie, "Tomorrow Never Dies." I have to jam the pencil into his neck multiple times before he dies. The next thing I remember was like a movie. I wasn't there but I see a third person view of the Mr. Valentine's assistant terrorist in a jet with another person following another jet. The jet they are following turns its machine gun on the back to fire at them but it's too late before Mr. Valentine's assistant's jet blows him up. *I took that as meaning that evil lives on even if it appears you defeated it at a time.* The next thing I remember is my family, mostly just me, my dad and my mom buying a large apartment condo near the top of a new skyscraper in Manhattan. The apartment has a rectangular room inside of it that people called "extra" and "not needed." I remember seeing a huge blue airplane flying slowly towards the building through the window when I am in the apartment. The airplane misses the building by going underneath where we are, sort of like flying between the two towers in Malaysia that are connected by a bridge even though this skyscraper doesn't have that and is made up of just one building. The blue airplane (much like a 737 or 777) quickly turns around and crashes in the skyscraper. Filled with fear, my parents and I head towards the elevators to evacuate the building. We can see out the windows of the elevators smoke and fire coming from the building. We get to the second floor and my dad exits quickly and my mom and I don't have time to follow him. The elevator starts going back up when the door closes, but luckily just goes to the third floor where nobody gets on. We then go back to the second floor to join my dad. We leave the building and go to a secure spot. I then see a giant robot or being lift (rip) the top of the skyscraper where the plane crashed and throw it away from the building, but it crashes rubble next to the skyscraper. The skyscraper at this point is all alone in a valley surrounded by dirt hills (the robot took the top of the tower off so that the rest of the building wouldn't collapse like with the WTC (twin towers)). I then remember there being a grand opening for a Chinese restaurant that is located at the top of the building, and it stayed in place because it is located exactly where the cutoff point is where the robot ripped the top of the building off. My mom, dad and I go up to the Chinese restaurant and my parents know the owners. They have a history with the restaurant that went back to some bet that they would have won but didn't because they didn't report that they got married. I see my mom and dad's marriage date on a screen alongside other couple's marriage dates and my dad explains that they would have won the bet (I don't exactly remember what the bet was) because our name, "Logician" was alphabetically before another couples. The Chinese restaurant then organizes a game where people throw eggs at a wall that has a picture of three trees. The object is to hit the trees straight on, as high up as possible. That is all I remember, then I wake up.[72]

## DREAM: THE WATERSHED

I was playing dodgeball with a red ball in the university Quad with a bunch of friends. Pierce was there, Victoria and Quinton. Later I just played with my brother and my sister in our kitchen. My brother was washing dishes from the Mexican Restaurant in our sink. My sister threw a dish instead of the red ball and it broke.

I am inside of Priest's classroom taking some class. People in the room are Victoria, Ray and others. We are watching videos that the students made for a project. Ray's was a karate/hacky sack video where he and another person would put two couches and tables stacked on both sides of a basketball hoop and try and hack it in.

I decide to run away from home and go to Florida with Victoria. My mom is baking some sort of castle cake at the time I leave, and my dad is talking to someone in through his car in our driveway about how he used to be Catholic. Victoria and I and two other people who I forget are on a bus and we arrive in New York City. I ask anyone on the bus how long it takes to get to Manhattan from here. She replies, "10 minutes" and I ask her if that is if I walked. She laughs at this, and I apologize, saying that I am from Denver and can get to any place in that city in 10 minutes from anywhere. We get off the bus and try locating a cab. I see a woman in an all yellow dress outfit walk on the (brightly lit) street in front of us. We finally locate a cab in a dark alley/street that is not lit. The cab only has his front very dim lights on. I knock on his window and he says he could take us. The driver's name is Harold (I know this because I asked him) and he looks a lot like Charlie. We start driving off when we realize we have forgot one of our friends who we then see riding his skateboard trying to catch up with the cab but ends up wiping out right next to it. He gets in and then we see a burning old bridge/building. Despite the buildings frail condition, cars are still allowed to drive under it even though it is starting to give away because of the fire. The taxi driver says that he knows the people who own the building or that he used to be in their company. I forget where we are and are going, so I ask Harold, "are we in Brooklyn?" and he replies, "more or less." I then ask where we are going and everyone in the car looks at me, surprised, and says, "the watershed." I tell them that I have never heard of the watershed in NYC and Harold looks surprised and confused. The dream ends with a night view from the ground looking up at the MetLife building (from the taxi).

## DREAM: QUITTING SMOKING AND SNORTING MISCELLANEOUS THINGS

I'm at my house in the living room by the kitchen with Rose. My parents are there, and I tell them that Rose is my girlfriend. I always have my left arm around Rose, and we keep kissing each other. She also leans her head on my shoulder a lot. She tells me that if we are going to be boyfriend and girlfriend, that she wants me to stop smoking. The only other thing that I remember is meeting Rose at some place (I am pretty sure it was a tanning company). When I get there, I see Rose sitting down at a table and I talk to some people who check us in and they ask if I want to snort some salt or sugar or something to get rid of my stuffy nose. I snort the salt and my dream ends.

## DREAM: MOUNTAIN STRUCTURE

I am at a mountain that looks kind of like the path that leads up to Zora's domain in Zelda. There is this huge white structure that is made out of white paper or white cardboard that is glued together. The structure is connected together up this mountain by individual cube rooms that keep going up. I am told by someone that each graduating class from my high school makes their own structure every year after they graduate. I am going up the structure with my brother and we go up by climbing ladders in the cubes to go into another level. We make it all the way up to a level in the 60's or 90's and then I lose my balance and make the top level crumble over. I then remember being at the 2010 HS graduating class ceremony at Red Rocks. I see Robert and we say that we are going to hang out after he graduates and climb the new structure together. After each person walks, they go up on the Red Rocks stairs and each contribute a yellow paper/cardboard (like the ones used for poster boards) to create and make the structure. I see Ashley roll her yellow paper up and contribute it to the structure for more support. After it is finished, the yellow structure spans from the stage, all the way up the audience seats to the top. I can't find Robert, so I start climbing the structure by myself. Once I am in, I see Robert and we stick together. Inside the different levels of the cubes it is dark and there is a 2-sided winding staircase that goes up to the next level. I try to climb the staircase backwards, but it eventually winds down so I cannot go any further, so I go around the correct way. Every level looks the same and after climbing one or two levels, Robert and I become separated. I then see Kyle's dad and he goes over to Robert who just comes in the same level as me and his stomach and chest are covered in blood. That's the last I remember and believe is when I woke up.

## DREAM: FALLING MOON

I am at a house with people (some I recognize were Peyton, Stan, Frank and Julia). I am behind a bar and Julia says that she will give me a hand job. I mostly am the one jerking off and she touches my dick once. Julia and I wrestle on the floor while everyone watches. I then begin to realize that I might be dreaming and I see Frank and say that I think we are in a combined dream together. We ditch school or some convention that everyone is going to and go to McDonald's to eat. We then go over to that street that Henry lives on right in front of that kid Chase's house and break into a yellow car parked in front of Chase's driveway. I use a knife that was already in the car to start it and then a cop car comes over and gives us the keys. Frank and I believe that the cops are after us so instead of going straight up the road towards Chris's house, I go in reverse and drive away. The next thing I remember is that Frank and I are at some house or country club. I can see the moon come swirling (orbiting) around the sky towards a lake or ocean right next to the country club. I then see a jet flying in the air, shooting rockets at the moon (the moon looks a lot like the moon in "Zelda Majora's Mask"). The moon breaks in half and then hits the ocean causing a massive tidal wave. Frank and I run to find a place to hide for shelter from the tidal wave. We find a sauna and go into it and I lock the door behind us. The last thing I see before I wake up is a person running to the sauna for cover, so I open it up and let the person in.[73]

## DREAM: SUPERHEROES AND PHILOSOPHY

I was in some tall building and I read the book, "Superheroes and Philosophy" twice. I was in the building trying to run away or escape from something and I remember being high up in this ceiling or vent and looking down into a room below. I then remember being in a hockey game. I was the goalie and the other team kept scoring on me. My teammates were pissed at me for not stopping the puck so I tell them I will make it up to them if I am not the goalie anymore. I score five goals in a very short time and my team wins. I then remember being with my dad in some arena with something like an obstacle course/black crust and hot lava beneath it. The obstacle course was a test to see how long I could go before I failed. Some person tells me that when I fail, the devil will possess me and that I should just give up immediately and jump into the lava to avoid the inevitable. I then see some person with long hair and a ponytail (looks about 30-35 years old who is still doing the obstacle course). I take that person to be me 10-15 years in the future who is still doing the obstacle course because he refused to become possessed. The person says that no matter how long you do the obstacle course and delay becoming possessed, you will one day lose. My dad says that maybe I should just jump in the lava. I start doing the obstacle course, by jumping on to the different platforms when I wake up.[74]

## DREAM: SMOKING ANTIPSYCHOTIC MEDICATION

I was at a mall with Abe. We picked up his friend Travis (who looked like Garebear) and Stephen. Stephen told me that smoking and taking a bunch of Risperidone gives you the same high as marijuana. I take 2 Risperidone's and we go over to Donnie's house in Boulder for a party. His house is way larger with many other rooms but maintains the overall actual appearance. I see people having sex all across the house. I see Frank having sex with two girls and one is screaming so loud that I think she is being raped. It turns out that Frank is not raping her, but she is just loving the sex so much. I know this because it appears that she has her arms around Frank after the sex, talking with him. The dream ends with me and Stephen smoking crushed up Risperidone out of a pipe.[75]

## DREAM: DOCUMENTING A DREAM WITHIN A DREAM

I go skiing with Teddy and a friend of his from out of town. We decide to ski on a double black diamond and to my surprise, Teddy and his friend do pretty well (Teddy's friend goes straight down the black diamond, going over the mogul's instead of around them). The skis that I am wearing have attached to my left foot boot a box from Walmart (the boxes that are collapsible and have the Walmart logo on them). I tell myself that the best skier I know is Carter and I think I may have seen him. I tell Teddy that I need to take a break and get something to eat so we get on a ski lift. As this is happening, I realize that I have just been dreaming and that I need to record this dream in my dream journal. I then begin to write down what happened previously in the dream in my dream journal while on the ski lift. We are then on a bus that takes us to the stop by were the RTD bus picks people up from close to Walmart, while I still continue to write in the journal. The dream then ends.[76]

## DREAM: WHAT HAPPENS WHEN SOMEONE DOESN'T START FOR THE FIRST TIME

I am at a football stadium and am with Marcus Mariotta, and my mom and dad. Marcus Mariotta is wearing a Florida Gators jersey and he tells me that he will go back to play college football for the Gators the next season. The next thing I remember is that I am walking around the stadium with Mariotta, my mom and dad, and Jason. My dad asks me who you think should start next season for the Gators, and I reply that it should be Jason because he has been with the team longer and that he earned it more. This makes Mariotta very angry and so he starts chasing people around the stadium with a laser type gun. I am very scared and run around the stadium trying to hide and run away from Mariotta. I finally escape from Mariotta, and he gets on a plane with my mom and dad and Jason. In order to completely escape from Mariotta I get on the back of the plane, and it takes off into the sky. I am holding on for my life as the wind strongly blows in my face. After that I am on the back of a plane by myself and the plane and am in control of the plane. I go back to the stadium and the plane crashes in a building with a runway. I reach the ground safely and then my grandparents immediately pull up in a red minivan. They tell me to get in and I do. I ask them where we are going and grandpa replies, "anywhere you want". My grandma says, "I'm sorry this happened, this is what happens when someone doesn't get to start for the first time in his life" (referring to Mariotta not being able to start because I chose Jason over him). The next thing I remember is us trying to reach a bus on the campus of Florida State University. I see people all around wearing FSU clothing. We miss the bus, and someone says that we can catch another bus somewhere close to the vicinity of where we are at. The dream then ends with me seeing some FSU student pointing to where the bus will be.

## DREAM: $1 SIGNS

I am at a University of Colorado and University of Oregon football game. The game is being played at Oregon's stadium. I am sitting in the stands with Paul and Philip. The first thing I remember is Oregon easily scoring first with an Oregon player easily out running the Buffalo players with a fast offense. The next thing I remember is Paul and Philip holding up these red lit "$1" signs. I forget what the signs mean but a guy sitting next to us in the stands tells us to stop holding them up. It is now the Buff's possession of the football and some of the Oregon and Colorado players come up into the stands. I see some of the players sitting on the rail out looking down to the field. As this is happening a guy walks throughout the stands holding a plastic cup with a green liquid in it and asks people if they want to touch it. Me, Paul, and Philip, all touch it and Paul and Philip take out their "$1" signs again and a lady sitting next to us laughs. The person then gives the cup with green liquid in it to a Colorado player and the player goes down to the field and begins to run with it down the field toward the touchdown. I see the player from behind try and outrun an Oregon player, but he cannot. The last thing I remember is running to the end of the field, trying to outrun Terrence to some small structure. I make it there before him and in the small overhang structure there are markings on the ground of four circles in a diamond shape with a Philadelphia Flyers logo on the top of it. I begin to move the ball with my legs in the shape of the diamond (passing the ball to each circle in the diamond shape) and then I wake up.[77]

## A Brief Dream Montage

The final part of this section I list bits and pieces of many dreams that I have had over the course of my life. Thus, I take the reader on a journey through my various dreams, the sensical, and the nonsensical.

1. I am Gandalf from Lord of the Rings. I am walking up a hill with my staff. The dream ends when my best friend calls me and wakes me up.

2. Richard Dawkins is holding a book signing event at my high school. Dawkins takes questions from the crowd. One person said: "I have a dying friend tell me something about an event that will happen in the world, and a few months after my friend died the event happened. How would you explain that?" Dawkins responded like most skeptics on the matter by saying it was just a coincidence. I then talk loud enough for everyone to hear. I say the following: "This person has presented some decent evidence as to the affirmation of some pseudoscientific belief. Your response to that person's question is highly irrational and not in alignment with how the truth of the world may be." I forget what Dawkins says in response. I am now in one of the hallways of the high school. I see a demonic creature appear in front of me. The creature tries to make me do whatever he wants me to do. In response to this, I grab the evil creature and begin to pound its face and body into the ground. At this moment, I realized that I owned the evil creature, and thus, evil has nothing on me and can't touch me. I wake up and immediately write this dream down.

3. It is the end times final battle in Megiddo. Both of these dreams illustrate an interesting metaphysical depiction of what possibly may be in the waking life (if the battle ever happens).

   3.a. I could see into both the physical and nonphysical (spiritual) realities at the same time. I see that whenever a person has died in the battle, they then stand in a line that leads up to the final judgement of each person (who goes to heaven or hell). The line is very long and gets longer as the battle progresses.

3.b. I have another dream of the end times final battle. I am the person commanding and issuing orders to the people on the battlefield. I have mastered the laws of physics so that I can fly anywhere or just hover in place (floating in the air). I have a staff and am wearing a bathrobe type jacket. I not only issue orders, but I also fight in the battle by occupying a position above the battlefield.

4. First lucid dream: I am in a large dark green forest. I am jumping over a huge cut down tree that still has its stump in the ground. The tree was even bigger than the Red Wood trees in California. As I jump over the stump, I realize that I am having a dream. I shout out to somebody else in the dream (not sure who): "it's ok, it's just a dream." I then remember I had a sense of relief.

5. I am talking to someone about being married and how you know that the people you want to get married is to someone you really know. I then say: "I may not really know Rose very well, but I would marry her in a second." Just as I said this, I see Rose sitting around a table. I tell her that I would marry her, and she responds that I am going to hell. She then says that she is going to heaven for being a Christian. I then tell her that she is not a Christian, she is a Catholic, since I viewed then as having differing beliefs from other Christian sects.

6. Girl in red dress: I see the girl in the red dress sitting at a booth right across a restaurant that I am at. She is sitting there with another person. I know it is her because she is wearing the red dress and looks exactly how she does when I first saw a picture of her.

6.a. I can't believe my luck. I am in love with the most beautiful and awesome girl in the world. We are sitting in my basement on the couch. We kiss and hold onto each other. The girl knows that my favorite movie is, "American Beauty", and asks some person if they have it so we could watch it together.
6.b. I am having sex with the girl and cannot believe how beautiful and gorgeous she is when we make out and have sex. She is wearing a pajama like outfit, and we jump on a trampoline in the middle of some forest. I wake up and try my hardest to fall back asleep so the dream will continue. I do not fall asleep again, but I know that it was the best dream of my life.

7.    Dreams with Annie: These are a few memorable dreams of Annie. Like the girl in the red dress was to me at one point, I consider Annie to be the model of perfection, even equating her beauty to a model of God perfection. In my rating she is a drop dead 12, which makes her the most beautiful thing I have ever seen.

7.a. Me and Annie are tiny bits of matter which, although we do not have our actual bodies, we know who we are. I am sitting on a wall and Annie is sitting on another wall, which I remember because it was where my Nerf/small basketball hoop is in my room. All I know is that there are some people trying to make us do something we do not want to do. All we want is to be left alone. This was the first dream I ever had with Annie.

7.b. I see the Incredible Hulk fly up to the sky (like shooting up to the sky when a rocket takes off). I see Jesus to, but I am not sure how he fits into the overall dream event/story. The Hulk is grey colored and looks roughly the same as he does in the comic books. The last thing I remember is that the place where the Hulk took off was serving corn dogs for people to eat for lunch or dinner. I then see Annie and her friend. It is apparent that Annie does not like corndogs, which I associated with her thinking that it had something to do with oral sex, and Annie did not like corndogs because of that. A friend of Annie then tells her that another place is serving French Toast to eat. Annie decides to get the French Toast. That's all I remember.

7.c. I am in a dream with Jim Carrey, and we formed a friendship because he took DMT which made him more insightful into the true nature of reality. There came a point where someone said to me that you cannot truly know someone just by seeing them in a picture or some other experience that doesn't show you the persons personality and how/who they are. I then see Annie, and I say to the person, that she is everything I thought she would be (perfect and beautiful).

7.d. I am at a Catholic church and want to go into confession. For some reason I couldn't do it (either the line was too long or something else), but one of the Fathers said that if I come back tomorrow night, we could do confession then. I remember in my waking life that tomorrow I am driving a taxicab and so I don't think I can. I then schedule a time I will be off the cab shift and tell the Father that I will be there tomorrow. I see Rose and try to talk to her, but she is always busy in some church meeting or service. I then see Annie and think that she brings out my more authentic or true side/self. Someone in the dream tells me that if I am myself, I would like it if Annie farted in front of me. I then see Annie start farting and she looks very nonconformable and embarrassed. She looks exactly like she did when she starred on the first season of Hart of Dixie. I am not turned on or like seeing Annie fart, which I and everyone else took to mean that I really don't have a fart fetish.

7.e. I had a dream where I was making out with Annie and that I made her laugh. I consider these dreams to be some of the best I have ever had.

8.   I am in a world where technology itself becomes sentient. There is a battle between technology and the anti-technology people. The technology side is commanded by someone who is a dictator/tyrant that doesn't care if other sentient technology items (like a lamp, for example), feel any pain or hardship, and just uses them as if they are not consciously aware, and are just objects it uses to further its own technological superiority. I am in the back of a building with a large ramp that goes up a few feet from the bottom to the top. I am putting on some full body suit to prepare me for the battle I am about to go into. The tyrant is ruthless on the other sentient technology, and the suit I put on is the best way to prepare for battle against it. The suit looks like a huge black padded suit that has pads on the head (top; looked like a black bicycle helmet and covers the mouth), the shoulder, arms, legs, feet, torso, and everywhere on the body. The only thing I remember about the dream was the beginning of the battle between technology and anti-technology, where fighter jets were firing and trying to destroy each other (the technology fighter jets have no pilot, the anti-technology fighter jets have a pilot). I see a jet get blown up, and I run over to a shelter so that the destroyed jet does not fall on me.

9.   I am hanging out with a few friends from high school. The only one I for sure remember was Frank. I have horrible acne that I can see when I look in a mirror. I am very self-conscious about it, since everyone else has clear skin with no acne. Some random girl then walks into the room where me and my friends are at with four or five other girls. The girl says to the other girls: "ok girls, chose whichever boy you want to be with." The girl that chose me ended up with me because all the other girls chose every other boy, and so I was the only boy left. I immediately know that the girl is not attracted to me at all, because of the bad acne that I have. She then says to the girl that chose Frank: "do you want to switch?" I later took this to mean that having a clear face (no acne) is a cool thing to have, and acne is not a cool or attractive thing to have. The dream then ends. When I woke up I had to go to work soon and just remember being in

one of the best moods I have ever been in upon waking up after a nap. I thought it was hilarious that a girl chose Frank over me.

10. I am on one of the grass fields in back of my middle school. The field is a rectangle that is enclosed on the long end by a gate, and on the short end by a giant concrete wall. I am playing ultimate frisbee and look up at one point to the top of the concrete wall and see a cougar/mountain lion sitting on the top. This makes me very scared/frightened, and I try my hardest to avoid the cougar at all costs.

11. I am with my six attractive cousins, and we are situated between one another alongside a steep road. Alongside the road are rooms and places to go into. One of my cousins said she needed to go to the bathroom. I was very horny for her and wanted to have sex with her. I then ask her: "could I come in?" To which she responded no.

12. I have a large amount of heroin, roughly a couple of kilos in brick form. I know that someone will be looking for the heroin, so I decide to hide it in my outside shed on the top level. News of the heroin that I have (not sure where I got it from or who I got it from) becomes a national incident, and people make a huge deal about the heroin and I understand that if I was found out to be the one with the heroin, I would get into trouble (like going to prison maybe). The last part of the dream that I remember is my sister saying to me that the government has just instituted martial law, because the heroin has sparked a sort of revolution. I then go to the shed, take out the heroin, and put it into a safer, better hiding spot to not get found with it.

13. Reoccurring school dreams: I have a long reoccurring dream that revolves around three main things, all associated with each other by the notion that I have either been ditching class all semester long, that I am not ready to take a test (did not study), and I still have to do a class presentation that I have been putting off for months.

    13.a. I am in my middle school. I attend my math class on the very first day of the semester and do not take any of the midterm exams, quizzes, tests, or homework the teacher has assigned for the class. It is a Calculus 2 math class and I sort of understand it but I know that I am not prepared at all to take the class final exam. The teacher does not know me very well, since I have been absent pretty much the entire semester. I sometimes take the test and see how I could do, other times I walk out of the class and don't take the test, knowing in the back of my mind that I am going to have to retake the class in the future.

13.b. I am in my high school. I am taking French with Ms. H as the teacher. Everyone that I was in French with in real life, is also in the classroom. I sometimes decide to attend, and when I do, I only stay in class for no longer than a couple of minutes. I decide to take the final exam because I know that if I do good on it, the teacher will take this to mean that I know French very well, even though I didn't attend class throughout the semester. Everyone takes the class seriously, but I don't, which gives me the impression that the other students know I am a slacker and unmotivated.

13.c. I am in my pre-algebra classroom in my high school. Sometimes the class is in this room, and sometimes it is in another room I have not seen before in my waking life. It is an English class, and the teacher is Ms. T. Throughout the entire semester the students in the class would stand in the front of the class and give a presentation about some topic. My partner for the presentation is Sam. Whenever I know to be the day that we are supposed to do our presentation, I ditch class for that day. It gets to a point where the only people left to present are me and Sam. Since I am skipping so many classes, the end of the semester comes, and time runs out for me and Sam to present. Ms. T doesn't really care that we never present(ed) and gives me a good grade in the class.

14. I think Becca is cute in my waking life and also cute in my dreaming life. I am walking around the Halo 2 map, "Ivory Tower" for some reason, and don't remember exactly why. I see Becca and she gives me a blowjob in the part of the map where there is a steep ramp that leads up from the bottom level to the top level (the place on top is where there is an air vent). I wake up realizing that Becca is actually cuter than I have previously thought.

15. Keno dreams: I have had many dreams of playing Keno and winning a bunch of money. These are the most noteworthy.

15.a. I am with Tucker Max, and he is playing Keno on his computer. He is very good at it, since every pull he takes he wins the jackpot every time (9/10 or 10/10 every time). He tells me that there is a secret to Keno that makes it not just beatable, but also makes you win the top amount of money whenever you play. I remember seeing the words "jackpot", "$250,000" (or some other large amount of money) and "winner". I'm not exactly sure what else happened, but I woke up and immediately was depressed that it wasn't real, since I learned from Tucker Max the secrets to winning money at Keno, and so I, myself, can make a ton of money at. 15.b. I decide to go up to a casino and play poker to win some money. I suck at poker and lose money. When I get very low on chips, I decide that I will use my remaining money to play keno and hopefully win more money than what I just lost. I sometimes play keno for 5 cents a pull, 25 cents a pull, or 1 dollar a pull. I remember knowing how to win consistent money playing keno, because I have found out how to beat the casino odds. I start off, when sitting down at the keno machine, by betting 1 dollar a pull. I immediately hit 7/8 and win $2,000 - $2,500".

15.c. Sometimes I play keno at a regular arcade instead of a casino. The keno machines at an arcade are such that you have to put in coins, and if you win, coins are dispensed at the bottom of the machine, just like money coming out of a slot machine. As I am currently writing this part of the book, I have the realization that this is not that bad of an idea for regular game/entertainment arcades to have, seeing as the odds are in the arcades favor (just like it is in the arcades favor to make people put more money into the arcade games, then the money they may get out of it (coins or tickets for example)).

15.d. The distinction between my dream life and waking life when put into contrast through keno, is that in both I have an unbeatable strategy. Start with small money (5 to 25 cents a pull), with the occasional big money bets ($1 to $5 a pull) put in occasionally. You always need to be playing with (the money you bet) money you have already won. So, you could do 5 $1 pulls, or 1 $5 pull. This betting structure, along with the insight that hitting 7/8 is not as insurmountable as one may think, enables one to beat keno. The only other keno dreams I remember is having a lucid dream, and hitting 10/10 on every pull, not just in regular one card keno, but 10/10 on all multi-card keno bets. All keno dreams end in the same way, mainly, disappointment that they were not real.

16. I am playing Zelda: Ocarina of Time and have discovered a new part of the game that nobody knows about. On top of this I have discovered certain glitches in the game that enable you to go from place to place (like a certain temple to another temple) whenever you want. The game within the dream becomes real when I stop seeing the body of Link and controlling him with the controller, and instead see a first person view of Link as I roam around the uncharted territory of the game. In the actual game, you only see a first person view of Link when he either has a bow

and arrow or uses a grappling hook. If the entire game were that way, I think the playing experience would be greatly increased.

17. Waterpark dreams: I have dreams of many waterparks. Some are outside or inside, and range from an average size park, to almost a city, such that they are an engineering marvel.

    17.a. I am with Rick and some other friends, and we are at a giant indoor waterpark. I remember going up to one of the slides and seeing a view of the huge park that was mostly made up of long, twisting slides, and everything has turquoise blue in color. I go down the water slide and that is all I remember. What is interesting about this dream is that the day when I had it, when I woke up, I went to Frank's house with Rick to trip mushrooms. I'm not sure if I told Rick about it.

    17.b. I am at a recreational center pool. The pool is made up of mostly jungle gyms and play structure areas that people could climb on and play with. However, under the water level are huge buildings made out of structures that you can scuba dive down to and explore. 75% of the park is underwater. The water depth must have been around 50 to 60 feet. The dream ends before I can explore the underwater park structure.

    17.c. I am at a very small indoor water park. The only really existing thing to do is to climb up a rock wall (like a rock-climbing wall) that must have been 40 to 50 feet high (maybe higher). At the top I see people jumping off and landing in the small pool at the bottom. The small pool is very shallow, and only a few feet deep. Some people land in the pool and really hurt themselves. I decide to jump off the wall. I make it safely on the ground, with the shallow pool depth not affecting me.

18. Unknown to me, there is a huge section to my house that I have never been in or seen before. Where my parent's bathroom is, there is an extension to the house where the size of the unknown part of the house, makes the regular size of the house into a giant mansion. The mansion is filled with awesome rooms, bathrooms, and other areas that I would love to have my dream home decked out with. I wake up and realize that there is no extension to my house anymore like there was a few seconds earlier.

19. College dorm and Adderall: I have many dreams of being back in college with my freshman college dorm room, and my roommate, Max. In all these dreams I always try to get Adderall.

    19.a. I have not seen Max in weeks or maybe even months. I have not been to my dorm room for a long time, as I have been out doing other things not college/school related. I forget the room number of my dorm and try my best to remember. I knock on the door and Max answers. We are happy to see one another, since it has been a while. Max has changed the dorm room around, since I have been gone for so long, he figured I may never come back. My visits to Max are short lived as I either wake up or decide to leave the room and do something else.

19.b. When the realization hits that I am in college in my dream, my first priority is to get some Adderall. I ask random people if they knew someone I could get it from, and every person either knows someone, or themselves have some for me to buy. Sometimes the Adderall looks like it is in waking life, and sometimes looks completely different. I occasionally run into someone who tries to get me to buy an Adderall knock off (like Wellbutrin), but I never take it, unless they just give it to me at a very cheap price. It's always the same guy that deals the Adderall to me, and I have his name in my cell phone, under the name, John. Sometimes he calls me, and I have to remember other dreams in order to recall who he is. In waking life I feel the effects of the Adderall. In my dream life I do not.

20. I am playing football at some stadium in the middle of a blizzard. The snow is a few feet high and still snowing very heavily. I play on the offense and every play revolves around me getting the ball handed off to me, or getting the ball thrown to me. I am the best player in the game, since every time I get the ball, I score a touchdown. It is halftime and the score is 93 – 0 (or something close to that). I decide to sit out the second half, even though I still want to play. What makes this dream completely epic was that one of my favorite things to do is to watch a football game in a blizzard. That combined with actually playing, was very fun and entertaining.

21. I see my therapist/shrink at someplace. I could tell that she had some feelings of attraction to me as I intuited from my waking life therapy sessions that I had with her. Knowing this, I asked her if I could have sex with her. She is a little hesitant, but then agrees. I have sex with her and look at her as she rides my dick up and down and I remember it feeling really good. The next time I see her I ask if I could have sex with her again. She promptly says no, and I could see that she regretted having sex with me before. Seeing at that I have masturbated to her in my waking life, I think the dream of having sex with her was very awesome. That combined with the last dream I have had with her, that being, that she had the best ass I have ever seen (in my waking life and dream life).

22. I'm at my parent's friend's house. The friends tell me that they love their daughter very much, which resonates with me that they like her a lot more than they like me. All they care about is their daughter, and they could care less about me. The only distinct memory I have of this dream is being in some area of the house with couches. 2 or 3 of the couch pillows had the words, "Primatene" written on it, with the actual Primatene logo. Since I was addicted to Primatene in my waking life when this dream happened, I thought it was kind of funny.

23. I see pictures of Mia naked on my computer screen. The pictures become strung together to make a short video. I see a video of Mia showing off her naked body, most notably her ass and pussy. I was happy in the dream and happy when I woke up.

24. I remember where my locker is, but never remember the locker combination. Half the time I get the locker open, the other half I don't get the locker open. I remember the locker combination from other dreams I have had. The locker is always situated along one of the sides of the wall in the center of the high school.

25. I am with a few friends, and we all see Philip in some arbitrary place. In my waking life, Philip died a few years ago in a motorcycle accident. We all hug him and are all happy to see him again. We then start asking him questions about what it is like to die and what happens after you die. Philip responds: "I'm not supposed to say." I decided to ask Philip a question that I still to this day, consider to be a major contradiction to the existence of a benevolent God/creator. My question: "Is there anything that I need to be fearful of when I die?" Philip asks what I mean, and I say, "for example, what happened to Hitler when he died?" Right after I said this I immediately woke up. I take this to mean that the question I asked was missing the point in some way. Upon seeing Philip in this dream and a few others after this, I think that when one dies, there really isn't something you should be worried about (like going to hell for example), which is what a benevolent God would want. Philip told me in a different dream after this one that he is, "in a good place."

26. I am on the 1990 CU Buffaloes National Championship team. We have a game to be played and are heading to Folsom Field in a bus to take us there. When we arrive, I see a crowd of people protesting the team and its season with picket fences and other rants. They are protesting that even if CU wins the game today, they should not be National Champions,

because of the 5th down game they won earlier in the season. I then begin to play in the game in an oval cylinder-shaped environment in front of Folsom Field.

27. An entire town has been flooded to create a lake in some mountain area (like in Dillon, CO). The town is in a valley that is surrounded by mountains on all sides. Many years later, I decide to scuba dive in the lake, and explore the buildings and houses of the now flooded town. I am a little worried about getting lost in some house or building and not finding my way out and am also worried that there might be something in the lake that scares and frightens me (like a dead person or a giant fish). I make my way from room to room and house to house, all without a flashlight.

28. I am in the middle of a huge forest at the base of a mountain where there is a very steep hill. At the top of the hill is one army and at the base of the hill is another army. The army at the base runs uphill towards the top of the hill where the other army is. I see soldiers firing weapons towards the top of the hill. The most noteworthy event of the dream was seeing a tank being driven up the hill, firing its missiles and taking fire from the other army. I woke up and immediately knew it was the greatest war/ battle scene I have ever seen (more than D-Day scene in Saving Private Ryan, for example).

29. I see the woman who plays "Ellie" in That Awkward Moment. Her real name is Imogen Poots. I recognize her and tell her my name to introduce myself. She responds that her name is, Imogen…she then farts and then says 'sssss'. At least in reference to waking life, I feel like this dream may actually be a playing out of what is going through everyone's head when they hear her last name 'poots'. I wake up and laugh.

30. I am ice skating around an indoor rink. I become lucid. I see Patrick who I worked with at Walmart. We exchange some words and I end it with, "but it's all good because it's just a dream" to which he responds, "yeah." As I am doing laps around the rink some guy says he needs help with something. I skate to him and act as if I am about to help him and then I say, "psych". Write as I said this I try to skate away, but the man grabs me. I wake up hating the guy.

I wish was a dream:

It is my birthday. I am working a dishwashing shift. I think people could hear my thoughts. The entire restaurant surprises me by singing happy birthday to me while holding a chocolate cake and a lit candle. As they were singing, I tried to think of something that I might say for my birthday wish. I think of some basic idea, but I never affirm it to myself, and actually say in my mind what the wish is. Just as they finish singing and are about to watch me blow out the candle, a coworker of mine says, "make sure you make a wish". Two thoughts then come to my mind: 1) I have thought of a wish but never actually said it when I did think of it; 2) If I make a wish now, all the people will be able to know what it is since they can all hear my thoughts. I then respond with one of the most foolish things I have ever said: "I already have." I blow out the candle and everyone cheers. I then become grief stricken by the incident, and down on myself as to why I just didn't say the wish. I am disappointed that I lied and now, if my paranoia is true, everyone in the restaurant knows that I lied. I obsess over how much I fucked up and, still as of today (four weeks since), would do a lot to go back in time. I go to sleep to dream about something that cannot possibly be worse.

# SECTION 6
# The Degeneracy of Mind Travel

## FORWARD

The following are stories of epic fails and complete debauchery. Sometimes I feel like I am a tornado, whirling around from place to place, doing nothing except leaving a complete ruin of everything in my path. This, of course, is completely unintentional and if I one day come across someone who wishes to judge me based on the negative ways of living I have lived in the past, this is the section that they will refer to. The voices claim to me that I was Adolf Hitler in a past life. I don't buy it personally, but there does exist one character trait that we both possess, mainly, that we tend to fuck up anything that we put our hands on. Being extremely poor for the past 14 months with no source of income, I have had to come up with ways to finance the things that I want to do but can't because I have no money. My solution? Find a way to get into your parent's safes without them knowing and take their money. I figured that if there ever came a time when either of my parents grew suspicious about me taking their money, and then confronting me about it, I possessed a very important way of denying that I had taken anything, mainly, that I don't know the safe's combination code so how could I possibly take anything from the safe? My dad owns a safe which, when I looked up on the internet ways to break into it, I was stunned at how easy it is break into it without knowing the combination. All you do is hit your hand on the top of the safe while at the same time twisting the lock, and then, viola! I have done it so many times that I could get it open in less time than it takes to use the safe combination. I have taken thousands of dollars, and, for some reason, my dad still keeps his money that he has won playing poker (he really fucking good, continuously making hundreds if not thousands of dollars every time he plays at a casino) in the safe. My mom's safe on the other hand, is not really a safe but rather a cabinet that has a lock on it that you have to have a key to open.

My solution: take two paper clips and put them in the keyhole while fitting the clips in the hole in different ways until finally you have imitated the key with the clips, and then twist the key hole around clockwise until it opens. My brother saw me doing this once and he told me that I am like Dexter from that show, "Dexter". It was not my intention to break in the cabinet and search for money, but instead search for prescription drugs which she had built up over the past ten to fifteen years of shit happening to anyone in the family. For example, my sister broke her leg back in the year 2000, and in the cabinet was my sister's prescription for Percocet or Vicodin (not sure which), which still had at least ten to fifteen pills in it. The majority of drugs that were in the cabinet were pain killers and for a brief time I had developed a minor addiction to them. If ever questioned by my mom as to whether or not I was the one who took the pills, I again had a good way of denying it, mainly, I don't know where your key is so how could I have taken them? This is a good introduction to showing how I have the potential to fuck shit up, and at the same time nobody would know it was me (for certain at least). Having now lived the stories I recount in this section, I am faced with a moral quandary as to how I will behave in the future, as opposed to have I behaved in the past. For example, in "The Republic", Plato asks someone that if they had a ring which, when putting it on your finger, causes you to become invisible, such that you could do whatever you want, like taking money from a bank, and get away without anyone knowing, would you use the ring or not use the ring? Justice (which I personally believe the best attempt to show how true justice is in the world comes from the way in which Plato conceptualized it), or to be a just person, you would not use the ring for harm, such as taking advantage of someone. I completely agree with that and so I think my days of taking shit that doesn't belong to me are pretty much over. If you could do everything in this section like me, and then still be able to honestly call yourself a just person, then you will have knowledge of the truth that Justice revolves around.

## MY GAMBLING ADDICTION

When I was 21, right after my fifth semester of college, I fucked up bad. I started gambling on an online casino called, "Cool Cat Casino." The thing that you should know about gambling online is that it is completely unregulated and completely fixed. Once you start playing, you win money. But this is just to get you to put more money into the casino. Multiple times I was up thousands of dollars, but I just kept playing, hoping to win more money. This was a mistake. I am not sure about other online casinos, but for Cool Cat Casino, there is a way to beat it. The way that this is done is through the bonuses that they give you. I am not sure if they still have the same bonus that they had when I was playing but there was one bonus called, "Coolcat777". With this bonus you could put in $100, and it would give you around $700; maybe a little bit more but I am not sure how much. Multiple times I have hit seven out of eight when playing Keno which would give you around $1,500. The online casino's that give people bonuses for playing on their site, set it up so that you have to play through the certain amount that they gave you the bonus for, and after that it is complete profit for you. I was up around $3,500 on one occasion, and somewhere between $2,500 - $3,000 on other occasions. I just kept playing, hoping to win the $30,000 that you receive if you hit eight out of eight. I am not sure what the chances are of hitting seven out of eight, but considering all the times that I have played, the chances of hitting seven out of eight, along with the bonus that they give you, puts the odds in your favor. I have hit seven out of eight, probably around 25 – 30 times when I have played Keno, and because I kept playing instead of cashing out, I ended up losing it all.

There was one time when I was playing and I had put in roughly $120. I lost it all, but within five minutes of signing out of the Cool Cat website, I got a call from some guy who worked for the casino.

Guy: Hello, is this Psychotic Logician?
Me: Yes.
Guy: I am calling you to tell you that you have just been upgraded to the "high roller's club" with our casino.
Me: What is that?
Guy: You have put in over a thousand dollars and are now considered to be what we call a high roller.
Me: Ok. Thanks.

Guy: You are very welcome.

What is sketchy about this conversation is that it took place literally minutes after I signed out. The conclusion that I have come to is that they watch the players on their website, either making sure that they do not win too much or waiting for them to log out so that they can call you and not interrupt you when you are playing. Between playing Keno online, or playing it at a regular casino, I have lost roughly $1,500 - $2,000. The time that I was called by a website employee, I was playing on Ron's computer. It took probably ten minutes for him to figure out how the hell to uninstall it on his computer.

I ended up being $700 in debt to my bank, because I overdrew so much money on my debit card. What's even more ridiculous about online casino's is the conversations I had with members of their staff, via instant message.

Staff Member: Hello, how can I help you?
Me: Hello, I have a question about depositing money into my account.
Staff Member: Ok.
Me: I am unable to deposit more money into my account and I am not sure why.
Staff Member: It appears that you have exceeded the three deposits a day max that we have on our website.
Me: So, does that mean I have to wait until tomorrow in order to play more?
Staff Member: Yes.
Me: I also had a question regarding why I am unable to use my debit card to play on the casino. I have had to purchase gift cards in order to play.
Staff Member: You need to contact your bank about that. Ask them to allow you to use your debit card on this site. <u>Do not</u> tell them that it is an online casino.
Me: Ok. Thank you.

The fact that she told me not to tell my bank that it was an online casino that I was using to overdraw my account, should have been a sign to me that this was a fucked up thing to do. I got in contact with my bank and asked them if I could take out a small loan. My idea was to win a couple thousand dollars again and then be able to pay the bank back, as well as win back the money that I had before I became indebted to the bank. I talked to a bank employee and asked for a small loan, but he said that the bank didn't give out the type of small loan I was asking for, mostly because it was a loan with no collateral (and the loan would only be for a couple hundred dollars).

If you are thinking about gambling online, use a site that has the biggest bonus, and once you hit it big, immediately cash out, and then use the money that you have won to put more money into the casino, using the bonus again. For example, what I should have done was after winning $3,500, was immediately cash out, and then use $100 of the money I have just won with the bonus to start playing again. If you do this, then you should be able to win money.

On top of playing Keno and losing horribly, I decided to try my luck at poker at a regular casino that I live relatively close to. I ended up always being on the losing side to someone who had a really good hand, and me having a really good hand as well, but just a little worse than the other player. I would wait until I had a pretty good hand, but then some other lucky asshole would have a hand just a little better than me. I, unfortunately, never ended up on the winning side of the good poker hands that I had. When it was all said and done, I ended up losing around $1,000 playing poker.

One of the main reasons why I think that beating online casino's is possible is because whenever I played Keno at the regular casino's, I ended up winning money. Hitting seven out of eight happens a lot more than the statistics would have you believe. At least for me. But having lost so much money gambling, I'll probably never go back to it.[78]

## MARIJUANA CHRONICLES

In a lot of my writing I discuss that a lot of the times that something ridiculous happens, it usually will start of by passing a pipe between me and my friends. This became the norm for me in my senior year in high school, and all through college. When I tried marijuana for the first time, however, what makes it different than all the other times that I tried drugs for the first time, is that I had never taken anything that altered my mind or body in any way. The only drugs I had ever touched were innocent things like Tylenol or Advil, and I had no idea what people were talking about when they talked about being "high". I don't know if it is a coincidence, but somehow it worked out that the drug that gives you the best introduction to how it feels to be high, is the drug that also happens to be what makes people want to experiment what other drug highs are like. About a year ago I wrote a status update (or whatever the fuck they are called) on my Facebook account, that said roughly the following: "If you ever try LSD then you will never be certain of anything ever again (bullshit); cocaine is addictive (bullshit); meth: not even once (bullshit); pot is a gateway drug (true)" The status update I think received mixed reactions from people, which I didn't really care about (although like a tool I structured what I wrote so that people would tell me what they thought about it). I was hanging out with one of my friends, "Eric" one day and he told me that he read the update and that he didn't completely agree with it. My intention in writing it was to try and get people to realize that despite the fact that they think some drugs are hardcore, the high's that you get from them are not that much more extreme than a marijuana high. I think back to when I first started smoking weed, and I realize now that the high I experienced I like more than LSD and opiates. All a high is, is just a mind or mood altering feeling in which you become more aware of things in your mind or surrounding. For example, my friend Frank apparently watched "Pineapple Express" around twenty times, each time baked out of his mind. When he then watched it sober, he noticed that the drug dealer has plants in his apartment, something that he did not see for the first twenty times watching it stoned. I talked to a friend of mine, Eli, while we did acid one time and he understood pretty well what a high is when he said, "even being sober is a high." All drugs really do is unlock a new outlook in your perception, that makes you see the world differently. And all drugs have degrees or levels through which you can experience the high through, like being a little high, moderately high, or very high. A friend of mine in high school decided to try marijuana for the first time, but he hated smoking, so my other friends gave him a sixteenth of an ounce of weed in an edible for him to try it out. He apparently got so high that he thought he was going to die, and he never touched weed again. How exactly is this different than taking some LSD and having a bad trip? Drugs affect people differently, depending on how the drug is taken, and just how the person's brain is wired. A guy I knew in high school called bullshit on me claiming to be a hardcore stoner. All of my friends knew that my brother was a huge pot head, and so just assumed that I was one to. The guy asked me what it feels like to be high, and I responded by saying that it just makes everything funny. I don't remember what he said back to me, but I don't think he was convinced. This brings me to the story of when I first tried weed.

I was on a tennis trip in high school when my team went to play Steamboat Springs. The entire team was situated in a hotel. I was asked previously to us going on the trip if I wanted to smoke weed with my double's partner, "Levi" and I said that I would try it. We went out to a secure location behind some dumpsters in the back of the hotel and Levi took the first hit. I was scared shitless because I had no idea what to expect. I took two decent size hits from his apparent "medical" bud that he had. For about the first ten to fifteen minutes I didn't feel anything, but I thought I would start acting how I think a high person would act. We were playing poker, when I took a chip, held it up close to my eyes, and just began staring at it. Levi laughed at this, under the impression that I was actually baked. But then weird shit started happening to me. I remember people coming in and out of the room where we were playing poker, and I couldn't keep track of who came in, when they came in, and when they left. Apparently, a buddy of mine that I usually called, "Mr. K", came in and I started calling him "K balls", and this pissed him off a little. That is the first thing I don't remember doing. The second thing I don't remember doing is apparently winning a huge hand in poker, and I look down at my chip stack at one point and I see that I have way more than everyone else. I look into the bathroom mirror and see that my eyes are bloodshot and that I have cotton mouth. I don't think I am acting any differently than how I usually am when I am sober, and so the things that my friends tell me that I do and say confuses me. I pissed Levi off for some reason and he told me that I wasn't invited out to smoke with him again. I was so new at this that even the thought of people smoking multiple times in one night confused me.

The point I am trying to illustrate that is apparent in my first time experience with marijuana, is that whatever drug you do for your first time, you don't know what to expect, and the drug will have whatever effect it has on you. A person who snorts cocaine for their first time experimenting with drugs, will, if the experience is good, have that be his gateway to trying other things. In this respect, all drugs are gateway drugs, as long as the high that the person experienced when first using the drug had a pleasant effect on them. So, what then exactly separates the levels at which some drugs are categorized as being more "intense" or "hardcore" than another drug? My friend in high school who ate the edible for his first time, would probably say that weed is a very intense mind-altering drug, to which other people would tell him that he doesn't know what he is talking about. However, the fact that he had a negative first experience, turned him off to all other drugs, some of which, if he tried them, he would find are way less intense then marijuana is. A bartender I used to work with at a restaurant understood how addictions work pretty well. Even something as innocent as eating a cheeseburger can give you a pleasurable mind-altering experience, which makes you want more of it. People who claim that weed is not as hard of a drug as other substances like cocaine or shrooms, say things like that it is not addictive, and that it is just a plant, and not even really a drug. As far as their claims that it is not addictive are concerned, they claim that they could stop at any time, but that they just don't want to. But that is exactly what an addiction is, something that you don't want to stop indulging in because you like the feeling it gives you so much. Even if they are claiming that an addiction is something in which you do not possess any personal power to stop doing it at your own will and need some external help to get you over it like going into rehab for example, their claim that they do possess this power is meaningless in reference to users of other drugs who also would be claiming that they do possess this power as well, but are just refusing to exercise it because they like the drug so much. As far as the argument that people use that some drugs are harder than others because of the physical strain it puts on the body than others, then they are not even referring to the high the drug gives you, but rather are talking about the secondary effects it has on you. A drug like heroin for example, can fuck with your body so much that you build up a dependency on it just to keep from dying. In this case, the very reason why they are even in this position in the first place was because they tried some drug before and liked it, and this peeked their interest in potentially experiencing other highs, which led them to causing serious harm to themselves. The point to understand is not whether or not the drug that the person is doing is more harmful to themselves than other drugs, but rather what made them want to try that drug in the first place. I am just guessing but I would say that a lot if not most people that have serious drug problems, started with pot. Wouldn't this mean that pot then is just as harmful to somebody as the other "harder" drugs are, because it is what turned them onto the harder drug to begin with? In other words, the not so hard drug played a direct result in bringing about the use of a harder drug. The extent to which a drug or anything intended to bring about a more pleasant state of mind for someone happens to affect someone, then that person is more likely to engage in other activities which are supposed to produce a similar if not greater effect. I am not really bashing on drugs, I love drugs, I think all drugs should be legal, I am just making a simple observation that has gone completely ignored by people who support the legalization of certain things that are just as problematic as the things that these people say shouldn't be legalized. A person may be addicted to gambling, starting with penny slots, which could then grow into betting greater and greater amounts, until they are broke. It ultimately comes down to the individual who engages in the habit forming activity as to how they will react to other opportunities that may present themselves to them in the future. But to say that one drug is harder than another drug and has more of a potential to be abused or become addicted to is completely subjective, in that a person may like the pot high as opposed to a meth high, and then just decide to smoke pot, thereby making pot the more hardcore of a drug.[79]

## APRIL FOOLS JOKE

On one April 1st when I was in high school, my brother and I decided to play an April fool's day joke on the people in my family. Our idea: take all of the Kleenex and toilet paper in the house and put it in our bathtub with the shower curtain closed to keep it hidden from the rest of the family. Unfortunately, the only victim of this joke was my mom, but it turned out to be even more cruel than we could have possibly imagined when we thought of it. My mom was confused as to what happened to all the toilet paper and Kleenex in the bathroom in the middle floor of our house.

Mom: Psychotic Logician, do you know what happened to all the toilet paper and Kleenex in the bathroom?
Me: No, I'm not sure.
Mom: Ok.

Since there was no toilet paper or Kleenex in the middle floor, she decided to use the bathroom in the top floor in her room. Instead of checking to see if there were any toiletries in her bathroom, she decided to use it.

Mom: Psychotic Logician, can you please get me some toilet paper.
Me: Ok, mom.

I turned to my brother to ask him what he thought I should do.

Brother: Just ignore her.
Me: Ok.

Five minutes later…

Mom: Psychotic Logician! PLEASE BRING MY SOME TOILET PAPER OR KLEENEX!

My brother and I were laughing pretty hard at this point, but we still decided to ignore her. After about ten minutes my mom was infuriated. She came into my brother's room where we were at.

Mom: Why the hell didn't you bring me any toilet paper?!
Me: Sorry, I couldn't find any.

She then looked into our bathroom and saw all the toilet paper and Kleenex in the house.

Mom: A joke is a joke and it's over!
Brother and Me: Sorry.

Cruel, yes. But it gets worse. A couple days later my mom was talking with some friends in me and my brother's Boy Scout troop. All the adults were talking about the April Fool's Day joke's that their son's played on them. And then my mom revealed what she got so pissed off about: apparently that night my mom was on her period and ran out of tampons and she needed some toilet paper or Kleenex to do whatever the hell she needed to do. That was the last April fool's joke I have ever played on someone.[80]

## UNDERAGE DRINKING STORIES

I have gotten two underage drinking tickets in my life. The first one was right after I graduated high school, and the other one was when I was a freshman in college.

# FIRST OFFENSE

I went to a party with four friends a few weeks after I graduated from high school. It wasn't that big, maybe around twenty to thirty people, in a small house. At the time it was the biggest party I had ever been to. The five of us agreed that we would just stay at the party for a couple of hours, and then walk back to Ron's house, which was roughly two or three miles away. I didn't drink very much, but I smoked a lot of pot. Rick and I were on a beer pong team and got our asses kicked, and the beer I drank from that game was pretty much all the alcohol I had that night. A memorable occurrence from this night is that it was the first time I ever tried a cigarette. Just like with any drug or substance, your first time experimenting with it always gets you the greatest buzz. I took one drag off of a friend's cigarette and I felt a very euphoric high. I could see why people can be so addicted to them. At one point I was out on the deck of the house with Frank, Ron, some random guy and a girl. The random guy was sitting in a chair, head leaning back with his eyes closed. He was obviously very fucked up and we began to mess with him, offering him a hit of pot and he just responded with incoherent mumbles. I got to a point while we were smoking weed that it was the first of two times in my life in which I have temporarily blacked out from smoking weed. What I remember is my foot touching something on the deck, and it was pissing me off that it was in the way of where I wanted to put my leg, so I first began to push at it, and when it didn't move at all I began to kick at it. I did this involuntarily and temporarily lost control of what I was doing. It turned out that what I was kicking was a plant in a plastic pot, and I completely broke it, making soil spill all over the deck. The only other time that I had lost control of my body when I was high was when I was standing in my friend's kitchen, and just fell over, face first onto the floor. I barely missed the counter which would have fucked me up bad if I would have hit it. I have seen other friends completely lose control of their bodies at other times as well. One time Ron, Frank, Edwin, and I were smoking pot on my outside basement patio, when all of a sudden Ron began to start stomping his legs on the gutter drain, severely denting it. We asked him why he did that, and he had no idea what we were talking about.

Frank (laughing): Why did you just kick that pot?
Me: I didn't know it was a pot. I didn't know what the hell it was.

Ron: Are you going to tell Cory (the guy whose house we were at) that you broke it?
Me: Let's just keep it on the down low.

I collected together all the soil and put it along with the broken pot in a corner of the deck, temporarily hiding it until we left so nobody could pin it on me. It was right around this time that the random guy who was fucked up got up from his chair, ran to the side of the deck and began puking over the side.

About two hours after we arrived, Edwin, Ron, and Frank decided that they wanted to leave. I was ready to leave as well, but Rick talked me into staying the whole night with the intention of getting a lot more shit faced. Unfortunately, I agreed. It was around when I took my first and only shot of the night, when I see a cop walk through the front door.

Cop: How's everyone doing tonight?

I immediately saw Rick and he gave me a "oh fuck" look. Besides getting a speeding ticket in high school, this was the first time that I ever had a run in with getting busted by the police. The cop made everyone sit in a group in the living room while the other cop went to go get the breathalyzer. Since I hadn't drank very much, I was gripping onto a hope that I may blow zeros on the breathalyzer. I ended up blowing a .03, which pissed me off, because I figured if I was going to get in trouble for drinking, I might as well be drunk as fuck when I do. If you are under 21, the penalty for blowing a .01 is the same as if you blow a .25.

Luckily, since I was 18, the cops didn't call my parents to come pick me up. It was kind of sad to see, but also funny at the same time, that people that were partying hard and having a really fun time 30 minutes ago, were now sitting on the couch crying, waiting for their parents to come pick them up. I learned a few days later that the girl who was out on the deck smoking weed with us, after seeing the cops come through the front door, jumped off the deck. She ended up being fine, apparently only scrapes on her arms from landing in some bushes on the ground.

I intended to keep this drinking ticket a secret from my parents, which meant that I would have to go to the alcohol classes without them knowing. I ended up doing this perfectly, taking care of all the things I was sentenced to do, with just one minor fuck up. A day or two before I was going to go with my dad to Florida for a vacation, I had just went to the courthouse and turned in all of the paperwork, proving that I took the alcohol classes and paid the fines. I ended up leaving the ticket inside my pant's pocket, and gave it to my mom to do the laundry. My mom always checks the pockets of my family's pants or shorts to make sure nothing is in them before she washes them. I was a little paranoid the entire trip in Florida, because I was trying to remember where I had put the ticket. When my dad and I arrived back in Colorado, my mom called my dad and told him that she really needed to talk to him. I pretty much knew at that point that I was screwed. When we got back to my house my dad showed me the ticket.

Dad: What's this?
Me: I was at a party one night and I had a few drinks, and the cops came.
Dad: When do you have to go to court?
Me: I already did. I took the classes, and everything is all done with.

My dad was pretty chill about it, not really caring. I guess he would have felt like a hypocrite if he got pissed at me, seeing that he was 12 years old when he started drinking. The class that I was forced to attend was typical drug and alcohol bullshit 101. We watched video's claiming that if you do LSD even one time you will never be certain of anything ever again. The people that campaign to try and get kids not to try drugs will say anything in order to scare kids into not doing them, even things are just flat out not true at all.[81]

## SECOND OFFENSE

It was the NCAA Final Four Championship game in 2009 when this story took place. I was hanging out with Donnie in his dorm room and we crushed a handle of vodka between the two us. I was black out drunk and for some reason decided to walk back to my dorm room, which was about a mile to a mile and a half away. I was so fucked up that I forgot to put my glasses back on. Donnie's roommate offered for me to sleep in his bed, but for some reason I chose not to. There are only a few things that I remember from that night. First was walking along a sidewalk leading back to campus when a police officer pulled over to the side of the road where the sidewalk was.

Police Officer: Are you drunk?
Me: Yes, I am!

Apparently, I was stumbling so much that it attracted the attention of a cop just driving along the street. I remember getting inside the cop car and the officer took me to a drunk tank/detox place. They took a mug shot of me and right as the person took the picture, I put on a big smile like I thought it was kind of a funny situation that was happening to me (interestingly also, they let me where my red hat when taking a picture of me, although I suppose they just allow it because it is not an official police type mug shot). The next morning an officer woke me up at around 6:00am and told me to blow into a breathalyzer. I blew a .16, which means that four to five hours before that when I got arrested, I must have blown at least somewhere in the .20 range. I started talking to the other people that were in the drunk tank with me and told them the story of when I peed in the Chinese Restaurant supply closet (a story I discuss later in this section). They laughed. It took me all the way until 4:00pm to finally blow a .00 on the breathalyzer, which, until you are completely sober, they do not release you. It was one of the longest days of my life. I just sat there all day reading magazines and talking the other people in the detox center. One woman I talked to said that when she got arrested, she blew a .40 (I don't think she would make up something like that if it wasn't true). The conversation with the woman who checked me out of the detox center went something like this.

Woman: Are you on any medications?
Me: No.
Woman: Are you allergic to anything?
Me: Yes. Puppies and kittens.
Woman: Would you please not crack your knuckles, it makes me nauseous.
Me: Sorry.

She gave me the underage drinking ticket and I left the facility. I called Donnie and told him what happened and that I had to go back to his dorm to get my glasses.

The more misdemeanor offenses you get, the more fucked up your situation with the law becomes. With my first offense, all I had to do was attend an eight hour class. With my second offense I had to attend a 24 hour class and do 24 hours of community service. It turned out that when you go to your court appearance, you have to sign up for community service with one of the court clerks. I did not do this and for the next two to three months after I was sentenced, I unknowingly had a warrant out for my arrest. I did my community service at the university library, mostly vacuuming and cleaning the bookshelves. It sucked hardcore but was better than the community service that the court helps you get, which mainly consisted of hard physical labor. The 24 hour class I took was 12, two hour classes, that had other minor offense degenerates. The highlight of the class was when we sat in a circle and had all the other people go around and tell the person who was the topic of discussion, what you thought about them as a person. Throughout the class I developed a reputation as a psychonaut/acid head, and all the other people in the class praised me for being a cool person who provided great insight into how much psychedelics can alter your perception and give you wisdom.

Girl In Class: When you told us about the knowledge that you gained during your mushroom trip it made me want to try mushrooms.

Everyone in the class laughed and the counselor was chill enough to understand that kids in their early twenties were passed the age in which you can manipulate someone into not trying drugs by telling them lies about what they do. The majority of people who have actually done the drug that they are belittling, would know straight up that that person is full of shit, and so they figure they might as well just stick to middle school kids to tell their lies and bullshit propaganda.

## MY FAKE MYSPACE PAGE

When I was around a freshman or sophomore in high school it was just the beginning of the social networking era. This was before Facebook became popular and so many people joined Myspace. My first impression of Myspace was that it was just a website for Emo's. I used to rip on people in my class who said they had a Myspace page, saying it was fake as shit (what I think about Facebook and Twitter as well). One of my friends, "Andy" used to laugh when I made fun of people for having a Myspace, but little did I know until I looked into it, he had a Myspace page as well. It is a known fact that Myspace is filled with sexual predators, so I came up with an idea that would show the people in my class that I really didn't give a fuck about social networking. I decided to create a Myspace page in which I would present myself as a sexual predator, or "pedophile", and fuck with everyone in my class that had a Myspace page.

I used a fake email address and set up the account. I let a few of my close friends in on my idea and they thought it would be a funny. A friend of mine, "Timothy" sent me a picture of an old man with two girls kissing him on the cheek and I used that picture as my main account photo. I filled in my account information, such as my favorite activities and interests and created the account in the creepiest way that I could. I wish I could write about what I wrote on my account, but Myspace has changed since 2005 or 2006 when I created it and I can't access it anymore on my account. However, if you want to see the page I created, it is still online. Just go to www.myspace.com/iloveteenbodies. You can see the account picture but none of the information I posted is available to see.

I began to fuck with people that I knew in my high school. Sending them creepy messages in which I came across as a pedophile. None of the people I sent messages to responded, however, there was one girl I sent a message to in my class, "Clara", in which, after reading my message, immediately told her boyfriend that some creepy child stalker was trying to contact her. Considering all the people I fucked with, it is amazing that nobody reported me. I think I even sent a message to the main person of Myspace, "Tom", who is everyone's friend when you create an account, but he never responded. Eventually, after messing with some of my friends, I told them who I actually was, and they added me as a friend. I put my name as "Freddy Johnston" and I have nine friends. However, there is one thing that happened to me that I found to be completely epic.

I logged onto my account one day and I found that I had received a message from a porn star named Julia Bond. I think she knew that I was just on the website to fuck with people (because the information that I wrote on my account was so ridiculous I doubt she thought I was the actual person I tried to present myself as). We exchanged a couple of messages, and I did the best impression of a sexual predator that I could come up with. This is a brief summary of the messages we exchanged:

Julia: Hey Freddy, are you looking for a good person to fuck?
Me/Freddy: Yes, I am, but you are a little too old for me. I am not that attracted to people over the age of 15.
Julia: I don't think you are an actual pedophile. I think you just want some attention from someone who is willing to fuck you.
Me/Freddy: I'm looking for attention from younger people. Maybe if you were ten years younger I would try and get with you, but honestly, if I did try and have sex with you it wouldn't work. My penis only gets hard for prepubescent children. Do you know anyone that fits that description that I might be able to fuck?
Julia: You mean fuck you like this? I'm used to it.

Attached to the message in which she said, "You mean fuck you like this? I'm used to it", there was a picture of her having sex. I laughed at the idea that I was communicating with an actual porn star and that she was legitimately trying to get me to play along with her antics. I then wrote back:

Me/Freddy: This is an interesting picture. Although I am fairly unfamiliar with this type of sexual activity. The only sexual action that I know of and have engaged in is little boy on man, or man on little boy.
Julia: Oh, Freddy…

That was the last message she ever wrote to me. I guess she thought that it was a lost cause to try and break me from the game I was playing. She is a decently hot woman, but I would be damned if I let some slutty siren mess with my identity as someone who is supposed to stand firm as a sexual predator. The last thing I can remember as to the impact that my Myspace account had on some of the people that I knew in my high school, was that I fucked one time with a kid I knew who told all of his friends about my account. His first impression was, "Holy shit, it's a pedophile!". When I came clean one day to him that it was just a joke, he friended me on the account and wrote on my wall (or whatever the fuck it's called (a message that everyone can see if they go to your account page)): "Pedophile! Pedophile!" My intention in creating the page was to make a statement about how easy and ridiculous it is to communicate with people that you don't even know on social networking sites and befriend people that you, in reality, have no idea who they are. When I was a kid (around 5 or 6), I had an account on "Kids Only", which was an AOL account set up for kid's that wanted to use the internet and email. I went into a chat room and asked if someone wanted to be my pen pal. Some random kid agreed, and we exchanged messages for a couple weeks until he told me that his parents wanted him to stop communicating with me immediately, probably because they thought I was some sexual predator. I was confused because I, at the time, had no idea that chat rooms and other networks used for social interaction on the internet could be used by child molesters.

My last efforts I ever made to mess with people was that one day, me, Brad, and Abe made up a fake Myspace page to mess with Timothy. We set up the account as a girl in her teens that wanted to become friends with Timothy because she saw him at one of our high school basketball games. After sending the first message he called us the night we created it and asked if we were just fucking with him. Of course, we denied it, but nothing really came out of it. Timothy eventually figured out what he were up to and got kind of pissed off. The final messages sent between us posing as the high school girl and Timothy went something like this:

Girl: I can't believe I thought I could be friends with you. You are just like any other asshole guy out in the world.
Timothy: Why don't you sit down nigga; and calm down.
Girl: Fuck you. I don't want to talk with you again.

The moral of the story is that, in my opinion, social networking sites make it too easy for people to gain the trust of people that they don't even know. Before I deleted my Facebook when I was a sophomore in college, I had around 300-350 friends. Of course, out of all those people, I was really only friends with about twenty of them. A lot, if not most people that have a Myspace or Facebook page, will meet some random person at a party one night and then the next day, friend them, only to never talk to that person again. A few years after I deleted my Facebook page, I decided to create another account to get pictures of my hot classmates for my spank bank. When I was on it I was sent a friend request from a guy who I had not talked to since middle school. I accepted his friend request and thought I would see what he was up to these days. After all, why would he want to be my friend if he had no intention of talking to me, right?

Me: Yo man, long time no talk. What have you been up to? Do you remember that one time in our middle school art class when you brought into class the "Kim Possible" porn?

Of course, he never responded. I think the obsession with friending people you don't even know stems from the fact that people who are on social networking sites just want to have another friend on their account to use as a statistic to show off to other people how many friends they have. Apparently, the more friends that people see that you have, the more they will think more highly of you.? I have no fucking idea.[82]

## TEACHER IN A PORNO

Before I tell you this story, I would first like to show you the impact of what I did had on years of students in the grades below me when I was in high school. When I was working at the car wash, several of my coworkers were kids that were seniors at the same high school I graduated from. I was in the class of 2008, and my coworkers were in the class of 2014, so when I was a junior in high school, the year that this story takes place in, they were in fifth grade. When working one day I was curious as to whether or not the high schooler's I was working with had heard about a rumor that I started. A rumor that, to this day, I believe is true. I asked two of the high schooler's:

Me: Did you guys ever hear about the rumor that "Ms. T" was in a porno?
High Schooler 1: Haha, I heard that. A lot of people talk about it.
High Schooler 2: My friend gives her son shit about it all the time.
Me: Have you guys ever seen it?
High Schooler 1: No.
High Schooler 2: No, I wish. I want to know what she does. Why, have you seen it?
Me: Yeah, I have. I was the one who started that rumor around the school.

They both laughed at this. I was fascinated that the rumor I started had such an impact on the people who attended my high school, at the time I was attending it, and with the people who attended it years later.

High Schooler 1: So, what does the porno show?
Me: Well it's only 45 seconds long, but you see her tits and……..

I then begin to laugh.

High Schooler 2: What? I thought it was a porno that was at least like 20 minutes long. What does she do?
Me: Well, basically, she takes her shirt off and stands in front of a bed. Lying on the bed is some guy. She goes over to the guy and ties him to the bed. After tying him up, she then bends down, ass first in front of the dude's face and…farts.
High Schoolers 1 & 2: Ah! What the fuck!?
Me: Yeah, it's pretty funny.
High Schooler 1: Are you sure it's her? How do you know for sure?

219

Me: Well at the beginning of the video when you see her take her clothes off and see a full body shot, it kind of looks like her, but you don't see her face very well. Then, at the end of the video, after she farts on the guy's face, the camera does a close up on her face. She looks into the camera and smiles. If it's not her, it is an exact clone.

On top of the fact that the woman in the 45 second porno video looks exactly like my high school teacher, there is also other things about her, like what she said in class, that gives me high confidence in saying that she almost for sure is the woman in the video. So here it is, the story of how I found out, and spread to my entire high school, that my high school teacher, Ms. T, was in a porno.

When I was a junior in high school, I was friends with some girl, "Amy", who was definitely into me, and who I thought was kind of cute, but I wasn't sure if I wanted to go out with her. I was looking at her Myspace page one day and came across a post that she did on someone else's profile (which means that everyone could see it). The post said something about her friend whose profile she was writing on, that she reminded her of farting. When someone farts, it reminds her of her friend. I was intrigued by this and the fact that I had never really thought of hot women farting as somewhat erotic. It started that I would just fantasize about Amy farting, but then got to the point that I would look up videos on the internet of hot women farting. It also didn't help that some of Amy's photos on her Myspace page were of her intentionally showing her ass to the camera and looking back towards it. I have since come across multiple photos from many girls who I know who do poses like this. Girls are funny.

I was surfing the web one day and came across a video on Metacafe.com that had the video title, "Sex Fart". I clicked on the video, and it showed what I described above: a woman tying a guy to a bed and then farting on his face. I couldn't believe what I just saw. Is it really Ms. T? It looks a shit load like her to the point that she would have to have an identical sister. Now, previous to me seeing the video, there were already a bunch of people who I knew of, myself included, that thought Ms. T was pretty hot. One of these people who thought she was hot, was my friend, "Ron". For about four or five months after I first saw the video, I kept it to myself. I wasn't sure who I would tell it to, or if I even wanted to tell it to anyone. There was the question of what I would say to people when they asked, "How the hell did you come across the video?" I didn't want to say, "Yeah I was intentionally searching for video's showing hot women farting and I came across it." (I have since learned that people being turned on by women farting isn't as uncommon as one may think.) Ron and I were on the high school tennis team together, and, as we were walking down to the courts for practice, the subject of Ms. T came up. We were talking about how hot she was, and I decided that if I could trust anyone with the knowledge of what I know, he would be a good person.

Me: Ron, there's something about Ms. T that I know, that I think you would find funny.
Ron: What?
Me: Well, I think, maybe, she might be a porn star.
Ron: Haha. Why do you think that?
Me: I saw a porn video that I think she is in.
Ron: Holy shit! You have to show me.
Me: Well, there is a thing about it that I think you should know.
Ron: What?
Me: In the video, she kind of.........farts on some guy.
Ron: Hahahaha.

I wrote down for Ron the link to the site. In the years since this happened (I think it was 2006 or 2007), they have since removed the video from metacafe. com, but you used to be able to access it by simply typing in google, "Sex Fart", and then pressing the "I'm Feeling Lucky" link. As of today, if you type into google, "Sex Fart Metacafe", it will be the first web page that appears in the search, but if you go to it, the video has been removed (unfortunately).

After watching the video, Ron agreed with me that it is probably Ms. T. At first, news of the video started with just me and Ron's group of friends. I wanted to keep the video on the down low, but Ron thought it was too epic not to tell other people. Of course, when my friends asked me how I found out about it, I just responded, "Me and my brother were looking at gross video's online (you know those video's like, "Two girls, one cup" that shows girls eating each other's shit, and then people recording their reactions to the video and posting them on YouTube) and we came across it." Now seeing that my attempts to keep the video a secret were in vain, I was talking to another friend of mine (someone not in my immediate best friends group though), "Todd" in one of our classes about Ms. T.

Me: Did you know that Ms. T is in a porno?

Todd: What? Are you serious?

Me: Yeah, just google "Sex Fart" and press "I'm Feeling Lucky" and it will take you to the website.

Todd: Haha! You know exactly how to get to it? I'll look it up tonight.

Me: Just be prepared for what you see.

Todd: What do you mean?

Me: You'll see.

The next day in class I asked him if he saw the video. He responded with a very enthusiastic, "It's her!" From that day forward, news of the video spread like wildfire throughout the whole school. Todd was in the popular group of kids, and, after having told them about the video, it went from person to person, grade to grade, throughout the whole school. One of my favorite quotes was told to me by my friend, Edwin, who overheard a conversation between two random people in the hallway.

Random Person 1: Yeah, apparently she farts on some guy.

Random Person 2: Really?

Do you remember that game where a person tells something to the person next to them, and that person then tells the same thing to the person next to them, and so on until it reaches the final person to see whether or not the same thing was said to the final person that started with the first person? Anyone who has ever played that game knows that most of the time the thing that the final person says has been changed either slightly or completely from the thing that the first person says. It was just in this way that the rumor of the porn video circulated throughout the school. I was at a Halloween party my senior year and the subject of the video came up with my friend Rick, and another person, "Ted".

Me: So, did you guys see the porn video that Ms. T is in?

Ted: Yeah, I have seen it.

Rick: That video is fucking weird. And the part when she farts on the guy's face is so gross.

Ted: Wait…what?

Ted was confused because he knew she was in a porn video, but he didn't know that she farted in some guys face in it. This would then mean two things: 1. Ted was lying that he saw the real video, or, 2. Ted saw another video that had Ms. T in it. The more the rumor travelled from person to person, the less people knew about what actually happened in the video, and that they thought it was just a regular porno. On multiple occasions the video was the topic of conversations between people in class. Still trying to cover my tracks as someone who would look up fart videos for pleasure:

Someone: Have you seen the porn video Ms. T is in?
Me: I almost puked when I saw it.

Thankfully, not that many people knew that I was the one who found it and spread the news to people. Another funny conversation in class:

Boy 1: Do you really think it's her?
Boy 2: It has to be her. It looks so much like her.
Girl: It's not her!

Apparently, Ms. T had a tattoo somewhere and the in the video you can't see the tattoo on the woman. This might be evidence that it indeed is someone else, but you can't rule out the possibility that maybe she got the tattoo after the video (how people who say she had a tattoo even know that she had one, I do not know. You couldn't see any tattoos on her when you just look at her with clothes on). What's funny about the above conversation is that it took place in Ms. T's class, at the beginning of class when she wasn't in the room yet. A friend of mine, Brad, had yet to see the video and when I spent the night at his house one night, I told him to look it up to see what he thought. When the video began, he wasn't convinced.

Brad: It's not her.
Me: Just shut up and watch the video.

Then, when the end of the video came on, I told him to pause it, right when she smiles into the camera. His face lit up like he couldn't believe what he was seeing.

Me: So, what do you think? Is it her?
Brad: ......maybe.

Unfortunately, it wasn't until I wrote this that I realized more evidence I could have gathered as to if it really was Ms. T or someone else who looked exactly like her. One of the questions I would ask if I could go back in time was, "when did you get your tattoo?" If she got it when she was in her teens, then it probably wasn't her, but if she got it recently, then that would completely leave open the possibility that the woman in the video was her. I was interested to know whether or not she may have been in other video's as well but looking her name up on google only came back with other people who have her name, and the things that were about her, were just school web pages. So, one day when I was a senior I thought that maybe she did porn with her maiden name and not the name that she currently has beginning with T. As part of a sociology project that I had to do for the class, I thought of a good way to ask the question. My project was on whether there are any noticeable differences in intelligence between blonde and brunette girls. In gathering information, I would ask girls, "do they have the fourth of July in England?" If the girl answered no, then that would count as a mark in favor of one group not being as intelligent as the other group (because of course they have the fourth of July in England, they just don't celebrate Independence Day like in the USA). So, I then asked Ms. T the following:

Me: What is your maiden name?
Ms. T: It's T----. Why do you ask?
Me: I'm doing a project dealing with the difference in intelligence between blonde girls and brunette girls and one of the questions I have is whether or not girls with different hair know what "maiden name" means.
Ms. T: Oh.

So, unfortunately, her maiden name is the same as the name she currently has. It may seem that, besides the way she looks, there really isn't all that much evidence in favor of her being the woman in the video. However, I have talked with multiple people in my high school class that have told me of things that she has either said to them or done that would make it seem like she is kind of a nymphomaniac. For example, take the following conversation I had with a friend on my tennis team.

Tony: Ms. T is kind of a freak.
Tennis friend: I think she likes me. She just seems sometimes to come onto me.
Me: You know she was in a porno right?
Tennis friend: Holy shit are you serious?
Tony: Yeah. And there was this one class conversation where we were talking about the difference between happiness and pleasure and she said, "They say pleasure brings happiness, but I masturbate every day and I'm not happy."

Tennis friend: That's fucking crazy.

Upon reflection I'm not sure whether I regret keeping the video a secret or not. One of my friends, "Eddie" used to work with Ms. T's son at Walmart and after asking her son whether or not he knew his mom was in a porno, the kid just shrugged his shoulders like he had heard it hundreds of times before. Although the video has been removed from the internet, you can still see some photos of the woman in the video if you put into google images, "Sex Fart Metacafe." The photos that have the words, "Set Loose" at the bottom of the image are the pictures of her in the video. I believe, "Set Loose", is a hilarious depiction of the video. Which I have masturbated to on multiple occasions. What is wrong with me?[83]

Disclaimer: DO NOT (as of 12/8/21) try to look up the video on any search engine, unless you like to see people shitting on each other.

## THE XBOX VIDEO CAMERA SEX STORY

When I was a senior in high school, a big thing in the video game world was having an XBOX video camera so that you could see your friends when you play games. The most use me or my friends ever got out of it was playing UNO on XBOX Live. You can even have chat parties where eight or more of your friends can all hook up their cameras. One my favorite things to do with friends was to play UNO and smoke pot as we were playing. On one occasion we were in a game with a guy named, "Blazer4Life". He was smoking a blunt and so we smoked out of Brad's bubbler along with him, toasted our devices up to the camera, and blew smoke rings into the camera. Having the use of a video camera at your disposal can open up plenty of innovative ideas to work with.

One day in the morning after Frank and Rick spent the night at my house, we got an idea. Rick had a booty call that he was hooking up with for several months and, not really giving a shit about her or her privacy, decided to set up his XBOX camera while they were having sex. We all thought this would be a great idea, so we invited Brad over as well to watch the action. Rick got to his house about twenty minutes before the girl showed up and set up the camera. He had a TV in his living room, where there was a couch that he sat on to play XBOX. He set the camera up with a perfect shot of the couch that they were going to hook up on. He had the TV shut off, with the XBOX on to make it inconspicuous to the girl that she was about to have sex on camera. She got to his house, and they began to hook up. We told Rick to keep his boxers on because we didn't want to see him naked, but he chose to go full nude. The girl was full nude, and she was riding him for about five minutes when I decided to give Rick a call. While he answered my call he told the girl to go out of the room, making up a story that his brother might come in the house any minute.

Rick (laughing): Yo, what up.
Me: Yo dude, the camera is a little off. You should tilt it a little to the right to get a better shot.
Rick: Ok. Tell me when it is good.

Rick adjusted the camera until it was in a better position to capture the action.

Me: Ok that's good. Oh, and by the way, epic so far bro.
Rick: Haha.

Brad showed up in the middle of coitus and the three of us just sat there laughing our asses off. Eventually it got old and we decided to stop watching it. The girl was kind of hot, but nothing special, and there is only so much you can watch of your friend having sex. It should be noted before I continue, that the girl he was hooking up with was a total slut and by the time she was a sophomore in high school, had either fucked or blown at least twelve guys.

A couple years later when I was a freshman in college, I decided that I wanted some ass and this girl presented a good opportunity. At the time I had never met her, never spoken to her, and she didn't even know that I existed. I decided to hit her up on Facebook with a poke, and, just to show you how fake Facebook is, she poked me back. I decided to send her a message and a friend of mine who knew about her slutty ways came up with a perfect in. The message went something like this: "Can I see the picture of your snatch that you sent to Peter's cell phone?" She responded saying that she didn't know how I knew that but that I better watch out who I tell that to. Unbeknownst to her, Peter had already told half of the school. I eventually got her phone number and we began to talk. Now, let it be said, I completely regret what I did next, and in a way, I feel like I kind of betrayed Rick, but at that point in my life all I wanted was to get laid and I thought if I was truthful with her I could get some. I ended up telling her that we videotaped her and Rick having sex. She was a little more than pissed off, but she promised me she would not say anything. True to form of most girls that say they can keep a secret, she ended up confronting Rick about it with a text saying, "I know what you did last summer." Rick didn't really care that I told her, and he actually thought it was kind of funny. My attempts to fuck her ended up failing miserably and I eventually gave up. But just to show you how much of a skank she really is: a couple months later she texted Rick saying that she would be down to hook up again and to call her whenever he wanted. Some girls like being treated like they are worthless I guess.[84]

## MASTURBATION CHRONICLES

The best birthday gift I ever received was at my 13th birthday party. I had five or six of my friends over and we were all in my hot tub. The subject of masturbation came up and I had yet to at that point in my life ever masturbated. I had been around my friends when they were jacking off (from the time you are in middle school up to freshman or sophomore year in high school it was just a normal thing (I think for most people to) for friends to sit on a couch next to each other in front of a TV or in front of a computer and jack off) plenty of times but didn't really understand what they were doing. One of my favorite stories was when five of my friends were all in the same room and Brad and Donnie were jacking off to some porn on Donnie's computer. Brad ended up cumming all over Donnie's computer, and, so enraged by what just happened, Donnie went ape shit and chased us all around his house with a paintball gun.

So, while all my friends were in the hot tub, I was introduced to the way in which one masturbates. The first time I achieved orgasm was with all my friends in the hot tub and I thought, "holy shit, this is fucking awesome." An hour later we were all down in my basement, watching the nude scene in Titanic, and jacking off. Little was I to know that this would start a very interesting career I have had with masturbation.

The first thing I ever masturbated to was the pictures of the "Hookup" skateboards. My parents had a filter on the internet, and I had no access to any porn. Gradually it built up to some anime, and then Sports Illustrated Swimsuit editions. However, when I was a sophomore in high school, I began to notice that it would be kind of nice to jack off to pictures of my hot classmates. I started with Myspace and then Facebook when that became popular. After I deleted my Facebook in college because I was sick of all the fake bullshit, a few years later I created another account for the sole purpose of friending my hot classmates so I could have access to all their pictures. I ended up keeping a Microsoft Power Point presentation with all my favorite pictures. I read some study, I think it was collegehumor.com, that said that roughly 20% of guys masturbate to pictures of their classmates. For some reason there is something cool about jacking off to hot girls you know.

In college I had to develop a way in which I could jack off in private. My freshman year roommate, Max, caught me jacking off once and I think it made him uneasy. I guess I know how he felt because I caught my sophomore year roommate jacking off and that was kind of weird (when I came into the room, I immediately saw him get up from his desk, shut his computer, cover his dick, and then climb into his bed and put the covers on). So, my solution: I would masturbate in public and private restrooms in the stalls. Of course, I would try my best to wait until everyone else was gone while I was doing it. It's very difficult to fantasize and achieve climax when you are hearing other dudes talk and piss. This worked out pretty well since it's better than having your roommates catch you jerking it. I think the most ridiculous thing I did was when I was sitting at a desk studying in the university library with other people around at nearby desks. I pulled out my power point presentation, being careful to make sure no one else was looking, and, right in the middle of the library, I rubbed my dick through my pants and came. Don't ask me why I did it, I was just horny.

When I started using stimulants in college, I noticed that masturbating while on them gives you a very euphoric rush. On top of making you hornier than you are when sober, it is fun to get it up, approach climax, and then stop, let it go down, and then beat off again. You do this several times until it gets to a point where you are able to get it up within ten to fifteen seconds, and then it no longer becomes fun anymore, and you cum. I would make a sport out of this jacking off somewhere in the neighborhood of 5 – 9 hours, only cumming once. My record is 21 hours which I would like to think is getting close to a world record, but then again with all the nympho's (or just kids bored out of their minds like me) out there who really knows. I'm not sure how many times I have cum in a day, something like seven or eight, which, even talking to my own friends, is not that much. It is important to understand if you attempt to do this is that you should always jack it with some sort of lubricant. I was on Ritalin once and beat off for about six hours, never once using any sort of lotion or anything (commonly referred to as, "dry dogging it"). By the time I came, I noticed that my dick had a kind of rug burn on it and was bleeding a little. I ended up getting a scab on my dick and was unable to jack off for as long as it took to heal. I have learned not to make such a sport out of masturbating anymore, considering that if you just cum once and be done with it, it saves you a lot of time to do something more productive.[85]

## THE STORY OF HOW I LOST MY VIRGINITY

At the beginning of my senior year in high school, the most I had ever done with a girl was peck kiss. I had not been to first base, second base, third base or home with any girl. However, there was one girl, "Heather" who I thought I had a legitimate chance to potentially round the bases with. I have to admit, I was not that physically attracted to Heather, but I was willing to make peace with that if I could get my dick wet. The biggest reason why I wanted to try and get with her is because she pretty much blew all of my friends and I thought I could be one of those guys to. I asked her to homecoming in my senior year and she said yes. After that we began dating. The physical relationship progressed fairly rapidly in the weeks since we started dating. Within the first week we made out a lot. By week two I had fingered her multiple times, and by week three we had oral sex. This all happened within the first to third week of October. Early November is when my birthday is, and so she thought it would be nice to have sex with me as a birthday present.

A week before my birthday we decided to have sex. She was a virgin and I was a virgin. She did a massive amount of research on what it is like to lose your virginity, such as placing a towel underneath the girl's body when you have sex just in case she bleeds. Never mind how she or I was going to explain to our parents why there is a towel with blood on it in the laundry basket, but I guess it's better than the bed sheets. We started the night by going from first to second, and then we decided it was time to have sex. We went with missionary position which I think is traditional for first timers. I had bought a pack of condoms a few weeks ago, but only two remained, because in the weeks leading up to that night I had used them to masturbate into (which is actually kind of nice since you can just cum freely without placing the other hand with the Kleenex on top of your dick (or, as one of my friends told me, you just cum freely and then afterwards rub your cum into the carpet)). I put the condom on and was ready to go in, when I then, for some reason, immediately lost my erection. It was still at half mass, so I tried to wedge it in, put it wasn't working. Since I had completely lost my erection, I thought if I got it up again with the condom still on it that would fuck with the ability of the condom to work properly, so took it off. She jacked me off for a while until I got it up again and I threw another condom on. I then tried to go inside her again, and then, true to form with all the girls I have tried to fuck in the future that I have not been attracted to (which has been pretty much every girl I have tried to have sex with), I lost my erection again. Fuck! I didn't know what the fuck was wrong with me. I took the condom off and went to the bathroom to see if I needed to piss. Maybe that was fucking with my ability to maintain an erection? I couldn't pee because I was too self-conscious that Heather would hear the water splash as my urine hit the water. I took the two condoms, along with their wrappers and tried to flush them down the toilet. Heather asked what I did with the condoms, and I told her that I flushed them down the toilet. Hearing this, she immediately got up from the bed, went to the bathroom, and grabbed the condoms and wrappers from out of the toilet just as they were about to go down the drain. I wonder whether she would have done the same thing if I had pissed in the toilet before I tried to flush down the condoms.

Me: What the hell are you doing?
Heather: You're not supposed to flush condoms down the toilet. Didn't you know that?
Me: I highly doubt anything bad is going to happen.

I still think I had a point. I had flushed down condoms all the time when I used them to jack off. If a toilet is able to flush down things like huge shits, then why is not able to flush down condoms? Apparently, it fucks with the filtering process or something. Not that I cared, I would rather the filtering process get fucked up and not have my parents know about how it happened then have them find two unwrapped condoms in my trash can.

The night had then taken an unexpected turn of events. I had thought two condoms would be plenty for the first night we had sex. We would fuck once, and then maybe later in the night try it again. But now, as it stood, I was still a virgin, and I no longer had any condoms to use to fix that.

Heather: Maybe we should call it a night.

Me: Fuck! No, you wait here. I'll go to King Soopers and get some more. I should be back in fifteen minutes.
Heather: Ok.

I drove to King Soopers as fast as I could. I got the same condoms that I had just used previously, "Trojan Ecstasy". Apparently, they are supposed to feel like nothing is there. Not that I gave a shit, I just wanted something to have sex with and those condoms were just familiar for me, since I had masturbated with them a lot in the past. As I was leaving the store, a friend of mine, "Jason" who worked at King Soopers at that time saw me.

Jason: Hey man! What up?
Me: Yo. Nothing much.

I then showed him the box of condoms.

Jason: Nice.
Me: Yeah, I hope so.
Jason: Is this your first time.
Me: Yeah, it is.
Jason: Good luck.

When I arrived back at my house I was determined to not fuck around anymore. I got an erection, put the condom on and……eureka! I am officially not a virgin anymore. It felt different then I thought it would, but very nice. Heather told me to go slow and I could tell it was somewhat painful for her. She had been fingered by me and other people I know probably dozens of times, but I guess my dick was the biggest thing that had ever been in her vagina. About thirty to forty seconds into it I realized I was about to cum. Fuck me! I had heard from people about ways to distract yourself from cumming to early, but none of them seemed to be working. Then, at almost exactly the minute mark, I came.

In five to ten minutes I was ready to go again, but this time Heather thought it would be better if she was on top, and that was fine with me. Upon reflection the only time she told me to go slower was the first time. After that she would always say, "deeper". I was able to maintain my erection again for long enough to get inside her. This time, within two minutes, I was ready to cum again. After I came, as my dick came out from her vagina, I noticed a white liquid foamy substance that was on the front of her vagina, as well as all on the outside of the condom. I wasn't sure what to think. Is this just the residue from

the combination of the lubrication on the condom with her vagina, or.......
or, fuck. Did the condom break? I immediately begin to freak out. I jam two
of my fingers into her vagina and when taking them out, the white substance
is covered on them. I get off the bed and begin pacing around my bedroom,
naked with the condom still on trying to figure out what to do. I took an
alcohol class one time in college for getting an underage drinking ticket, and
a girl in the class told me that whenever she and her boyfriend would have sex,
right afterwards they would put the condom under the sink and fill it with
water to make sure that the condom didn't break. I wish I would have thought
of that just to be sure, but at the time I was just flipping a bitch.

Me: Holy shit. Goddammit. What the fuck are we going to do? What if
you get pregnant? I'm fucked.
Heather: I'll get an abortion.
Me: Fuck!

I was at the time very pro-life and the idea of her getting an abortion was
unsettling. But just like my high school civics teacher said, "you may be prolife, until you get your girlfriend knocked up." He had a point, but at the
time I was just trying to figure out what else I could do. I went down into
the basement to my older brother's room to get some advice. He was playing
video games as I came into the room.

Me: Hey man, could I talk to you.
Brother: Sure.
Me: So, I just had sex with Heather and the condom broke. What do you
think I should do?
Brother: You did not just have sex.
Me: Um…yeah, I did, and the condom broke. So, what do you think I
should do?
Brother: I don't know.
Me: What if she gets pregnant?
Brother: There's that plan B pill that people take to prevent getting
pregnant.
Me: Yeah, but isn't that kind of like aborting a fetus?
Brother: Well would you rather have that or have a fucking kid?
Me: Ok.

I went back upstairs to my room and told Heather about the plan B pill. She said she had heard of it before and that she will go to a Planned Parenthood clinic tomorrow. Since we knew she was getting the plan B pill soon, we decide to have sex one more time (who cares if the condom breaks this time, she is getting the pill anyways).

In the next few weeks we had sex a few more times. The condoms never broke but Heather was so paranoid about getting pregnant that she went down to Planned Parenthood and got the plan B pill the day after each time we had sex. I was proud that the last time we had sex I lasted roughly 30 minutes, albeit that I lost my erection multiple times during it. But when she started blowing me (with the condom on), I would get it back up again. She was kind of a nymphomaniac. That is, a nymphomaniac that is new to sex. I found it very annoying that she was so paranoid about getting pregnant and decided that I was going to break things off with her. She was pretty devastated, but I didn't really care. She was a freak in my view of her and what happened after that made me realize just how glad I was to not be dating her anymore. The night I broke up with her, she called one of her friends, "Alexandria", and had roughly the following conversation:

Heather: Psychotic Logician just broke up with me! And on top of that I think I am pregnant!
Alexandria: You're pregnant?
Heather: Yeah, I think I might be. But that's not what is important. What's important is that he broke up with me.

I talked to Alexandria a few weeks after that. She was confused that me breaking up with Heather was worse than her being pregnant. I agreed. But what was far worse was that, Alexandria, after talking to Heather, told all of her friends, which in turn told their friends. Within a week I had people coming up to me in the hallways:

Random Person: Yo dude. I heard Heather's pregnant.
Me: No, she's not pregnant. She's just a psycho.

I never really spoke to her again after that. She would call me and try to hang out with me, but I was just done with that girl. I was 18 at the time and told her I loved her. I of course was confusing love with the feeling of being horny. Some people choose to wait until they are married to have sex or just wait for the right person because they want it to be a very special time. The story of the time when I first had sex was something that the people who wait for the special person or special time dream about in their nightmares. Upon reflection it was special in one way: that I ended up not fathering a child.[86]

## HOOKUPS WITH WOMEN IN MY LIFE

I have hooked up with six girls in my life. These hookups have ranged somewhere between first base to home. I have a rating system for women that ranges instead of the traditional 1-10 scale that most people use, I use a 1-12 rating scale. The lowest/least attractive girl I have ever seen in my life is around a 4 (a 1-3 would have to be such an ugly girl (inside and out) that it would make a 9-12 be infinitely hotter in relation to her (I actually really don't think a girl like that exists)). I have only seen three or four elevens in my life, and the rating of a twelve belongs to only one girl, who holds the title of the most beautiful girl I have ever seen. The hottest girl I have ever hooked up with has a ten, and all we did was her giving me a hand job and me fingering her. We were both very drunk and I think there were only two reasons why she hooked up with me: 1) She knew I was into her and, based on what I have learned from women in the past, is that if you are into a girl and she knows this, this will make her somewhat more attracted to you. They are attracted to the fact that you find them attractive and this matters to them. This differs from men in that even if a man knows that a woman is attracted to him, if he is not attracted to her inside or out, the fact that she is into him does not make a difference at all to how he feels about her. 2) She saw a few weeks earlier at a high school party that we were both at, that a girl who was a total slut, wanted to hook up with me. I was not attracted to the slut in any way, and I did my best to avoid her whenever she tried to make advances towards me. However, what matters is the fact that because the girl who I hooked up with saw that, what she considered to be kind of a high up girl in attractiveness was into me, this made her more into me. Just like the first point I made above in things that matter to women in reference to men that they find attractive, the second point I just mentioned does not matter to men at all. A man could see that another man is into a girl, and this does not matter to him at all. Either the girl is hot, or she is not. Keep these two points in mind as I describe the following sexual encounters that I have had.

When I was a freshman in college, over winter break I was hanging out with four of my friends on New Year's Eve. Three of my friends were seniors in high school, and the other one was a freshman in college like me. After crushing a handle of vodka between the five of us, we then made a pact to all have sex with a girl in the month of January. In the story I am about to tell, I held up my end of the pact, while the other four failed. This pissed me off because in order to hold my end of the pact up, I sacrificed my dignity in order to do it.

In the middle of January, when the spring semester started, a friend of mine, "Donnie" invited me and some other friends up to his cabin in the mountains to party. The problem: there were five or six of us guys, and one woman. And the problem concerning the woman: she was fat and ugly. If I had to put a ranking on her according to my rating scale, I would say that she was roughly a five. We began drinking, and, for some reason and I don't remember what that reason was, the girl and I started talking and I could tell that she was kind of into me. Apparently, she was kind of drunk, because according to Donnie (who used to be fuck buddies with her in the past), only one or two beers gets her wasted. I only on the other hand, was not drunk at all, nor was I tipsy (I think I had two or three shots and that was it). As we were talking, she started making advances towards me and the next thing I knew we began to start making out. As this was happening, I knew that this was not something I wanted to do, but I kept at it. The next thing I knew she had her hands down my pants and my hands were down her pants. I was thinking about stopping what was happening right then and there, but then I remembered the pact I had made with my friends. Fuck! Seeing that I am not that big of a ho-runner/player and don't hook up with women very often, I figured that this would probably be my only shot at fulfilling my end of the agreement. As everyone else was passing out, the girl and I decided to have sex. For some reason it didn't matter to me or her that I didn't have a condom, but she was content with me just to pull out. I got an erection and tried to put inside her. Just as this happened, I immediately lost it.

Me: Fuck, I just lost it.
Girl: You had it up a second ago.
Me: Hold on.

I then started jerking it to try and get it up again and when that failed, she started jerking me off. I finally got it to a half chub and that was good enough to get it inside her. Once inside her, I got it up completely. It was kind of weird fucking a girl that weighs at least fifty more pounds than you, and when I was humping her, only half of my dick was able to penetrate her vagina, because her waist was so large that it kept my body from fully being able to hump her balls deep. A few minutes into it, she for some reason decided that she no longer wanted to have sex and so she took my dick out of her vagina. This confused me because she didn't convey to me in any way (like talking) that she wanted me to stop. So, once she took my dick out, I immediately put it back in. Ten to fifteen seconds later, right as I was cumming, she took my dick out again. I came on the floor between her legs. I thank whatever god's may be that she did this because, for some reason, I was not thinking at the time at all that I should pull out. If she wanted to keep having sex and not want to stop, I probably would have cum inside her, which would have presented a much bigger problem for me on top of the problem that I now had ever since this incident took place, mainly, the memory that I would have to carry with me for the rest of my life that I had sex with such an unattractive girl. After I came (which I am pretty sure she was oblivious to), we were lying on the floor and she took my arm and put it around her body, as if we were going to cuddle and sleep next to each other for the rest of the night. That was not happening. So, I got up, went to the opposite side of the room, and went to sleep. The girl and I did not speak the next morning, or ever again, except for one time when I went to the bank to deposit a check and she was the teller. I don't remember what we said to each other at the bank, but I know it was short and pointless. I was kind of paranoid that I may have an STD, since I didn't wear a condom, and, according to Donnie, she gets around a lot. She is what most guys would call a, "practice girl", or "hood rat."

Me: When I fucked her I didn't wear a condom. Do you know if she has an STD?
Donnie: I fucked her without a condom to. You're fine.

A few days later I sent my friends a message on Facebook telling them what happened and that I held up my end of the pact. They all thought the story was hilarious and said that I must have been really committed to my obligation to them that I would go so far as to fuck a fatty in order to make good on the agreement. When February came along, I was the only one of them who had sex the month before. I guess situations like this come along every once in a while, and, although in order to do it you must sacrifice a certain amount of self-respect, fucking an ugly girl really isn't that big of a deal.

I hooked up with three other girls after that in college. On two occasions, I couldn't get it up to have sex with them, and so we just settled for third base. On the third occasion I tried fingering her multiple times and she kept taking my hand away every time I did this, never explaining to me why. I learned from her friends a few days after that, that she was on her period, and that if she wasn't, she would have had sex with me. Not that it would have mattered, since there really only exists two possibilities for me when it comes to having sex with girls, especially girls that are a seven or below on the rating scale: 1) I won't be able to get it up. 2) I will come within two minutes.[87]

## THE TIME I WOKE UP WITH A BLACK EYE

When I was a freshman in college, I woke up one morning, feeling very shitty. I remembered the night before getting extremely drunk with Aaron and another friend, but I blacked out (as it usually went for me back in those days) and didn't remember what had happened the night before. I looked in the mirror and saw that I had a massive black eye. I called Aaron so that he could fill me in on what happened the previous night.

Aaron: We were watching TV and drinking a handle of vodka between the three of us when you decided to walk back to your dorm room to crash. You were slurring your words and tried to get up to walk a few times but kept falling down. On one of your attempts to stand up straight, you tried to gain your balance by walking around the room. You couldn't get your balance to stand up straight on both your feet, and in your attempt to do so, you started crookedly walking towards the door. You eventually started to run fast towards the door in order to stand up straight, and when you did this, you tripped over your own feet, and fell, hitting your face against the door knob, and knocking yourself out.

Me: Oh fuck.

Aaron: We were both laughing hysterically. We tried talking to you, but you just laid on the floor, unconscious. You finally woke up, not knowing what had just happened.

Me: How did I get back to my dorm?

Aaron: I helped you get back on your feet and you were able to walk, but still trying to gain your balance to stand up straight. We walked back towards your dorm and stopped on the way to talk to some people that were building a snowman.

Me: Please tell me I didn't fuck with the snowman.

Aaron: No, you were calm. You tried to talk to them, but they couldn't understand what you were saying. Once inside your dorm hall, you went into a person's room that is on the same floor as you. There were three or four guys and two girls. You kept telling one of the girls that she was hot, and started yelling, "I want to bang you!"

Me: Jesus Christ.

Aaron: After that we went into your room and you immediately passed out on your bed, without saying another word.

I decided to skip my classes that day, since I was so hung over, and didn't really want to have to explain to people what happened to my eye. I ended up missing an important test that day in my calculus class, and it kind of fucked me over in that class for the rest of the semester (I ended up getting a D in the class). Upon hearing from Aaron what happened that night I consider myself to be very lucky. Instead of my eye that I ran with full body force into the doorknob with, what if it was my mouth? I could have lost all of my front teeth, which would have sucked infinitely more than my eye.[88]

## BEING CRUNK: GOLFING AND JUMPING INTO A LAKE

Me, Ron, Edwin, and Frank all decided that it would be a good idea if we got completely hammered and high off our asses and went golfing. We got to the golf course in the early afternoon with a couple of joints and a bottle of Jagger. Frank and I decided to rent a golf cart while Edwin and Ron decided to walk. Since Frank and I had a golf cart and didn't have to walk, we were going to be the ones to get the most shit housed. The first couple of holes were uneventful, just smoking bud in between shots and taking swigs of Jagger every ten minutes or so. I was perpetually smoking cigarettes at the same time and my golf game was pretty shitty. We decided to only play nine holes because as we were playing, we came to the conclusion that since we were getting so drunk and high, eighteen holes seemed like an insurmountable task. I believe it was the ninth hole that Frank and I came up with an idea. My ball landed in the sandtrap and we thought it would be a good idea for Frank to drive up to the sand trap going as fast as he could, and me, being in the passenger seat, would then jump out of the golf cart as he was driving past it and dive into the sand. To capture the moment, he would be videotaping it with his cell phone while at the same time I would be videotaping it with my cell phone. Edwin and Ron thought it was a good idea to and they would be watching from about twenty yards away.

I put my cigarette out, took another swig of Jagger and smoked the last of the joint in preparation for the event. There were several more onlookers who were teeing off on the next hole close to the green that the sand trap was near.

Frank: Ready?
Me: Hell yeah. Time to rock.
Frank: Let's do it.

We had our cell phones in our hands as he stepped on the gas and accelerated towards the sand trap. I'm not sure what the maximum speed that a golf cart could go, but in our crunked out of our minds state, it seemed pretty fast. He passed by the sand trap, coming very close to driving the cart into it, and I jumped, headfirst into the sand trap, all while recording my first-person view, and Frank's third person view. I got up, pumped my fist in the air as several other golfers looking on just shook their heads. Edwin and Ron laughed and I'm not sure where Frank went with the cart, but it seemed to be fine. We then continued to putt and headed for the club house to buy some beer and get more shit faced.

At the club house I bought at least four or five more beers for each of us. This is a common thing that I do when I am drunk out of my mind: I buy the alcohol for my friends and random people I see at bars. I guess I am just a nice drunk like that. The guy at the club house who we were buying the beers from didn't seem to care that we were buying so much alcohol. He was obviously ignorant that Ron was 19 at the time and hence, couldn't legally drink. I then began to talk to random people. There was some hot girl driving the beverage and snack cart around the golf course and I asked everyone I came across if they knew anything about her. People just laughed and continued on their way doing whatever they were doing before I interrupted them. We finally see the hot girl and I go up and talk to her, but I don't remember how the conversation went. Ron was the most sober out of the four of us, and so he decided to drive us back to his apartment. However, he told us about a lake nearby that maybe we could go swimming in. Everyone was game for that and so we headed to the lake.

Once at the lake I was determined to swim. The first thing I saw was two people, a guy and a girl roughly in their early twenties who were sitting at the top of a cliff, at the bottom of which was the lake. So, I got an idea: I'll jump into the lake from the top of the cliff, only wearing my boxers. I went over to talk to the guy and girl.

Me: Yo, yo, yo. What's up guys, how's it going?
Guy: Pretty good, just chilling.
Me: What are your names? In case you're wondering, I'm shit faced right now.
Girl: Haha. I'm Catherine, and this is Darren.
Me: Nice to meet you. I'm Psychotic Logician. I'm here with some friends, but for some reason they haven't come over here yet.
Girl: Nice to meet you.
Me: So, did you guys go swimming? Did you jump from this cliff? Is the water cold? I am thinking about jumping in.
Guy: Yeah, we just finished swimming. The water is not that cold.
Me: So, is it safe to jump from the cliff? I don't want to fuck myself if I jump, if you know what I'm saying.
Guy: Yeah, we jumped from the cliff a couple of times. The water is pretty deep at the bottom so I think you should be alright.
Me: Cool. Fucking right, yo.

At this time Edwin, Frank and Ron come over to the spot where I am talking to the guy and girl. Edwin got the idea that he will videotape me jumping into the water.

Me: Aren't you guys going swimming with me?
Edwin: No, we're good.
Me: Pussies. Pussies. Pussies.
Ron: You're pretty drunk, man. Do you think you can swim?
Me: Of course I can fucking swim. Here take my clothes and make sure nothing happens to them. If I get out of the water and you keep my clothes from me, I'm gonna be a little more than pissed off.
Ron: Don't worry, your clothes are safe with us.
Me: Cool.

I then proceed to get undressed all the way down to nothing but my boxers. However, unbeknownst to me, and out in the open for everyone to see, my dick is hanging out of the front of my boxers. Everyone starts laughing, but me, being crunked out of my mind, do not understand what they are laughing at. So, I let it slide. Edwin, desperately trying to get the video camera on his cell phone to work tells me to wait a minute until he starts videotaping. The guy and girl are laughing hysterically. I finally clue in.

Me: What the fuck are you guys laughing at? Haha, I don't work out. Fuck you guys.
Girl: Just jump dude.
Edwin: Just wait a second.
Me: I don't give a fuck if the camera is working or not. Here I go.

I then jump off of the cliff, which had to be at least ten to fifteen feet high and land in the water. The water was cold but it was a warm day outside, so I didn't mind it. I then proceed to do a backstroke with my dick still hanging out for everyone to see. I swam in the water for about ten minutes and then decided I had had enough. While this was all taking place there was a group of about five people on a motorboat about fifty yards away near the middle of the lake.

Guy on motorboat: Hey you little bitch, what are you doing?
Me: What the fuck does it look like, I'm fucking swimming. You're a bitch. Don't call me a bitch when you are the one who is a bitch.
Guy on motorboat: Fuck you, I'll come over there and kick your ass kid.
Me: Good luck with that you fucking pussy. You're on a boat and I'm over here. Get fucked.
Guy on motorboat: Fuck it.

The only way out of the lake from where I was swimming was a rock cliff where there were boulders that you could climb onto to scale the cliff. I get out of the lake, dick still hanging out, and proceed to scale my way across it to get to a place where I could get back on dry land. Ron comes over to me.

Ron: I got your clothes. Hurry up.
Me: I'm trying. These fucking rocks are hard as fuck to climb on. Don't fucking bale on me.
Ron: We have no reason to take your clothes away from you. We have already had our entertainment for the day.

I put my clothes on and Edwin and Frank come over. I flip the people on the boat off one more time and tell them to fuck themselves. They ignore me.

Edwin: Goddamn it, I couldn't get the fucking camera to work.

Frank: Dammit, that would have been an epic thing to get.

We get back into Ron's car to drive back to his apartment when they tell me what they had been laughing about.

Ron: Your dick was hanging out for everyone to see. It was classic.
Edwin: Absolutely classic. I can't believe my camera didn't work.
Me: What the fuck? Are you serious? Why the fuck didn't you tell me. Did the chick see it?
Frank: Everyone saw it.
Me: I don't even care. I'm shit faced. Worse shit has happened to me.
Ron: You kind of have a tiny dick.
Frank and Edwin: Hahahaha.
Me: Fuck you. The water was cold.
Ron: Your dick was small before you got into the water.
Me: Whatever, I don't even give a shit right now.

We get back to Ron's apartment and I begin puking violently into his trash can. This would have upset him except he is used to this type of behavior with me, mainly, getting fucked up and puking. All of my friends are used to it. After a while I begin to sober up and Frank and I drive back to our home town. I don't remember how Frank was able to drive, seeing that he was shit faced and high as a kite as well, but the important thing is that we made it home. The lesson that this experience taught me was simple: if you are ever in a situation where you are with a group of people and go swimming, make sure your junk is not out in the open for the world to see. This happened to a friend of mine years later when he went into a hot tub at a party with a bunch of hot girls. The girls saw his dick and teased him about how small it was. Not that my dick is small, it's average. But who the fuck is anyone else to judge someone for their dick size? Especially girls. If girls really think they can legitimately comment on the size of some dude's penis, let's see you grow one and then it will be a fare conversation. If a dude comments on the size of a woman's breast in front of their face, then apparently they are an asshole. I have no idea.[89]

## MESSING WITH THE PIZZA DELIVERY DRIVERS

Every time I hung out with Abe at his house, we would always come up with pranks to play on the pizza delivery man. Here are three of the most notable things we did to fuck with the delivery driver.

## TRIP WIRE

One night we got the bright idea that we would set up a trip wire near his front door. Why we decided to be such blatant jackasses I do not know. If that weren't enough, I decided to dress up like a woman with balloons in my shirt as breasts and tell the pizza delivery man that if he wanted his tip, he would have to reach into my back pocket and get it. As the inspiration for this, I was to use a line from "Family Guy" in which the pedophile says to Chris, "I have a tip for you in my back pocket, but my arthritis. Why don't you reach in there and grab it for me?"

The pizza delivery man pulled into his driveway, and we waited by the front door window, ready to watch the evil plan we concocted. The delivery man walked up to the front door and about two feet away from it, we hear a "Whack!" We begin to laugh hysterically. We opened the door and right smack in the middle of his forehead we see a huge red mark. He wasn't able to put his arms forward to brace the fall because he was holding the pizza. He handed the pizza to Abe and then it was my turn to act.

Me: I have a tip for you in my back pocket, but my arthritis. Why don't you reach in and grab it for me?

The delivery man just stood there not knowing what to think. He was probably still recovering from the massive hit he just took to the head, and just stood there silently looking at me. Abe was still laughing hysterically.

Abe: Dude, just give it to him.

I then gave the delivery man a $1 tip. A small payout considering what we just put him through. About thirty minutes later as we were eating the pizza his home phone rang. It was the Domino's Pizza manager.

Abe's Mom: Abe! Dominos just called and they are threatening to sue you. You need to call them back and apologize immediately.
Abe: Oh shit. Ok.

He called Domino's back and talked to the delivery man. Luckily the delivery man was cool and said it was no big deal. This act of debauchery could have turned out to be a lot worse if the delivery man was more seriously injured. Lucky for us.[90]

## AXE AND LIGHTER

On one occasion Abe, Rick and Brad decided to set up a pretty dangerous prank. The pizza delivery man knocked on the door and right as Abe opened the door, Rick ran up to the door with a lighter. Right behind him was Brad, who held a bottle of Axe spray deodorant. Brad sprayed the deodorant and there was a huge flame, resembling a flame thrower that went right in the direction of the delivery man. Scared shitless, the delivery man dropped the pizza, went to his car, and drove off. He never charged them for the pizza, and, luckily, never reported them to Domino's management or the police.

## STEALING THE DOMINOS SIGN

When the pizza delivery man, distracted from his car by accepting the payment from Abe for the pizza, Brad went over to the delivery man's car, climbed onto the top of it, and tried to steal the Domino's pizza sign. He couldn't figure out a way to get it off, and as he was trying, the pizza delivery man was confused.

Pizza Delivery Man: Is there a reason why you are on top of my car?

Brad and Abe laughed as the delivery man then drove away.[91]

## THE TIME I PASSED OUT IN A DITCH

One night in my sophomore year in college I went to a party with my friend "Eli" and his roommate. The party was at some guy's apartment that he knew located about a half a mile off campus. We had pre-gamed pretty hard before the party and when we got there, I was already pretty smashed. It was a pretty small apartment, with roughly twenty people there, playing beer pong and taking shots. I took a few more shots and decided I wanted to play beer pong, however, the waiting line for people to play the game was long, so I just put my name on the list, grabbed a beer and went outside to smoke a cigarette. When I got out on the deck to smoke, I realized I didn't have any more cigarettes, so I asked if I could bum one from another guy smoking on the deck.

Me: Yo dude, could I bum a smoke?

Guy: Yeah, for sure. Here, take two. I hate to see someone go without smokes.

Me: Thanks G. So, do you know the guy whose house this is?

Guy: No, I'm just here with a friend.

Me: For sure. I want to play beer pong, but the goddamn wait is too long.

Guy: Well, all you can do in the meantime is just keep drinking.

Me: I agree.

This was the last memory I have of the night. Apparently, the pre-game drinks, combined with the shots I took and the last beer I remember drinking was enough to send me completely into black out territory. I woke up the next morning in my bed in my dorm room and the bed was completely soaked. I kept trying to tell myself that there was no way that I pissed in my bed, but my roommates kept giving me shit about it and told me that I most definitely did pee the bed. I had no idea what the hell happened that the previous night, but my first clue came from a buddy of mine, "Gerald", who lived on the same dorm floor as me.

Gerald: How are you feeling? You were pretty fucked up last night.

Me: What the hell happened? I don't remember shit.

Gerald: All I know is that you came back to the room at around two in the morning, being carried by Eli and his roommate. You passed out, and me, Eli, and his roommate all chilled and smoked a bowl. They said they had to carry you all the way back here from like a mile away.

So, clearly I got so shit faced that I couldn't walk or stand on my own. In order to fill in the night even more, I decided to call Eli.

Me: Yo, Eli, what the hell happened last night?

Eli: Jesus Christ, where the fuck do I begin.

Me: The last thing I remember was being at that guy's party and I don't remember much after that.

Eli: You came back into the apartment after you smoked and were acting completely belligerent. You kept trying to play beer pong and people were getting pissed off at you for interfering with the game. Then you puked in my friend's sink, and he got really fucking pissed. He grabbed you by your shirt, pulled you to the center of his apartment and yelled, "Ok, who the fuck brought this kid?" I said you were friends with me, and he told me that he didn't want you there anymore, so we had to leave. At this time, you were still able to walk so I asked if you would be fine to walk back to your dorm by yourself and you said yes. So, my roommate and I headed in the other direction back to our dorm (Eli and his roommate lived in a dorm hall that was located about a mile and a half off campus) when like forty five minutes later, just as we made it back to our dorm, I got a call on my cell phone. It was a guy calling me from your cell phone, asking if I knew a guy named Psychotic Logician. The guy told me that he found you passed out in a ditch with your cell phone in your hand. He tried talking to you, but you were completely incoherent. He looked at your cell phone and saw that you tried to call me like five times. He said that we should probably come and get you before the cops did.

Me: Holy shit. I don't remember any of that.

Eli: So, we turned around and found you lying in the ditch, no more than fifty yards from my friend's apartment. We tried to get you to walk on your own, but you just kept falling over so we had to carry you over our shoulders for like a whole mile to get you back to your dorm.

Me: Christ. Thanks for helping me, man. I guess I probably shouldn't get that drunk anymore.

Eli: It's cool. I was just pissed that we walked all the way to my dorm and then had to immediately walk back to get you.

Me: Was the guy who called you chill?

Eli: Yeah, he was way chill. He seemed pretty concerned about you and wanted to make sure that we were ok to walk back to campus carrying you.

Me: You hooked me up man. Anything I can do to repay you just let me know.

Eli: You definitely owe me one that is for sure. I'll let you know when that moment comes.

It's hard to make a list of the top five drunkest times I have ever been in my life but if I had to guess I would say this definitely ranks in the top five. Usually when I blackout I am at least able to still walk, stand up straight and talk to people. That night I couldn't walk by myself, and I couldn't talk coherently. On top of that I pissed in my bed. If it wasn't for the random guy who helped me, I would have either woken up in a drunk tank, or woken up in a ditch, having no idea where I was. Thank goodness for the kindness, generosity, and understanding of people who know what it's like to be fucked up.[92]

## SMOKING WEED WITH A HOBO

When I was in college, I would get black out drunk three to four times a week. How did I accomplish this by being under 21 and having no access to buying my own alcohol? I would walk around the houses that were near campus and find random parties. If the party was big, I would just walk right in no questions asked. If the owner of the house didn't know who I was, he would just assume that I was there with somebody he knew. If the party was small, I would just quickly sneak in, intake as much alcohol as possible in as little time as possible, then bail. There was one night when I did this that I came in contact with a very unique individual.

I was walking back to campus, drunk out of my mind and I got the munchies. The only problem was that I was dirt poor and had around ten cents on my debit card. I stopped by a local pizza place and asked the guy at the register if he could just give me ten cents worth of breadsticks. Unsure of what to do, the guy just gave me two breadsticks for free and called it even. I was happy with that and went outside to sit on the sidewalk and eat. When I got out to the sidewalk I saw a man, probably in his early fifties playing a violin and taking tips out of his violin case. Being as drunk as I was, I decided to engage the guy in conversation.

Me: Yo how's it going? I'm Psychotic Logician.

He ignored me and kept playing his violin. I was determined to talk to the man so I kept at it.

Me: Yo, how long have you played the violin for? My sister plays the violin, and she is pretty good. Do you think you are as good as her?

Man: I don't know. I don't know you or your sister.
Me: You seem pretty good. Sorry, but I don't have any money. If I had change, I would give you some but all I have is ten cents and it is on my debit card. You want a breadstick?
Man: You think you could buy me some cigarettes?
Me: No man, I'm sorry but I don't have any money. You can bum one though.
Man: Thanks.

I handed the man a cigarette and we continued to talk.

Me: So, what's your name?

Man: Do you know of any parties? I did some heroin a little while ago and I need something to help me deal with the comedown.

Me: No not really. I just came from some parties. I'm pretty drunk. But I do have some weed back at my dorm room, if you want you can come with me and we can get stoned.

Man: Do you have any Adderall?

Me: Yeah, I got weed and Adderall. Come on man, let's chill.

The man seemed content with this, so he packed up his violin and we began to walk towards my dorm room.

Man: What did you say your name was again?

Me: I'm Psychotic Logician. What's your name?

Man: My name is Gabriel. I'm the archangel Gabriel.

Me: Like the angel Gabriel from the Bible?

Man: Yes, that's me. I serve Jesus and I'm on this earth to help rid the world of evil.

Me: Oh shit, that's cool. Could I ask you a question then?

Man: Ok.

Me: So, is there really a heaven and hell?

Man: Yes, they are both very real.

Me: What is hell like? Is it as shitty as the Bible says?

Man: Hell is a horrible place. If I were you, I'd get good with God because you don't want to go there.

Me: What kind of people are there. Like who specifically?

Man: It's full of evil people.

Me: Yeah, but who specifically? Like I saw this one documentary called "Religulous" where one of the founding fathers, Thomas Jefferson believed in Jesus, but he denied all his miracles –

Man: Thomas Jefferson is in hell.

Me: Oh shit, that sucks.

Man: Are you sure you have pot and Adderall? I don't want you messing with me. To walk all the way to your dorm just to have you fucking around.

Me: Oh ok. Yeah, I'm just fucking with you.

Immediately as I said this he turned around and started walking the opposite direction.

Me: No man, wait. I'm kidding. I have all that shit. Come on, just keep walking with me.
Gabriel: Alright.
Me: So, are you homeless or something? Do you just get money from playing your violin?
Gabriel: Yeah, I live on the streets. Most of the time I play my violin on Pearl Street and just sleep there.
Me: I heard a story from a friend I know who said there is a guy on Pearl Street who drank a whole vile of acid and now thinks he is a glass of orange juice. He gets scared when people approach him because he thinks if they touch him he will tip over and break. Do you know him?
Gabriel: No, I don't think so.

We get to my dorm hall and, too drunk to make a sober call on whether or not this guy can be trusted in any way, I invite him in. My two roommates were both asleep when we came into the room. I look around my desk and find my bag of weed, and forget about the Adderall, which he never asked about again. I realize that I don't have anything to smoke out of so I wake one of my roommates up and ask if I could borrow his cheap plastic bong to smoke out of. Now picture this, my two roommates have just woken up, and they are looking at some sketchy homeless hobo who they have never seen before, standing their carrying a violin case in the middle of the room.

Me: So, could I borrow the bong?
Roommate: Sure, it's in my closet. Who is that?
Me: Oh, he's cool. His name is Gabriel. He's an angel from heaven.

My roommate just stares at me not knowing what to make of the situation. I grab the bong and Gabriel and I leave the dorm room to go outside to smoke. Once outside, I load the bong and we begin to smoke. Anyone who has ever smoked weed once they are in a very drunken state can attest to the fact that if you smoke just a few hits, it will likely lead to you getting a case of the horrible spins. I take about two or three hits from the bong and I start to spin. Spin very badly. We were sitting right outside of the dorm hall on the steps that people would go to smoke cigarettes at. There is a railing that has a place where you could sit while you smoke, and I laid down on it.

Gabriel: Hey are you ok?

Me: I don't know man. I feel kind of sick. I don't know if this was such a good idea.

Gabriel: You're fine just relax.

I then begin to puke over the rail.

Gabriel: Goddamn.

I don't really remember much of what we said to each other after that, being as crunk as I was, but I do remember one thing: there was a campus cop sitting in his car about twenty yards away from us. I just laid there near the rail, closing my eyes as I tried to deal with the world spinning around me as Gabriel continued to hit the bong. As sketchy of a situation as it looks like, some homeless guy who would probably get questioned by a campus cop just for being on campus, let alone five feet from a dorm hall, and me, an underage drinker puking his guts out. Luckily, the campus cop never got out from his car to question what we were doing. The last thing I remember was Gabriel pretty much carrying me around his back, leading me back to my dorm room, and after that he split, never to be heard from again.

The next morning when I woke up I noticed two things: the bong was missing, but my whole bag of weed (there was a decent amount in the bag, at least an eighth of an ounce) was sitting on my desk, untouched. The fucker stole my roommate's bong! So much for being a fucking saint. Here to rid the world of evil only to take advantage of a stupid nearly black out drunk college kid and steal his bong. My roommates asked me who the hell that guy was and why I trusted him enough to let him into our dorm room. I just responded that I was plastered and didn't know what the hell I was doing. But to me it didn't seem like that sketch of a thing to do. Why shouldn't I trust some random guy who I have never met and let him into a college dorm hall? Probably because this guy could have been anybody and who the hell knows what he might be capable of doing. My roommates told everyone else on my dorm hall and everyone was as confused as they were. My favorite quote from some kid on my dorm hall about the incident:

Kid: I heard you let some homeless guy into your dorm room.

Me: Yeah, I smoked a bowl with him and he stole my roommates bong.

Kid: I told a kid about it from across the hall and he told me to never talk to you again.

Me: Haha. What is the big fucking deal?

I'm just glad that the only thing missing was the bong. Of course, I had to pay my roommate back for the bong. Luckily it was just a shitty $15 bong, so I just paid him back with $15 worth of bud. I guess I should know better next time than to trust some sketchy hobo with access to a bunch of shit that he could have fucked me for. But I was drunk so I guess I get a pass.[93]

## THE SHIT STORY

When I freshman in college I was having trouble in my classes. From 6th grade to 12th grade, I maintained a 4.0 GPA, but my first semester of college I got a 1.9 GPA. One of the classes I sucked the most ass in was chemistry. I ended up getting a C in the class thanks to a Korean guy I was friends with who let me copy off him on the final. The second midterm of the semester I had studied a lot for and went into the exam feeling very confident that I would get a good grade on it. The exam was a multiple choice fill in the bubble type test where all the professor had to do was run the exam paper through a machine and it would read out the test score. So, an hour after the exam, the grades were posted on the class website. When I got back to my dorm, I went to check my grade and to my utter disbelief, I got a 55% on it. I was extremely pissed off and depressed so I turned to the one thing I knew would cheer me up: alcohol.

I had just bought a brand new, never opened bottle of Captain Morgan Spice Rum, thanks to my roommate, "Max" who had a fake id (actually it was just a regular id of some kid he knew that was over 21 who kind of looked like him). Right as I began to pour down some shots, two of my friends, "Abe" and "Aaron" came into the room and I remembered that we had planned to play racquetball at the rec center that night. I decided that it would be really fun to play racquetball shitfaced, so I began to drink heavily. Twenty minutes later, I had drank 9 shots, which was by far the most I had ever drank in so little a time before in my life. The racquetball game was rather uneventful. It just consisted of me being a drunken moron and sucking at the game.

After we left the rec center we decided to go back to my dorm room and chill. I was so drunk by this time that I became very emotional when I remembered that I had just failed an exam that I had worked my ass off to do good on. My friends tried to cheer me up as I started crying like a little bitch, but it was pointless, since

I was so shit faced. The last thing I remember before the following events took place was my friends leaving the dorm room and I went to sleep.

The next thing I remember was having these weird dreams where I was spinning and going completely vertigo in some strange setting. I woke up and felt extremely dizzy and still very drunk. I then became aware that something didn't feel right. The lower half of my body was soaked and drenched with something, and it was very uncomfortable. I then lifted up the covers and was overpowered by a horrible smell. I looked down and saw that the entire lower half of my body, from my lower abdomen, all the way to my feet, was completely covered in shit. Goddammit! I can't fucking believe I just shit in my bed! As I laid there trying to contemplate what to do, I became aware of one thing: I was going to have to shit again, and if I don't act now and do something, it was going to be in my bed again and that was not an option. I immediately got out of bed, and some of the shit that was on my feet made imprints on the floor of the dorm room as I raced out of the room. I ran down the hall as fast as I could and just as I was about to lose it all, I made it to the toilet. I begin to violently shit into the toilet. As this was happening, still dizzy and drunk out of my mind, I begin puking all over the bathroom floor at the same time. Just to give you an idea of how drunk I was: I was puking blood. I sat on the toilet for what must have been roughly ten to fifteen minutes, and when I stood up to walk back to my dorm room, I see that roughly 50 – 60% of the entire bathroom floor is covered in watered down blood puke. I got back to my room and see what I am dealing with: my entire bed is covered in shit, and there are foot trails of shit leading away from it. I roll all of my blankets and sheets into a ball, trying not to spill any of it onto the floor. I use them to wipe up the shit on the floor. I think I am ok at this point, so I take my extra blankets and use them as covers and go back to sleep.

The next morning Aaron calls me to see how I am doing, since the last time he saw me I was in tears over how much I sucked at college. I told him the story of what happened and he laughed hysterically. I decided not to go to any of my classes that day, because I was feeling not so much hungover, but very tired and depleted since I had just shit and vomited out all of the water and liquids in my system. I was dozing in an out of consciousness, trying to sleep but I kept on being interrupted by Max coming in and out of the room shouting, "It smells so fucking bad in here! What the fuck is that?" I never respond and just keep trying to sleep. After a while I feel good enough to get up and so I go out to the bathroom. When I get to the bathroom, I see that the entire bathroom has been crossed off with yellow, "Do Not Enter" tape and I see two or three cleaning people with mop buckets go in and out of the bathroom trying to clean it up. A while after that Abe and Aaron show up to see if everything is ok. They laugh when they see that the very top of the mattress where the sheets go over has a brown colored stain on it. They look on as I take all of my shit covered sheets and blankets and head down the hallway towards the stairs so I can wash them in the laundry room. As I pass the crossed off bathroom, I see a cleaning woman who, when seeing the blankets and sheets that I am carrying, begins to laugh and walk away.

This incident was one of the drunkest I have ever been in my life. I'm not prepared to say it was the drunkest I have ever been because I did not black out. In college when I would get drunk three or four times a week, I would drink way more than nine shots. I guess the difference between the times I have blacked out and this night was that I had nine shots in twenty minutes. That was by far the most I have ever drank in such a short span of time in my life. I think I definitely infringed upon alcohol poisoning, seeing as that I puked blood. The only thing I don't remember from the night was what I did with my shit covered boxers and socks. Did I take my socks off before or after I went to the bathroom? If I didn't then there very well may have been shit marks on the floor from me running to the bathroom down the hallway. I simply don't remember. Lesson learned: next time you decide to drink your problems away, spread out drinking over the course of a night, never within twenty minutes of finding out about your problem.[94]

## URINATING IN A CHINESE RESAURANT SUPPLY CLOSET

One night in college in my freshman year, I was friends with a guy I knew from high school, "Blake". Blake was in a fraternity, and he invited me to go to a party with him that one of his fraternity friends was having at his house. We got to the party pretty early before that many people showed up and I began to pregame by drinking shots of vodka and a few cups of a Gatorade and Everclear mixture. By the time people began showing up to the house, I was pretty drunk and kept drinking more beer from a keg. I don't remember a lot of what happened that night so I will just explain what I do know for sure from my memory of how the night unfolded and from what people told me.

I got into a conversation with a girl who was the goalie on the Universities Lacrosse team. I could tell that the conversation was headed towards me potentially hooking up with her, and, since I was not attracted to her in any way, I tried to avoid this. I told her I had to go to the bathroom and to wait until I got back. Of course, I had no intention of returning. Once in the bathroom, I was at the beginning stages of blacking out, but I do remember seeing one thing that caught my attention. I saw a book that was on a shelf inside the bathroom. The book was, "The 33 Strategies of War" by Robert Greene. I flipped through the book and thought it was awesome, so I decided to steal it. When I was finished using the bathroom, I tightened my belt and put the book between my waist and pants. I tried my best to avoid the Lacrosse girl as I headed to the kitchen to try and find Blake. Once in the kitchen I ended up running into three girls I knew from high school and one of the friend's roommates. I'm not sure what we did put they posted pictures on their Facebook page a few days later and it was just pictures of me with them looking like a Tucker Max wanna be (one of the pictures I was in showed me with one of the girls and I had my figure pointed towards me and the girl like Tucker Max does in the cover of his book, "I Hope They Serve Beer In Hell". At this point in my life, I considered Tucker Max to be a hero of mine and wanted to aspire to be like him. Upon reflection years later, I realized, although awesome, he is probably not the best role model to have.).

I left the party with the four girls and Blake, and we decided to eat at a local Chinese Restaurant that was open late. At this point I was black out drunk and the only memories I have are frames and pictures that you awake with of things you did the previous night (anyone who has ever been black out drunk knows what I am talking about. You don't remember whole series of events, but only specific 2-3 second scenes.). What I am recalling are the little scenes I remember, as well as what I was told the next morning when I woke up and called one of the girls that I was with that night to see what had happened.

We got our food at the restaurant and sat down at a table. I then decide that I need to take a piss. The only problem: the restaurant does not have a restroom (or at least not a restroom that they allow customers to use). I was being very belligerent at this point, stuffing a superfluous amount of food into my mouth and yelling at random people in the restaurant. I then get up and go to a door that I believe to be the restroom. Instead, it is a maintenance supply closet with brooms, a mop and other cleaning devices used by the restaurant staff.

I go into the closet and just as I am about to shut the door, "Emma", one of my high school friends says:

Emma: Psychotic Logician, you know that is not a bathroom right?
Me: Oh. Ok.

I then shut the door and then I have one of two mini scene black out frame memories of the night. I begin to piss over everything in the supply closet. Apparently, I was being very loud in the supply closet and the attention of everyone in the restaurant was on me. After finishing urinating on all the maintenance supplies, I walk out of the maintenance room and everyone in the restaurant is laughing.

Emma: You should probably go tell the owners that you peed in their closet.
Me: Ok.

I then walk over to the front counter and yell to the staff behind it.

Me: I pissed in your bathroom!

How they responded, I do not know. The last memory I have of the night is the six of us walking towards campus. I see a cab and decide that I would like to treat everyone to a cab fare to get us back to campus sooner. I try to hail the cab, but it does not stop. After failing to hail the cab, I then decide that I would like to go streaking. Right as we get on campus, I begin to take off my shirt and get my pants halfway down, when, I think, one of the girls tried to stop me. That is the last memory I have of the night.

The next morning, I woke up and was not sure what had happened. I called Emma and she told me everything that happened. Apparently, everyone at the restaurant thought it was one of the funniest things they have ever seen. Emma's roommate, "Mia", one of the girls that was with us that night, ran into a guy on campus who was at the restaurant that night.

Guy: Hey aren't you one of the people that is friends with the guy who pissed at the Chinese restaurant last week?
Mia: Yeah.
Guy: Haha. That kid was fucking sick![95]

# SECTION 7

# Abstract Mind Travel

## FORWARD

In the following section, I give my account of A) what I think about the issues and problems of the world (issues which people disagree with each other about), and B) what I believe to be a reasonable take on logic, enabling me to construct a theory of everything from pure thought. This pure thought can most readily be understood as the organization of concepts in such a way that all you must do in order to establish some truth, is examine the relations between these concepts. This theory of everything, along with the current issues of the world, are both constructed through simple logic, where you can even deduce the correct way of seeing the world, such that the issue can no longer cause disagreement over it, because the abstraction to truth or how something is, enables both sides of the issue to clearly see the correct understanding of the issue. The theory of everything deduction I make in this section is one of the last remaining philosophical papers I have left in my possession. The majority of things I have an opinion of in this book deals with the practice of philosophy as a discipline in itself, rather than actually writing papers through abstraction or logical deduction, which differs from the practice of philosophy (training oneself to think philosophically and rationally) by way of actually doing philosophy, rather than just talking about it. In my theory of everything, I do my best to reconcile a priori knowledge of the world, with the a posteriori knowledge of the world, exemplified by science. My attempt at arriving at an irrefutable knowledge of the world will show how human reason could give answers to most of existences major questions and problems. Stephen Hawking in his book, "A Brief History of Time" gives the following commentary on complete knowledge of the world: "However, if we do discover a complete theory, it should in time be understandable in broad principle by everyone, not just a few scientists. Then we shall all, philosophers, scientists, and just ordinary people, be able to take part in the discussion of the question of why it is that we and the universe exist. If we find the answer to that, it would be the ultimate triumph of human reason – for then we would know the mind of God." Previous to the examination of this theory, most (if not all) attempts at constructing a theory of everything revolve around the use of mathematics to explain the phenomena of nature (the forces, how it behaves, etc.). Although mathematics is extremely useful in how it can explain the universe by giving the scientist a precise measurement of the thing which the scientist is examining, it can say nothing about the knowledge of ultimate state of existence, because, as you rewind the universe back to its earliest stage at the moment of the big bang, the laws of mathematics break down and cannot by itself explain the ultimate truth of the universe. Einstein, when he came up with his Special Theory of Relativity, wanted to know how the real world operates and so then he must come up with a General Theory of Relativity to better understand the entire universe. Similarly, I don't want to just understand how our current universe works, but instead want to understand how all of existence works, whether existence does indeed have parallel universes and higher dimensions. If I have accomplished such a feat in what I write below, it will then be shown to the people in the world how existence operates, that doesn't base its truth upon an opinion or a mere hypothesis, but rather it would be an irrefutable depiction of reality, which everyone will agree with.

## ON THE THEORY OF EVERTHING DEDUCTION

## INTRODUCTION

What is written below is my best attempt to explain a scientific notion of a theory of everything about the universe, and existence in general. Contrary to popular opinion of physicists of the day (mainly, you can only understand the universe in a mathematical way), it is entirely possible for the universe to be known, and a complete theory of everything to be constructed, based off of a pictorial or descriptive way. Mathematics, I believe, can only go so far as to explaining the phenomena of the universe. This can be easily seen through that fact that mathematical knowledge fails in respect to understanding the smallest units of matter, as well as the largest units of matter (mathematics becomes too complex at the quantum level, and also becomes useless the further back in time one traces to the beginning of the universe because the laws of mathematics break down). It is in this respect that I have come up with a theory of logic in which all ways of describing the world can be understood through. Much of what I have written below is a logical deduction through pure a priori thought. I mention in this deduction the scientific world view, known through a posteriori explanation of the universe. In reference to empirical science, I show how some of the physics knowledge that has been made in reference to a complete theory of everything, are either correct at describing the universe, or incorrect ways of describing the universe. For example, the current understanding of the universe is that there only exists relative states of time and space (as was shown through Einstein's theory of general relativity), and not absolute states of time and space (as was thought by Isaac Newton). I show how this view of the universe is incorrect and I have made a best attempt to explain the mistake. I believe that I have solved major questions posed by scientists, and, since it is based almost entirely upon logical abstraction and deduction, the theory can, if properly understood, is irrefutable and hence, anyone who understands what I have written will see it as a proof, upon which anyone can understand. In this respect, I believe what I have written can be demonstrably shown as true, and all claims as to how the universe behaves, aligns with empirical observation of the universe.

1.  *Time is what differentiates how space is measured through observation. Space is how observation is measured through time. Relative observations of space and time are what differentiate how absolute time and absolute space relate to one another, within, and through the absolute state of rest.*

2.  There exists four fundamental ways of observing the universe (referring to an existence). 1) Relative to relative reference; 2) Relative to absolute reference; 3) Absolute to relative reference; 4) Absolute to absolute reference. These four ways of observing the universe are the four fundamental interactions that occur in the universe.

3.  There exists 5 dimensions in the universe. These are: 1) Relative to relative time and space; 2) Relative to absolute time and space; 3) Absolute to relative time and space; 4) Absolute to Absolute time and space; 5) Absolute absolute to relative space-time unity; The five dimensions of time and space become unified through the observation of a dimension of a space-time unity. *The 4 dimensions are to be understood as the four interactions of the relative time and space, and the absolute time and space together, as well as the fifth dimension of absolute relative space and the absolute relative space-time

unity.* Thus, the fifth dimension is the unifying observation of the four interactions (dimensions) of the universe, simultaneously.

4.  There exists three ways in which the relative states of space and time can interact, and two ways in which the absolute states of space and time interact. These are: 1) observation of space before observation of time; 2) observation of time before observation of space; 3) observation of time and space simultaneously; 4) absolute time and absolute space differentiated from each other; 5) absolute time and absolute space union.

5.  A relative observation of space and time becomes an absolute union of space and time when it is observed through the absolute state of rest. This is accomplished through both space and time being observed relatively in simultaneity, which then refers to the absolute state of rest. This is because when space and time are observed simultaneously, they form and interaction with the union of the absolute states of time and space, through the relative states of time and space being observed in an absolute way (an observation which is equivalent in its interaction to the existence of the absolute state of rest, this being mainly, not a differentiation between time and space, but rather a union of time and space (when an observation is made that simultaneously refers to relative time and space, this observation accords with the state of absolute rest, in that there exists no differentiation between time and space, and hence, absolute time and absolute space become unified).

6.  The weakest of the four interactions is the relative to relative interaction, and the absolute to absolute interaction. The strongest of the four interactions is the absolute to relative interaction, and the relative to absolute interaction. The organization of the universe to accord with these four interactions is the following: (weak force) and ((weak force) strong force) In other words, the weak interactions can be described through their existence within the strong interactions. Furthermore, in referring to a fifth interaction, we have the following: (((weak force) strong force) strongest force).

Interaction #1 (the first dimension): (weak force) (weak unification)

Interaction #2 (the second dimension): ((weak forces) strong force) (strong unification)

Interaction #3 (the third dimension): ((weak forces) strong force) (strong unification)

Interaction #4 (the fourth dimension): (weak force) (weak unification)

Interaction #5 (the fifth dimension): (((weak forces) strong forces) strongest force) (strongest unification)

7. The following is the causal process through which relative observations refer to absolute observations: (Relative observer ⇸ simultaneous observation of space and time ⇸ reference to the absolute state of rest ⇸ absolute time and absolute space unification.) The existence of the absolute state of rest provides a way in which relative states can accord with absolute space and absolute time. In this way, all relative observations of space and time can become synchronized together, to show which observation corresponds more with the absolute states of space and time. The more relative observations that refer to the absolute states of space and time (through the absolute state of rest), the more that the absolute states of space and time will begin to unify further and further together in the universe.

8. There exists two fundamental ways of observing the causal interaction between relative states and absolute states. These two ways correspond to the different laws of logic which are inherent in all the interactions in the universe, which can be organized through how they are governed by the smallest interactions and the largest interactions. 1) Relative to relative interaction (Ax ⇸ Ax). No observable reference to a state of existence apart from oneself; 2) Relative to absolute interaction (Ax ⇸ Bx). This observation establishes the differentiation between a relative state, and an absolute state. 3) Absolute to relative interaction ($\forall$x ⇸ $\exists$x); 4) Absolute to absolute interaction ($\forall$x ⇸ $\forall$x); 5) Absolute absolute to relative interaction ($\forall$x ($\forall$x ⇸ $\exists$x)).

9. The denoting of a particular interaction as either weak or strong are made based entirely upon how the interaction unified the absolute states of time and space, thereby giving a structure of the universe which can be seen as a unity of all ways in which time can exist (past, present, future), in alignment with all ways in which space can exist (relative and absolute).

Interaction 1 (weak (non-unified force)) unifies with Interaction 2 through the differentiation of observation (Ax → Ax (Ax = relative) becomes Ax → Bx (Bx = absolute)).

Interaction 4 (weak (non-unified force)) unifies with Interaction 3 through the differentiation of observation ($\forall$x → $\forall$x ($\forall$x = absolute) becomes $\forall$x → $\exists$x ($\exists$x = relative)).

Interaction 2 ((weak (strong) (unified force)) and Interaction 3 ((weak (strong) unified force) unify through a relative observation that differentiates absolute time and absolute space, simultaneously.

(Ax → Bx (relative to absolute)) ↔ (∀x → ∃x (absolute to relative)) = every possible way through which a relative observation can interact with absolute space and absolute time.

Interaction 5 (weak unification (strong unification (strongest unification))) unifies the four interactions through the simultaneous observation of all four interactions through the absolute state of rest ((∀x ↔ ∃x) ∀x)

10. The relative to absolute interaction and the absolute to relative interaction are two interactions which are capable of being described by the inverse of how an absolute state and how a relative state can exist and form an interaction. Hence, they are different aspects of an equivalent interaction. Because these two interactions invoke different laws of logic in order to explain them, we may still understand the interactions as existing through the same causal interaction, but different ways of interpreting the causal interaction: Ax ↠ Bx (Relative to absolute interaction); ∀x ↠ ∃x (Absolute to relative interaction); ∃x (Ax) ↔ ∀x (Bx) (unification of the interactions, through denoting existences which correspond between relative space and absolute space, and relative time and absolute time.

11. The relative to relative interaction and the absolute to absolute interaction can be unified according with how the union of the interaction of relative to absolute and absolute to relative relate to one another. We may state this as follows: ∃x (Bx) ↔ ∀x (Ax). In this understanding, what exists in the universe refers to an absolute state, and what exists in all the universe refers to a relative state.

     1. (∃x (Ax) ↔ ∀x (Bx)) (unification of interaction 1 + interaction 4)
     2. (∃x (Bx) ↔ ∀x (Ax)) (unification of interaction 2 + interaction 3)
     3. ((∀x ↔ ∃x) ∀x) (unification of interactions 1, 2, 3, and 4)

12. The Absolute absolute to relative interaction, or fifth interaction, can be denoted by the equation that unifies all the interactions in the universe together. 1) Ax ↠ Bx (law relating to the causal interaction of two things in relativity (relative to absolute interaction)); 2) ∀x ↠ ∃x (law relating to the differentiation of all the ways in which an existence can interact at a causal level. (absolute to relative interaction)); 3. ∃x (Ax) ↔ ∀x (Bx) (union of both causal law interactions in the universe (absolute to absolute

union with relative to relative)); 4) $\exists x \, (Bx) \leftrightarrow \forall x \, (Ax)$ (union of relative to absolute, and absolute to relative interactions). This means that although the relative and the absolute are governed by different types of logic which refer to the universe, they are still capable of being related to one another by the causal law of time and space interaction (if, then), according with the causal rules by which time and space interact (if and only if).

13. The fifth interaction has a necessary characteristic that the other four interactions do not. The fifth interaction possesses no opposite, as opposed to the four interactions possessing opposites, through which they can then be unified to accord with simpler basic understandings of the interaction. Hence, the simplest basic understanding of the interactions of the universe is a representation which no further deduction can be made in reference to it in describing the complete understanding of the single interaction through which all other interactions can be understood through.

14. The universe, in reference to how all observations can be made within it, possesses three fundamental ways in which time can exist, along with space. These are the following: 1) Moment 1: This is the first absolute moment of the universe. This was the moment in which time and space came into existence (beginning of the universe). 2) Moment 2: This is the second absolute moment of the universe. This is when a relative observation unifies absolute time and absolute space together, through the simultaneous observation of both (and hence, in accordance with the absolute state of rest). 3) Moment 3: This is the absolute moment in which every relative observation of the differentiation between space and time become absolute through their observation (simultaneously observing space and time). Once there no longer exists a way in which one can observe space and time relatively and apart from absolute existence, then the only thing that could be observed occupies an absolute existence. The absolute state of rest, since it no longer is able to differentiate relative states with absolute states (because there no longer exists relative states), it transcends its existence in the universe to accord with all ways that time and space can be united through an absolute existence. The absolute state of rest (once absolute time and absolute space are completely unified) becomes the way through which all absolute states are observations of simultaneity, that exists through which the absolute state of rest itself can be defined, not in reference to relativity, but rather referring to all absolute states that can possibly exist through an absolute space and absolute time unity.

15. Through Moment 1, it can be seen how the notion of an arrow of time came into existence. An equivalent understanding of the arrow of time is that it is a measure of change. In this way, a definite direction becomes observed in the universe, through which time and space become differentiated through the relative observation of the ways in which time and space interact. The arrow of time is a representation of the different ways in which relative space and relative time can possibly exist in reference to each other. The existence of an arrow of time necessarily entails the other ways that time and space can interact with each other, mainly, the existence of the past, present, and future.

16. Through Moment 2, the differing ways in which the interactions of the universe exist, become more and more in alignment with an absolute observation of a state of existence in the universe. So, time becomes a measure of the present state of something, as opposed to the past or future existing state of something in the universe. Instead of there existing different ways in which one may come to observe time as, in relation to space, the different ways become closer and closer into alignment, towards describing the same absolute existence.

17. Through Moment 3, time and space, relatively and absolutely, become completely unified and organize the universe according to how all possible observations of it can exist. In this state of existence, there does not exist any differentiation between how space and time can be understood, since the differentiation of space and time is a byproduct of the existence of relative observations.

18. The following depicts an order to the universe, according to how the universe as a unified whole reflects: Moment 1 (the big bang) → Moment 2 (the progressive union of relative space and relative time with the absolute state of rest) → Moment 3 (the union of absolute space and absolute time).

19. The absolute state of rest enables relative observations to refer to absolute observations. The absolute state of rest necessarily becomes a way of differentiating all the possible ways in which space and time interact. If there did not exist a state of absolute rest, then there would not exist a way through which relative observations could become absolute observations.

20. Moment 1 organizes an existence within the absolute state of rest according to every way in which the absolute state of rest can be defined. This can be seen through the fact that the separation of a time-space unity results

through the introduction of different way of defining how time and space interact in accordance with the absolute state of rest.

21. All interactions are a by-product of the differentiation between space and time that exists in the universe (relative and absolute).

22. The absolute state of rest is not a union of other existences which define how it fundamentally exists as, and it can best be described as an interaction or force through which things come into existence. The absolute state of rest cannot be ascribed any label through which time occupies a reference to it, because it does not possess a reference to an interaction between time and space. This could be seen through an infinite regression towards some beginning state of the universe. The absolute state of rest, causally speaking is a first cause way of interacting with all the other states in the universe. Nothing acts upon it because nothing precedes its existence, either within the universe or apart from it. Its form of interaction behaves in reference to the rest of the universe in an equivalent way, mainly, as an unmoved mover. It acts on the time-space differentiation through a first causal interaction and is never acted upon to conform with a union of something differentiated from itself.

23. Through Moment 3, the state of rest becomes equal in every form of ways in which absolute space and absolute time can exist in a space-time union. Because the fifth interaction (state of absolute rest) becomes equivalent with all space-time unities in the universe, it occupies an existence through itself, by itself, and in itself.

***

I will now present a complete logical deduction and clarification of what I have discussed above, such that a more technical understanding of the universe (one which would be of most benefit to physicists and mathematicians) can be understood.

1. (Interaction 1 + Interaction 4 (Interaction 2 + Interaction 3 (Interaction 5)))

2. Relative + Relative (Absolute + Absolute (Absolute Rest)))

3. $(\exists x \, (Ax) \leftrightarrow \forall x \, (Bx))$ (unification of interaction 1 + interaction 4)

4. $(\exists x \, (Bx) \leftrightarrow \forall x \, (Ax))$ (unification of interaction 2 + interaction 3)

5. $((\forall x \leftrightarrow \exists x) \, \forall x)$ (unification of interactions 1, 2, 3, and 4)

6. (weak unification (strong unification (strongest unification)))

7. Weak unification (interaction 1 + interaction 4 through strongest unification ($\exists x \leftrightarrow Bx$): ($Ax \rightarrow Ax$) + ($\forall x \rightarrow \forall x$) = ($\exists x (Ax) \leftrightarrow \forall x (Bx)$)

8. Strong unification (interaction 2 + interaction 3 through strongest unification ($\forall x \leftrightarrow Ax$): ($Bx \rightarrow \exists x$) + ($\exists x \rightarrow Bx$) = ($\exists x (Bx) \leftrightarrow \forall x (Ax)$)

9. Strongest unification: (interactions 1 + interaction 2 + interaction 3 + interaction 4) = ($\exists x (Ax) \leftrightarrow \forall x (Bx)$) + ($\exists x (Bx) \leftrightarrow \forall x (Ax)$) = ($Ax \leftrightarrow \forall x (Bx \leftrightarrow \exists x (\forall x))$) thus, the universe is unified through this equation.

10. ($Ax \leftrightarrow \forall x$ (weak) ($Bx \leftrightarrow \exists x$ (strong) ($\forall x$ (strongest)))) =

    ($\forall x$ (strongest) ($Bx \leftrightarrow \exists x$ (strong) ($Ax \leftrightarrow \forall x$) (weak)))

11. Thus, the fifth interaction ($\forall x$ (absolute rest observation)) is a unifying force that exists in all four interactions. It unifies according to: weak $\rightarrow$ strong $\rightarrow$ strongest; and, strongest $\rightarrow$ weak $\rightarrow$ strong $\rightarrow$ strongest. It unifies all observations in the universe and existence through the simultaneous observation of all the observable interactions. It exists in itself, through itself, by itself, and is the strongest unifying force in existence. It is your own observation, and through a simultaneous reference to all observations, unifies everything. This deduction coheres with the previously stated insight into the complete deduction of existence. Everything in existence can be unified and known through your observation, thus, we may say that "$\forall x$" is the simplest form of observation that exists, and the greatest reference existing between an absolute observer and everything else, which is known as existing everywhere.

## RULES OF LOGIC THAT GOVERN THE SMALLEST MATTER AND THE LARGEST MATTER

In accordance with the physics of today, we may call the rules that govern the smallest matter, quantum theory, and the rules that govern the largest matter the theory of general relativity. Physicists find it difficult to unify the mathematics of matter at the quantum level, to the mathematics at the level of general relativity. In this respect, one could put forth a decent argument stating that, based purely upon the difference between the mathematics that attempts to describe the small and large as, that mathematics has a limit. So, if any attempt can be made at unifying the small and large scales of the universe, one must look for other methods which could shed light upon, and answer questions about the universe we live in. One can see in the theory written above that I used a type of logic in which causality (cause and effect (if, then) can be used to describe the universe, but also accord with different forms of logic relating to all the ways in which the universe can exist as. What I have written below is a description of the laws of the universe, deduced entirely from the rules of logic that I have attempted to elucidate in order to understand how the universe works.

1.  We may say that the laws of cause and effect, or causality in general, can be shown to govern the universe at a quantum level, as well as at the general relativity level. The only difference is how the laws of cause and effect operate or work in reference to the phenomena being attempted to be described. In other words, although causality, and how it occurs in nature, it, itself can be interpreted in different ways. It would be a mistake, however, to assume that just because cause and effect (can be shown as the logical equivalent to if, then statements), encompasses how anything can be observed in the universe, at an empirical level (a posteriori), that it cannot be described at a rational level (a priori). Any observation of the universe that is able to describe how the universe behaves, is a form of thought which will be seen to accord with cause and effect. This is shown through the following: At a quantum level (in reference to the observer effect of the double slit experiment), if you observe units of matter, they behave differently based upon whether or not an observation is made about it. So, we have the following understanding: if you observe the units of matter at a quantum level, then the units of matter will behave differently than if you did not observe it. At the level of general relativity, we may say that if you travel at the speed of light, then time slows down. Newtonian mechanics (at least the parts that Einstein overthrew with the theory of relativity) also behaves according with a cause and effect type interaction of matter. So, we can use the logical symbol, $\rightarrow$, in order to show how a cause and effect relationship that exist in the universe can be constructed via an "if-then" causal connection.

2.  The universe, at a general relativity level can be shown to be in alignment with two or more variables, which denote how some phenomenon can be logically described. For example, $Y \rightarrow X$, with Y and X denoting the relationship that one wishes to describe. Y might stand for acceleration, and X might stand for the speed of light. Hence, the logic used to describe these two physical aspects of the universe is: if you accelerate, then you will approach the speed of light.

3.  The universe, at a quantum level can be shown to be in alignment with two (relating two or more variables together) ways of denoting something which can possibly exist. Just like the theory of relativity, quantum mechanics is able to be organized to accord with the same logical theory that aligns with the causal relationship shown in general relativity. This being, mainly, an if-then logic, that follows different rules of both theories, since the rules being described are differentiated from one another through the different ways of denoting an existence, be that as some single thing that exists ($\exists$), or everything that exists ($\forall$). Hence, the logical equation (x denoting some variable), $\exists x \rightarrow \forall x$, means, "if x exists, then x exists in everything." So, in reference to the current understanding of modern physicists and scientists in attempting to unify quantum mechanics with general relativity, it can be seen that instead of obeying different laws or rules that govern how each behaves, the view of causality that exists at the level of both theories (if-then), the only thing which comes under question as to the difference between the two, is that different variables exist in different ways. So, the mistake made by scientists is that they believe that the two theories are difficult to unify because of they think the logic behind why they are different is that the logical interpretation of both underlying causality are different from each other. This is incorrect, since the only way that they are different from each other is how one categorizes the phenomena as existing.

4.  Under the interpretation of the logic governing the large matter of the universe, with the logic governing the small matter of the universe, it can be seen that any form of existence in the universe can be described, through forming different relations that exist in all the matter in the universe. The different relations demonstrate a way in which the two forms of matter can be unified. In order to form a reasonable logical symbol to discuss how different forms of matter relate to each other as one (rather than just logically examining the small matter with the large matter) we may show the following: the logical symbol that must be used in order to unify two opposing ideas is, $\leftrightarrow$ (if and only if). This is because it demonstrates an equivalent understanding of both ways of interpreting the universe as. This logic has the benefit of showing how the two main notions of how the universe works can be reconciled, purely based off of the different ways of relating how one may change the variables to better accord with in a way of relating the two or more together in a way that doesn't change the meaning of each variable, since the unified theory is

a demonstration of how each theory of the universe, apart from the other theory of the universe, doesn't change what they mean semantically, but rather what they mean logically, which can always form different relations to each other and make a truer understanding. One could understand this as a way in which, through pure logic, they could come to know the aspects of the universe, based purely off of the different relations made by the different variables, and what the equation means. At a certain point, in order to make sense of the variables and how they relate to the other variables in the equation/interpretation of the universe, what is a true representation of the universe can be known, since the problem deduces completely to pure logic.

5.  Modern physicists believe in the ideas of the universe which general relativity says, mainly, there is no such thing as absolute space, absolute time, and an absolute state of rest. Newton thought absolute time and absolute space existed, but, as part of the understanding of the universe as known through the theory of general relativity, there does not exist absolute time, absolute space, and an absolute state of rest. The problem with the theory of relativity is that it claims that bodies in motion can only be known how fast or slow they are moving based upon other bodies in motion (other bodies moving in relation to other bodies). The problem with this understanding of only being able to know one's position in space and time through the relative motion of oneself in relation to another body, is that it doesn't take into account how bodies relate to another, other than referring to relative time and relative space. Take, for example, a body in motion on the earth (could just be someone walking). According to relativity the only way in which one can know how fast or slow they are moving (walking), is through its motion in comparison to another body, the earth moving around the sun. In this view of physics, relative time and relative space are not unified (observed at the same time), but rather are different observations which can be made in reference to something else (a body). The motion of a body has little to do with relative time and space. The motion of a body relatively speaking, does not consider how an observation of the universe can unify relative time and relative space, not by how they move through time and space, but rather by the observation of time and space, which, can either be different from each other (how relative time and relative space interact through one's observation of the two), or equivalent to each other (observed

as an equivalent time-space unity). So, bodies in the universe that can form an observation of the universe, can observe any relation in the universe, and any way in which relative time and relative space may relate to one another. If the observer observes relative space and relative time equivalently, then it is not a measure of relative motions through space and time in reference to oneself and another, but is instead a measurement of a complete union of time and space, through the observation. The importance of an understanding of space and time, well as the universe in general, is that it doesn't account for the importance of an observer. The rate at which an observer can observe something in the universe, corresponds to a union of relative space and relative time, then that corresponds to the absolute states (time, space, state of rest) of the universe. Any observation of relative space and time will always be a measurement of how one body moves in reference to another, unless one observes time and space as a union (space-time), in which case there does not need a reference between one's observation and another body in the universe.

6. The relative time and relative space union, by observing everything in the universe as in accordance with one's observation (and not in reference to other bodies) of it, accords with the existence of an absolute state of rest. Another problem with the theory of relativity is that it states that there must exist somebody which is stationary in reference to all other bodies in the universe, through which anything in the universe can become synchronized together to know everything's absolute position. We may understand an observation of a relative time and relative space unity, corresponds to the existence of an absolute state of rest, because the fact that an observation of relative time and relative space, by being observed as equivalent and hence, no differentiation between anything in the universe, the observation is stationary so to speak, in reference to all other bodies in the universe (all bodies can be measured to be in accordance with the observation). Through the state of rest, absolute time and absolute space, all other bodies or observations of the universe can be seen as in accordance with an absolute time and absolute space unity. When any observation unites relative space and relative time, they refer to absolute time and absolute space, through the absolute state of rest, which enables the observer to be seen as in accordance with a synchronized state through which any observation can relate to.

## EMPIRICAL SCIENTIFIC EVIDENCE

In this part, I will describe potential scientific test which one can see lends support as to the validity of the theory described above.

-In the philosophy of science, there exists a problem which philosophers of science take as meaning that science is affirmed by empirical observation of the universe, and that logic or abstract reason tells us nothing about how the universe truly is. This problem is the following:

If someone sees black swans somewhere in the world, how sure can they be that there are no white swans? Empirical examination of this would seem to entail that you only have evidence that black swans exist, and not that white swans exist. The question is, should the fact that you only saw black swans be any reason to believe that only black swans exist? In hearing the question, many seem to view it as being described to accord with the problem of induction. In other words, induction would tell us that the more black swans you see, the more likely it is that you will keep seeing black swans by themselves, and not white swans. Other people have gone about answering the question by stating that it does not matter how many black swans you see, this tells us nothing as to whether or not there exists white swans. This way of going about answering the question denies how induction can shed light onto whether or not white swans exist, because it doesn't matter how many black swans you see, to claim that the more black swans that exist somehow makes it a reason why you should believe only black swans existing and not white swans is not logically valid, since it relies on for its answer to know exactly how many swans are in the universe. Even this answer, however, relies on an invalid notion that just because you are getting closer to seeing all the swans in the world, instead of it meaning that the more black swans you see, the better chance is that you will only see black swans in the future, it can also be interpreted as meaning that the more swans that you see in the world, the more likely it is that you will see a white swan. In other words, the more swans you see that are black, does not give one any justification for saying that it is more likely that the next swan you see will be black, because there is no way of knowing whether or not seeing more black swans accords with induction, simply because you don't know if induction correctly refers to the rest of the swans you might see. In other words, why should one belief that just because they see more black swans, that gives any logical reason why they should see more black swans in the future, since apart from past experience of seeing black swans, there is no reason to predict whether or not you see a black swan or a white swan. In this respect, one could make a reasonable argument that induction is not a completely valid way of trying to understand what is true in the world. It relies on the false assumption that the future will resemble the past, when truly, apart from one's own perception of what has happened in the past, and corresponding it with what may happen in the future, there exists no reason (apart from how conceptualizes the question or problem at hand) why there should not be, in the case of the black swan and white swan, an equivalent probability as to which color the next swan will be. In reference to this, empirical science (induction is empirical) cannot hope to answer the question because it relies on one's experience in order to establish whether or not something is true or not (which, as far as how science has been able to establish a certain truth, there does not yet exist a 100% certain knowledge of the physical world).

The only way of attempting to go about shedding some light on the answer to the swan question, must be through pure reason. Using a pure logic deduction of the question, we must demonstrably show: 1) How reason tells us more than experience (how to know whether or not a black swan and/or white swan exist); 2) The Karl Popper philosophy of science (scientific method of trying to disprove the existence of something).

A single observation of a white swan (only one is needed), would make the question of there existing only black swans in the world, disproved. It then seems that science, as far as empirical observation is concerned, does prove or disprove some existence (phenomenon). To disprove something, automatically entails proving something. For example, if I see a white swan, then the statement, "there exists only black swans in the world", would be disproved. In order to prove that there exist only black swans in the world, one would have to see every swan in the world and see that there only exists black swans and no white swans. So, a statement such as, "there exists swans in the world that are white" is proved by the observation of a single white swan. It seems from what is written above that science can prove or disprove things in the world, if the way in which the questions of the world are phrased in a certain statement, as opposed to questions which can only be answered by empirical test. In this way, structuring questions into statements could be phrased like the following: Question: "does there exist any white swans in the world? Statement: "there exists white swans in the world." If the statement is affirmed, then this also answers the question. Through pure reason using the above question and statement, we can come to deduce other things about the world such as: "there only exists black swans in the world" (in reference to this statement, this is something that must certainly be true or false). The more statements of fact that one is able to deduce from the simpler assumptions, corresponds to answers that are known a priori, and deduced entirely through the use of a posteriori questions or statements about the world, which one is then able to construct a scientific understanding of the world, based off of the abstract knowledge you gain from the logical entailment of some known thing (something that is either proved or disproved), to another thing. The a posteriori knowledge gained through the scientific method of proving or disproven some hypothesis or theory, is a solid foundation upon which further knowledge can be deduced from the a posteriori scientific understanding.

Empirical Scientific Evidence of Experience Deduced Through Rational Abstraction: 1) The mathematical laws of the universe break down when attempting to describe the beginning of the universe (the big bang), as well as the small matter of the universe (quantum theory). A union of the small and large matter in the universe is accomplished through pure reason. 2) Observation changes the way in which matter behaves. This can be seen through the double slit experiment. This is because of all the different ways in which relative notions of space and time can be observed in reference to other relative observations. 3) The four fundamental interactions that occur in the universe can all be simplified together, to relate to a fifth interaction. This fifth interaction can unify all four interactions. 4) The absolute states of time, space, and state of rest exists in how Newton conceived of it. Einstein's theory, although correct about a physical understanding of the universe as being all relative, it has been shown that Einstein stating, "God does not play dice", a view of the universe that is not in accordance with how quantum theory works, is able to be resolved through the way in which quantum theory and general relativity unify. Hence, the universe as thought of by Newton and Einstein are only a partial understanding of the universe, which, through each other, can be reconciled. 5) The laws of cause and effect being simultaneous, as well as being understood as a conditional in logic. A relatively new understanding of cause and effect is that they are simultaneous with each other. In understanding causation this way, it enables one to see cause and effect as occurring within relative space and time in the universe, as well absolute space and time apart from the universe (relative space and time accord with the condition, if-then, and absolute space and time to accord with simultaneity (if and only if)). 6) An arrow or direction of time that is apparent in the universe pervades all observation within the universe. The direction of time existing through relative states of past, present, and future. The closer a relative observation of a union of space and time occurs, the closer one gets to observing a single dimension of time, in which only the present exists (absolute state of rest). 7) Performing a measurement in the universe is equivalent to observing some existence in the universe. A common (and relatively new) conception of the universe is that there could not exist a universe without observation existing in it. The observer is the measure by which any form of existence can exist. (The Quantum Physicist Fred Alan Wolfe understood this when he said: "Quantum physics really points to this discovery. It says that you cannot have a universe without mind (consciousness, observer, perceiver, etc.) entering into it. The mind shapes the very thing that is being observed.") 8) The ultimate fate of the universe, instead of ending with a big crunch or ending in a freeze, it can rather be described as when all observations in the universe are in accordance with the absolute states of the universe (space, time, and state of rest). 9) The universe exists in five dimensions, which unifies the other four dimensions in the universe. The four dimensions are the four different ways in which all four observations that occur in space and time, can exist in reference to one another (for example, the relative to relative time, and the relative to relative space are united together, existing in a one dimensions). The fifth dimension is just a unification of all the relative space and relative time, such that a relative space-time union exists, which also refers to the absolute states of the universe.

## BRIEF ABSTRACT OPINION ON CURRENT ISSUES

On Global warming: If Al Gore was a republican, then it would be the Democrats who deny its truth, as opposed to the Republicans who deny its truth.

On Abortion: Whether or not life begins at conception is a hypothetical question, as opposed to life ending right after the baby is born (partial birth abortion), which apparently is a proven question.

On Hate crimes: If I intentionally kill someone because he is white, and intentionally kill someone because he is black, does the color of my skin have anything to do with which of these two murders is racially motivated?

On the Second amendment: You are three events away from pointing a gun at someone and someone pointing a gun at you. Event 1 = pay your taxes. You refuse. Event 2 = follow any order given to you. You refuse. Event 3 = cops are at your front door ready to arrest you, and you will be physically forced to go with them. You refuse. The police have their guns, and you have your gun.

On Gay marriage: When you do not allow something that does not immediately affect your own privacy, and right to life, liberty, and the pursuit of happiness, you immediately affect someone else's privacy, by stripping that person of the right to life, liberty and the pursuit of happiness.

On Affirmative Action: If two people graduate from the same college, and apply for the same job, intuition tells you that the person who will get the job (with all else being equal) will be the one who did better in college (better GPA and test scores), since there really is nothing else that can be used to differentiate the two people. As it turns out, the person that got the job was not the person who did better in college, but rather a minority student (black person for example) who had lower test scores than the other person, who was not a minority student (white for example). The very fact that the black minority student was chosen over the white student, meant that the job was, instead of looking for the best possible employee, they were instead looking for a minority employee who got the job based purely off of the fact that what made the difference between the two people, was that the black minority person grew up in a place where that it was tougher to succeed than the white person. In light of this standard used by the boss selecting the employee, it is clear that the hiring person had no interest all along in how the two people did in college, the decision to hire the black person was made, not on the basis of which person is more highly qualified to work, but rather which person may or may not have had a tougher time growing up. Hence, if we then analyze the two people's resume's as equivalent (both grew up in the same neighborhood, and both have the same college grades), the only thing separating how the two people appear to the boss, is the color of their skin (white and black). Affirmative Action will then mostly if not all times, favor the black minority over the white majority. How is this not racism?

On Pretextual stops and racial profiling: Ranging anywhere from having a small amount of police officers driving on the streets, to having a large amount of police officers driving on the streets, there exist cops who patrol the streets every day, looking for minority members, like a black person and a Hispanic person, who they believe may be involved in criminal enterprises. This belief that the minority person is involved in something illegal, was a judgment made by the officer, based purely off the person's race and ethnicity.

These types of cops patrol the streets, out to get someone who they suspect may be involved in illegal activity. The problem: the cop that pulls over someone he believes is a criminal and engaging in criminal activity, may stock and follow the person's car goes for as long as it takes to catch violating some traffic law(s). The cop now, at this point, is in a better position of control to find any illegal activity the person might be engaged in. Lesson learned: pretextual stops should be illegal, and any time a cop is doing it, it shows just how fucking racist and fucked in the head these people are. Next time follow a woman with five kids in her car going to soccer practice, and pull her over for some insignificant reason, so that you could eventually search her car, and find nothing illegal.[96] (except meth maybe, since, supposedly, the biggest users of meth are soccer moms)

On the Drinking age: Is there really that much difference in the maturity of a person who drinks alcohol between the ages of 18 to 21? The issue isn't whether or not an 18 year old person should be allowed to have a drink when they toast at their wedding. The issue is whether or not an 18 year old can be as responsible with alcohol as a 21 year old can. This seems a little subjective. When I was 18 in college, there was a petition that was being signed by presidents of universities who were in favor of the drinking age being lowered to 18. The very fact that a person can join the military and die for their country, but not be allowed to drink alcohol, seems a little odd.

On Illegal drugs: Is it a coincidence that all the politicians and lawmakers in the USA that are in favor of making drugs illegal have never tried them before ("I smoked it out of the pipe, but I did not inhale" is somehow ok, but to inhale is not ok)? I highly doubt it, and that in itself should raise a red flag to someone who tries to outlaw something that they personally have no firsthand experience with (and hence, are trying to outlaw it not because of what they personally know, but because of what someone else told them (who, of course, is an expert on the issue regardless of whether they have tried the drug or not themselves)). Proof: Ronald Reagan once said that "marijuana can very well be the most dangerous drug there is", and someone in favor of making drugs illegal told me, "Obama shouldn't be president because he admitted to taking cocaine."

On Prostitution: Any person who has sex with a prostitute, assumes all responsibility and accountability for what happens as a result of having sex with a prostitute. If a man gets an STD from having sex with a prostitute, then it should be his responsibility to not spread the STD to his wife or significant other, and not the responsibility of lawmakers who try and do something about it.

On Religion: A world with religion, as well as any fundamentalist type of belief system, suffers from the negative consequence of putting any other religion or belief system against them. A world without religion, as well as without any fundamentalist type of belief, at the very least, has the positive outlook of not using ideas as a way to divide people. In that respect, atheism seems to possess a valid point in its outlook of the world, mainly, it is not the belief in some idea or ideas, but rather the absence of belief in some idea or ideas (and hence, does not put something against something else).

On the Use of racial slurs like the N word, or calling a football team the Redskins: To claim that it is ethically ok for a black person to use the N word, but it is not ethically ok for people of any other race to use it (particularly white people), is itself, a form of racial profiling. Using the slang version instead does little to help the cause of the issue, since without consent of a black person, using the slang version is just as bad as using the not slang version. To those who wish to put an end to the use of the N word, they must stop its use by any race except for black people, as well as its use by black people. What is clear is that many black people have absolutely no idea why they are supposed to take offense when hearing the word. They just know that they are supposed to get offended, without really knowing why. That, it seems, is highly irrational.

On The Japanese hunting whales: The hunting of whales, apart from concerns regarding the extinction or endangering of the whales, seems entirely reasonable. If the whales are endangered and hunting them makes the whales closer to extinction, then it seems irrational to think that someone could be justified in killing them. Apart from this reason to not kill the whales, there doesn't seem to be any other justified reason why it is an ethically wrong thing to do. Intuition tells me that the size of the whale has something to do with why some think hunting them is wrong. Something tells me that a whale that is thriving in nature, and a beetle is not thriving, some people would still consider the killing of the whale as worse than the killing of the beetle. This makes no sense.

On Liberal vs. Conservative: A favorite quote that I have regarding the division between the left and right ideologies, goes like this: "I hate conservatives, but I really fucking hate liberals." (I think this quote was said by South Park co-creator, Matt Stone) Existing apart from the big government aspirations of the liberals, and the more than no government identity of the conservatives (they tend to desire small government, yet at the same time think that some form of government is necessary), there lies the libertarian perspective which, in its claim to novelty over the government controlled beliefs of the liberals and conservatives, understands that in any form of government that attempts to control how people live their lives (makes them accord with what the government says), there will be rights of the people being violated. In reference to communism that is ok. In reference to anarchy that is not ok.

On Evolution vs. Creationism: If the Bible said that life has evolved on earth over millions and billions of years, then everyone that is a creationist would believe in evolution. And even more ironic about that fact, is they would then go on to say how much evidence there is for evolution. This evidence for evolution, of course, since it is considered by creationists to be a complete falsehood and misrepresentation of life on earth, raises questions about what people are told is true (creationists), and what people find out is true (evolution). The former being a state requiring one to not ask questions and just accept what is told to them, and the latter being a state requiring one to investigate and believe what the evidence points to. Facts, rather than being something to fit in a closed off world view that does not change how the person thinks or what they believe, are something which, if you are rational, should change your beliefs or reaffirm one's world view. That is scientific and rational.

On Nuclear weapons: the use of nuclear weapons should always be used as a completely last resort, where there does not appear to be any other options. The nuclear weapons that were used to end WWII, had this to its understanding of why/how it is morally justified to use nuclear weapons. To end a conflict (use the nuclear weapons as a means to an end), as opposed to starting a conflict (use the nuclear weapons as an ends to a mean), is what gives moral justification for the use of nuclear weapons. In this way, it can be seen that the existence of nuclear weapons (the weapons in the hands of someone good), tends to be more rational than a world without them. It is only when the weapons are immediately available for use by someone who is inherently a bad person, that questions regarding the moral justification for a world without nuclear weapons becomes apparent.

On Equal pay for men and women: If a man and a woman do the same work, and are paid unequally, then it seems (apart from a misogynistic person who happens to be the boss of the man or woman) that this stems from the results of the work that the man did, as opposed to the results of the work that the woman did. If someone is better at doing a specific thing, than another person who does the same specific thing, then the person performing the job better should be paid more, regardless of whether they are a man or a woman. Apart from this, if a man and a woman have the same job and are equally good at it, then it seems completely irrational as to why the man should be paid more over the woman.

On 100% total government vs. 100% total anarchy: Control vs. freedom. Why anyone would want the former, I do not know.

On Conspiracy theories (9/11, the moon landing, JFK, the Illuminati): Some people believe that anyone who subscribes to a conspiracy theory from which there is not a lot of evidence, or that the evidence is based on a false understanding of something, are lunatics and very irrational. In reference to an irrational belief which is based on a poor understanding of science, it seems to me that the people who believe in the conspiracy that the moon landing never took place, would fit into this category. In reference to a more rational understanding of science and common sense being used to back up what the conspiracy theorists think, it seems that the conspiracy that 9/11 was an inside job is in this category. The problem with most people who think that 9/11 was not an inside job, is that they just simply refuse to believe that it could be true. In this way, their perception of the conspiracy is one based more on a commonsense appeal to what is far more likely to be true, as opposed to its opposite. For example, an anti-conspiracy believer could say, "Do you honestly believe that George Bush and the United States government had a hand in 9/11?" The point to this question being that the very idea that the conspiracy could be true is completely ridiculous and also it is very morally wrong to even think that way. In any case, whether one believes in a specific conspiracy theory or not, what is most important is the appeal to evidence that one sees in favor of the conspiracy being true or not. If some evidence is being used to suggest the truth of 9/11 as being an inside job, then it should be up to the other side of the conspiracy to also use evidence that appeals to hard reality, as opposed to evidence that appeals to one's feelings and emotions about the conspiracy.

On Torture: the irrationality of torture can be seen through the following thought experiment: The military specifically trains some of its recruits to not give into torture and reveal some important piece of knowledge, by torturing them. In this way, they can better handle it if the time ever does come that they will be in a situation like that. The main point in not telling an important piece of knowledge to someone who is torturing you, is because if you do ever cave in and tell the torturer what they want to hear, there is no reason, especially if the torturer is a very bad/evil person, that the person will not just continue torturing you after you have told him the information he needed to know. Knowing this, one who torturers another person to obtain important information, suffers from the basic understanding that the person being tortured can say anything to you, and if what he tells you is false, then you are reverting back to a method of gaining information that does not allow you to know whether or not the person being tortured is telling the truth. In this way, whether what the person being tortured tells you is true or false, then there are two options: 1) if they tell you what you want to hear, then there is no reason to suspect that they will not keep torturing you afterwards; 2) if you don't tell them what they want to hear, then they will keep torturing you. Understanding this makes one see that torture, on top of being a completely fucked up thing to engage in, is also highly irrational.

On LGBT: The basic rights for the LGBT people, must be the same and equal for anyone else, including those who wish to constrict the rights of the LGBT community. Any form of inequality that exists between the LGBT community's viewpoint, and any other viewpoint, is not morally justified, since an LGBT person has as much of a valid viewpoint as any other viewpoint has, this being mainly, that they are in favor of only their viewpoint, and how it exists in reference to the opposing viewpoint. Taking this at face value, it is easy to see how one's appeal to their emotions and feelings about one's own viewpoint in reference to the other, does not constitute a rational way in how to judge oneself against another. So, if someone says that being gay is wrong, this opinion that they possess appeals only to their own subjective understanding of what they truly think and see is wrong. This person's opinion (viewed by them as entirely true) carries no more validity than the person's opinion that is the opposite of one's own (that being gay is not wrong), and in this respect, constitutes the very same level of reasoning as each other. Therefore, all viewpoints of anything in the world, are only valid once one accepts what they are against, and understands one's own viewpoint, as it contrasts to the other. For example, a person who has the physical body of a man, may think that they are actually a woman (an appeal to what they believe is true apart from how they think about their physical gender). Upon realizing this, the person then could want to have a sex change operation, so that their physical body matches their internal perception of oneself. However, one's internal perception of oneself, although the person gives it more credibility as to one's own true gender, as opposed to the perception of their physical body, has no limit. There doesn't even seem to be any rational explanation as to why there should be a limit to one's perception of oneself. Earlier in the book I talked about a man who honestly/truly believes he is a glass of orange juice. Seeing the man's physical body, one can say to the man, "No, you are not a glass of orange juice, you are a person." This observation appeals to the person's physical body as evidence that they are a certain way (a person as opposed to a glass of orange juice) and does not sympathize with or take into account how the person truly views oneself. Taking this into account, a transgender person who believes that they are the opposite sex of what their physical body is, we may say they define themselves differently than other's do, but at the same time possesses the same amount of validity as the opposite way of seeing oneself. Hence, there should be no discrimination of someone in the LGBT community, whose views of oneself are just as valid as other's view of oneself. (Technically, they are now called LGBTQ, since, for some reason, 'queer' is now seen as an ok word to use towards gay people. Why not add 'faggot' to the end also?)

On the Death penalty: There is an internal contradiction existing within the viewpoint of the pro death penalty supporters. Many of the people that are for the death penalty, are prolife in reference to abortion. There have been attempts made in past elections to try and instill a certain definition to life, so that, for example, abortion will become illegal, since it would be killing "a person", as they have defined it to be. But how can someone honestly say that a fetus is a life, but that a person who has been born and is living in the world, does not fall under the same level of how a life can be defined. If a fetus is a life, then a person born and living in the world, regardless of what crimes they have committed, is a life as well. It can then be seen that the death penalty supporters make a heavy appeal to emotion and their feelings about what they think is right. The problem: although a fetus may be innocent in reference to it being free from any negative actions it may have committed, and a person may be guilty in reference to some negative actions that they have committed, this matters little in reference to how a "person" should be viewed, and for the rights that they have, regardless of what they may or may not have done.

On Gangs and cults: The problem with indoctrinating any set of moral or ethical values into a person, is that the ideas that they possess have the potential to cause very bad consequences as a result of subscribing to those ideas. For example, a person may believe so deeply in the fundamental ideas and world view of the cult or gang that they are involved in, that they become convinced of the truth of what the cult or gang espouses is true, no matter how irrational or morally evil the ideas are. Ideas tend to become more ingrained in one's world view, and the more that other people also believe the same thing, reaffirms to people as a truer/better way of seeing the world. If someone believes in some idea and there doesn't exist any other person in the world who also holds that belief, then this resonates with the believing person that their world view may not hold as much validity as they would if multiple people believed it. On top of being influenced by the amount of people believing the same thing as oneself, there is another problem with the spread of dangerous ideas in the world, mainly, the idealization of what the world would be like if their idea took effect and shaped how the world will ultimately come to be. Promised by the idea of being rewarded for their adherence to the particular world view, people commit evil things, and behave in evil ways, just as long as they truly think they will be rewarded at some point. This is the problem with cults that adhere to dangerous and evil ideologies, as well as gangs and other organizations which try to instill in their followers a sense of solidarity, and unified perception of what they belief is right or wrong. In uniting for a common cause and an ultimate reason for what they think is right, people will do things that they would never do if they were not so indoctrinated in a certain belief system. A cult may try and organize a mass suicide, and, being so entrenched in the very fundamental way of seeing the world, the adherers to the cult do not see any reason why they are not being true to themselves, as well as how what they do can be seen by another as morally wrong.

On Young earth vs old earth creationists: There exists an internal conflict within the different belief sets of Christians. Christianity is set up so that all of those who believe in it must accord with one of the following viewpoints: 1) Young Earth Creationist; 2) Old Earth Creationists; 3) Theistic Evolutionists. These three viewpoints categorize a belief in Christianity as according with how the world and universe exist as. It makes no sense to speak of a young earth theistic evolutionist, because evolution, by its very operation, cannot exist in accordance with a belief in a young earth. Fundamentalists on all sides of the viewpoints attack the other's position and give reasons why one should deny the opposing beliefs in Christianity. The conflict gets so heated with all sides claiming that their belief is not only correct, but also superior to the other sides. This is easily seen when, Young Earth Creationists, when arguing with an Old Earth Creationist, claim that they are worshipping different

God's, and that their version of the Christian God is correct. Christian Evolutionists, although they (at least in reference to scientific discovery) are most likely closer to the truth than the other two viewpoints, receives the most amount of critique for it failing to adhere to the traditional, Adam and Eve story of creation. The division of the three major sects of Christian belief, is sometimes used in a way that completely contradicts the Bible, as opposed to leaving it up for different interpretations (which is how the three divisions exist). For example, Catholics believe (as believed by Pope John Paul II) in evolution, and the only question as to how life and humanity have existed or come to exist in the world, they claim that it is only a matter of when God decided to put into place the human soul (the injection of the soul into the human bodies). Anyone who knows anything about evolution, however, knows that it is completely ridiculous to say that there existed a very first human, and that the life forms that existed even a single generation before, could not also be categorized as a human. Even more absurd in the way in which these divisions come to believe about the world and how it appears in relation to the Bible story of creation, is the cherry picking of what they think makes sense to them and then believing that, even if it has no basis in reality or the Bible. This is easily seen when examining what the scientist, Francis Collins, believes about Christianity. He believes in evolution, but at the same time also believes in the literal story of Adam and Eve. How he reconciles these opposing views is of little importance. However, we can know that any reconciliation he offers can be shown as meaningless, since it tries to explain how life began in a non-evolutionary way, and accord that with an evolutionary way, which, both, had different beginnings. I believe there to be a resolution to the different belief divisions in Christian world views, shaped by how the earth and universe began: Base your belief in the Christian God, not on how you believe the world started, but rather on Jesus dying on the cross. To say that Young Earth Creationists are worshipping a different Jesus that died on the cross, as opposed to another Jesus dying on the cross believed in by the Old Earth Creationists, is absurd and only negative connotations can be ascribed to it that do more harm than good. However, the three viewpoints do agree on at least one idea, mainly, that the earth and universe are not 7,000 years old.

<u>On God</u>: One of the most accurate descriptions of God that I have ever read about, was given by Alfred North Whitehead. He ascribed God as the ultimate ground for limitation. If we wish to know the beginning of the moral absolutes of good and evil, we are forced to ascribe their beginning

with the first cause, God. One, however, should not judge God based on the existence of good and evil, and how they have come to exist in the world, but rather God must be judged in accordance with how He separates the good from the evil. Therefore, there exists a certain sort of metaphysical dialogue or activity that God engages with in existence. So, knowledge of God can be understood as the way in which one fundamentally interacts with and believes is true in accordance with how God reveals Himself to oneself. Through this understanding of God's true nature becoming more and more apparent to how one interacts with the perception God making Himself aware of to you, we can see a valid rationality of God's existence. Love is wise, hatred is foolish. When the moral absolutes of good and evil are understood in reference to the rational of belief in something, we have then come to see the ultimate knowledge of God. Harmony out of conflict, order out of chaos, and rationality out of irrationality, provide the underlying notion as to why there is a certain reason of why things are the way that they are. What gives our life meaning is the way in which we act in accordance with what you can conceive of as the greatest absolute good. God knows this is the best we can possibly do.

## HISTORICAL AND EXISTENTIAL OBSERVATIONS/ABSURDITIES OF THE WORLD

(This is a brief list of ideas I have thought about in the past that I have not yet found a rational answer to. Thus, I provide a skeptical analysis of certain observations of the world. If the observation is stupid and wrong, I would love to know why. If the observation is good, and hence, cannot be explained, then the purpose of this section will have been achieved.)

1. Trips made across the ocean in older times would have had to pack all food and water for the entire trip. (This would mean that all the food on board the ship would be able to keep edible without the use of a refrigerator/freezer (to keep it fresh) or microwave.)

2. Slave trade (enough room on the ship, for food, slaves and water enough for months at sea). The slaves were packed into the ships like sardines. How did they feed everyone, hydrate everyone, maintain a semi cleanly living quarters for the weeks or months at sea?

3. Finding places without GPS or maps (how did cab drivers know where to take the customer without knowing the exact location, as well as the customer not knowing the exact location)

4. The world seen from outer space before satellites (a coincidence that the maps made before a view of the earth seen from space were an exact match to how the world really looks)

5. Knowing how to get from one place to another without a compass (like in ancient times) (how were sailors able to go from one place to another when at sea (going from England to America for example), without any reference to where they want to go out in the ocean?

6. Marble or granite statues (like the Venus De Milo) being made from either perfectly measured marble in nature, or they were chipped away from a larger piece of marble.

7. Why did the dinosaurs become extinct roughly 65 million years ago after an asteroid hit the earth (why wasn't all life wiped out from the asteroid?)?

8. If wood deteriorates after a tree is dead, then why doesn't all the wood used for building or constructing things also deteriorate?

9. When in the development of humans over thousands or millions of years decide to brush their teeth for example (why do humans have to brush their teeth in order to keep their teeth (prevent it from getting gingivitis for example) healthy, but other animals don't?)

10. "Life" documentary being able to capture on film certain things in nature that are very rare (also it was able to look underground to get on film certain ecosystems, and at the same time not interfering with the life that lives underground). Also capture on film multiple angles of the same event, as if they know where a life form will be and what it will be doing.

11. Manuscripts (like the constitution) seem to have been written almost perfectly (excellent cursive and writing in straight lines), such as the "We the People" being written in a very large amount of ink, as opposed to the small amount of ink (like they would have to color it in).

12. The money in ancient times having carvings or pictures on them (like of Caesar), and had to have been made by hand, because there did not exist any mints or printing presses.

13. How did the German Reich know who was Jewish, since there is no definable set of physical indications of one's ethnicity, the only way that a Jew could be separated from other people is if there was some ethnic test to determine the ancestry of someone (the problem with this is that being Jewish is not an ethnic group (or other people that were a victim

of the holocaust for example, like, homosexuals (the only way they could determine who was to be sent to the concentration camps, is through physical signs (like the gay walk or the gay accent), and even then this only provides a hypothesis as to how someone is)).

14. How did people know in the ancient times, what time it was, and how to structure their lives according to the times of the day? Ex: to meet someone somewhere (say going to Plato's academy), without the exact knowledge of a definite time to meet them (also, before the invention of the alarm clock, how did people get up (no way of telling the time at night (like with a sundial)) at a certain time to do something (sun dials only give a rough estimate of time, as opposed to a definite time)

15. Years being 365 days as measured through one orbit of earth around the sun (is it a coincidence that people back in ancient times knew how long a year was as they measured it according with their society)

16. Seconds, minutes, hours, days, weeks, months, years, etc. all according to a perfect synchronization of time. Ex: there are 60 seconds in a minute, 60 minutes per hour, 24 hours per day. Is it a coincidence or a product of structure that all the times worked according with each other to enable a measurement of time (why is it not 56 seconds to a minute, or 47 minutes to an hour)

17. Information being spread throughout the world in ancient times being passed through such means as carving the written message on a tree. Also, what made people believe in the etched message, as opposed to something else? (Could only propagate through one person at a time).

18. How did people know in ancient times where and when a battle would take place? Ex: was there a messenger? What if one side wanted to meet somewhere but the other side did not? Why did people structure how wars occur through battles in which both sides meet at a certain place?

19. How were animated films (or TV shows) able to be made without the use of a computer that has that kind of ability to create a show or movie?

20. When did it become necessary for humans to have to drink purified water, as opposed to other life in the world which do not need their water that they drink to be purified? How was water originally purified (when

did it become known that boiling water would purify it (at least to some extent)), and how was it known that it must become purified to being healthy?

21. If the flood historical event (many accounts of a flood occurring in the world) really happened, then it must have been either fresh water or salt water. If it was fresh water, then all the life that lives in the ocean (can only live in salt water) would have been dead. Also, if it was salt water, then all the life that doesn't live in the ocean (live in freshwater lakes for example) would have been dead. (So then how did the earth, once the flood ended, differentiate between the different aquatic life forms that need different habitats to live in?)

22. When in the line of evolution did humans (or its ancestors) decide to wear clothing, which they would need to survive in harsh conditions of cold weather? Why do they need to wear clothing, but other life forms did not?

23. How is the temperature at the surface of the sun (roughly 10,000 degrees Fahrenheit) able to provide enough heat to travel 93,000,000 miles to the earth? If the temperature drops 1 degree Fahrenheit for every 9,300 miles between the sun and earth, then no heat (0 degrees Fahrenheit) would be felt by the sun. (this might be a stupid one, but, wtf, I'm crazy)

24. Why is it necessary for other life forms to eat food without cooking it, but humans have to cook theirs or else they might get sick (food poisoning for example). When in the development of humans (evolution) did humans have to cook their food in order to make it edible? In the development of humans (design), why were people singled out amongst all the other life forms in the world to have to cook their food?

25. Stonehenge is said to be the works of giants, or that it is just not known how it was constructed. However, other ancient buildings (such as the Parthenon or Pyramids in Egypt) are said to be constructed by people. How were people able to construct structures that today require an architectural knowledge to build, as well requires machines (like a crane used for buildings)? Where is/ was the type of material that is needed in order to create the structures come from? For the pyramids for example, where did all of the big square/rectangle stones come from? Were they pieces broken from a larger piece of stone or were just found that way somewhere?

26. Why have the ancient structures erode away and become ruins? (In other words, for example, why/how did the Coliseum deteriorate into a structure that no longer is able to be used for what it was constructed for (the audience stands no longer can hold people)? Also, how far along in the deterioration (becoming a ruin) of the structure did people stop using it for (when did the Coliseum deteriorate to the point that they no longer held gladiator fights at it; when did Pantheon stop being the place where meetings were held (where did the meet after they stopped meeting at the Pantheon?) the purpose of what it was built for?

27. What was the instrument used to write something down before the use of a pencil and pen? Writing on trees required the use of a carving instrument (like a knife for example). How did it become known throughout the world that the invention of a pencil or pen could be used to write (or, how did knowledge circulate throughout the world which started off by just being invented or discovered by someone in a specific place/civilization?) It was either independently discovered or spread from person to person starting from one place to another.

28. How are the meanings of words in a dictionary agreed upon by people who make the dictionaries? (In other words, do they vote to determine the correct meaning of words?)

29. How did the stock market crash and work before the internet and mass communication were invented? Morris code?

# SECTION 8

# The Rationality of Mind Travel

Many people in society, whether they are educated or not, tend to believe that the best way to set up a country's government is through a democracy, and the best way to set up a countries economy is through capitalism. The political and economic theories of what makes a government civilized, tends to promote more of a just society in reference to democracy and capitalism as opposed to a dictatorship and communism. Fundamentalists residing on either side of these political and economic ideas seem to argue over which form of government and economy that aligns more closely with a just society, and hence, tends, in one case, to promote a society in which there are freer citizens, and in the other case to stifle any freedom that its citizen's may live in accordance with. In reference to either of these extremes of government of economic control, it can be shown that both suffer from ideas which could promote a new political and economic theory. To show this, we can turn towards perhaps the wisest person in history.

Socrates' philosophy, in having lived roughly 2,500 years ago, is astonishingly rational and for someone who wanted to live in accordance with knowledge and ethical values, is a life that seems incredibly ambitious. Socrates claimed that in order for a society to be just, it must possess rational bases for it being established in society. What is rational or reasonable in this life must stem from a certain amount of knowledge or truth that one sees. Seeing truth, what Socrates called, "The Form of the Good" must be at the for front of how any just society can operate. We can then see a potential problem with a democracy: in a majority win political theory, Socrates' problem with it is many of the citizens that exist in the society, are themselves, not very well educated or knowledgeable regarding what can be called "good" or "right" ideas about justice, and hence, if ignorant people are allowed to voice their opinion, then a societal structure revolving around its politics or economics will/can become a structure that is based on the wisdom or ignorance of the people living in that society. Socrates argued that rather than structure a society based on the majority of the citizens, a society should be structured according to a rational and logical basis to define how in touch it is with the ultimate truth of the world. If a society cannot be based upon a sound/valid understanding of what it means to be ignorant vs what it means to be knowledgeable, because then that structure will be a reflection of not complete goodness, as well as a form of irrational thinking. In this way, one could see how a form of government in which there exists a dictator of tyrant, will reflect an unjust society, founded upon a control of the citizens, as implemented by the irrationality of the authority figure.

Just like the mathematician claiming that there exists mathematics throughout nature, we may say also claim that there exists a certain level of rationality that becomes reflected in nature and society, formed through the logical reason that exists in the philosopher, and does not exist in the tyrant. The philosopher is a lover of wisdom, whereas the tyrant is a personification of ignorance. It seems completely absurd to think that it is better to be feared than loved as Machiavelli once stated, because fear is a form of ignorance (not knowing how something is, and hence, fearing how it is because you don't know how it is), and love is a form of wisdom. Socrates claimed that in the most just society, the one person who it should be left to in order to organize an unjust society into just society, is what he called a, "Philosopher King". This Philosopher King, rather than inflicting a certain level of control or influence onto all of the citizens living in the society, serves the purpose (I believe) of being a messenger in a way, in that he sees the Form of the Good which is equivalent to absolute truth, and then uses that knowledge gained to form a just society. It should be noted, however, that the Philosopher King, rather than instituting his own subjective thought onto society as a whole, and not referring to one's own feeling or emotion in structuring society through himself, is not to be thought of as a ruler or someone initiating control of the world to accord with one's wishes. The Philosopher King has the sole purpose of being the one person in the society who is able to arrange the structure of the society, to accord with truth. Socrates claimed that the Philosopher King is the only one in the society who is able to completely see the truth (The Form of the Good), and in that respect, must be understood as a deliverer of the truth to the citizens, rather than an inventor of the truth through which the citizens follow along with, that possesses no other rational for why something is true other than just because the truth is the way that it is, merely because the Philosopher King says so (which is what a tyrant or dictator would say).

There exists a distinct difference in my ability to attain knowledge of the world, between me being a philosopher or logician. Apart from stimulants, especially amphetamines, I cannot abstract or logically deduce anything of importance. Wittgenstein once said about Schopenhauer's philosophy something like this: "Where real depth begins, Schopenhauer ends." I can somewhat see what Wittgenstein meant, since Schopenhauer at one point in his life said that Hegel's philosophy was worthless. Now, with the aid of amphetamines, I am able to abstract or logically deduce with relative ease.

I will now present two logical proofs that solve two major mathematical and logical (computer science) problems. If they are correct, I will consider them to be the pinnacle of my attempts to think rationally, with clear and concise intent. This is because of the roughly 3,500 pages of logic and philosophy that I have written in my life, 90% was very obscure.

***

**Proof of Goldbach's Conjecture:** Every even number greater than two can be expressed as the sum of two prime numbers.

## Two Atomic Forms:

1. even + even = even
2. odd + odd = even

## Six Axiomatic Forms:

1. even (prime) + even (prime) = even (**example**: 2 + 2 = 4)
2. even (prime) + even (not prime) = even (**example**: 2 + 8 = 10)
3. even (not prime) + even (not prime) = even (**example**: 8 + 12 = 20)
4. odd (prime) + odd (prime) = even (**example**: 3 + 5 = 8)
5. odd (prime) + odd (not prime) = even (**example**: 5 + 9 = 14)
6. odd (not prime) + odd (not prime) = even (**example**: 15 + 9 = 24)

## Proof:

1. Consider the number 6. There are only 3 ways of expressing the number 6 through odd numbers and even numbers:

   (A) 1 + 5 (**Proof**: odd (not prime) + odd (prime))
   (B) 2 + 4 (**Proof**: even (prime) + even (not prime))

(C) 3 + 3 (**Proof**: odd (prime) + odd (prime))

**Lemma**: Through the above number 6, we can correctly infer that any axiomatic form that does not hold true for this number, does not hold true for every even integer, because it doesn't hold for the even integer 6. So:

(I) even (not prime) + even (not prime) (**disproved** by the number 6)
(II) odd (not prime) + odd (not prime) (**disproved** by the number 6)

We are left with:

(A) odd (not prime) + odd (prime) = even
(B) even (prime) + even (not prime) =even
(C) odd (prime) + odd (prime) =even
(D) even (prime) + even (prime) = even

2. Consider the number 10. There are only 5 ways of expressing the number 10 through odd numbers and even numbers:

(a) 1 + 9 (**Proof**: odd (not prime) + odd (not prime) (which was **disproved** by the number 6))
(b) 2 + 8 (**Proof**: even (prime) + even (not prime))
(c) 3 + 7 (**Proof**: odd (prime) + odd (prime))
(d) 4 + 6 (**Proof**: even (not prime) + even (not prime) (Which was **disproved** by the number 6))
(e) 5 + 5 (**Proof**: odd (prime) + odd (prime))

**Lemma**: Through the above number 10, we can correctly infer that any numerical form that does not hold true for this number, does not hold true for every even integer, because it doesn't hold true for the even integer 10. So, after deducing the numerical relations when considering the number 10, we are left with:

(I) even (prime) + even (not prime) = even
(II) odd (prime) + odd (prime) = even
(III) even (prime) + even (prime) =even

3. even (prime or not prime) + even (prime) = even (any) + 2

The reason why any even will refer to all even numbers is because:

even (any even $\geq$ 2) + 2 = 4 $\longrightarrow \forall$ even

4. Therefore, [even ($2 \leq$) + 2] = [even + even] = even (unification with **atomic form**)

5. So, [odd (prime) + odd (prime)] = [odd + odd] = even (unification with **atomic form**)

6. [even (any) + even (prime)] = [odd (prime) + odd (prime] = ∀ even

■ Goldbach's Conjecture is correct, every even integer greater than two (as shown in premise 6) is the sum of two prime numbers.

***

**Proof of the P vs NP problem**: If the solution to a problem is easy to check for correctness, must the problem by easy to solve?

1. There only exists four references through which the verification of a problem can be measured by the solution of a problem.

   (i) easy solution; hard verification
   (ii) hard solution; easy verification
   (iii) hard solution; hard verification
   (iv) easy solution; easy verification

2. There only exists two references through which the quickness of a problems solution and verification can be measured.

   (I) instantaneous interaction (fastest interaction between solution and verification)
   (II) non instantaneous interaction (slowest interaction between solution and verification)

3. For (i), the problem takes a longer time to verify than it did to solve, thus measuring the problems solution as easy, and the problems verification as hard.

4. 4. For (ii), the problem takes a shorter time to verify than it did to solve, thus measuring the problems solution as hard, and the problems verification as easy.

5. For (iii), the problem takes the same amount of time to verify than it did to solve.

6. For (iv), the problem takes the same amount of time to verify than it did to solve.

7. (iii) and (iv) are measured through (I) and (II), which provides a reference between (iii) and (iv), such that the difficulty of each other can be defined.

8. (iii) is measured by (II), because although the solution and verification take the same amount of time to compute, the two are not instantaneously related, and hence, (iii) is slow.

9. (iv) is measured by (I), because the solution and verification take the same amount of time to compute, the two are instantaneously related, and hence, (iv) is fast.

10. The difficulty of (i) and (ii) form a relative measurement between one another, through which the easiness or hardness of a solution or verification can be defined:

(a) solution time > verification time
-The solution is harder to compute than the verification because it takes longer to solve the problem, than it does to verify the problem.

(b) solution time < verification time
-The solution is easier to compute than the verification because it takes longer to verify the problem, than it does to solve the problem.

11. Thus, the difficulty of (i) and (ii) are relatively defined through each other.

12. The difficulty of (iii) and (iv) are absolutely defined through (I) and (II). So, because (I) is a faster interaction between solution and verification (instantaneous), and (II) is a slower interaction between the solution and verification (non-instantaneous), we may define (I) as easy, and (II) as hard.

13. A non-instantaneous interaction is defined through P ≠ NP, and thus, defines (i), (ii), and (iii).

14. An instantaneous interaction is defined through P = NP, and thus, defines (iv).

15. Since (i), (ii), and (iii) are non-instantaneously defined, they are computable in nondeterministic polynomial time (slow).

16. Since (iv) is instantaneously defined, it is computable in deterministic polynomial time (fast).

17. Since P ≠ NP is relatively defined, and P = NP is absolutely defined, we can determine that P = NP is correct, and P ≠ NP is incorrect.

18. Therefore, if the solution to a problem is easy to check for correctness, the problem must be easy to solve, since:

(A) easy solution ↔ easy verification (absolutely determined)

(B) hard solution ↔ easy verification (relatively determined (not absolutely determined))

■ P = NP

\*\*\*

Apart from amphetamines to enable my rational thought, I suffer from what Socrates once said: "All I know is that I know nothing." With amphetamines to enable my rational thought, I understand what Socrates once said: "The unexamined life is not worth living." Upon reflecting philosophically for the past 10 or 11 years, I can see how some people put at the forefront of their search for happiness, satisfaction or contentment, the journey of self-discovery and self-realization. Having gone down the rabbit hole perhaps more than anyone who has ever existed previous to me, I can say that at the intersection between pure reason, and mental observation of phenomenon relating to truth, one can then come to apprehend how life truly is a state of mind (as beautifully shown through the movie, "Being There"). What I call myself, ("Psychotic Logician") is a definition of my own sense of identity in how I view the logic of the world, discovered by me either because of my apprehension of pure reason, or because of my mental illness. It is to this extent that I can say that I have travelled through the avenue of my own subjective mental existence, and the objective mental existence that pervades the entire world. In this sense, I have travelled the minds of reality and philosophized about the basic framework of the world. What I have written in this book can therefore be called, "The Philosophy of Mind Travel". Although I may never reach the ultimate goal of my life, which just so happens to be a representation of a theory of everything (not just physically, but mentally (philosophically)), it is meant by me that what I have written in this book may one day come to provide support in helping to deduce truth, and comfort in reading through stories which one can document with brutal honesty. In this case, I believe to have succeeded, and I believe I have failed, simply because my rational logic and philosophical abstraction abilities are to slight for the task.

Hear no evil. See no evil. Speak no evil.

# Tools for Mind Travel or (The Operation of Mind Travel)

## RESOLUTION OF GETTIER'S OBJECTION TO KNOWLEDGE

B elow is my solution to the knowledge rejected by Gettier in his famous article, "Is Justified True Belief Knowledge?" I demonstrably show the mistake that Gettier made when forming his objection to knowledge. I draw upon the same two cases in the paper that Gettier used. My method of going about solving the problem does not demonstrate a further 4th further condition to be added, but instead to add a minor part to condition 3 (S is justified in believing P). This paper can be thought of as proving a sufficient foundation upon which all epistemological forms of knowledge can form a reference to. Thus, my solution presents a new theory of knowledge, and how it exists.

In cases 1 and 2, Gettier makes the claim that the person does not know the certain proposition in question. However, in reference to providing a theoretical theory of knowledge you should not use know to describe the theory of knowledge, because know itself is not yet being defined by the person, who is concerned with the necessary and sufficient conditions of knowledge, which precedes the notion of know, because knowledge enables a person to know.

S knows that P, iff

1. P is true (a fact)
2. S believes in P (a belief in a fact)
3. S is truly justified in believing P

*Justification of P is S's true belief in P

*True justification of P is: S's false belief in P + S's true belief in P

*P is true (belief in P) = ~P is false (justification of P)

*Thus: 1 is a necessary condition for knowledge; 2 is a necessary condition for knowledge; 3 is a necessary condition of knowledge. Therefore: 1, 2, and 3 demonstrate the necessary (single), and sufficient (all) conditions of knowledge.

Case 1 Resolution:

> (d) Jones is the man who will get the job, and Jones has ten coins in his pocket.
> (e) The man who will get the job has ten coins in his pocket.

Smith knows that (e), iff

1. (e) is true
2. Smith believes that (e) is true
3. Smith is truly justified in believing that (e) is true (true justification is: (e) is true + ~(e) is false)

   (e) = Smith will get the job
   ~(e) = Jones will get the job

   (e) is true = Smith will get the job (fact)
   ~(e) is false = Jones will not get the job (fact)

Hence: (e) is true = ~(e) is false

The above conditions demonstrate the necessary and sufficient conditions by which Smith will have knowledge. (Although mentioned in the paper of (d), I do not refer to it because it said in the article that (d) is false, and hence, is of no use). We may demonstrate these conditions as follows:

S knows that P, iff

1. P is true (P is a fact)
2. S believes that P is true (S believes in P (believes P is a fact))
3. S is truly justified in believing that P is true (because: P = true fact; ~P = false fact; hence, P is true = ~P is false)

From 1, 2, and 3, we can establish that Smith knows (e) (Smith has knowledge of (e) (the true fact))

So, my argument above, as well as what I will demonstrate later in this paper, differs from the contemporary view of knowledge stating that knowledge is 'justified true belief'. This view is what Gettier objected to. I agree with Gettier on the point of requiring a different condition to be added to the three necessary conditions of S knowing P. My argument is that knowledge is 'truly justified true belief'.

-Justified true belief = (fact) is believed
-Truly justified true belief = (fact) is believed as true, and ~(fact) is believed as false.

We have thereby established, through Case 1, a resolution to Gettier's problem of specifying the necessary and sufficient conditions for knowledge.

Case 2 Resolution:

(f) Jones owns a Ford
(g) Either Jones owns a Ford, or Brown is in Boston
(h) Either Jones owns a Ford, or Brown is in Barcelona.
(i) Either Jones owns a Ford, or Brown is in Brest-Litovsk

Since (f) is false, we can therefore simplify the propositions:

(g) Brown is in Boston
(h) Brown is in Barcelona
(i) Brown is in Brest-Litovsk

It is important to note that (g), (h), and (i) all contradict one another, in that when one is affirmed as true, then the other two must necessarily be false (because Brown can only be in one of the three places at one time).

So, because (h) is true, this necessarily demonstrates (g) and (i) as false. We then have:

(a) (h) is true
(b) Smith believes (h) is true

(c) Smith is truly justified in believing that (h) is true (because: (h) = true fact; ~(h) = false fact; hence, (h) is true = ~(h) is false)

(h) = true fact = (~(g) and ~(i))
~(h) = false fact = ((g) and (i))

So, Smith knows (h), because:

1. (h) is true (a fact)
2. Smith believes (h) is true (believes that (h) is a fact)
3. Smith is truly justified in believing that (h) is a fact ((h) is true (justification of belief) = ~(h) is false (true justification of belief)

Therefore, we have the complete necessary and sufficient conditions of knowledge:

S knows P, iff

(i) P is true (necessary condition)
(ii) S believes that P (necessary condition)
(iii) S is truly justified in believing that P (necessary condition)

*When all three necessary conditions are satisfied, then this constitutes the sufficient conditions upon which knowledge is founded. Thus, knowledge is sufficiently described through the unification of (i), (ii), and (iii).

Thus, upon examining Cases 1 and 2, we see that the only difference between my epistemic theory, and Gettier's objection, is that condition three is revised to mean "truly justified of belief", as opposed to "justified belief"

\*\*\*

## A RATING OF EVERY DRUG I HAVE TRIED (NOT INCLUDING THE DRUGS I HAVE DONE MENTIONED ABOVE)

## DRUG RATING – COCAINE

Of all the thousands of dollars that I have probably spent on cocaine, I have nothing to show for it (unlike other drugs I have purchased where I have philosophy essays to show for it, for example). For starters, the cocaine I get where I am from is horrible quality. I am not sure what exactly the procedure for cutting down blow is, but if I had to guess, I would say that the asshole's cocaine that I eventually ended up snorting, was so thinned out, that he profited way more than he should have, had he not fucked with the part of it that makes you high and replaced it with something that doesn't get you high. I would definitely be down to try cocaine that they get from Columbia in the movie, "Blow". The main problem is that it doesn't last very long. Even if you smoke it in crack form, I don't think it would be as fun of a drug as amphetamines for example. I read a saying once by Bruce Lee who said the following: "Long-term consistency trumps short term intensity". To me this applies exactly to how cocaine lines up in comparison to other uppers. Cocaine may give you a better high than other uppers (although it never did for me), especially with crack, but a highly euphoric Adderall or Ritalin high trumps the short term high of cocaine, because the high lasts much longer and in my opinion, when taken a decent amount, will even give you a better high. Come downs suck when you are on any drug, but for cocaine especially, you can blow through a couple hundred dollars easily, only to have it end a few hours later, feeling like shit and wishing you had more.

## DRUG RATING – MOLLIE

I have never tried ecstasy, but I have snorted Molly several times, which I hear is as good if not better than ecstasy because it is the pure form of it, without other drugs cut into it. I never understood why people complained that ecstasy was cut with other drugs. It is not like cocaine where they cut it down with baking soda (something that doesn't get you high). They cut it with other drugs, which, since they are drugs, can only do more to improve your state of mind. Molly is, in my opinion, a decent high, that lasts about as long for me as a cocaine high, which is pretty fucking lame, considering most people say it lasts for four to six hours for them. I guess that is the price I pay for being addicted to stimulants. After the not very good high is finished, I get very tired and just want to go to sleep. Why people think that things feel really soft or rolling to the point that you are waving glow sticks around in a club, I never understood.

## DRUG RATING – KETAMINE

I had first heard about Ketamine from Eddie and when we had conversations about it he would refer to it as "fire". Eddie got so addicted to it that he ended up pawning off his Play Station 3 in order to get more of it. I figured I'd try it out to see what was so special about it. I bought around $50 worth of Ketamine powder and snorted it with Eddie and the guy I bought it from. Once it started to kick in, it immediately reminded me of tripping on mushrooms. Not really hallucinating, just a different type of perception which you could see the world through. After doing this drug, I thought for sure that I could go up to a casino and win some money, since it put me into a tripping type state of mind where I think I could control the physical world. The reason I thought this was because when I was on it for the first time, I looked at the bag that the Ketamine powder and thought that I could fill more in it, so I thought about this, and the bag filled up a little bit. I tried to win money at a casino a few months later and it failed miserably. Probably because of the fact that the Ketamine wasn't very good and apparently, I am completely delusional when it comes to legitimately thinking that I could affect the physical world. Apparently, the dealer that got us the Ketamine the night that I went up to a casino got shot a few months later.

The most intense thing about Ketamine, in my opinion, is that it takes you to another universe where your mind becomes detached from your ordinary perception of your life. I started injecting it at a certain point and this gives you a more intense high. Injecting it is not like injecting heroin in that you don't have to inject it into vain. I mostly injected into my leg and my upper ass at least once. The point is to inject it into a muscle and that makes it kick in within about ten to fifteen minutes. The other times I got high I tried to control the physical world, but with little success (much like with everything else I have tried to do and fucked it up). Ultimately, my opinion of Ketamine is that it is a fun drug, just be prepared when you take it to experience a detachment of your consciousness from your physical body to the point that the world that you see in front of you is a reality that takes you along with it. Complete control of your mind, to a much greater extent than other hallucinogens. Eddie and I had a conversation once about how much Ketamine can alter your perception.

Eddie: Just don't go into a K-Hole.

Me: What is a K-Hole?

Eddie: When the drug takes you to a place where it is in complete control of you.

Me: I don't see why that is a bad thing.

Eddie: Yeah, I suppose that's right.

The last time I did Ketamine I was talking to some guy, trying to explain to him why Ketamine is such a fun drug. He told me that he had a friend who died on it once and that he doesn't like that drug. Ultimately, I don't really think it's that big of a deal (which is pretty much my opinion on every drug that exists).

## DRUG RATING – BATH SALTS

A few years ago, it was legal in the state that I live in, to buy artificial stimulants, called, "bath salts". They came in multiple forms, some simulating a Mollie high, while others simulated an LSD and stimulant combination effect. By the time that I became interested in trying them for myself, the state made them illegal, unfortunately. However, I did try one of the bath salts one time. It was called, 2CI, and it had the effect that I described above, being the one that makes you trip while feeling a euphoric stimulant high. The first mistake I made when I first tried it, was that the person who we got it from put it into little pills to take it orally. I didn't question it at the time, but upon reflection, the amount I paid for was not going to get me anywhere close to where I could even feel a little bit different. I should have snorted it, but instead I only took half the pill to begin with, because apparently if you take too much of it, your heart rate will increase dramatically, not that I haven't dealt with that before. Frank started rolling within thirty minutes of taking it and I was confused as to why it wasn't doing shit for me. I had specifically asked one of the cooks at the restaurant I was working at at the time to cover my shift, so I could party with my friends. The plan I had was that since I was going to trip, I could accomplish my fantasy of stopping absolute time and freeing myself. The drug never kicked in, which makes me think that all bath salts probably suck just as much.

## DRUG RATING – OPIATES

I have tried heroin once and I have done Suboxone, twice. I can't really say how good the heroin high is because I smoked it and it didn't really hit me. But I once read a report on the internet, in which a guy was talking about the first time he shot heroin. He said that within the first 2 – 3 seconds that he felt the high kick in, he knew he was going to be an addict. The only thing I can really comment on is that in the case of Suboxone, it gives a nice mellow tired feeling, which I can only guess to its similarities to heroin being somewhat like this, because they give Suboxone to heroin addicts to help them recover so they won't die from the withdrawal symptoms. I am not much into downers or sedatives. I have never been in so much pain in my life that the doctors at a hospital put me on morphine. I hear good things about it, and would probably take some morphine if offered, but I don't really care enough about it to go and seek it out.

## DRUG RATING – MODAFINIL

In college I became aware of a stimulant called, "Modafinil", and its lesser version, "Adrafinil". When I ran out of Adderall, I would take Adrafinil and, just like I have described in reference to other drugs, once you experience a very intense focus, although other substances may also make you feel focused, it's just not the same or as good. I watched a lot of videos on YouTube describing Modafinil and what it did. Some people even went so far as to compare it to the limitless pill, NZT48 in the movie, "Limitless". Others said it made you feel really good. I decided that I wanted to try it and see what everyone is raving about. The problem is that they are a Schedule 3 or 4 controlled substance and if the cops find you in possession of it without a prescription, you could potentially be charged with a felony or misdemeanor at the very least. The people talking about how good of a drug it was in their video's referred me to some websites based outside the US that you can buy it from, and have it shipped into the country, with little or no careful inspection as to the illegal contents that the package possesses. I was a little sketched out in attempting to buy it. I didn't want to end up like Dwayne Johnson's son in that one movie where he buys drugs and when he opens it, there is a police tracker inside of it that goes off, as cops swarm the house. I decided to risk it and bought 120 pills for around $200 - $250. When the pills arrived, I started off by taking two. Two pills, at 200mg a piece, is usually the maximum does that a doctor will prescribe to a patient, mostly for sleep disorders like narcolepsy. I watched one video where a kid said that anything above 500mg (two and a half pills) gets you into an "unsafe zone", at which overdoses happen, I guess. After taking the two pills I did come to realize one aspect of the pills that I saw a guy talking about in an interview about the pill, mainly, that when it starts to kick in, lights become brighter and seem a little more vivid. At first, I was happy with what it did to me, the good feeling actually was decent, and I could feel more concentrated to get shit done. I thought if I began to push the limits with what the pill might be able to do for me (if 400-600mg makes me feel decent, what would another 800mg make me feel like?), I could discover hyper focus like Adderall. The more pills I took at one time, I discovered they gave me an almost trippy type feeling, in which it reminded me of a psychedelic drug first coming on. I found out that the more I took, I didn't feel any more euphoric or happy, and my focus wasn't that much improved either. The most I took in one day was around twenty pills, and it was very disappointing. I tried jacking off when I was on it and that was lame to. This drug is in a class of substances which are referred to as "Nootropic" drugs. These drugs help improve your minds performance across a wide range of abilities, such as focus, memory and reaction time. I bet if you tested me to see my brain's performance in these certain categories that it is supposed to help with, I would probably score higher when I am on Modafinil, but nothing compared to how much higher I would score if I was on other stimulants like amphetamines (which are apparently considered Nootropic drugs to). What I take away from my experiences with Modafinil is that it is not that great of a drug if you are looking for a mind boost that other euphoric stimulants give you. And what's even weirder about it, is that apparently it is not even classified as a stimulant (according to some guy being interviewed on TV). It helps keep you awake without forcing you awake. Whatever the fuck that means.

## DRUG RATING – EPHEDRINE

When I was working at a Car Wash, one of my co-workers was a woman named, "Suzie". She was way chill. We would always be talking about drugs, and she even asked me one time if I needed some acid because her son had some. We were talking about stimulants one day and she told me about, "Ephedrine", which at that time I had never heard of before. She told me about its effects, that mainly being the euphoria and focus that other stimulants give you. It wasn't until a year to year and a half later that I decided that I would try it. I looked up online if they were selling it, and all I saw was something called, "Ephedra", which I don't know if that is the same thing or not, but I decided not to risk it. I found out that at pharmacies they sell certain medications over the counter, ranging from ones for asthma to ones for your cough, which contain ephedrine. I asked the pharmacist what medications they sell that contain it, and she told me about one asthma medication called, "Primatene". When purchasing medications that contain ephedrine, you are required to show the pharmacist your driver's license or photo ID so that they can put you into a database, which tracks how many times a month you buy it. In the state I live in, you can buy up to 3g of ephedrine that is contained in a medication that you get in a single day and can buy 9g in a 30 day period. Every box of Primatene contains 750mg of ephedrine in it, which means that you can buy it up to twelve times in a given 30 day period. I already wrote about what happened to me the first time I tried it, mainly, hallucinating my balls off and getting very psychotic. However, the more I purchased it and started experimenting around with it, I found that the more I took, the better I ultimately felt, as well as my psychotic symptoms, especially hearing voices, subsided. Eventually, I got to a point (which as of this day that I am writing this, I am still at this point) where I would take all sixty pills in the box at once. When I first started using this drug, I would buy it three, and sometimes even four times a week, since I was able to get it up to twelve times in a 30 day period. I have been rejected multiple times for trying to buy over the allowed amount that you can purchase. The first time this happened I was actually a little relieved, because I had read an article on the internet that said the cops arrested someone who bought more ephedrine medication that was legal to buy. Apparently, people can use this drug to make methamphetamine, and that is why it is regulated. I am at a current point in my use of this drug such that it produces two shitty results. First, the euphoric, nice high only lasts for no more than two or three hours now, whereas when I first started taking it, I would be good for up to six hours. Second, even though you may not feel jack shit in reference to the ephedrine having an effect, it still works through your system for at least 24-30 hours, keeping you awake when you really want to sleep. In order to combat being awake for so long and not having any fun whatsoever, I have to take multiple pills of one of my antipsychotic drugs, "Zyprexa" to help me fall asleep. In spite of the fact that ephedrine doesn't give you nearly the type of effect that Adderall or Ritalin do in reference to feeling good or ability to focus, I sometimes did possess the ability when I was on it to abstract decently and write two pretty good (I think, others don't) philosophical essays. A big problem that I noticed takes effect the higher in dose you go up, is that when the drug first kicks in, you begin to see double and feel a little bit of a head fuck as it first begins to take effect. Ephedrine takes (at least the ephedrine in Primatene) only five to ten minutes to start working, and I usually know when it's coming on when I feel a slight numbness in the bottom of my lip, and in my head. I have researched online what are some of the potential effects that Primatene abuse might have on your liver, but there is literally nothing that anyone has written about it. Regardless of whether I am fucking up my liver or not, whatever you do, do not mix it with alcohol. Maybe one or two drinks tops should be your limit, because anything above that and you will see double up the shit and feel very fucked up. Whenever I take this drug, I will usually always use some form of nicotine (whether it be smoking, chewing tobacco, nicotine gum, etc.), although this increases the high, if you take too much of it, you may get the spins, start sweating, and puke, as I usually do when this happens. Also, caffeine and energy drinks increase the high and make it last a little bit longer, but too much will put you in a very shitty state where you end up contemplating why the fuck you put your body through the abuse you do. I have asked myself this question on several occasions, and I always give the same answer: because I like feeling high, and even though I may be using drugs in blatant disregard for how to keep your body healthy, I am at least content to know that fuck up degenerates like me weren't meant to live long lives anyways. All in all, ephedrine is ok, but nothing special.

## DRUG RATING – RITALIN

I have been prescribed other stimulants besides amphetamines in my life, most notably, Ritalin, Concerta, and Wellbutrin. I can say that Ritalin is the best of these three, with Concerta being second best, and Wellbutrin the least good. Ritalin is number one in my opinion, because taken in large enough quantities, it can make you just as euphoric and focused as any amphetamine can. I have read that immediate release Ritalin possesses a similar chemical structure to cocaine and gives you a similar euphoric buzz. But cocaine sucks because the good part only lasts around fifteen to twenty minutes, whereas a Ritalin high will last a good six to eight hours. Then there is Concerta. All

Concerta is, is extended-release Ritalin. So, if you are looking for some sort of euphoria out of it, this can only be accomplished through taking multiple pills at the same time, enabling all the pills to slowly release the Methylphenidate at once, and give you a better feeling. I was prescribed 20mg of Ritalin, and 36mg of Concerta, the former I took once a day, and the latter I took twice a day. I found that the rough equivalency for amphetamines to methylphenidate is that amphetamine mg is half of Ritalin or Concerta mg. For example, a 20mg Ritalin is equal to roughly 10mg of Adderall, and 36mg Concerta is equal to roughly 18mg of Adderall. I used to take 6 Concerta and 3 Ritalin at one time, which is like taking roughly 140mg of Adderall. In doses like this it is just as good as amphetamines, but it doesn't last as long. I mentioned earlier in this book that I once went through a one or two month supply of Ritalin in five days. The shit I could perceive and philosophize about when I took around eight to ten 40mg pills in a single sitting was pretty bad ass. I told my psychiatrist this at one point, but he didn't believe me (and maybe he is right and I am wrong), when I told him that I took so much Ritalin at one time during the five days I stayed up, that my heart rate probably got anywhere from 200-250 beats per minute. My doctor said if it got up that high, I probably would have died, so I can't really be sure, but it sure as shit felt fast, like in the movie, "Wanted" when his heart beats around 400 times a minute and he could slow down his perception of time. There is a lot of truth to this, seeing that when my heart was going apeshit, I was able to abstract like a mother fucker and see such high up logical constructs. It was sickness, for sure. I got so high on Ritalin that once I came down just a tiny bit from the very rapid heartbeat high, I started feeling a little depressed. I was still feeling very good and focused, but it's just like seeing a perfect, beautiful woman in reference to another beautiful woman, once you see the perfect woman, the other woman, although beautiful, doesn't quite match up with the other woman. In other words, once you have seen the peak of something, anything less than that, although it could still be awesome, still doesn't give you complete control of the potential in your mind, quite as much as the peak does. All in all, I would say that Methylphenidate is a fun drug, that enables you to do whatever what you want for quite a bit of time. I will briefly discuss Wellbutrin, but it is really not good enough to even be considered in the class of other stimulants like Adderall or Ritalin. When I was prescribed it, I didn't know that if you abused it, you could potentially get a decent high out of it, and have it give you enough focus to get shit done. The only time I took enough to feel any different from sobriety, I got from a co-worker. I forgot how much she gave me or what the mg were, but I snorted at least three or four of them, and it put me in a good mood for about ten minutes before it wore off.

## DRUG RATING – NICOTINE

Despite being only a mild stimulant, I always liked what Nicotine did to me. It's always a nice thing when you could just relax for ten minutes outside, smoking with friends to get away from your shitty job for a while. I started smoking when I was 19 and it was the first time I experienced what Nicotine does to me. I recently quit smoking when I developed a shitty cough that wouldn't go away and was just sick of doing it. The health aspect didn't play that much into my decision to stop smoking, besides the fact that I wanted my cough to go away and thought that if I quit smoking, it would. It hasn't. What separates using nicotine through cigarettes different than other ways of taking it like gum or chew, is that the nicotine buzz isn't even the best part. I was mostly addicted to the oral fixation of puffing on something, blowing smoke rings. Smoking is a lot of fun, but if you are looking for a big nicotine kick, it is not the way to go. Once I figured this out, I lost all interest in smoking. I was introduced to nicotine gum by a co-worker one work shift and he gave me two pieces, each containing 2mg. Like I do with all substances, I began to bump up the amount I intake at once, and now whenever I use nicotine gum, I take six to eight 4mg pieces. It doesn't get me that buzzed and the only reason I still do it is mainly to increase the high of the stimulants I take. If taken in large enough quantities, a substance like nicotine can become a sport where you chase the high to see if you can attain a buzz usually only reserved for illegal substances. I do this with chewing tobacco. I always get the pouches, because every time I tried using the regular chew in high school, it always ended with me puking and people laughing at me. I heard a story about some guy who was a few grades above me in high school, in which he dipped (on at least one occasion) with an entire can in his mouth. I was inspired by this and it made me experiment around with what doing a lot of this stuff can do. Chewing tobacco, through what I have found out in my own experimentation of it, gives you the best nicotine buzz out of any other way in which it can be taken. The most I have ever dipped at one time was ten pouches, which, if I am on a stimulant like ephedrine, always ends with me sweating, feeling tired, and puking. The only drawback (and there is always one with every goddamn drug or substance in the world): it fucks your gums up something bad, starting with gingivitis, then upgrading to potentially losing your teeth, and maybe having part of your tongue removed. There's a whole interesting science as to how it develops. But you get what you ask for, in that unlike most ways of ingesting nicotine, dipping allows you to take the most at one time to give yourself a temporary mind and body high. I have tried nicotine patches and electronic cigarettes but am disappointed with the little to no effect that either one had on me. I'm sure there are other limits you could push like putting twenty nicotine patches on your body (the most I have ever done at one time was six), or even swallowing some liquid nicotine that hasn't been vaporized yet in your e-cig, but this type of way of chasing the nicotine high never really appealed to me. Just like with any drug, there are ways that you can abuse it and potentially causing real harm to your body. But if you are looking for the safest way to get a nicotine buzz, the gum is the way to go.

# MOVIE SCRIPT IDEA (ALSO, A LESSON IN ABSTRACT REWORKS AND COMBINATIONS)

What is written below is my movie script idea in which I rework scenes from specific movies to accord with another idea that will elucidate a humorous way in which the scene can be reworked to accord with an original idea. It will exhibit how the scene can be used to show a different set of circumstances through which each of these scenes can be understood in a humorous way. It is my hope that when this book gets published that it will create insight by other people to do the same thing and hopefully make a movie out of these ideas. Therefore, the movie, if picked up by some producer or company that makes movies, will then show how something humorous can be reworked into the scene with the purpose of showing the world how these different scenes accord with the actual scenes that I am taking them from, and create a film that is funny. For every person that contributes to these movie scene ideas, will be part of the writing process, and hence, be mentioned as part of the writing process of the movie. After every scene I rework, I end it with, ……….. This is because I believe that there could be much more to be said about the scene and other original reworks can be incorporated in to. Below are 200 of my best reworks that I have come up with. Seeing that I come up with multiple each day, I have probably thought of 10,000+ since I started thinking of them.

## INTRODUCTION TO MOVIE SCENE REWORKS

I am a savant when it comes to taking scenes from movies and either rearranging them in my mind to make a somewhat coherent string of clips that can range from really funny and mood brightening, to making me angry that I thought of it (this is called a *combination*. When you string together clips or just reference one clip in your head that makes sense in context to what is being experienced or happening in the world apart from me. What I have written below is of another type of creative activity that I engage in because it enables me to be entertained by my own thoughts. This is called a *rework*. Basically, it is just taking a scene from a movie, television, the internet, radio, personal experiences or anything else that you can visualize and think about it in another way that it could be portrayed as with the hope that you preserve the overall feeling and tone that the actors try and convey in the scene they are in. It is fairly easy to construct a rework which deals with almost entirely adult material (ideas related to sex mostly). The best reworks are those that are the most innocent, because they require more amount of thought that goes in to completing it than do the adult reworks. The innocent reworks also tend to be way funnier, and in turn, makes me happy. I have often wondered what are the kind of things that the average person thinks about when they are not talking to or interacting with another person. A lot of women apparently think that men think about sex almost all the time. If this is true, I don't relate to it at all. Although constructing reworks is just as pointless as thinking about sex all the time, there is a tiny bit of aesthetic quality that goes along with constructing a good rework. Kind of a feeling like you did do something constructive, even if you have nothing physical to show for it. The main reason I decided to write these scenes and ideas down is because my intention was to rework a scene, and then have the original actors and actresses come back and play the part in the rework. Unfortunately, a few of the actors in the scenes I reworked died, and I think it wouldn't be the same if some other actor played the dead actor's role. A movie based around this idea, would have the sole purpose of being humorous and not an actual plot oriented movie. The main point to this section is to stimulate ideas surrounding the movie/tv show scenes that I rework. Someone may come along and rework the scene in a funnier way than how I reworked it. A lot of these reworks may seem to not make any sense, but the hallmark of a good rework is that the more absurd the rework, the funnier it could be (construct a rework through the sense that past, present, and future all meet together).

# `THE REWORKING OF SCENES TAKEN FROM POPULAR CULTURE MOVIES AND TV SHOWS

1. "A Beautiful Mind" scene where John and the Professor walk into the faculty lounge and see the other professors giving pens to a man. REWORK: instead of having the people give pens to the man, have them give brownies to the man. As John and the Professor walk to the faculty lounge, they are talking about something that has to do with baking and cooking food. After John gets rejected by the Professor (about something that has to do with baking (the professor goes up to the guy who everyone is giving brownies to and gives him a brownie also)), we see him in his room and looking at cookies that are baking in the oven. He hits his head and starts to bleed. Charles then pushes the oven outside the window.………

2. "American Beauty" scene where Brad is reading Lester's work note. REWORK: instead of the note being presented in preparation for him blackmailing Brad, the note should be written in the present tense, in which Lester describes exactly what he will do in blackmailing Brad: "I expect that my boss, Brad Dupree, upon reading this note will ensure that I receive the severance package that I have just described, not for fear of me releasing the information about the company editorial director buying pussy with company money, but rather as a means to ensure that my intent to blackmail him through the exploitation of oral sex upon me, was conceived of through him…

3. "I love you, Man" scene where Paul Rudd and Jason Segel are talking about how to pronounce "Chocolat". This scene can be shown in unison with the scene from "Avatar" where the guy in the wheelchair tries saying the names of the Avatar people to Sigourney Weaver, and she corrects his pronunciation. REWORK: "Avatar" scene saying "Chocolat"; "I Love you, Man" scene saying "Atucan"; Jason Segel saying "Will.I.am" pronouncing it "William", cut to Sigourney Weaver pronouncing it "Will.I.am"; "Avatar" scene saying "Holla", 8,008 pronounced BOOB because it's on calculator, Flo Rida instead of Florida, Dumas being said Dumbass

4. "Yes, Man" scene where it shows the guy telling Jim Carrey that he must say yes to everything, no matter what it is. We see Jim Carrey walk out to his car, and a homeless man asks him if he can borrow a lighter. Jim

Carrey gives the man the lighter and we see the man light up a crack pipe. The man blows out the smoke and asks Jim Carrey if he wants a hit. We hear the guy's command "you will say yes, no matter what it is" play again, and Jim Carrey takes a hit from the crack pipe............

5. "The Number 23" scene in which Jim Carrey claims that things relate to him have to do with the number 23. REWORK: "Michael Jordan and Lebron James, my favorite basketball players, their number is 23."; "My favorite drink is Dr. Pepper. Dr. Pepper has 23 flavors.",............

6. "Before the Devil Knows your Dead" scene starting with seeing the top of a car driving with the words, "The day of the robbery". We then see the robber put on a hockey mask, and enter the store. Once inside he pulls down the window cover and we see a woman holding a tray of cookies with oven mittens on. The robber points the gun at the woman and she immediately stops in horror. The robber says, "Ok, down touch anything, don't say anything, put the cookies down. Take off the mittens and back up. Back up!" The woman backs up and............ (At the end of the scene when the woman shoots the robber and he crashes out of the glass window door, we see Hank in the car. Blood sprays onto his face and we see him wipe some of it off on his hands, as he freaks out and drives away.)

7. "Corky Romano" scene where Paul tells everyone he can't read. REWORK: make it about that Paul doesn't know how women's periods work............

8. We see a television commercial for "Garden State 2". It is the movie where Largeman plays the retarded quarterback........ (we see excerpts from some of the scenes that they discuss in the movie, such as when Largeman gives the speech to the stadium and his dad gives him the thumbs up).

9. "Garden State" scene where Largeman visits the neurologist. REWORK: the neurologist reads off the list of drugs that Largeman put on the paper. They are all illegal drugs. Neurologist: "Methamphetamine? How long have you been on the meth?" Largeman: "this is the first time I haven't had a controlled substance in my body in a long time.".............

10. "Jumper" beginning scene where he is standing on the Sphinx explaining to the audience how his day went. REWORK: "Let me tell you about my day so far, robbed a bank and got off scot free (cut to "what kind of crook leaves a note?" scene), hooked up with a girl who came onto me because I live in London (cut to "and now I'm living in New York" scene), gave my girlfriend a private tour of the Coliseum because the front doors were

unlocked (cut to "is that door just open to?" "It's open now"), put in near the end of the scene the clip from when he finally comes clean about lying, and then right after that, put in the clip where he looks at Rachel Bilson and says to her that he is not lying (so basically a rework of every time he lied in the movie)...............

11. "Elf" scene where the boy is reading from the book of what people wish to Santa what they want for Christmas that is being broadcast on television with the reporter. REWORK: "Person A wants a new...........(this scene will show the reactions of the people watching the news in response to them either knowing the person, or the person himself (it will contain some revealing information and some consequences that follow)).

12. "The Secret" scene where the guy is talking about the gay standup comedian. REWORK: instead, the guy is talking about Lester Burnham. This will just be a description of Lester's life starting with being depressed, and ending with his ultimate happiness. Another idea could be to have the guy talk about someone who sucks at using the secret and his life just keeps getting worse and worse...

13. "Cold Mountain" scene where the guy says, "Where's Georgia?" REWORK: put in scenes from other movies where someone asks a question starting with, "Where's..." and then cut to the rework scene where the guy imitates it sarcastically..... ("Who's John Galt?")

14. "Collateral" scene where the guy falls on top of the taxi. REWORK: we see Jamie Foxx flipping through the pages of a Maxim magazine, while eating a sandwich. We then see a person dressed in an S n M outfit with a ball gage in his mouth fall onto the taxi. Jamie Foxx freaks out as Tom Cruise comes down to see what happened. "I think he's dead", "It's a she, and yes she's dead." "You killed her?" Tom cruise then points the gun at Jamie Foxx. The two then carry the body into the trunk of the cab. The next scene then cuts to Tom Cruise tying Jamie Foxx's hand's to the steering wheel, and then proceeding to put the ball gage over his mouth..........

15. "Inside Man" combination scenes showing the dumbness of the bank robbers and cops (whatever stupid things either of them do in the movie): 1) the part where the robbers first make their presence known to the bank by telling everyone to get down on the floor. For some reason the robbers decide that it would be a good idea to throw smoke grenades around the bank. As also noted from the late Roger Ebert, why would they try to

attract attention to themselves, which is exactly what the smoke grenades ended up doing. 2) the part where the robbers pretend to shoot one of the hostages. This only sped up the police's decision to go into the bank. 3) the part where Denzel Washington tries to get someone off the streets who knows the foreign language being spoken by what he believes (incorrectly) are the robbers. A man tells him that they are speaking Albanian, and for some reason Denzel Washington equivocates this with speaking Albanian as opposed to just being somewhat familiar with language. 4) The part where Denzel Washington is about to leave the bank after being accompanied by the robbers, and, when he goes to shake the robbers hand, he tries to grab his gun, and this leads to both men falling down the stairs on top of each other, trying to get the gun, which the robber ends up doing and then immediately pointing it at Denzel Washington telling him that he crossed the line. What exactly was Denzel Washington's intention in trying to take the robbers gun, even if he did get the gun, aside from the fact that it was a fake, did he really think he had a chance to make the situation better by getting the robbers hand gun (as opposed to the other robbers who were carrying automatic weapons). 5) The part where the cops are trying to solve some riddle or logic problem that the robber told them, which, if they got it right, he would then allow them to bring in more food. After a few minutes of deliberating, and calling the robber, and then calling the robber again, they decide to just take one of the cops word for it without any discussion about why he thinks it must be true. The cop ends up being right about the question, making the other cops deliberating the answer to the question a minute before seem like they have literally no idea. 5) the part where, after putting recording devices in the pizza boxes to hear what the robbers are saying, when they hear the foreign language, one of the officers was quick to say that the robbers were speaking Russian. The language ended up not being Russian, which begs the question of what exactly it was about hearing the language that made one of the cops just get some random intuition that it sounds like Russian. 6) the part where the Muslim comes out of the bank and the cops take his turbin off. One of the cops calls him an arab and asks if he had a bomb. If he did have a bomb it would have come from the robbers, and not the Muslim, so the fact that he is a Muslim and has nothing to do with what the robbers made him carry out of the bank, and is definitely a case of racial profiling of Middle Eastern looking people. Later, the cops talk to the Muslim and the Muslim says that his religion is some sect of Islam. After telling the cops that he is not an Arab and is actually a different type of Middle Eastern descent, he recounts the experience of one of the cops first calling him an Arab. Immediately one of the cops interjects and tells him that he didn't hear that because he didn't. Claiming that there was a lot of commotion going on when the Muslim left the bank, apparently the Muslim, because there was a lot going on in the surrounding area nearby, hallucinated that one of the cops called him Arab.….

16. "That Awkward Moment" scene where he says woman's brains lit up like fireworks. REWORK: "Women's brains lit up like fireworks when they were showed pictures of…a penis." Once the guy says this, we see reactions from the women in the room, showing their approval…

17. "Sex Drive" scenes where Lance is hooking up with that girl who handcuffs him to a bed. REWORK: "Ever hear of Cleveland steamer?" "Ever hear of a dirty Sanchez" "No, let's try it."

18. "Good Will Hunting" scene where he says "Do you like apples? How do you like them apples?" REWORK: "Do you like dick's? Well I got a gift card (presses up against the window a Dick's sporting good gift card), how do you like them dicks?"

19. "Wolf of Wall Street" scene where Jordan speaks to his company. REWORK: "Is your wife a worthless skank? Good pick up the phone and start dialing." "Is she trying to get full custody of your kids? Good pick up the phone and start dialing." "I want you to deal with your bitch wife, by becoming rich." Make the rework to be all about the people's wives.……….

20. "Limitless" scene where Eddy and his brother-in-law are at a bar. "I guess I can help you with that." He then takes out of his pocket a joint, a bag of heroin, and two pills of Adderall, he then pushes his shot next to the other things so they are all lined up in front of Eddy. "What's in it?"……………. "I had gotten little information from Verne just what these drugs would do. And then I felt it."……………

21. "One Flew Over the Cuckoo's Nest" scene where Jack Nicholson is being carried by Mangeni and talks to chief about putting the ball through the basketball net. REWORK: they are playing quidditch (from Harry Potter) and Jack Nicholson has the ball. Everyone is riding around on broomsticks, but they are not flying. Jack Nicholson then comes up to chief. "Put that son of a bitch through the goal, Chief!"

22. "The Internship" where the people tell them to look for Charles Xavier. REWORK: instead they tell them to look for Adolph Hitler." They then go to the college and see someone looking just like Adolph Hitler" After they try and talk to him he says, "We're all here, Clause Barbie, Gorbells, Romel………………"

23. "Grandma's Boy" scene where he is at the wedding talking to the kids. REWORK: "Have you shot the crack dealer and taken his money? Great. Here's what you do, rob the bank. After you shoot the teller, grab the money and go back to your car. Once you get there, there will be a hooker waiting for you. After you screw her, get in your car and go back to your apartment, and that's it, level 3 is done." The children then applaud…………….

24. "Blair Witch Project" scenes where they are asking people if they have heard of the Blair Witch. Instead they are talking about, "Have you ever heard of a kaffir?" "That actually sounds kind of familiar by sister actually went to kaffir elementary?" "It's a story by grandma used to tell me to make us go to be early, she said if you stay up to late, walk around the house to much the kaffir will come and, get ya." "Oh yes, that's an old, old story.".………………

25. "Religulous" scene where Bill Mahr is talking to the people at the trucker's chapel. "Are you guys ever challenged by anything that nobody has any evidence for like, "Zeno stacking people around volcanoes, people having thetens, the universe is 80 trillion years old?…………." "I don't know who you think you are but I don't like were you are going. You start refuting L. Ron Hubbard, and you got a problem." "When I've seen what I've seen I know scientology is true, you can't change my mind, no one can. I walked for thirteen years…………." "it's a science fiction thing." "let me ask you a question, what if we wrong you ain't, you gonna make it we ain't" "I've walked for 15 years, from the time I grew up I was an atheist." "Real atheism?" "Yes, real atheism. Not believing in scientology, and being married to strippers, I walked around with gold rings on my hands, I gave all that up, when I became a scientologist." "And when the guy said, you know I had strippers for wives, and I had gold rings, and I'm going, and your problem was?"…………..

26. "Being John Malkovich" scene where John Cusack tells Maxine that he just went through the portal. REWORK: "In my office, there is a portal, that takes you inside the mind of Danny Elfman." "Who the

fuck is Danny Elfman?" "Oh, he's a great composer, one of the greatest composers of the twentieth century." "Oh yeah what has he composed?" "Lots of things, he played in that one movie with the guy who had the scissorhands"............

27. "Limitless" scene where Eddy is at the bar with Vernon. REWORK: Vernon gives Eddy a bag of DMT" "What's in it?" "You know how they say the average life time of a person is 75 years? Well what this does, it lets you live for trillions of years."...............

28. "Baseketball" scene where squeak and Matt Stone go into the room and shows squeak where he is going to sleep. REWORK: they go into the room and there is a dog cage. "Dude that is so fucking weak, how am I supposed to get a chick in that?" "Don't worry dude you couldn't get a girl if you had a $100 hanging out of your zipper." "Yeah I could." "No, dude you suck dick for coke." "I do not. I don't even know why I hang out with you guys." "Because your attracted to transsexuals." "I am not attracted to transsexuals." "Yeah but you suck dick for coke.".................

29. "Club Dread" scene where the two cops are in the boat and arrows are being fired at him. REWORK: "What is this some kind of show?" We see a person firing through a potato gun menthos." We see the cop taste the liquid that the boat is filled with. "Diet coke." We then see the person fire the menthos. "Yeah dude, that's something. Little menthos action." "Absolutely." We see the person fire the gun again and it hits the boat and the boat explodes. The Reel Big Fish then begin to play, "Take on me", as everyone applauds.

30. "Teacher calls student N-word" scene. REWORK: replace nigger with cracker or gangster.

31. "Leaving Las Vegas" scene where Nicholas Cage is shopping for booze. REWORK: have him shopping for condoms.

32. "Dumb and Dumber" scene where Jim Carrey talks to the guys who have the big gulps. REWORK: have the people making balloon animals. "Hey guys, balloon animals huh? Well see you later."................

33. "Blow" scene where George's mom calls the cops on him. REWORK: "do you really not think people don't know you're the antichrist? How do you think that reflects on me? So you go to hell, it's for your own good. You need to straighten your life out."...........

34. "Bill O'reilly freakout" scene. REWORK: instead of "to play us out" use "shemale" – "what does that mean shemale? A transvestite?"

35. "Wedding Crashers" scenes where he is about to tell Rachel McAdams the truth and says it is not a big deal. REWORK: combine all the scenes showing that he lies.................

36. "Captain America" scene where the girl shoots Captain America because she is pissed that he kissed that girl. REWORK: she first shoots him with a machine gun and then a rocket launcher and it sends him flying back. He gets up unharmed; or, have him get severely injured (like after she is done firing the weapons at him he goes over and picks his arm up).

37. "The Exorcist" scenes with the demon strapped to the bed. REWORK: instead of the demon it is the Grinch. "Altered states of consciousness can elicit an above average amount of strength (then it shows the Grinch throwing the Christmas tree)."....................

38. "Road Trip" scene where EL tries to get a bus from the blind girl. REWORK: "I was sent over here to inspect grow house number 2 and I'm afraid I have some bad news. The plants seem to have an adverse effect of lip augmentation." "Marijuana makes your lips get bigger?" "Ha, yeah." He then lights up a joint for a small monkey ("please don't smoke up my monkey")....................

39. "Meet the Parents" scene where Ben Stiller tells everyone about operation co-sumi. REWORK: it is instead operation "New World Order". "Your dad is still very much in the Illuminati." "Jack can't use The Secret." "Yes, Jack can use The Secret very well. And around and around we go Jack.".................

40. "Avatar" scene where Giovanni Ribisi tells Sigourney Weaver that they offered to build the Na'vi schools and roads. REWORK: we see the Na'vi people walking on roads with books in their hands and riding their horses. We then see a bunch of helicopters and planes line up in the sky over the place where the Na'vi society is. Giovanni Ribisi says, "but they prefer to stay the way they are", and Sigourney Weaver says, "yeah that tends to happen when you shoot guns at them". We then see the helicopters and planes fire missiles and bullets at the Na'vi society as soldiers climb down ropes to the ground.............

41. "Minority Report" scene where the machine that carves the names of the people into the wooden balls, makes two balls, one for the victim and

one for the assailant. REWORK: the black guy grabs the assailant's ball and hands it to Tom Cruise. Tom Cruise then begins to search through the images and videos that will help them solve the case. We see the two witnesses and they are ready to watch the evidence. On the screen we see a man enter into a barn with about three horses all separated by individual stables. We then see the man walk up to one of the horses and begins to take his pants off. Tom Cruise flips through more images and is confused/intrigued by what he is seeing. We then see the man begin to have sex with the horse. The horse begins to freak out and the woman witness throws up. We then see the victim's ball drop down and the black guy hands it to Tom Cruise. It says, "Alexander the Great" (or another name for a horse, like "Annabelle"). We then see the man after he is done having sex with the horse, put his pants back on and make a quiet escape. Tom Cruise asks how much time they have until it will occur and the after the black guy tells him, he puts on his helmet and goes out the door to the helicopters, followed by three other officers………….

42. "Unbreakable" scene where Samuel L. Jackson tells Bruce Willis to go to a place with a lot of people and see what he finds out. REWORK: we see Bruce Willis wearing a poncho and first bumps into a little boy holding his mother's hand. We then see a scene where the mother takes a cookie jar away from the boy and says no more. The mother then leaves the room and we see the boy drag a chair over to the counter, and steal another cookie. We then return to the terminal place where Bruce Willis is walking. He then accidentally gets in the way of a person who is wheeling someone in a wheelchair. The wheelchair is designed to accompany someone who is paralyzed from the neck down. We then see another scene where the person wheels the man into a room and leaves for a second. During the quick second that the person is not in the room, we see the paralyzed man get up from the wheelchair stretch, crack his back and return to the wheelchair, acting paralyzed again. We then return to the terminal and see Bruce Willis avoid running into anyone until a man with a cowboy hat runs into him. We then see the man with the cowboy hat at a saloon playing poker at a table with six other people. The man has a cowboy vest on which covers up his arms. Under one of the arm sleeves, and hidden from view is a mechanism that holds cards for people to cheat. We then hear the man say, "straight flush" and as all the other people at the table look like they can't believe it, the man with the cowboy hat laughs and pulls in the chips. We then return to the terminal…………….

43. "Lord of War" scene where it shows the machine gun bullet being made. REWORK: the thing that we see a first person view of being made is the Sauron's ring from "Lord of the Rings". We then see a first person view of the following: a lava waterfall leading into a lake of lava in Mount Doom. Once in the lake we see other creatures swimming around and fires rising and then extinguishing all around. We then go down another lava water fall which leads to a conveyer belt. We see an orc pick us up and examine what he is holding. He puts it back on the conveyer belt and then another orc picks it up. We see him begin to write something on the ring with an exacto knife. After finishing the inscription, we then go through a machine that has champers that mold the ring together. Finally, at the end of the conveyer belt we see Sauron who picks us up, and then we see a view outside of the first person showing us that it was the ring that was being made. We then see Sauron put on the ring and laugh...........

44. "I Love you, Beth Cooper" scene where Dennis is giving his speech at the class graduation ceremony. We see Dennis dressed up like Link from the Zelda video games and he goes to the podium and begin speaking. "I love you Princess Zelda. I have loved you Princess Zelda, ever since I first met you at your castle...............". He then continues his speech about other video game characters: "Let us confess, I'm a stuck up bitch, because deep down I know I look like a man" (it then shows the video game character Samus). "Let's admit, I'm a shitty brother, because deep down I know I am in love with his girlfriend." It then shows a picture of Luigi, while we see Mario and Princess Peach look over at him to. "Let us vow, let us all vow that when................. (do more statements about video game characters)........................

45. "The Mighty Ducks" scene where Gordon's law firm boss tells Gordon that he found out about his DUI. REWORK: instead of Gordon getting a DUI, he instead gets an illegal drug trafficking offense. "Did you really think you could keep me from knowing that you didn't get away with smuggling 300 kilos of cocaine across the border? Or did you think I just wouldn't figure it out." The law firm boss then tells him that he is keeping him employed, but that he has arranged for Gordon to become a coach.............................

46. "The Mummy" scene where the main character is about to be hanged and Rachel Weiss tries to stop it. REWORK: instead of being hanged he is going to be drowned by a tank that fills up with water. "I will give you 50 pounds to save this man's life." "My lady, I would pay 50 pounds just to

see him drown. Proceed." We then see a man walk over to the tank with a bucket filled with Piranhas. Rachel Weiss then offers him more money but the guy still won't budge. He then orders the man holding the bucket to pour the Piranhas in. Finally, Rachel Weiss says, "He knows the way to the forbidden city." "You lie." "I would never. Plus I will give you 20% of what we find." "15%" "Deal." "Break it." We then see a man standing next to the tank holding a sledge hammer who then hits it against the tank and it shatters. The final thing we see are the piranhas flopping up and down as the main character rolls on the ground, in obvious pain from the piranhas attacking him (he is bleeding from head to toe), as Rachel Weiss looks on ..................

47. "Role Models" scene where the main characters are talking to the director of Sturdy Wings about how she used to eat for breakfast and lunch cocaine. REWORK: The group director and the main characters get into a conversation about cheating on your husband or wife, which is what the "Sturdy Wings" group is based, mainly, it is a foundation that deals with all things related to adultery (***perhaps put in a brief video explaining what the foundation is). "I know why you are here. I had an Ashley Madison account also. But let's make one thing clear.............. "You know what I used to do for breakfast? Lust after men. You know what I used to do for lunch? Lust after woman." "What did you do for dinner? Was it lust after...................?

48. "Demetri Martin Finds Clearification" scene where he is playing a board game with three friends. REWORK: they are instead playing "Disney Trivia". The dialogue will be the same except for: "you think Jasmine was the princess in Aladdin. If I had the movie, I would show you the movie." We see Demetri get upset in that he starts throwing things like board pieces that no one is using. We see one of the girls get excited over something that happened in the game and another girl cheers along with her. "And I'm not saying this to be a jerk, do me a favor and not team up. Just please, I invited you guys over, do not trample on my enjoyment of this game. Go."........................

49. "21" scene where Ben is in Kevin Spacey's math class and he tells him how to resolve the game show question that he asked the class. RESOLVE: instead of Kevin Spacey asking a math question, he asks a question about what to do when a hooker charges you more than the pimp. "Now, let's say originally the pimp said it would cost 65 dollars for thirty minutes. After you and the hooker finish your session, she claims that you owe her

120 dollars. What do you do? Yes (points to Ben who raises his hand)." "I would tell her that the pimp didn't say that the other sexual acts that we did would cost anything extra." "Ok, let's give Ben the opportunity for some extra credit. Let's say that Ben's response to the hookers demands are true, the pimp really did not specify that anything, no matter what it was, would cost extra. However, the hooker, who, by the way, knows that the pimp only charged you 65 dollars, after having been refused the extra 55 dollars by you, decides that she will then call the authorities and claim that you raped her. What is your response?" "I would say that she should take it up with the pimp, because my unwillingness to pay is based off of what the pimp told me not what she is telling me" "But wait, how do you know she is not just trying to blackmail you, try and get you to pay her the 55 dollars more?" "I wouldn't really care, my answer is based off what her pimp told me, not what she is telling me." "Explain." "Well, when I originally got the hooker there was a one in two chance, either she would or she wouldn't claim that I owed her more money. Having that in mind, I knew that if she did claim that I owed her more money, and I didn't pay, there was at most a one in two chance that she would go to the police about it, those being, that she is 100% certain that she will claim I raped her, or that she is not completely sure that she would go through with it. Having known that, you now know that the hooker will.......................(****end this with showing that it is logically sound to not pay the hooker the 55 extra dollars)...........

50. "Election" scene where Matthew Broderick throws away the two votes so that Reese Witherspoon doesn't win. REWORK: instead of voting for class president, the school is voting on whether or not to allow boys on the poms team. Reese Witherspoon is an advocate for not allowing boys on the poms team. She looks into a classroom and a guy who just counted the votes gives her the thumbs up as to say that what she wanted won the election. Matthew Broderick sees this and decides that he wants boys on the poms team because we see a picture of him in an old high school year book as a member of the cheerleading squad. Next to the picture is a note that says, "Dear Matthew, sorry you had to settle for this, but it was fun right?" On the next page of the year book we see a picture of the poms team with the caption "Go girls!" We then see Matthew Broderick take out two votes and throw them into the trash can. The votes are later discovered and Matthew Broderick gets fired, as well as boys who tried out and made it onto the poms team had to be told that they could not be on the team (the boys look very disappointed)..............

51. "Galaxy Quest" scene where the characters are at the Galaxy Quest convention and Tim Allen finds out that none of the other characters like him. REWORK: we see Tim Allen signing autographs and Justin Long comes up. Justin Long asks him a question about how he was able to keep the crews spirits up and keep them from getting angry at each other and falling apart as a crew (kept them working together as a team). Tim Allen doesn't pay him much attention and excuses himself to use the restroom. Once in the restroom we hear the following being said: "Did you hear the space pilot say he was boning the girl behind Tim's back?" "And I even heard something about a ménage a toi with the first mate." "The guy has no idea the shit that goes on around him.".................We are then back at the autograph tables when Justin Long walks up again. In response to Justin's question Tim Allen gets pissed off and flips the table over, stubs his toe/hits his foot against it and hobbles away as everyone at the convention looks on at the scene.............

52. "Beerfest" scene where it shows the German's talking to the reporter about the main characters restaurant ("and look what I found, a rat's fetus inside")). REWORK: instead of the reporter talking to them about the German restaurant, the reporter is interviewing them about their participation in a pyramid scheme such that they were always exploited to sell vacuum cleaners...........

53. "No Country for Old Men" scene where Javier Bordem breaks his leg at the end. REWORK: he breaks his bones in multiple locations (legs, arms, neck, etc.), has massive scabs, bruises and burns and looks very beat up. Then two kids come by, one pushing the other who is in a wheelchair. He then offers the children a hundred dollars for the wheelchair, but they refuse. We then see Javier Bordem crawling around the sidewalk as we hear police sirens in the background...............

54. "Shutter Island" scene where Leonardo DiCaprio sees Andrew Laidis (whose face is all disfigured) and he tells him "no hard feelings right?" REWORK: we see Leonardo DiCaprio go into a room with a fire that also has a hot tub in it. Inside the hot tub are two beautiful women who are all over Andrew Laidis. He is smoking a cigar in one hand and has a glass of scotch in the other. Laidis then says to DiCaprio, "no hard feelings right?" Right before this scene we hear a conversation between DiCaprio and Mark Ruffalo in which DiCaprio says that the accident that killed his wife was started by Laidis so that Laidis could benefit off of the death of his wife.............

55. "One Flew over the Cuckoo's Nest" scene where Jack Nicholson tries to gather enough votes so that they can watch the World Series. REWORK: instead of the World Series he is trying to get people to vote to watch series finale of "Lost". After getting the final vote from Chief and Nurse Ratchet still doesn't let them watch the episode Jack Nicholson says, "Now you're going to be a flaming bitch"..............

56. "Slumdog Millionaire" scene where the main character is on the game show and asked a question. REWORK: whatever the question that the main character is asked is then shown how he knows the answer to it by what he experienced earlier in his life...

57. "Spider Man" scene where Peter lets the robber get away with the money. REWORK: Peter takes the money from the robber (spins a web and grabs it), who is frightened and grateful just to get out of the situation with his life. The wrester guy then gets upset that he didn't stop the robber from leaving. He then tries to take the money from Peter who then says no)).........

58. "Zoolander" scene where the three friends are having a gasoline fight. REWORK: instead of fighting with gasoline, they are firing flame throwers at each other. Then one of the friends tries to fill up his car with gasoline, which then causes the entire gas station to explode..........

59. "Edward Scissorhands" scene where Edward is on TV. REWORK: we see Edward sitting on a stage in front of a live TV audience with the woman whose house he lives in. Displayed on the stage are things Edward has sculpted and cut with his hands. Among these things are a figure of "Venus de Milo" which is sculpted out of butter, a picture of the "Mona Lisa" which is carved out of wood, and "The Seated Scribe" which is made out of a thick piece of saran wrap. The people in the audience then ask questions to Edward. "Have you ever gotten angry and threatened people with your hands?" Also have someone ask a question about the louvre. "Since the inventor died before you could become complete with real hands, and before you could completely educate yourself do you consider yourself different and special?" Before Edward can reply, the woman says, "Edward will always be special" The final question is: "How do you wipe your ass after going to the bathroom?"..............

60. "Rain Man" scene where Tom Cruise and Dustin Hoffman are gambling in Las Vegas. REWORK (combinations): we see Dustin Hoffman sitting at a blackjack table with Tom Cruise standing in back of him. We see

the pile of chips grow bigger and bigger. We then see them at a poker table and the chips again keep piling up. As this is going on, we see that a crowd is beginning to form watching them play. In the backdrop we see the scene from "The Hangover" where they are playing blackjack and Bradley Cooper flips off the camera. We also see math equations and a video from "Good Will Hunting" showing Will Hunting reading a book very quickly. We then see a video in the backdrop of the scene from "21" where Ben says, "splitting tens". We then see the two walk up to a roulette table and Dustin Hoffman says that it will land on 12 black. Tom Cruise makes a large bet and amazingly it ends up falling on 12 black. We then see the scene from "Rat Race" when Jon Lovitz puts a quarter into a slot machine and wins and says very excitedly, "whahoo!". Tom Cruise then makes another bet, this time with all of the chips and instead of landing on 12 black again, it lands on 4 red. We then see in the backdrop the scene from "Rounders" where Matt Damon loses all his chips in the poker game with John Malkovich ("I already knew he had me beat, he didn't even have to show me his hand"). The final seen we see is the scene from "Pulp Fiction" where Bruce Willis gets pissed off and says, "Do you have any idea how stupid you are?! No!"....................

61. "Billy Madison" scene where he has to go from kindergarten to 12th grade in two week increments for each grade. REWORK: make it so that he even must even graduate from college with his bachelor's, master's, and doctorate degrees in two weeks. We see Billy having a conversation with his girlfriend. As he talks to her about how college is going for him, we flip back and forth between what he says, and how he experienced it in his classes. For example, he says, "I'm trying my best but I just get so distracted" to which we then see a scene of him and some girl that sit across from each other in a classroom. We see the girl look at Billy and do suggestive things like spreading her legs so that you can see her vagina because she is not wearing any panties), to which Billy then replies with his own suggestive behavior.................

62. "Happy Gilmore" scenes showing the rowdy fans that come to the golf tournament to see Happy. REWORK: among some of the things that the fans are doing are: when Happy makes a putt, they fire blanks out of pistols; we see all the fans wearing exactly the same outfit that Happy wears (like the Boston Bruins jersey for example); people crowd surf and get into mosh pits..............when all these things happen, Shooter gets pissed off (maybe show scenes from the movie where he says,

"damn you people this is golf" and "damn you people, go back to your shanties"......................

63. "The Matrix" scene where they upload data into Neo's mind (like learning Kung Fu), and then practice what he learns. REWORK: this will be a combination of small scenes that can be put into different areas of the script. Among some of the things that Neo says when he wakes up are: "I know how to make crystal meth" (we then see Neo inside a kitchen with an apron, protective glasses, gloves, and a breathing mask); "I know how to fight a koala bear" (we then see Neo beating the crap out of a koala bear who is knocked unconscious and unable to fight back)..............

64. "Blades of Glory" scene where they tie and both win the gold metal and then get in a fight on the podium. REWORK: have both Will Ferrell and Jon Heder tie for the bronze medal. After Will Ferrell does his skating routine, he is very happy about his scores ("another 7.6"). We then see both skaters sharing a spot on the third place podium and the announcer says, "they must really be proud, the only thing better than a bronze medal is sharing it with your fellow countryman". The two begin to push each other and end up getting into a brawl with the following happening: we see Will Ferrell take off one of his ice skates and begin to charge at Jon Heder with it; somehow Jon Heder comes into the possession of Gandalf's wizard staff from "The Lord of the Rings", we see two or three referees skating around where they are fighting, not breaking it up yet, just like they do in professional hockey games when two players fight. Will Ferrell then somehow gets into the possession of a wand from "Harry Potter". The two then take turns exchanging blows, until one of them gets control of the other's weapon and sends the other one flying in the air and hitting the center big screen television, which then explodes. The final thing we see is the referees take control of the person with the staff and wand (battle between Gandalf wizard (staff) and Harry Potter wizard (wand)...............

65. "Fight Club" scene where the police threaten to cut off Edward Norton's balls. REWORK: instead of Edward Norton turning himself into the police, he commits himself to a mental institution. He is then inside a room with three psychiatrists. One of the psychiatrists says, "you said, that if someone tried to go on antipsychotic drugs, even you, we got to take one of his kidney's" "I'm mentally ill" "you said you would say that" "ok, I'm not mentally ill, I just want to score some tranquilizing drugs" "you said you would definitely say that" We then see the three

psychiatrists pin Edward Norton down on a table and one of them takes out a scalpel and tries to take one of his kidney's...........Another REWORK: Edward Norton is in a mental hospital and refuses to take the antipsychotic drugs. "you said, that if you ever tried to not take antipsychotic drugs...............

66. "Little Miss Sunshine" scene where Richard is explaining to Steve Carell his nine step program. REWORK: instead of the nine step program that he is trying to explain, he is instead describing his participation in a high interest rate loan company. Richard is driving a van and Steve Carell is in the back seat trying to act interested but is not at all. "So here I am, interviewing for this loan company, and the guy interviewing me says, you would fit in here." "wow" "he tells me that this is a highly... "yeah, and this is the guy who knows it all you know, first it starts off at a beginning position as a payday loan officer, maybe even leading up to being a loan shark, there's this whole interesting science about how these moneylenders operate" "wow, how about that" "I do detect that sarcasm Frank. But I want you to know something, if you ever borrowed money from me I will not hesitate to resort to violence if needed in order to collect that debt you owe me. Blackmail is a major tenet in this business and that's the first thing that you should be aware of if you ever borrow money from me" "you really opened up my eyes to how much I shouldn't take a high interest loan"...........................

67. "The Cable Guy" scene where Jim Carrey tells Matthew Broderick that the girl he had sex with was a prostitute. REWORK: Jim Carrey is making breakfast as Matthew Broderick walks up. Unbeknownst to Matthew Broderick, Jim Carrey slipped a rufee and a crushed up pill of Viagra into his drink and food during a party last night. Matthew Broderick is happy because he had a good time at the party. Matthew Broderick is a virgin and saving himself for when you gets married to his girlfriend. Jim Carrey then says, "well it's my treat" "what do you mean it's your treat?" "you know, hooking you up with getting your cherry popped" "what do you mean getting my cherry popped?" "well metaphorically speaking" "do you mean to tell me that I was raped last night?" "well of course you were, that rufee and Viagra combination made it an opportune time for you to get laid for the first time" "My girlfriend is never going to forgive me" "well I'll tell you how to deal with that, don't tell her".................

68. "Lost in Translation" scene where the director of the commercial speaks for a long time to Bill Murray and then the translator only tells him a

part of what the director said. REWORK: instead of shooting a whiskey commercial, they are shooting a commercial to try and bring attention to the controversies surrounding offensive sports team names that relate to Native Americans, like the Cleveland Indians, the Washington Redskins, the Atlanta Braves, the Chicago Blackhawks, and Kansas City Chiefs. The director in charge of shooting the commercial speaks in Navajo. The reason why the translator only tells Bill Murray a part of what the director says.................Put in the dialogue something about how Native American's are upset because they were forced to assimilate to American culture, and now American culture is using Native American racial slurs in its society.......... ****Could potentially make this about all racial slurs, in particular nigger.

69. "The 40 Year Old Virgin" scenes showing Steve Carell failing to get laid. REWORK: we see Steve Carell watching the movie "Teeth" and it freaks him out in such a way that he doesn't want to have sex because there is a possibility that the vagina might bite his dick off. Also, we see a girl who has a huge bush wanting him to perform oral sex on her, and he is very apprehensive about it, but she tries to force his head down (we see on her lower abdomen a tattoo that reads, "George Herbert Walker"). Also, we see a girl who has very chapped lips or hands and wants to give him a blow job or hand job...........

70. "School of Rock" scenes where Jack Black is teaching the students about rock history, and tries to teach them how to be more like old school rockers. REWORK: we see Jack Black teaching to the class how Jimmy Hendrix used to take acid during his concerts, by putting tabs of acid on his forehead wrapped with a bandanna so that when he sweat on his forehead, he would start tripping. We then see everyone in the class practice this with bandanas and small pieces of paper. We then see a montage of scenes showing the children getting tattoos, being taught sex ed (on the board it says, drugs, sex, and rock and roll (specify that they are only in third or fourth grade).....................

71. "Eternal Sunshine of the Spotless Mind" scene where Jim Carrey is having his mind erased and keeps hiding so that they cannot erase all his memories. REWORK: he wants them to erase the time he went to prison, but they made a mistake in that they accidentally (we see the people who are operating on him partying) are erasing everything in his life except that experience of going to prison. One of the places that he is forced to hide is in the showers at the prison, which he is very apprehensive to hide at...........

72. "Face/Off" scene where John Travolta changes faces with Nicholas Cage. REWORK: show some of the ramifications of what it would mean if this were to happen because although the other guy has John Travolta's face, there are parts of his body that are not the same. Examples: John Travolta's wife says to him (Nicholas Cages body), "did you get circumcised?"; "you have never made me cum like that.".................

73. "Napoleon Dynamite" scenes where Uncle Rico and Kip try and sell their products to people. REWORK: they are selling penile enlargement products, such as cock pumps, Extenz, and a string with a weight attached to it. Uncle Rico goes to people's houses and tries to get them to buy the product by giving them a free gift, such as magnum condoms ("I want that").............

74. "Indiana Jones" scene where Indiana steals the gold skull and gets chased by the big rock. REWORK: instead of a gold skull, he steals a comic book. We see that it is a very rare and expensive comic book. As he is trying to leave the cavern, he runs into a wire (the wire clips him on his neck and he falls on his back) that is connected to both sides of the cavern. This sets off a giant rock, we then see the screen split into two. On the left side of the screen we can see that all he must do in order to avoid the rock is wait until the rock gets released from the ramp. On the right side of the screen we see him panic and immediately start to run down the hall while the giant rock rolls after him. On the left side, we then see him walk down the cavern hall towards the front entrance being careful not to set off anymore traps. On the right side, we see him running and setting off every booby-trap that exists in the cavern. The scene ends with the Indiana Jones on the left side of the screen being greeted at the front entrance by a bunch of Apes from "The Planet of the Apes", who immediately attack him and take the comic book. On the right side of the screen we see half his body pinned under the rock, with poisonous arrows and darts sticking out of his back. The Apes just calmly walk up to him and take the comic book............

75. "Wanted" scenes in which they show how to bend the bullets around objects. REWORK: we see the main character in a small classroom type room with three other people. They are the newest members of the organization and they are about to watch an orientation video. The video shows that the organizations main purpose is to assassinate people, but the video also stresses that they like to have fun in the organization. Not only do they teach you how to bend bullet's around objects, they also

teach you how to bend other things such as golf balls behind trees, hockey pucks around other players, bow and arrows, etc.............

76. "Good Luck Chuck" scenes where he has sex with women because they think if they do they will find love. REWORK: instead of everyone thinking that if they have sex with Chuck they will find love, it turns out that everyone who makes Chuck do something that he is not comfortable with, will find love. Some things that woman try and force him to do are: act out the scenes of a porno as it is playing on his TV; hand cuff him to a bed and do anything they want............................

77. "A History of Violence" scene where Vigo Mortensen meets up with William Hurt and William Hurt tries to kill him but it backfires. REWORK: instead of trying to strangle Vigo Mortensen, a man tries to shoot him in the head, but the man forgot to load the gun. After Vigo Mortensen escapes from the room, William Hurt goes up to the man who didn't load the gun and says, "how do you fuck that up?" He then grabs the gun from the man, loads it himself, and shoots the man in the head.............

78. "John Wick" scene where his car is stolen and his dog is killed which makes him seek revenge. REWORK: We see people egging his house and toilet papering his house. The father of the person who did it gets very angry because he knows that John Wick is a crazy fuck who is very good with violent behavior. He calls John and tries to talk John out of seeking revenge in some way but it is no use. He tries to tell John that it is really not a big deal and that it is not worth people dying over. The last scene we see is of John opening up his gun safe and equip himself from head to toe with weapons............

79. "Inception" scenes showing the different levels of dreams. REWORK: make it so that they are four levels deep. In the fourth level it is complete paradise. As the levels go down to the first level the dreams get worse and worse until finally they are stuck in the first level in which they have to live with the exact opposite of the fourth level, mainly, complete unhappiness and misery.

80. "Wall Street" scene where Charlie Sheen wears a wire to rat on Michael Douglas. REWORK: have it so that Michael Douglas admits to things that further incriminate himself that the cops originally did not try and get him to confess to/pin on him. Ideas for things that he could admit to can be that he is also a pimp, is an identity thief (doesn't think that

the cops will find out about the illegal things he does because he does it under a different identity), and that he gives all the money he earns from insider trading to charity...............

81. "The Wolf of Wall Street" scene where Jordan and Donnie are talking about Donnie's wife being his cousin. REWORK: have the dialogue by about Donnie having sex with his mother just like in Oedipus Rex. "I heard something about your son being your brother".

82. "National Treasure" scene where they find the treasure under Wall Street. REWORK: instead of the treasure being something very important and worth a lot of money and value, have the treasure be something that is not of any importance or value at all. Nicholas Cage is very disappointed when he sees the treasure, and on top of that, the cops arrest him and he goes to jail................

83. "Family Guy" scene where death tries to take Peter away as dead and then twists his ankle trying to catch him, as well as wants Peter to show the world that people can still die. REWORK: death want's Peter to show the world other ways in which you could still die. However, since death is injured, people are still not able to be killed. Some examples of ways in which Peter tries to kill people can be that he gives a pregnant lady the a lot of morning after pills but the fetus still does not die, takes the parachute out of a person's back pack when they skydive and they are unharmed, and have a scenario where people's body parts are missing (like their head for example), but they simply reattach it and keep moving on with their day................

84. "Step Brothers" scenes where Will Ferrell and John C. Reilly try and stop people from buying the house (like dressing up as a Nazi and a member of the KKK). REWORK: have it so that the people looking at the house are members of the KKK and Will Ferrell and John C. Reilly are black. Have them act as though they are a gay couple and that the people looking at the house are super religious (like the god hates fags people). Also, have them dress up like Muslim terrorists..............

85. "Super Troopers" scene where they pull over the semi-truck and the trucker locks them in the back. REWORK: instead of it being filled with marijuana, it is actually full of illegal aliens. In the aftermath we see in the papers the officers and the mayor having their pictures taken with the illegal aliens. Have it so that one of the officers tries to have sex with one of the immigrants but the other officer tries to persuade him not to,

because if the immigrant has a kid then she would be allowed to stay in the U.S. in order to take care of her kid (which would be an American citizen)..............

86. "Dodgeball" scene showing the dodgeball tournament's different teams. REWORK: come up with other crazy names and people that are teams in the tournament. Some examples of teams could be Muslim extremists who jump over the center line in order to get a member of the opposing team out (this would illustrate Jihad because the Muslim's are willing to take their own lives in order to kill others), as well as Buddhists or Hindus who only sit and meditate in the arena and just avoid the balls when they are thrown at each other, but do not throw the balls back (this would illustrate nonviolence)...............

87. "The Count of Monte Cristo" scene where Priest and Monte Cristo try and dig a tunnel to escape from prison, as well as when Priest tries to teach Monte Cristo things about the world. REWORK: Priest and Monte Cristo keep trying to dig their way out of the prison, but always end up going the wrong way. It will say "2 years later" for example in reference to them finding out that they went the wrong way. Also, Priest will teach Monte Cristo other things about the world such has how to play basketball (we see that they made a hoop out of something and use a rock as the ball), badminton (they use their food plates as rackets and a dead mouse as the birdie), and other educational areas of study in which Monte Cristo gets very frustrated at Priest for going too fast because he doesn't have pencil and paper.....................

88. "American Pie" scene where the four friends make a pact to all lose their virginity. REWORK: Instead of making a pact to lose their virginity, they are instead making a pact to see who can go the longest without having sex. We see Sherman, for example, hug the girl at the party in the morning, and instead of bragging that he had sex, he instead brags to the friends that he just talked to her all night and did not have sex. We also see into the future with them telling their girlfriends that they are saving themselves for marriage, but when they get married they still consider the pact that they made as more important than wanting to have sex with their wives.................

89. "Django Unchained" scene where the KKK people can't see out of their masks. REWORK: have this be multiple mini scenes in which it shows the group of people doing some activity and not being able to see out of

the mask or whatever it is that is covering their face. For example, they are wearing sports helmets and masks like a hockey visor or football visor that is tinted. They are in the dark and say that can't see anything. Also, they are at a Star Wars or X-Men convention and can't see out of the masks of the storm troopers or Cyclops eye mask.....................

90. "Strange Wilderness" scene where they find Bigfoot and kill him. REWORK: have them find other creatures and kill them, even though the animal is not harming them at all. Some examples could be: the chupacabra is about to attack a cow and so the crew shoots the cow in order to save it from being killed by the chupacabra (because they think that would be a much more painful death); the crew is in a submarine in Lake Lockness and when they see Nessie, they fire torpedoes at it and kill it.......................

91. "The Truman Show" scene where Truman is showing his wife all of the absurdities of how it can possibly be that the world isn't set up just for him. REWORK: he goes to greater extents to show that the world is just for him, and for everything that he does, a miracle is performed that makes it so that he cannot know for sure that the world is just for him. Examples: he tries to jump off a cliff, but right before he is about to do it a cop points a gun at him and tells him to step away immediately. Truman swan dives off the cliff only to then be immediately picked up by a giant eagle. Show that no matter what Truman does, something will always occur which will preserve his live, while also trying to make it seem like a normal occurrence in that the world is not just for him.................

92. "Hall Pass" scene when Owen Wilson and Jason Sudeikis are talking to each other about the family who's house they are in, while being unaware that everyone else is watching them on camera in another room. REWORK: they talk about how conspiracy theories and make fun of the people that just accept what the government tells them without questioning anything. Some of the things that they talk about are the Kennedy assassination (other shooters, Jack Ruby), the moon landing, and 9/11. What they say offends the people in the room watching them, because they trust the government (this can show how different political viewpoints differ from each other in how much they believe government should be involved in the world)...............

93. "Forest Gump" scenes showing Forest doing multiple things that make him famous. REWORK: show a trailer or commercial showing Forest

doing a bunch of other activities. Some activities that he could be doing are: rock climbing on a very technical cliff (shows him jumping from rock to rock without a rope attached to him), being a farmer (shows him milking cows and riding a horse while lassoing sheep)........................

94. "South Park" scene where Richard Dawkins talks to the class about evolution. REWORK: instead of the theory of evolution he is talking about the theory/hypothesis of the world being a virtual reality. Dawkins brings up evidence for the virtual reality theory, yet Garrison doesn't believe it because he thinks it is in contradiction most of the religions and world views (just like evolution). Later Garrison claims that the world is definitely a virtual reality...................

95. "Pirates of the Caribbean" scene where Johnny Depp and Kiera Knightley are trapped on the island with the rum and they are dancing around the fire. REWORK: on top of booze, the island is filled with every drug and they get as fucked up as possible. We see for example, Johnny Depp hallucinate and jump into the fire (last part of the scene) and catch on fire while Kiera Knightley just laughs as Depp runs toward the ocean. Also, we see them run around naked, and both of them laying down on the sand completely out of touch with anything that is going on around them (like taking DMT)..............

96. "Orange County" scene where Jack Black talks to Ben Stiller about the fire. REWORK: instead of them talking about a fire, they are instead talking about an explosion of a radiation power plant. Jack Black has a large tumor on the side of his neck. It turns out that Jack Black and a girl who works at the power plant had sex and accidentally set off the explosion (Jack Black's brother applied for an internship at the power plant but was rejected). "Why do you have a tumor on your neck Jo John?"...............

97. "The Departed" scene where Martin Sheen and Leonardo DiCaprio are followed into the building and Martin Sheen ends up getting thrown off the roof. REWORK: instead of taking the outside stairs down to the ground, Leonardo DiCaprio stays with Martin Sheen when Costello's people arrive. Instead of thinking that Leonardo DiCaprio is the rat who works for Martin Sheen, when they catch the two together they just assume that DiCaprio got their first ("you're fucking early"). Also, when Costello's people come out of the building, the police begin firing at Costello's people, also thinking that DiCaprio is one of them and not with the police.....................

98. "Titanic" scene where the ship hits the iceberg. REWORK: instead of an iceberg it is a giant cupcake. When the ship hits the cupcake, frosting, sprinkles and a cherry fall on the ship. We see people kicking the sprinkles and cherry around afterword. Also, as the ship is about to hit the cupcake, the ship's crew scramble's around to try and avoid it by taking extra precautionary measures such as shutting the water tight doors before the ship even hits the cupcake................

99. "The Shining" scenes where Jack Nicholson begins to go insane. REWORK: he has a methamphetamine addiction (any hard drug) and once he runs out he begins to slowly become psychotic (multiple mental disorders), because he is trapped in the hotel with no way out...............

100. "Van Wilder" scenes where Van comes up with ways to make money, like the topless tutors. REWORK: have Van try and get money to stay in school through other methods, such as setting up a lemonade and baking stand, stands next to busy intersections with a sign which reads something about him willing to do anything for money, and dealing hard drugs to sketchy people.................

101. "O Brother, Where Art Thou?" scene where George Nelson robs the bank. REWORK: the robbers name is Mike Hunt and when he robs the bank he proudly says his name, and then a customer whispers to another customer, "more like my cunt."...............

102. "Independence Day" scene showing people on rooftops with signs and yelling, trying to welcome the aliens to earth. REWORK: we see people on different building rooftops holding signs welcoming the aliens to earth, people having BBQ's and partying, as well as religious people holding their religious books (like the Bible or Quran) and speaking in tongues to the aliens in the ship. Despite all of the good nature of the people on the rooftops, the aliens still destroy the buildings............

103. "Rounders" scene where Matt Damon loses all his money to John Malkovich. REWORK: have Matt Damon have a horrible hand (like a pair), and think that he is going to win, only to be beaten by John Malkovich who also has a horrible hand (in comparison to what can be good hands on the board)..................

104. "Easy A" scenes with the guys that pay her with gift cards. REWORK: we see Emma Stone attempting to become someone with the reputation of hooking up with a lot people. Instead of people giving her things to have her make up stories about what she did with them, she is actually

the one who goes to the guys and tells them to make up stories that they hooked up with her. She goes to people of all different groups, such as gay men and woman to show that she is the type of girl who gets around……………..

105. "Knocked Up" scene where Seth Rogan and Paul Rudd are tripping shrooms in Las Vegas. REWORK: put more things that they do when tripping on shrooms, such as: hallucinating that the water fountains are actually a dragon breathing fire……………..

106. "Starsky and Hutch" scene where Snoop Dog is Vince Vaughn's caddy. REWORK: Vince Vaughn finds the wire on Snoop Dog and then takes him hostage and will only let him go in exchange for the wire recording to be erased. Furthermore, Starsky and Hutch also try and blackmail Vince Vaughn by saying that they will give up the recording to the police unless they let Snoop Dog go. This results in a stalemate leading to the eventual death of Snoop Dog who is caught in the middle of the argument……………..

107. "Pulp Fiction" scene at the very beginning in the restaurant. REWORK: instead of them talking about robbing the restaurant, they are instead talking about rebelling or overthrowing either God in heaven, or some other high authority……………..

108. "Bad Santa" scene where Marcus is about to shoot Willie in the mall. REWORK: instead of saying, "do you really need all that shit, it's Christmas", he says, "do you really need all that shit, it's Kwanza." Mention something about how Marcus should be giving gifts and not stealing things because he is black and that is how Kwanza is celebrated…………..

109. "Anchorman" scene where they are having the battle between news stations. REWORK: instead of news stations fighting, it is different gangs in the United States. We see for example, the Crips, Bloods, Aryan Brotherhood, and KKK amongst others fighting. There are members in each gang which seem out of place with what the gang stands for, such as a black person being in the KKK and the Aryan Brotherhood, and a white person being in the Crips or Bloods……………..

110. "School for Scoundrels" scenes where the people in the class start confrontations with random people. REWORK: come up come up with more scenes about what the people in the class do when they are required to start a confrontation. For example: a person in a bike race

gets the page telling him to start a confrontation and so he intentionally runs into the biker next to him which then leads to a massive pile up of all the bikers in back of them; we see two people on a ski lift and one of them gets the page. He gets into a brawl with the person next to him which ends with the person who started the fight making a quick escape off the lift, while the other person's ski's get caught on the lift and can't get off...............

111. "Signs" scene where Mel Gibson sees the alien on top of the roof and him and his brother run around the house to try and scare it off. REWORK: Mel Gibson's daughter wakes him up and says that she can't sleep because Santa Claus is on the neighbor's roof. Once Mel Gibson sees Santa he wakes up his brother and the two, thinking that it is some robber or something, try to scare him off. Santa becomes frightened and falls off the roof, only his foot got caught in the ropes tying together the reindeer, which then makes the sleigh fall of the roof right on top of him, killing him.................

112. "Liar Liar" scene where Jim Carrey's son wishes that for one day his dad couldn't lie. REWORK: the son wishes that for one day Jim Carrey was gay. This plays out such that Jim Carrey is upset that he finds men attractive over women, but can't help how he now naturally feels. This scene should examine the debate about whether or not being gay is a choice...............

113. "The Slammin Salmon" scene where the guy tells the hooker what he will do to her ("are you mike'd?"). REWORK: the two are discussing something when a waitress comes over to them and makes a big scene to the entire restaurant, which sketches the guy out. "Am I being punk'd?"

114. "Lord of the Rings: The Fellowship of the Ring" scene where Gandolph tells the fire creature to "go back to the shadow". REWORK: instead of the fire creature that they are trying to run away from, it is the Hulk that chases after them. As the fellowship is running toward the end of the mine, we see various characters from superhero movies (hero and villains) fire weapons at them to try and kill them................

115. "Reservoir Dogs" scene where Tim Roth is telling the story about the police officers in the bathroom. REWORK: Tim Roth is telling a story about how he faked being a police officer (some criminal group sent him in to infiltrate the police department). On one occasion the police department had a psychic come in to help them solve a case.

The psychic picks up an intuition about a possible undercover in the police department. Pretty much the whole time she is paying most of her attention to Tim Roth. "And I can see, she is directing all of her attention to me."………………….

116. "Sideways" scenes where they are tasting the different wines at the vineyard. REWORK: they are at a cocaine growing facility in Columbia. They test out the cocaine through having it cut with other substances such as heroin (speedball), gun powder (brown-brown), and speed, as well as smoking crack cocaine. Paul Giamanni is a cocaine connoisseur and teaches his friend how to properly sniff the cocaine (like rubbing it on your gums)……………..

117. "Team America" scenes showing Team America go to other countries to try and stop the terrorists. REWORK: have "Team Jihad" come to America and try and rid it of infidels. Once they have gained control of the government we see that the Islamic flag is flying over the White House. They then say that America is greater than it was before, and we see that all the women are covered up from head to toe, and every man has a turban on. On occasion there is a person who does not follow the Muslim dress code, and we see "Team Jihad" come in to kill that person…………..

118. "Traffic" the scene where Catherine Zeta-Jones shows the drug dealer the kid's doll that is made out of cocaine. REWORK: there is a world shortage of milk due to a plague that has wiped most of the cows in the world out. People have begun trafficking dairy products. Catherine Zeta-Jones shows a smuggler a toy that is made up of highly condensed dry milk. The smuggler insists that she try it first to make sure it is not poison, but she refuses because she is lactose intolerant. The smuggler then mixes the dry milk in some water and tastes it and to his delight it is what she said it was……………..

119. "Thank you for Smoking" scene where Nick is a guest on the Joan Lunden show. REWORK: Nick is a top official working for an alcohol company. Along with him as other guests on the show are people that are against the use of excessive drinking as well as underage drinking (a member of Alcoholics Anonymous could be a guest for example). The last guest is an 18 year old person who is in a wheelchair (from an accident that happened while he was drunk), as well as the new father of a baby he had with a one night stand. Nick takes the stance

that the drinking age should be 18, which is something all the other guests are against (can even have someone who wants to return the U.S. to prohibition). The purpose of this scene will be to show the debate amongst people of whether or not the drinking age should be 18 or 21...................

120. "Mission Impossible" scene where Tom Cruise is meeting with his superior and discussing what happened to everyone on his team during the mission. REWORK: the mission is to rob Fort Knox. Ways in which members of the team can die during the mission can be: someone steps on a land mine, someone gets electrocuted by the electric fence, security personnel open fire using things such as tanks and helicopters (someone gets caught in the barbed wire and security opens fire for example). Tom Cruise is the only one who makes it out alive by virtue of the escape tunnel in the vault. We find out from Tom Cruise's superior that the mission was a set up and that all of the deaths of the members of the mission are all related together through the set up.......................

121. "Moulin Rouge" scene where Nicole Kidman thinks that Ewan McGregor wants to have sex with her when really he just wants to recite his song. REWORK: we see Nicole Kidman try and seduce Ewan McGregor through putting on different outfits of princesses (Disney princesses for example). With each outfit she puts on Ewan McGregor (who is dressed like Aladdin) gets more confused because he was under the impression that she knew that they were going to rehearse "Aladdin". Finally, once she dresses up like Jasmine, we see the magic carpet fly into the room to the amazement of the people looking in from outside. Ewan McGregor and Nicole Kidman then get on the magic carpet and fly out into the night sky, with one of the onlookers saying, "a whole new world.".............

122. "School for Scoundrels" scene where Roger goes over to people playing basketball and pops it with a knife, and asks for his shoes. REWORK: we see Roger go over to a bunch of people playing soccer. He catches the ball and deflates it with box cutters (he uses the cutters to completely deflate the ball and go around the ball, such that the soccer ball is cut completely in half, with two sides). He then says to someone, "That's my finger, you cut it off and I want it back." The guy refuses but then his mother comes over to him and says, "You told me you got that finger at a morgue. Give him back his finger." The guy gives him back his finger (middle finger) and we see Roger hold it up to where the middle finger

goes on his hands and put the other four down, such that he is giving the guy who cut it off the middle finger..........

123. "The Secret" scene where the Reverend says, "If you jump off a building, it doesn't matter whether you are a good person or a bad person, you're going to hit the ground." REWORK: "If you go fishing in the Dead Sea, it doesn't matter whether you are a good fisherman or a bad fisherman, you're not going to catch anything." "If you're a lesbian, it doesn't matter how much you want to have a biological child between your lesbian partner and you, it isn't going to happen.".........

124. "Jeopardy" game show scene where the two creators are playing with another person. REWORK: The two creators have an equal amount of money, and the other person is negative. One of the creators advises the other person that he should just give up unless he wants to owe the show hundreds of thousands of yen, pesos, euros, franks. When the game continues, Trebek advises all three players that they need to answer with a question, or they will be disqualified. The longer the game goes on, the more Trebek get pissed off. Right as he is about to lose his shit, both the creators then begin to answer the questions that Trebek gives them, and the creators get into an answering questions battle with each other, because they can read his face before he asks the question. This gets him even angrier until suddenly he grabs his shoulder and falls on the floor, motionless. Three players and everyone in the audience are completely silent, until one of the creators gets in front of a doctor, advising him to give him some space. The show cuts to commercial in silence, as another person brings the doctor a the two paddles used to shock someone back to life.....

125. "Who Wants to be a Millionaire?" game show scene where a guy is on a question that he doesn't know the answer to. REWORK: He first decides to use the audience, but he tells the audience not to vote if they don't know the answer. Only vote if you are 100% sure of what the answer is. The audience comes back and all answers were voted on and relatively even in how many people voted for the answer. He then calls a friend, and, right before his friend is about to answer the question for him, he tells his friend only to answer the question if he is 100% sure of the answer. His friend tells him that he is stuck between two answer, A and B, and doesn't for sure know. After he hangs up on the friend, he tells Regis that he wants the 50/50 odds of getting the right question. After the 50/50 is applied, the C and D buttons are removed. The guy

now begins to get pissed off, he is currently at the $250 mark, and begins using Regis as a sort of shrink and asks him what he would do. Regis (who is one of the creators), after a brief conversation of the guy (who is one of the creators), decides that he will throw the game and give the guy a substantial clue. In this way, he figures he will be called the champion, through cheating and manipulating the player. He tells the man that he is 100% positive that the answer is C, so the man makes C his final answer. The answer ends of being D, and the man just sits in the chair, arms crossed and looking down. Regis beings to give the guy a hard time, at which the guy gets out of the chair, and just as Regis is saying his last words (with the crowd also clapping their hands and yelling), the man grabs Regis by the throat and the two fall to the ground with the man still holding Regis's neck. The crowd begins chanting, "Jerry, Jerry" as if it was the Jerry Springer Show. The scene ends with two or three employees trying to desperately get the man off of Regis..............

126. "Limitless" movie scene where Eddie decides to go on Oprah to endorse his book, which was just inducted into Oprah's book club. REWORK: The problem is that right before he is about to go on stage, he checks all his pockets and the pills are gone. He begins to panic that he could be getting violently ill on stage if he doesn't take one of the pills. He is called out onto the stage and sits on a couch next to Oprah. After asking him a few introductory questions about himself and the book, he then begins to sweat profusely and you can see that his face looks just like it did in the movie right before he throws up on the sidewalk. Oprah asks him another question, but he not listening. Instead, he looks over at the far side of the stage where there is three people, all wearing black. One of the men (one of the creators is Bradley Cooper, and the other creator is Oprah) begins to reach into his pocket and pull out the clear bag that holds the pills. He passes two or three pills to the other two people and they each take one. As the interview continues, Oprah can see that Bradley looks uncomfortable and notices that he keeps looking behind her and over where the curtain is. Oprah then, trying to decide why he keeps looking to the side of the stage, turns around and looks for what she thinks Bradley is looking at. This then makes the audience (because the looking off stage has put a pause in the interview, and everyone in the audience also being silent), curious what Bradley is looking at. Upon seeing the back stage where the employees are dressed in black, Oprah tells the camera man to cut to commercial. Once the

commercial's begin Oprah goes over to the back stage and yells at one of the employees, "How dare you!" and grabs the bag they are in from the employee. Upon watching this scene play out, Bradley the goes over to Oprah off stage and tells Oprah that the pills are actually his. She denies this, while still managing to have a decent smile. However, Bradley does not belief this and then grabs the bag carrying the pills, so that the two are fighting over it with their hands, trying to take it from the grip of the other person's hand. The camera man interjects into the mini fight, and gives the on air sign that has broken out between her and another person. We see on live television the fight keep escalating between the two and the scene ends with them ripping the bag, spilling all of the pills out of the bag. Instead of going for the pills, the two continue to fight, with the result of Oprah tackling Bradley on the couch, which falls on its back.......

127. "Fever Pitch" scene where Drew Barrymore falls onto the field while the baseball game is on. REWORK: An employee sees this and begins to run over to the woman, attempting to catch her and, if she resists, to tackle her to the ground (basic police behavior). As the man approaches the woman he takes out a Taser, and runs toward her. The woman, then begins to run towards the a dugout to meet Jimmy Fallon. The police follow suit, but it is clear that they are not that fast as the woman and so they stand next to each other trying to catch their breath. The woman talks to the man, and every once in a while (roughly every 15 seconds) one of the officer's interject in the conversation, telling the woman that she must come with the officer. The woman (the other creator), hearing this and refusing, goes back to talking to the man (the man is talking (the man is one of the creators) about selling his season ticket to another person. The woman tries to interject into the conversation by taking the tickets and setting them on fire with a lighter (the crowd, upon seeing this begin to cheer). The officer, upon seeing this tells her one last time that she must go with him. The crowd begins to cheer again, chanting, "let her go, let her go". The scene ends with the announcer telling the officer over the loud speaker to let her go. The officer upon seeing that everyone in the stadium is for the woman and against him, he gives the middle finger to the crowd, which then results in foot and drinks being thrown at him. The last we see of the officer is him being carted off the field in a golf cart, with people booing him.......

128. "Apollo 13" scene where the astronauts are told by NASA that they made to construct a device that enables them to breath in oxygen. REWORK: They tell one of the astronauts to get a bag and use it for some purpose. After ripping the first bag, he then tries again (after being specifically told that he can't rip the second (because they would essentially be fucked if he did), and rips the bag a second time. Everyone in the NASA control room is silent. One of the other astronauts comes in the room, and actually in a good mood, whistling. He walks over to the other astronaut, looks at the left hand, immediately his smile is gone. The radio in the shuttle is playing some happy song, and Tom Hanks (the other astronaut who did not rip the bag is one of the creators, while the other astronaut who did break the bag is the other creator), goes over to the radio and turns it off. "Hey, I like that song." "Well, I would like to keep the channel the same, if you didn't break the fucking bag." "Fuck you". The scene then ends with the TV playing the movie, "The Secret". The Reverend in the film says the following: "If you rip the only two bags that you need in order to get safely back to earth, it doesn't matter whether you are a good astronaut or a bad astronaut, you are going to suffocate."............

129. "The Firm" scene whether a lawyer (one of the creators) that works in the same firm at the main character (one of the creators), shows him pictures that were taken by someone who saw the main character hooking up with a woman on the beach. REWORK: The lawyer then flashes pictures of the two hooking up, and with each new picture seen by the main character (who pretty much gives him a commentary about what the pictures show), grows more and more agitated and uncomfortable like he can't believe this is happening to him..............

130. "Under the Tuscan Sun" scene where Diane Lane (one of the creators) visits a guy (who she calls her boyfriend) who she hooked up with a few weeks or months earlier. REWORK: The guy (one of the creators) goes down to the street to talk with him. As they are talking, we see someone go onto the deck of the house or apartment, and yell down to the guy that he is ready to go. The guy on the deck is wearing a complete dominatrix costume, complete with a whip and mask. The guy down on the street leaves the woman and the scene ends.........

131. "Vantage Point" scene where multiple people catch the same event with their cameras. REWORK: Each person involved in shooting the scene with their video camera are different videos happening at the same,

only they are not shooting the main event. However, although the main event was never captured on film, the other things that the characters captured with their video cameras were other crimes being committed at different places of where you could watch some person speaking to the audience. Some of the other places were up in the sky, people watching, and a snack bar. A man with a camera (one of the creators) videotaped the sky when he gets tired of watching the speech. On his camera we see Iron Man, Captain America, and Thor. As more and more people begin to look up at the sky, they pay more attention to the superheroes than the man speaking (one of the creators). At this point, the man who was speaking is shot and assassinated by an unknown killer...............

132. "Zodiac" scene where the news company gets its first letter which is a sort of code written by the murderer, giving clues to who he is. REWORK: the news company enlists the help of Robert Langdon (from the Da Vinci Code) to crack the code, and at his first shot at deciphering the code he gets it correct. The police then arrest the Zodiac killer, making him come across to the world as an idiot..............

133. "Chess" game between a top level player (a creator) and a computer called, "Deep Blue" (a creator controlling the deep blue player). REWORK: The player beat the deep blue computer at a single game. Once the match was set between the player and the player controlling deep blue, the match as set. The person controlling deep blue, however, spent many millennium trying to decipher how to beat the top level player. The player that controlled the deep blue computer, when the player knew for a fact the deep blue is getting its ass kicked, the player making the moves for the computer stood in and, without the top level player knowing that it was actually a real person he was playing against as opposed to a machine, the player then was able to know what play to do next, while the machine, is seemed to be a novice player of chess, because the player controlling the computer, had (although it took a very long time in one of their training sessions) played and mastered every way in which any scenario may occur in a match. The scene ends with Bobby Fischer losing to the top level player, which, upon a rematch between Bobby Fischer and one of the creators, the creator player had experienced this match between himself and Bobby Fischer in virtually every scenario that can exist in the universe.................

134. "Avatar" scene where the people that have Avatar's enter into the Avatar's body, through a machine in roughly the same dimensions as the hookup

machines in "the room" at the beginning of the film, except there is not a top that closes on you. REWORK: The machines that exist between the film Avatar and the film Inception, both take you to a different state of reality through which you can either enter things lives, or enter into a different state of existence, through which time becomes dilated through the different ways in which it can be measured through more and more events occurring in it, as well as the similar ways in which it can be measured through more and more events occurring within the observer. For example, in Inception, five minutes in the real world is equivalent to experiencing an hour in the dream world. Time dilation can be better understood through the differing ways of measuring the real world, which, through observation, the more and more different observations measure the real world to accord with all ways in which time can describe how the real world is measured in reference between different states that time can exist in relation to the real world. ***Ten to fifteen minutes in a DMT hallucination gets you to relate to the real world through measuring it in reference between different states. These different states can be dilated to accord with a difference of elapsed time between two events (an event in a DMT trip is a different state which can be dilated to accord a further DMT trip, which is just an event in a different state.

135. "The Witches" scene where the witch tries to give a little boy some chocolate, but then walked away once the boy's grandmother came to him. REWORK: we see different ways in which a witch tries to sell her chocolate to other people especially children. We see her putting up a table in front of grocery store, trying to sell the chocolate. When nobody had bought any chocolate, she then stands in front of the grocery store, and, with a chocolate bar in her right hand, she quickly hugged the little boys, and put her hands around the child, and put the chocolate bar in between the child's pants and underwear...........

136. "Ghost Ship" scene where a wire is swept across the room like a sling shot where it is under pressure. Once released wire came across the room, roughly four to five feet above the floor. In the film the only survivor when this happened was a little girl who was to short to be cut by the wire. REWORK: everything is the exact same in condition of the room with the wire. The only difference is that there is introduced into the scene a trampoline. So, when the wire is released, instead of going just

above her head, she jumps on the trampoline and it hits her legs just below the knees, and severs them off………..

137. "World Series of Uno" shows who the best Uno game player plays. The game is commentated by Lon McLean and Norma Chad. (in this examination of the rules and strategy of Uno, in constructing a winning strategy, look back on the Uno paper you wrote, and complete it before moving on)…………..

138. "Mulan" scenes where she tries other things to come across as a man. REWORK: she cuts her hair and glues (modern glue, like super glue or hot glue gun) it to her armpits; she, after a sex change, was ok to hang around the other soldiers, such as swimming a lake. ***Song in the movie while Mulan is undergoing intentional changes with her body (ex: taking out the silicon in her breasts after a boob job; cutting other areas of her body with hair, she then glues it to her face to shave.) When the war ends, upon living the last months or years with the army, trying not to get caught, she return home and undoes ever physical change that she has gone through for a while…………………………..

139. "Something's Gotta Give" scene where Jack Nicholson tries to climb up a flight of stairs, because his doctor told him that if he can walk up a flight of stairs, then he is in good enough shape to have sex. REWORK: Jack Nicholson is halfway up to the top of the stairs, when a Frisbee comes from somewhere along a beach they are at, and hits him in the forehead. He continues to climb the stairs, and then coming from the same direction as the Frisbee, a football hits him in the shoulder, while a kid going over to Jack to retrieve the football apologizes, it is shown that the people who the objects of a Frisbee and football that hit Jack are shown to be intentional. The scene ends with Jack making it to the top and, and after making a bet with friends of whether or not they could hit him with a volleyball, the ball hit him and he falls down the stairs………………

140. "The Matrix" scene where they rescue Neo after he wakes up in a pod and then gets flushed down into a river type thing. Morpheus and the other people in the realer reality find Neo and take him into the ship. REWORK: Neo, after he wakes in his pod, instead of being flushed down a water slide type thing, as soon as he gets released from the pod. Right as he goes down the water slide for one or two seconds, he then sees that the water slide turns into a brightly lit tunnel. The tunnel after

being on it for only a few seconds, drops him into the mind of Danny Elfman (looks just like the mind in "Being John Malkovich"). After seeing Danny...................

141. "Her" scene where the main character talks to the robot/A.I. on his cell phone, as well as the main character's admission that they have sex with each other. REWORK: the robot/A.I. is Siri from the iPhone. The main character tries to emulate his relationship to the robot girl from "Her", with a new relationship with Siri (have the main character and the robot break up for some reason). Every attempt made by the man to try and forge a relationship with Siri, Siri ends up only responding with the notion that she doesn't know what you are talking about. The main character abandons the relationship he has to cell phone robot girls, and instead tries to find love through forming a relationship to computer bots (such as "Smarterchild" from AIM instant messaging). He again attempts to forge a relationship with a robot, through communicating via instant messages. The computer bot and the main character, begin to have a connection, and he then begins to push his luck with the robot, by asking personal questions. The robot's answer to all the questions is that it is just a robot and not an actual person, and hence, there is a limit to how it can answer questions that it is not specifically designed to answer by the people who invented the instant messaging robot. The main character is not impressed with the answers he is getting from the robot, and, upon the recognition of the robot that it is just a robot, the main character immediately loses interest, because, although he knows that the things he tries to communicate with are robots, it is the fact that the two cell phone robots do not identify that they are robots (because...), and instead, the main characters tries to form a specific relationship to the cell phone robots, based upon him believing that he is communicating with a robot, which, with the absence of the robot saying it is a robot, he is able to add a certain level of positivity in how he thinks towards the robot, which can be seen as a genuine relationship, since the main character does not truly see the robot as just a robot (because it didn't tell you it is), but rather a person who can be seen as someone who forms positive for the main character, in that their relationship is real, and hot fake, which only happens when the main character views the robots relationship with itself (it comes across as a real person, because, for example, you can hear the robot making a sound as if it is breathing deeply (even though it has no body

through which one can make that sound), which comes across to the main character as having real people qualities, and not as just a robot that knows it is just a robot, and hence, makes the appearance of the relationship artificial to the main characters....

142. "Waiting" scene where the guy says he hopes Justin Long calls. REWORK: that card that the guy gives to Justin Long is for McDonalds.

143. "Lord of the Rings: The Return of the King" scene where the girl kills the dragon while on top of it. REWORK: she falls to the ground and once she hits, her shoes fly off like in that half pipe video. Make it so that it goes along with the original commentary in the skateboard/half pipe video.

144. "Super Troopers" scene where the cops get stoned and laugh while they watch the Afghani cartoon. REWORK: they are watching Paranormal Activity, the part where the demonologist says he is just angering the ghost. They all laugh when watching this scene stoned.

145. "National Treasure" scene where they visit the girl in her office to tell her that the declaration of independence is going to be stolen, and the girl says, "did bigfoot take it?" and "I have seen the back of the declaration of independence and there is not map on it." and they say, "Its invisible". REWORK: instead of talking about the declaration of independence, they are talking about treasure being at either side where a rainbow starts/finishes. The girl says, "I have been to the start of a rainbow and I can assure you there is no treasure." The guy (Nicolas Cage) says, "It's invisible."

146. "The Ides of March" scene where Ryan Gosling tells George Clooney that you never, ever fuck the interns. REWORK: Ryan Gosling says to George Clooney, if you ever fuck an intern, you never ever cum inside the intern.

147. "Mr. Deeds" scene where John Tutorro finds out that the 40 billion dollars is actually his, "That's my birthday!" REWORK: have John Tutorro say that all the characterizes that point to him being the heir to the money is who he is (that the identity of the man who gets the money always describes John Tutorro to which he always agrees with that it him that they are talking about). Make other goofy things that identify John Tutorro.

148. "Commercial for medicines that they advertise on TV" scene where (a version) the prescription drug is heroin used for pain relief. It is the type

of commercial where they talk about what heroin is, its side effects and what it does. While they talk about heroin, it is just like other medicine commercials where it shows clips of people doing random things.

149. "Pulp Fiction" scene where Jules and Vincent are talking about the comparison between giving a woman a foot massage and performing oral sex on a woman. REWORK: instead of disagreeing with each other, they instead agree that oral sex and foot messages are in the same league as each other.

150. "Paris Hilton Carl's Jr. commercial"; REWORK: instead of a hamburger, she is holding a taco in her hands while she is washing a car (or some other random object (food or not)). Also, the rework will have Paris Hilton's naked body censored as opposed to her wearing some form of clothing.

151. "South Park episode with Cartman as the teacher"; REWORK: instead of having all the students get 100% on the AP Calculus test, they get 100% on the AP Music Theory test.

152. "Anslem Choudry on CNN and Fox News"; REWORK: have the tv hosts ask him about non violent religious and spiritual practice, and how Muslims will do a jihad on the people of those religions and spirituality.

153. "Drinking DMT auyastca" where all the characters who drink it end up throwing up in a bucket; REWORK: the bucket is completely filled to the top with a persons vomit, and, have the person faced with a dilemma: the person who will soon throw up must either A) puke in bucket with the consequences of getting vomit on the floor (because the bucket is completely filled), or B) puke on the floor with the consequences of getting vomit on the floor. After the floor has been vomited on, the owner of the house then sees the vomit, and gets angry and upset and begins questioning people as to who the person was that vomited (angry because she has just gotten new carpet). Everyone denies that they made the stain, including the person that actually did it, thereby getting off scot free.

154. "Cheaters" tv show where they catch the guy wearing a gimp head; REWORK: instead of wearing gimp clothing, the guy is urinated on, which leaves wet marks on his clothing, and his hair is wet.

155. "To catch a predator" scene where a fake 12 year old gets involved with an adult for sex; REWORK: it turns out that the internet picture of the

12 year old is Robbin Williams in "Jack", and so believes that the person that the adult is chatting with is of adult age. He then gets arrested and registered as a sex offender, because the age of the body, ends up actually being a 12 year old, and not an adult.

156. "Orange County" scene where Jack Black tells the main character that he was high, and then set the building on fire; REWORK: instead of Jack Black saying that he was high, instead have him say that he was tripping. Then the main character responds by saying "you're always tripping on shrooms"

157. "Bill O'reilly – Rivera" scene where they get pissed off at each other over some issue in the news; REWORK: instead of fighting over illegal immigrants from Mexico, they are righting over illegal immigrants from Canada.

158. "Garden State" scene where they are in handy world (store) and the guy sees Largeman. REWORK: the guy pitches the idea of vacuum cleaners to Largman. "Are your carpets dirty? I know mine are, I'd like to talk to you about an exciting new vacuum cleaner that people are talking about."

159. "Mouse Hunt" scene where they see Caesar's truck on the road; REWORK: have the truck displaying the "Eruption" picture in the 40-year-old version (or, the car portrayed as a dog like in Dumb and Dumber; ice cream truck), and have that be Caesar's truck.

160. "Road Trip" scene where Barry tries to feed the snake by dropping a mouse inside; REWORK: have the mouse do crazy acrobatic moves to avoid being eaten. Then, Barry picks the mouse up to try and get the snake to eat it, the snake then attacks the mouse holding in his hand, as well as Barry's arm.

161. "Donald Trump saying John McCain is not a hero"; REWORK: instead of just saying that McCain is not a hero, he then ads that all people who have ever been captured are not heroes. Have the interviewer nods his head and seems to agree with what he says.

162. "Skateboard Punks" scenes from Harold and Kumar; REWORK: combination of the scenes where they talk about being 'extreme'. Instead of "extreme", they say, "tripping". (ex: common guys lets get fuckin acid; that was so not trippy)

163. "Harold and Kumar" scene in the jail with Harold talking to the black guy; REWORK: have the black guy be Rodney King and tell him about the way the cops treated him.

164. "The four horsemen discussion" scene with the four atheists having a round table talk; REWORK: the four horseman atheists are believed to be the four horsemen in the Bible, which then explains what Christians hate mail of the four atheists. (burn in hell fuckin atheist)

165. "Richard Dawkins documentary about religion" scene where he interviews Ted Haggard; REWORK: when the interview is over, they head towards the parking lot, and are stopped by Ted Haggard saying that he will do other negative things to the film crew ("I'll have you horse whipped" or "I'll sick the dogs on you")

166. "The scene in Family Guy where Stewie is watching TV and does the 'head, shoulders, knees, and toes'" REWORK: Stewie is watching the same TV show and Brian goes along with it by doing the YMCA sign with arms. This prompts Stewie to be like, "What the hell is this? This is the YMCA show."

167. "The scene in Family Guy where Peter is good at playing the piano while drunk and plays the x-files song in a bar." REWORK: instead of playing the x-files song, he is instead playing the song that usually takes two people to play, but Peter can do it all himself (the song that was played by music teacher and cousins).

168. "The scene in South Park where Jimmy takes steroids" REWORK: on top of using steroids, he also gets blood transfusions. We see Jimmy in a doctor chair with a needle in his arm, first taking out blood, and then injective it back into his arm. We see Jimmy look into the mirror and flex his arms.

169. "The scene in South Park where Towlie buys air duster from the store and the cashier tells him that he must have a dusty computer. REWORK: instead of air duster he buys, he buys a bunch of meth pipes, a glass mirror, and a mini torch to light it. "My, my, you must use a lot of Pervitin" Towlie frowns and responds, "Fuck up bitch I have a prescription" meaning that he is prescribed Desoxyn by him doctor.

170. "Scene in the TV show, "You" where the main character gives a book to a kid he knows, and the book got damaged." REWORK: instead of the main character being cool about it, he tells the kid that he is unable to fix

it, and gets angry. "This is a first edition Koran. I can't fucking believe this!" "I'm sorry, my dad ripped-""I don't think we could be friends."

171. "Scene in Shawshank Redemption where the people work on top of the roof and Andy gets them beers. REWORK: Red says that "November is one fine month to be working outdoors." We see the prisoners on the roof snow shoveling, while Andy approaches the guards. Everyone is wearing cold weather clothes. Two possible REWORKS: #1: the main guard guy ends up throwing Andy off the roof. Andy, however, turns out fine since he landed on a big mound of snow; #2: the prisoner's drink cold beer while they sit around looking cold and shivering.

172. "Scene in Fracture where Anthony Hopkins is alone without a lawyer and then finally objects at a point in the trial. REWORK: he is sitting on his side solving a rubik's cube. The trial is about how you can solve the 3x3 cube, in record time, and blindfolded, while chewing gum. The prosecution claims that he is lying about solving the cube while chewing tobacco. They bring witnesses up to the stand who claim that it is impossible to do all 4 at the same time. The defense (Hopkins), objects when they claim it is impossible. His objection is that he was chewing tobacco, in gum form (big league chew). He ends up winning the chase, and as he leaves the court room, says to the prosecutor, "even a broken clock gets to be right, twice a day."

173. "Scene in that "Acceptance" YouTube video where the guy says, "who the fuck gets rejected from Cornell? REWORK: instead of saying he got rejected from Cornell, he instead is rejected by either a community college, or from a military academy like West Point. For community college it is the easiest college to attend, and hence, the guy draws upon this. For West Point, it is one of the hardest colleges to attend, and hence, the guy downplays its importance.

174. "Scene in Wall Street where Charlie Sheen says, "no sir that wouldn't be legal" and Gordon responds, "sure." REWORK: instead of insider trading that is illegal, it is the limitless NZT-48 pill that is illegal. Gordon asks Sheen if he wants one and Sheen replies, "no sir that wouldn't be legal" "I could lose my license, that's a banned substance, right?" "If you're not on NZT your out, Bud Fox."

175. "The incident with Charlie Sheen going off the deep end and calling his former 2 ½ men co-star a 'troll'. REWORK: instead of saying that he is a troll, Sheen instead calls him a little person. Sheen defends himself by

saying that he was talking to the person as a man, and not downplaying his height as being a 'dwarf' or 'midget'. "What if he were to call me, "Carlos Estevez"? He would be talking to me as a person, just like I talked to him as a troll."

176. "Scene in "Edward Scissorhands" where they try to steal stuff from Jim's dad and the alarm goes off. REWORK: instead of stealing from Jim's dad, they try to steal from Fort Knox. "We need Edward to get us in." When Edward uses he hands to get them in, he enters the room with the gold while the other people run away. When Edward leaves the building, there are dozens of military people surrounding the premises, all with bullet proof vests, and automatic weapons. They threaten Edward to stop or they will shoot (they think his hands are weapons). They decide to use rubber bullets and fire at him at will. Edward falls to the ground, while the police walk towards him and put handcuffs on him.

177. "Scene in "Thor" where Thor tries to break into the new camp set us around Thor's Hammer. He is found out and arrested. The police guy then asks Thor where he received his combat training; Chechnya?" REWORK: instead of the camp around the hammer, the camp is around the "sword in the stone". Thor fights his way into the center of the camp where the sword is. Since he is not 'Arthur', he cannot pull the sword out. The police guy then continues asking possible places where he was trained. Thor responds, "Time Crisis 4".

178. "A midget special Olympics" REWORK: it is just like the regular Olympics, except it is with a bunch of micro small/tiny people. We see a person go over to a shot putt which is five times as big as him, and try and lift it off the ground, but he can't. We see a tiny person using a tooth pick to pole vault with. The tooth pick breaks and the tiny person impales himself. We see a tiny person trying to do the gymnastics vault, but does not have enough weight to bounce itself on the vault. However, the one good sport that they are good at is the floor exercise routine for gymnastics. They are able to do a lot more tricks in the same amount of time as tall people. Finally, we see 3 tiny women and 3 tiny men all on the gold, silver, bronze stand, but winning the floor exercise. A black tiny person puts his arm up to do a black panther salute, which prompts another person to salute, furthermore, we see some of the other tiny people sit down on the stage when the National Anthem is being played. The scene ends with 3 tiny people sitting down, and 3 tiny people doing the black panther salute.

179. "Scene from "American Beauty" where Caroline finds Lester masturbating in bed." REWORK: When realizing that she knows, he goes through all the slang words of referring to masturbation, such as: saying high to my monster, choking the chicken, dry dogging it, masturbating, jerking off, jacking off, slapping the salmon, what I do in the shower every morning, etc. After saying all the names, Caroline is befuddled and speechless.

180. "A scene showing the similarities between Scientology and Catholicism." REWORK: we see a list and playing out of similarities between the two. (i) Both claim there is a defect or corruption; (ii) both claim that belief in either cleans the defect or fixes the corruption; (iii) reference to atomic bombs (volcanos; non literal translation of Revelation); (iv) the injection of the human soul in cavemen. The scene then ends with, "Scientology = Catholicism …sort of; and, Scientology ≠ Catholicism…sort of.

181. "Scene from "Titanic" where Jack draws Rose naked. REWORK: While in the middle of drawing her, Billy Zane and his associate enter the building. This surprises both. They both get up and go running out of the room. As Rose runs naked, Jack collects his drawing but drops the half picture of Rose on the ground. Billy Zane then picks up the picture, and crumbles it in his hand like he does in the movie. The scene ends with Rose and Jack together in a walk in closet, hiding from the other people.

182. "Scene from "Braveheart" where the Scottish people go to battle and moon the other side of the battle. REWORK: instead of just mooning their enemies, they also flip them off and jerk off in their direction (cumming the enemies direction). The enemies captain just shakes his head and orders his troops to fire, which they do, and the Scottish people all die and lose the battle.

183. "Scene in "The VVitch" where they say prayer before their dinner. REWORK: instead of saying a Christian prayer, the father quotes the AA creed, and refers to the 'higher power', as Jesus. All while holding each other's hands high together. When the prayer ends, Caleb shouts, 'Let's eat!"

184. "Scene from "Religulous" where they claim the pastor is not a doctor and has no degree, after the pastor tells them he wants them to call him doctor. REWORK: The words on the screen say, "Dr." and then his name. Combine this with "scene from "Horrible Bosses" where Harkin

gives the guy scotch. "You're a trustworthy guy, Nick, you understand the importance of being honest. Which is why I'm confused as to why you called the guy a Dr.?" "I was just trying to be polite, I had no idea he was actually a real Dr." "But according to this, he wasn't a doctor, so either you're a liar, or this guy is a liar." "I shouldn't have said he wasn't a doctor. "Oh, so you were lying." "No, it was more of an expression like, "said he wasn't a doctor""....

185. "Scene from "Religulous" where they are talking about all the ways around what you cannot do on the sabbath" REWORK: The guy lists all the punishments by death, and includes: tying your shoe, untying your shoe, pressing the floor on an elevator, registering with ashleymadison.com (anytime), etc.... After listing the punishments, the guy talks about the loophole ways around the punishments. Some of the ones he mentions are: a loophole of other animals dying from rat poison. "Why is there a loophole in the poison, such that other animals can die. Response: Because the people who made rat poison fucked up?" A loophole around a literal interpretation of the Bible: "How is it possible for there to exist multiple explanations for Adam and Eve (literal, nonliteral (evolution))? Response: Because the person who wrote the story fucked up?

186. "Scene in a scientific TV show about philosophy, science, and reality (theory of everything, for example). It asks whether we can know for sure that something exists outside of your own mind. The show claims that there is no possible way to know the world except through the five senses. REWORK: The TV show host shows the following: a list of the 5 senses (these are the only ways), and then is highly confused when someone in the audience yells, "what about thinking as a sense". Combination with Team America: The host: "you cannot out smart me person, don't even try." When the audience agrees that thinking is a 6th sense, the host doesn't know what to do: "empirical understanding... corporate America..."

187. "Scene from the Academy Awards where they mistakenly award "lala land" best picture", when it was really "moonlight". REWORK: Instead of mistaking who win best picture, they mistake who wins 'best animated film'. They at first award it to "moonlight" when it really is won by "Frozen".

188. "Scenes from "Jesus Camp" movie, and 'yes, God, yes' movie about what is moral or not. REWORK: IdRaHaJe (I'd rather have Jesus camp); WWJD (What would Jesus do?); IdRaHaJe (I'd rather have jealousy); Pastor looking at porn = what would Jesus not do? IdRaHaJe + WWJD = Protect yourself from God...

189. "Scene from "Pocahontas" where Pocahontas talks to the tree about Cocoham . REWORK: Instead of telling Pocahontas that he is too serious, she says that he is too old. Pocahontas responds by saying she is 18 and so she can legally be with him. Plus, since he is finest warrior, he has the best six pack of all the other warriors. The tree tells her that she talked to Cocoham last week and he told her that he is bi-curious and romantically confused. The scene ends with Pocahontas walking away from the tree and being disappointed.

190. "Commercial from the 2008 presidential election where the Republicans used Obama's association with Bill Ayers as a tactic." REWORK: instead of using Bill Ayers as a reason to vote for McCain, the democrats use him as a reason to vote for Obama. "(i) he believes deeply in what he does and his actions; (ii) he unapologetically doesn't leave the past in the past ('I won't apologize'); (iii) he was a terrorist, but not anymore; (iv) he is not friends with Reverend Wright; (v) Obama is/used to be friends; (vi) he thinks this election will ultimately matter; (vii) he is friends with unamerican activist, Ward Churchill; (viii) is half black/half white like Obama (with whiter skin than Obama); (ix) came up with the name, "weather underground' while on PCP; (x) is one of a very few group of people who don't think Sarah Palin is hot.

191. "Scenes in "Stranger Things" where the girl's nose bleeds whenever she uses her powers. REWORK: every time she has a bloody nose she wipes it on her shirt. If the bloody nose continues, she stops what she is doing, gets a Kleenex, rolls it up, and puts it in her nose. While doing this she is oblivious to the fact that her friends are running from monsters chasing them, while avoiding her (since they know she could kill them).

192. "Commercial where the guy asks a group of kids what the biggest number they can think of is." REWORK: when one of the kids says, "10", instead of saying "ok...", responds with, "that's sad". When another kid says, "1000 billion", he responds, "that's not that big." Finally, he says infinity x infinity is the biggest number, to which another kid says,

"what about Cantor?" The commercial ends with the guy just sitting there, confused.

193. "A person talking at Speaker's Corner, Hyde Park in London. REWORK: the guy speaking is making the claim that Trump is the most pointless president, to which a person in the crowd responds, "was he more pointless than William Henry Harrison?" "Yes, but only because Harrison died."...

194. "Scene in "The Dark Night" where the Joker is in the jail looking straight forward like he can't believe he has sunk this low. REWORK: he looks forward and we then skip to a clip of him being a jester at a kid's birthday party. The screen then shows the clothes he is wearing and instead of his usual Joker outfit, he is dressed up like a medieval jester. Sporting the same "I can't believe I sunk this low" look.

195. "Scene where two girls and one guy sit in a hot tube where the girl diarrheas in the hot tub, prompting the other guy and girl to immediately get out. REWORK: instead have the woman's water break in the hot tube. Once this happens, the other girl and guy aren't sure what is happening. She tells them that her water just broke, which then makes them immediately get out of the hot tube.

196. "Scene in "Shutter Island" where the guy talks about atomic bombs. REWORK: the guy mentions A-bombs, H-bombs and then finally mentions H20-bombs. He says that one H20-bomb could create clean water to the billionth, trillionth degree, destroying the earth through a complete flood. As he says this, Leonardo DiCaprio continues to kick the shit out of they guy.

197. "Scene from "Inside Man" where the middle eastern banker comes out of the bank with a briefcase. REWORK: instead of the police officer saying that he is Arab, he instead says other ways of referring to middle easterners. Ex: a towel head, a camel jockey, a sand nigger, Jihadist (to which the police then asks if the briefcase is a bomb, and the banker replies, "I don't fucking know.")

198. "Commercial showing 1800 tequila, with their new top that can be made into a shot glass." REWORK: instead of being easy and not difficult to poor the tequila into the shot top, the person doing it has a lot of difficulty, such as: (a) the more it doesn't work, the more the guys hands shake; (b) every time he turns the bottle upside down, everything spills all over his hands and on the floor; (c) saying, "fuck this", and

begin chugging the tequila straight from the top. The commercial ends with, "1800: Same Great Taste, Without the Bullshit"

199. "Last scene in "The Blair Witch Project" where Mike faces the wall. REWORK: combine this scene with the robbery in "Before the Devil Knows your Dead", where Bobby tells the woman to get into the corner. "Stay in your corner. Don't even think about looking at her. Get in the corner." The scene switches to the one guy interviewed who said, "She couldn't take the eyes watching her, that's why she had one stand in the corner like that." The scene ends with, "I don't go up there. I believe enough not to go up there."

200. "A scene showing an alternate time where Steve Bartman didn't interfere with the ball and the players ability to catch": REWORK: you see the player catch the ball, the Cubs winning the game, then going to the world series and winning. The lesson is clear: Steve Bartman screwing up = Cubs lose NLCS; Steve Bartman not screwing up = Cubs win WS. Either way, it shows that Steve Bartman controls the Cubs destiny.

201. "Scenes from "The Scarlett Letter" and "Easy A" where the girl wears a red 'A' on her shirt. REWORK: Instead of the red letter 'A', the girls wear the pink letter 'C'. The 'C' stands for cheater, and the pink stands for Victoria's Secret (where she purchased it from).

It is my intention that the people that played the original characters in the films shown above will come back and act in the scene that I have described above. There really is no plot, only to show that a movie can be understood in a different humorous way which I believe the audience will enjoy. I find it to be an insult to the comedic genera in books, television shows, and movies that they all (or the vast majority) are following set guidelines through which they could structure their script. The structure of any story whether it be book or film goes something like: beginning (character and scene introduction); middle (the climax of the story/pinnacle (where some event or circumstance makes the story/a major); end (a reconciliation of characters to each other; usually is a happy ending). What is typical about the middle/climax of the story is that it can only be represented as a break in how characters either relate to themselves, other people, and everything else. People prefer to see movies and read books that have as a basis of the story a certain connection in which the story will progress towards. What the above reworks show is that there does not need to exists some sort of an overall framework to make things fit into an entertaining thing.

# THE GRAIN SILO STORY
# (HOW IT DIDN'T HAPPEN)

I arrive at my cousin Scott's house at precisely 10:00am for a play date on a gorgeously sunny Saturday morning. I met him once when I was five, seven years ago, and so my mother and aunt thought it would be a great idea to get us together for a day. As we approach his house, I become unavoidably uncomfortable for two reasons: 1. I have just been made aware that Scott lives on a ranch. I hate ranches. I hate ranch dressing. The smell, the atmosphere... the animals. I hate it all. 2. My mother was unable to finish this week's laundry because our well ran dry. I was going commando to my cousin's ranch on a hot summer day, and it itched like the chicken pox. My mother seemed to leave me abruptly. I felt like a baby being dropped off at a fire station, although I was conscious and knew what was going on. I receive a warm family welcome from my cousin and aunt who are both wearing short shorts and a tank top. They give me the grand tour of the ranch while I set there fantasizing about things I would rather be doing, like playing Nintendo or swimming. Once they are done lecturing me about horse and cow paraphernalia, my cousin asks me if I want to see his grain silo. Not knowing what a grain silo is, I, of course accept his offer.

The 20 foot grain silo looked like the Empire State Building from where I was standing. The following events ensued:

> 10:16: We climb up the grain silo and look in. Scott pretends to push me in through the top, not funny, for I almost pee my pants.
> 10:20: Scott and I tie a rope around the top of the silo and climb the rope down into the dark abyss.
> 10:26: After a few minutes down at the bottom, Scott climbs the rope back up out of the silo, and I realize that I am starting to have fun. Psychotic Logician is happy.

I begin to climb up the rope and realize that it is harder than Scott made it look. My hands start sweating a little and my heart begins to pound as I struggle like an infant chimpanzee first learning to climb a tree to get to the top of the silo. I reach the top and put my hand on the side, only to feel a strange searing pain travel up my hand. The sun beaming down on the silo has caused the chrome-colored figure to heat up to an unhealthy temperature. The following events ensued:

10:29: I take my hand off of the silo and begin to fall 20 feet back down to hell. Psychotic Logician is sad.

10:31: I awake to my cousin yelling, "are you ok?" I don't answer, something seems weird

10:32: The dust of the grain silo begins to diffuse around my face, I begin to sneeze profusely. Snot rockets fire from my nose like an AK-47. I begin to sneeze from the dust inhalation. Current conditions suck.

10:33: I look up to find my cousin still shouting, this time it's gibberish. I try saying something to him, but I can't. I take my hand which now has a second degree burn on it and put it up to my throat. It not only has swelled up to well over the size of a baseball, but now I begin to feel tiny bumps all across my body. Was I evolving into some sort of demonic alien creature?

10:44: My hives are getting worse and my eyes were beginning to swell shut. Outside I could hear echoes of people gathering around the silo, what was going on?

10:45: The ground begins to shake beneath me and I realize that they are using the bottom trap door to get me out. Finally, I look around to make sure I have everything. I check my pockets. My pockets? Where are my pockets? My pants...OH MY GOD MY PANTS ARE GONE! I first look down to find my dust-covered penis swaying to and fro. I then look up to find my pants, shredded, handing down from the top of the silo.

10:46: I begin to panic, here I am butt naked and the ground on which I am standing on is crumbling beneath me. An arm then bursts through the bottom, grabs my leg and pulls me out.

I come out of the silo, appearing before an assembled crowd. A father who came over to see what all the commotion was about puts his hand over his daughter's eyes. I see an old woman make comments to a neighbor about this "sickeningly unpleasant display." I walk over to the old woman with my whole body still exposed in all its glory, intending to say something. Just then a heat rush hits my head. BLAAAAH! I yak all over the old lady, who seemed in shock over what just happened. It was then at 10:49 that my aunt pulled me, a hive-covered, extraterrestrial-looking, naked boy away from the grain silo.

# THE PURPLE BISHOP IDEA

When I was in boy scouts, one year for summer camp we went to a place called Camp Tahosa. One night, sitting around a fire with my fellow scouts (some my friend, the other's I think suck), a staff member of the camp told us a story that happened in the 1880's at the camp. The story he told us was about a man who the locals called the 'Purple Bishop'. Whether you have heard or read about the story before is a matter of indifference (just look it up online to know the whole story). The only thing you really need to know is that as a consequence of what this Purple Bishop person did, there have been reports by some campers and staff that they have seen purple lights in the forest, as well as the sound of organs playing in the woods. I forgot whether or not I saw this happen (maybe if I actually did, I would remember that I did, as opposed to not doing it and potentially thinking that I did), but supposedly every once in a while, you will see purple flames flicker in the campfire. I saw the Blair Witch Project and was amazed at how many stupid people there were that thought it was real. After the last scene, when the credits role, you can clearly see that the film had a director. Some people who believe deeply in the paranormal and supernatural are so convinced that things like ghosts and witches exist, that they don't want to fuck with any sort of experience which may put them in a position to allow a portal for the evil entity to fuck with you. I bought a Ouija board once, and later that day, Victoria and I sat along a path leading up to a graveyard to try it out. Nothing happened and I never used it again. I myself have never, apart from all the fucked up shit that has happened to me relating to my schizophrenia, really given much thought as to the existence of ghosts and paranormal things like that. I definitely think that paranormal entities have a decent shot of being true. I base this mostly on the first-hand accounts that I have heard from people. For some reason, an exploration attempting to show the existence of the Purple Bishop is entirely untapped. Therefore, I will outline a basic rubric as to how one may partake in such a journey, if they want to.

1.  You must assemble a crew to accompany you on your trip. This crew should be no more than four or five including yourself. Any more people

than five runs the risk of there not existing a solidarity between all members. The more people you have, the greater the chance that someone is going to have some problem at some point (especially if shit hits the fan), which can cause more problems with other members of the group. You must assign a team leader (which you, since you are the one who has organized the entire operation and have handpicked the other people that will join you, are the obvious team leader). I will give a fictional outline of how diversified your team is, as well as how you think they will work together:

-A skeptic fundamentalist who is most absolutely certain that paranormal phenomenon is false and has no scientific backing to support whether it is true or not.

-A spiritual leader like a Shaman or someone who is experienced with dealing with the paranormal, such as a demonologist. Having someone skilled in how to handle and deal with potential evil entities, will enable you to better equip yourself with the proper knowledge about how to cope if shit ever hits the fan.

-A camera man whose sole job is to always be taping everything at all times.

-A psychonaut, who has the job of always never being sober. This person will always be under the influence of some drugs, mostly psychedelic's, which enable him to perceive potentially both sides of existence, mainly, the physical dimension, and spiritual dimension (immaterial). It is important that the person you hire for this position be highly experienced with drugs. If, for example, when on LSD, the Purple Bishop makes his presence known, and bad things start happening, the psychonaut is equipped with how to deal with any negative things, since he has mastered how to control your mind when faced with what he sees is a potentially bad trip.

-Yourself as the organizer of the trip. Instead of coming across as the boss that everyone must listen to without question, organize your crew in a way which will maximize how to be safe and efficient when faced with decisions that could even mean the difference between living and dying. In this way, there really is no central authoritative boss giving instructions to the other people, since the other people possess just as much control over the choices to be made in the woods.

2. In understanding an important part of maximizing how safe you can be on the trip, the topic of whether or not weapons of any sort should be allowed to be carried by any of the members of the crew. The only thing to be cautioned about as to carrying a gun for example, is that if a member of the crew goes ape shit and starts losing his mind, you don't want any weapons around which he may use to harm others or himself. Theoretically, the only real reason why anyone in the crew should even consider bringing a gun or machete on the trip, is for protection against possible encounters with the paranormal, or protection from some wild animal like a mountain lion or a bear. In this respect (and the point that one could defend himself with a weapon, against a crew member who loses his mind and also has a weapon), carrying weapons alongside oneself while on the trip should be allowed, while stressing the importance of not abusing the power of being able to carry a weapon (like, for example, if two members of the crew decide to have target practice on some trees).

3. The trip should take no more than 3 to 4 days. Every night, since the object of the whole expedition is to find out whether or not the Purple Bishop exists, you will make a fire which through it, the sight of purple flames can possibly be seen. Also, other ways of eliciting spirit entities will be done (most notably the use of a Ouija board). Make sure that you make it clear to the members of the camp that about how long you will be out in the woods for, that way if you are not back by the time you said you would, people will start to look for you. Although only one camera will be used at all times on the tip, make sure that you have with you at least one replacement camera, as well as lots of batteries that will last a few days.

4. Never get lost in the woods with no known way to get back to the camp. Taking a paper map of the area with you and use that as a way to also chart how long you want to hike each day. Always stay on the map so that you know where you are at all times. A GPS may be preferable, but not ultimately that much of a necessity. A compass and map work fine, so long as each person in the group knows how to use it.

If you prove the existence of the Purple Bishop, I think they give Nobel Prizes for that.

# (THIS IS THE OBSERVER SPEAKING…) INSERTS THROUGHOUT BOOK

1. (**THIS IS THE OBSERVER SPEAKING:** As you will read later on in this book, I am not a hardcore skeptic, and am very open to the possibility that tarot card reading, as well as other people claiming to have psychic or pseudo-scientific ability, may in fact be a truth of reality. I've just seen too much crazy shit revolving around psychic or telepathic people, that anyone who deliberately labels it as a complete falsehood, are the ignorant ones (fundamentalist atheists, agnostics, and skeptics. ***I refer the reader to my philosophical roast later in this book, for a more rational understanding of why skeptics and hardcore atheists are really not as rational as they seem.))

2. (**THIS IS THE OBSERVER SPEAKING:** Although some may say that you should just kiss the girl, this runs the risk of the girl rejecting the man's (or women's I suppose (any two things that can possibly kiss one another) forced offering. Either I am not just a "player" in the sense that I am not a hoe runner for beautiful women, or I just think you should give the girl a choice, before your tongue is inside the woman's mouth. To understand how to come across infinitely less creepy, or forceful with someone who really wouldn't say yes if you asked her before she makes out with you (pec kisses are a little tricky about what to do, because by the time the girl has realized that the man has kissed her, your lips are already back apart from hers. This may seem more ethically questionable in reference to the forced makeout or libs together for at most four to five seconds, I believe that it is still ethically inferior to asking the girl.), you have a clean slate on your conscious as to whether or not you took the woman's judgement, as opposed to your judgement which you obviously think is morally or ethically defensive, not just your own desire, but also the desire of the woman (very important: it is always about the girl rather than your own desire))

3. (**THIS IS THE OBSERVER SPEAKING:** The only proof I have of this happens to be one of the very few things that I actually do know

about woman. This being mainly that if you tell them to keep a secret, but that secret that you told them in some way has to do with something that they consider to be a big deal (and big deal can most definitely refer to something that is not a big deal at all), then they most definitely will not keep what you told them to keep secret, a secret. I believe this relates to the fact that if you tell a woman you have a secret, they will not stop nagging you about what it is until you tell them, even if you are bullshitting them in the first place that you even have a secret to tell. If the secret refers to themselves, they will tell someone about it. If the secret refers to someone else, they will tell that person. If the secret doesn't refer to them or someone they know, they will tell someone about the secret you told her, and how weird it was. In any case, unless you can absolutely trust a woman with some very confidential information, do not trust them.)

4. (**THIS IS THE OBSERVER SPEAKING:** Brad was probably pissed off and slightly depressed because he likes her, but now, not really sure how to process the situation, the situation being, he wants to have sex with her, but since her snatch is exposed to everyone, it somehow came across as a turn off, enabling him to not see her the same way again. My friend Brad, as you will read about later in the book, is one of my best friends, and after seeing Miranda laying on the floor of his apartment, I do think a part of him died. Still enabled with the ability to have a good time, this fact didn't matter at all, because apparently when it comes close to what he may consider to be a good thing or a negative thing, the feeling of being high or drunk is not seen to affect his mood, or inhibitions. Lesson to be learned by this situation: feeling fucked up on any substance, only has an effect on you, if and only if, you ultimately allow that substance to compete against your mind state of desiring to not be affected by the substance. Just like most pot heads know, in order to drive a car, you can smoke as much as you want up until you drive, and then immediately come down to a more serious and responsible level, easily accomplished by consciously refusing to get caught up in what the drug is trying to have an effect on your body and mind. In other words (and I honestly do believe this), you can blow a .30 on breathalyzer, and, as long as you keep your mind together to a sane level of existing, you could drive or do other things which drinking supposedly makes more difficult, at a certain level of sobriety, such that it doesn't affect what your mind in the traditional sense. Being frightened or paranoid about something that may happen to

you enables you to get your shit together, and take any situation seriously, then, perform at a certain level of responsibility, making you see actions that come may come from potentially being too intoxicating, as being reckless and mindfully immature (thinking you can drive when really you can't), and hence you know you are feeling sober, even though you may be completely smashed and blow high numbers on a breathalyzer. In other words, tolerance to a substance has nothing to do with how well your mind can adapt to otherwise shitty circumstances. Later in the book, you will read about my own experience of driving on substances, and how, I was able to make it through them, usually by mentally elucidating within myself, an attitude which enables one to reverse how drugs naturally operate and work within one's system (*drug effecting person), to a way in which the substance will only has an effect on your to the extent that you consciously let it (*person effecting drug (how it interacts and operates within the substance abusers body. After all, a teen driving after blowing a .09, may be a much worse driver than another person who blows a .21. Some can handle their shit, and some can't))

5.  (**THIS IS THE OBSERVER SPEAKING:** this is a combination of two events, both revolving around the same thing I said to anyone who asked me who I was or who I knew at the certain place I was partying at, mainly, "Is this Scott's house", or "I am friend's with Scott". Scott, or course, being one of the worst possible names I could have used to try and explain who I was to people, seeing as that it is a fairly uncommon name.)

6.  (**THIS IS THE OBSERVER SPEAKING:** in reference to what the girl may have said to herself if she saw her blanket: "that's because it is your brown blanket that went missing from your door.")

7.  (**THIS IS THE OBSERVER SPEAKING:** I consider this event to be one of the biggest fuck ups related to trying to be funny in my life. I also view the time when I made a fat person joke in my creative writing class in high school, and instead of people laughing at it like I thought, there was silence. There are times in my life where I have failed hardcore in reference to thinking something is funny to yourself, and other's thinking that it is not funny at all. It's an interesting fact about the world related entirely to the semantics of logic, this being, mainly: shouting it is "awkward" to a group of people and nobody laughing. This in itself is awkward, and instead of people potentially laughing about my initial shout of awkward to them (so that they are laughing with me), it may in fact draw the attention and make someone laugh once they understand

(laughing at me). If, in ones attempt to be humorous in some way toward something else, the ultimate desire is to make another person laugh or be entertained, and, if or when failing to accomplish this, the only thing left to do to accomplish your desire is to draw the people's attention away from what you originally intended to be humorous, and instead, attempt to draw people towards something else, which may potentially be the fact that you fucked up, and the little idiosyncrasies that one could potentially point to in order to call upon for people to laugh at, is your own failed attempt to get what you want, and hence, reference the intended humorous act as forming the way that one could see as funny in some sense (funny that you fucked up, as long as it is not a serious issue). My failed attempts to make the audience laugh at something that was a) not funny at all (a delicate subject matter, for example, like poking fun at fat people) and b) funny only to you (nobody else identifies with the joke you make). The fact that I possessed the ability at the coffee shop to go into the open mic night, after constructing an entirely fake story in no more than ten minutes, and make someone cry from laughing so hard, shows the level to which, I was able to unify my, at the time, "gift" of making people laugh, with my vision of what I wanted others to view me as. If I could do it all over again, I would have just made up an entirely fictional story to tell the people before I got there for the open mic night. Pushed from my comfort zone of not wanting to speak that week at the event, I told a story, partly true, and partly false, about how I woke up with a black eye one morning in college. I actually consider it to be an act of justice that the times when the audience did laugh at what I was saying, this was when I was telling the true parts of the story, and when the audience did not laugh, this was when I was telling the false parts of the story that I made up.)

8. (**THIS IS THE OBSERVER SPEAKING:** it's not that I think frats are completely toolish or anything, it's more that I think they are an organized way for older students to justify being assholes to younger students, who apparently deserve the shit they do to them any more than the people who are dishing out the punishment (or whatever the fuck you want to call the things that the older students do to the younger students; Harassment? Torture? Rape (sometimes metaphorical and sometimes (like in Animal House where they spank each other) literal)?). My ultimate view on fraternities: it's like a bully picking on a kid in elementary school, but worse because instead of the victim of the bully being able to freely

retaliate without fear that they might be screwing themselves over in some way, the victim of the frat abuse cannot freely retaliate, for fear that he might lose his status in the fraternity. Where superiority complexes intersect with inferiority complexes, fraternities exist.

9.  (**THIS IS THE OBSERVER SPEAKING:** I later told my therapist who I was seeing twice a month that I had tried heroin. She immediately dropped her pen that she is taking notes with onto her notepad and seemed to sort of begin to put it away or put it somewhere else. This, along with her saying in a tone that conveyed that she thought, "The situation with this kid is even more complicated than I originally thought" and that she was now, having heard this, having to deal with a person who she had initially judged as a relatively straight person when it came to drugs, to now exploding into a judgement of me that she couldn't have possibly conceived that I may identify with. "…..Okaaaaaay…." was her response. I then tell her that I had thought I did heroin in college, but I was just hallucinating on shrooms, and it wasn't real. Hearing this, she is greatly relieved. Looking back on this experience of hallucinating that I had injected heroin, I am actually kind of disappointed that it didn't happen. I was able to describe to my friends, with an incredible amount of detail, the experience of shooting heroin. At the time, I was suffering from a vivid false memory, brought on by the shrooms, as well as testimonies of my friends telling me that they did in fact inject me with heroin. Having heard a few days later from Aaron that they were just fucking with me and that I never really shot heroin, it was a mix of anger, and confusion as to how I could have a distinct memory of doing it. A major giveaway that it was just a hallucinatory experience, was that after having told me that I was on heroin, I didn't feel anything different than how I felt before I thought I injected it. I recall Aaron saying, "Just let it take you" in reference to the fact that there does indeed exist some set of drugs which, in order to have the fullest experience of the trip or feeling, you have to mentally give in and stop trying to control how you think the drug's effects will be like when they kick in. This can be seen when, after smoking DMT, the trip does not begin to take its effect (or at least not nearly to the extent of what the drug is capable of doing) until the user closes his eyes and just calmly awaits for the drug to take hold. So, having not felt any effect from the heroin injection I had thought I took relatively recently, I then begin to have the first auditory hallucinations that I have ever had in my life. This was just the sound of fingers snapping

right up to my ear, and each time I heard it, I looked behind me to see if Aaron was snapping his fingers in my ear. He was not. After becoming a little more educated about heroin in the years since this happened, as well as drugs in general, I can definitely say that if there is a drug high come-on that does not depend on the mental state of the person using the drug to control when you begin to feel its effects, heroin is at the top of that list. I read a report on some website where a person wrote about his first time experience with shooting heroin. He recalled that after the heroin was injected into his arm, it took only two to three seconds for him, once the high came on, to realize and honestly know that he was going to be an addict. A heroin high, which I have heard is considered to be one of the greatest feelings/euphoria that any drug or substance can have on a person trying it (the other supposedly is crack), and if you have never tried it, I highly doubt that the high is going to be delayed and rely on your mental block about what you think it is like. So, in reference to Aaron's advice that I should just, "let it take me", I don't know what I am supposed to do in order for it to take effect, because I don't know what I am mentally doing or mentally supposed to be doing, in order to either feel the effects, or not feel the effects. It's like smoking pot for the first time, the high comes on without anything to compare it to, and hence, you could be thinking about anything other than what you think the high will be like, and you will be wrong about how the high is, because you have never tried it before.)

10. (**THIS IS THE OBSERVER SPEAKING:** I have told to a buddy of mine all the experiences I have had involving the pigmy type people that are covered in blue, and wearing jewelry, being in my presence. He thinks that these people are potentially the Mayan people who lived in Central America or Latin America hundreds of years ago. All of these hallucinations that I have had with a supposed Mayan person in my presence, occurred before December 21, 2012, the last day of their calendar, which many people believed would either be the end of the world, or a drastic new start or beginning to a new way of living and existing in the world. None of these things ended up happening, which is not a surprise. I began to think that these blue Mayan people that were interacting with me whenever I was tripping LSD or Shrooms, were trying to show me something. When the opportunity came for me to possibly go into a DMT type trip when I was only on acid, I never completely accepted the idea of what might happen if I did completely

allow the Mayan person to take me by the hand and bring me into a completely new reality. An unjustified paranoia that I had in reference to seeing the Mayan people was that I heard from some source around that time that it was only when a Mayan person was about to be sacrificed or that something negative was about to happen to them, that that was the time in which their bodies were completely painted blue. Regardless of whether that is true or not, it doesn't really matter in reference to my potential trip with one of them. A paranoid sense or feeling as to how something may or may not be, can be just as influential in how something may be experienced by someone. In other words, if I just think that the Mayans are only blue when something negative happens to them, this may take hold in your mind as having a very high sense of belief that one has, just as high as a belief that one knows is absolutely true, as believing that something might be true. It was for this reason that I never decided to completely explore the Mayan people's existence in my mind. Better to just live and die with your own theory about how you believe something is, as opposed to having to live and die with a belief that something might be.)

11. (**THIS IS THE OBSERVER SPEAKING:** tripping on Robotussin, or more commonly referred to as "Robo tripping", is getting a hallucinatory high on legal cough syrup. This was the first time I had tried it and only drank one bottle. If it wasn't for the pot that I was smoking after I took it, I would never have attained a hallucinatory state that is in any way special or noteworthy of describing. What felt like ten to fifteen seconds of experiencing the complete visual hallucination that is what I was going for when wanting to do it, was, according to my roommate roughly a minute to minute in a half of just me looking up at the ceiling. I was actually more pissed off that he woke me up, then what I would have led him to belief was my reaction to coming down. If I were to ever do it again (which I won't because I think it sucks), then I would need to drink at least two bottles to get me anywhere near the level of tripping that would be noteworthy to even talk about.)

12. (**THIS IS THE OBSERVER SPEAKING:** according to the CU cop/ tennis partner, on his myspace page he created in high school, music, to him, makes the difference between him just making it through the day, and holding up someone at gunpoint in a grocery store with their head backed up against the frozen peas. Despite that being pretty imaginative, the cops didn't think so, and as a result, he was expelled from school,

and his myspace page were taken off the internet. His lawyer must really kick ass, based purely off the fact that he got a security job in spite of the fact that he sported semi-automatic weapons in pictures of himself (how he did this I don't know. Perhaps he was holding the gun in one hand and with the other hand he took a picture of a mirror he was standing in front of. The only other way I could think of of him showing off his gun collection, is that either a friend took the pictures (which is kind of fucked up), or he had a camera that enables you to time the photo being taken, so that you could quickly set the camera in front of you, set the timer, and then pose for the picture when the timer is off. I don't know which potential is the one that he did, but what can be known after analyzing this situation, is that regardless of whether or not his fantasies of treating people who piss him off are actual threats, I am happy that the security officer's do not carry guns, and if they did, I think that him recognizing me as an old buddy from high school would potentially carry the effect of him going from one second to him threatening me with his gun, to the next second giving a way to have him put away the gun. On a brighter note, he is actually a pretty goofy person. When we were tennis partners, he called me "kidney", because on one day of practice, he spiked the ball and it hit my kidney, giving rise to the name. He would every now and then tell me that he hoped I pissed blood. I don't know if he was serious or not.)

13. (**THIS IS THE OBSERVER SPEAKING:** I call Max a, "master", because he was the kind of kid who everyone respected, and thought was a way chill person. If I was never his roommate, we never would have hung out, talked, or associated with each other in any way. Our friendship was based on each of us putting up with the other's bullshit, and never getting annoyed or pissed off at each other about it. You know you have truly found the foundation of what makes a person a bad ass when you can do something that buzzkills a great moment, and the other person will not place the blame on you, but rather on the fact that he is not high enough. In this respect, happiness really does come from within, at least in terms of the fact that the source of what makes you uneasy does not come from outside yourself, but rather from some deficiency within yourself. That is true mastery.)

14. (**THIS IS THE OBSERVER SPEAKING:** keep in mind this fact about the Boulder Police Department, mainly, that there seem to be more of them around campus when an event is going on that literally has no

crime or even disturbances of peace. What is obvious is that the officers don't want anyone to know that they are looking at them, and so they sport sunglasses and stand around, not even making an attempt to look as though they are upholding the law (you can't enforce something if no laws are being broken). When you read my experience in Boulder later on, remember that the cops are useless.)

15. (**THIS IS THE OBSERVER SPEAKING:** Also, good call on taking all of the Adderall you had just bought (roughly 150mg – 200mg) at once. Just in case the cop decided to search my car for some reason, I at least was all clear on the amphetamine (Schedule II controlled substance, felony for possession (even just one)) front.)

16. (**THIS IS THE OBSERVER SPEAKING:** This was the second time I had ever gotten high on weed. If I had been an experienced pot user at the time, I probably would have known that Red Rocks was not the pyramids in Egypt. But then again, I am glad that I thought they were, seeing as you have more fun when you are baked with a low tolerance, than you are when you are baked with a high tolerance.)

17. (**THIS IS THE OBSERVER SPEAKING:** I ended up driving high again. Many, many, more times. At least for me, driving high on weed is way riskier and more dangerous than driving drunk. The difference is the psychological aspect of the weed that fucks with your motor skills, that is entirely missing from the effect of alcohol on your mind, mainly being that you just don't care as much about things you normally would. Virtually every time I drove high on pot, I would get paranoid that a cop was behind me, just waiting for me to fuck up on a single thing, and in most cases that I was truly convinced that it was a cop behind me, it was, and I got pulled over for minor traffic violations. Now that police can test for someone driving under the influence of marijuana, just like they can test for someone under the influence of alcohol, I am not advocating that you drive in either state, but in reference to the paranoia you might potentially get while under the influence of either one, definitely don't drive while on the one that gives you the paranoia.)

18. (**THIS IS THE OBSERVER SPEAKING:** The only thing more entertaining than when you are blitzed out of your skull and watching "Sex Talk with Sue Johansen", is to watch old school Disney movies. This rule also applies to what entertains you when you are tripping shrooms. (A quote from my friend Frank while tripping hard and watching South

Park: "I can't watch South Park!" An interesting thing to say while tripping, since, as any person who has used psychedelic drugs before knows, there are some things you just can't handle while you're like that.))

19. (**THIS IS THE OBSERVER SPEAKING:** An interesting thing to note is that (at least in my experience and having heard the experiences of others) when you are black out drunk, the only memory that you possess the next morning after binging are pictures or frames of what you did the night before. I have always liked that.)

20. (**THIS IS THE OBSERVER SPEAKING:** In a sense I understand why some teachers use examples from student's work to explain a point to the rest of the class, while being sure that the student that they are referencing remains anonymous. The problem is that if the teacher, when citing the students work, in any way tries to show the ridiculousness or irrationality of the student, then they are essentially exploiting the student's idea and making a mockery of it to the rest of the class. If teacher's really do stand by the old saying that, "there is no stupid question", or, "the only stupid question is the one that goes unasked" then how exactly does this differ from a student's response to a question that happens to be wrong? In this sense it seems as if, seeing that the teacher is going to cite the response in a way which will ridicule it to the rest of the class, the student should not have even answered the question in the first place. Any answer to any question is the product of how someone understood it through their own mind, and hence, in analyzing it, rather than making fun of it in reference to your mind's own way of understanding the question, it should be looked at with interest and curiosity as to how and why this person thought of the question in this way. This of course only applies to honest judgements and any attempt by someone to answer a question with complete bullshit that really doesn't resemble how they think about the issue, will be wrong, because their answer refers to nothing and is therefore meaningless. This was the main point I was trying make with my claim that two contradictory viewpoints can both be right, because if both viewpoints were made by people who both honestly felt that their viewpoint was the truth and were not trying to bullshit anyone in any way, then they could both be true aspects of the same thing, just merely understood in different ways.)

21. (**THIS IS THE OBSERVER SPEAKING:** Interestingly, the professor said that only one student thought that science would one day establish a certain knowledge of the world, yet no one in the class raised their hand.

Upon reflection, if I did in fact raise my hand, then the whole class would know who the one student is, which, not really caring, I do in fact want to remain anonymous, lest I become known to the class as a moron. However, there was a time when I was the only student in the class who thought that string theory could potentially be a good theory to explain the universe. The professor's response: (referring to me, who sat at the very back of the class) "One theorist in the back." Classic.)

22. (**THIS IS THE OBSERVER SPEAKING:** I think Stephen Hawking had a good point when he stated that philosophy is "dead". Modern philosophy, run by PhD professor's, is a joke. There hasn't been much progress made to philosophy in a long time. It mostly now consists of PhD people arguing over numerous philosophical disciplines, with no progress being made. If modern philosophy is going to try and make a case to be considered as a serious discipline that actually gives something back to the world, then it's going to have to be known as a subject matter through which something can be proved. Without proof, modern philosophers will always be arguing over what is true and what is false. Although, in my opinion, even if someone did provide proof of the resolution of some philosophical problem, the PhD people would still not buy it.)

23. (**THIS IS THE OBSERVER SPEAKING:** to me, philosophy is about proof. If logic is rational argument, and rational argument is a demonstration of how something is, then if the logic is sound, then the rational argument describing something must be true. I find it to be a little bit of a novice understanding of the capability to which one may form a true belief about reality and prove its validity, if one just views philosophy as way through which one analyzes something and thinks about it to form questions about it, rather than analyzing it to the point of examining how it relates to everything and anything else that one may conceive that it can, and hence, provide insight into how the questions that can be formed about it relate to idea, rather than how the questions that can be formed about it relate to themselves. In other words, through all the potential ways in which one may question something in reality, if the questions asked in reference to some underlying notion (some metaphysical or epistemological view) are intended to provide insight into how the notion operates (works, exists as) in the world, then one must relate the idea to the questions that can be asked about it, as well as relate the questions that can be asked about it to the idea. Each way of possibly knowing the viewpoint is that they are analyzed and cohere

together such that they are understood as existing together in reference to one another, then, the question seizes to only relate to an inductive form of understanding, and then becomes a deduction of how something truly is. This is the difference between science and philosophy, mainly, that science can only form a one-way relationship between the viewpoint it is examining and the questions that it can ask about the viewpoint. A hypothesis is a formation of questions about an idea, which encompasses every possible way in which one may conceive of the viewpoint. A theory is an careful inspection of a viewpoint in that it forms questions about the viewpoint, and then tests its validity through the way in which it makes the viewpoint conform to what it is asking. A scientific theory operates in this way through examining a viewpoint and testing whether the viewpoint will conform to the questions that it asks or not, via the doubt or skepticism that it places on it. If the viewpoint is not disproved by the imposition of the question relating to it, then that question is considered part of how that viewpoint is. Although this does provide insight into the nature of how something is, it cannot provide a complete understanding and knowledge of something, because it considers questions which conform to the thing being tested (was not disproved), as describing the same thing as questions which do not conform to the thing being tested (was disproved), and hence, what is known about the thing can only be known via both ways of describing the thing, mainly, a false statement and a true statement. This differs from proof and philosophy because a thing being examined and being shown to be proven, must only conform to questions which show something as being unable to be disproved, because of how it may be proved has been shown to be not disproved. Hence, there is a dual relation of understanding which is required in order to truly know something, and, the paper which I received an A+ on as described above was a representation of this way of forming facts about reality, because it showed a two way connection between both ways of questioning reality which are necessary for knowledge, mainly, the union of logical deduction (questions about a thing in reference to everything a part of it) and scientific induction (questions about a thing in reference to the thing and everything apart from it), resulting in the formation of facts about reality in the form of philosophical abstraction (knowledge about a thing in reference to the thing as a part of everything, and apart from everything, thereby giving all possible relations of existence). Through this understanding, it becomes a truism that complete knowledge and understanding of the world comes from the union of the two essential things that enables an argument to be sound, mainly, a valid deduction of an induct question of an idea, related together through the valid induction of the deduction of the idea, thereby enabling the two differing ways of deducing truth to become equivalent ways of knowing facts about something. This is the simplistic solution to the problem of induction, and through this, anything (notion, concept, question, statement, proposition, etc.) can be known about something through the abstract relationship that it shares between itself and everything else in existence. Nice.)

24. (**THIS IS THE OBSERVER SPEAKING:** most people, in my opinion, do not truly understand what Descartes truly meant when he said, "I think, therefore I am." They make it sound like he was coming across as referencing something about identity, or who he is as a thinker. It really doesn't even have much to do with one being aware of one's own mental phenomena (thought in this case), or consciousness. Many people analyzing this quote make the mistake that Descartes is self-reflecting about his own existence, and that he is aware of his own existence through his thought. However, it can be seen that although Descartes uses the word, "I" in both instances denoting who is speaking in the statement, the "I" refers to different relationships that it stands in towards itself and everything else in existence. This means that although Descartes references himself as substantiating the thought ("I think"), the fact that he later states that it is himself that exists in reference to the thought ("I am"), shows that there are two different ways in which he is demonstrating existence, and hence, is a statement about existence as a whole, and not just about himself in relation to the whole. This is seen once you understand that "I think" does not just refer to himself, but also to everything else in existence, since it is just presupposed within the thought of "I think" that if I exist (or anything for that matter), then that means that existence as some whole must exist, whether the whole of existence is made up of just myself or something that exists apart from myself. Because of this realization, the conclusion of "I am" refers to the fact that because the reference to himself is not being directly referred to by "I am" in relation to "I think", because he presupposes his own existence, through the fact that there is still doubt as to whether or not existence is composed entirely of himself or himself with others, the statement of "I am" then becomes a statement describing exactly what he attempts to describe in "I think", mainly, that his existence becomes equivocated with exactly what is referred to when he thinks. Through this one can understand that

Descartes is describing different aspects, or points of references that he stands into, in relation to two different existences, those being existence a part of himself (part) and existence apart from himself (whole). The only way in which one may refer to both at the same time, through the same reference of themselves to him (stating "I" as the thing which is existing), is through his own existence being made up of everything existing apart from himself, and his own existence making up everything existing apart from himself. In this way, everything is related together, because it shows that existence as a complete whole (everything) is made up not just by itself apart from his own existence, but rather that it is through himself (his own existence), that everything can be known to exists, because it is through him that everything does exist. By his own identity only being directly referred to through the understanding of "I think" and "I am" in reference to each other's existence in existence itself, this demonstrates that the "I" refers to everything, and Descartes identity to everything, through how he conceived of it. The ramifications of what this means is the following: anything that forms a conception of existence (stating something to exist), what is conceiving the conception forms the relation through which anything in existence can be related together and known. This means that one's own conception of existence, is the very thing that unifies all of existence together, and through this conception, one may then come to apprehend a complete knowledge of the thing which was not directly referred through the way in which one formed the conception of existence, mainly, yourself. It is in the way through which the conception refers to existence independently of its own existence, that one can ultimately come to refer directly to its own existence. This is because although both ways of substantiating existence in reference to oneself are being related together through the one forming the conception, what forms the conception is, rather than being shown to also possess an existence, is instead being known independently of its formation of the conception of existence. This means that instead of something's existence being demonstrated, it is rather an unveiling of the very thing which all of existence rests upon, mainly, you, and in that respect, existence itself. In short, if one forms a conception about existence that allows everything to be interdependent upon existence itself, such that everything in existence relates to everything else in existence through what is presupposed in existence, then this will unite the one conceiving the conception, with the conception itself. We may then say that Descartes ultimate description of how existence can be related to itself in all ways (independently, dependently, and interdependently; in itself (a part; contained), outside itself (a part; contained), by itself/through itself (apart; containing)) constructs a picture of existence in which what is presupposed through the conception, is the exact same thing that is presupposed in all of existence itself. This means that when understood, any conception formed will provide an equivalent understanding of not only the conceiver, but all of existence itself, because they are the same thing. The complete conception of everything is just the realization that whatever is conceived, is how everything in existence is. As long as this is realized, anything conceived will be a reflection of how all of existence is. Therefore, Descartes model of existence, rather than referring to a subjectivity apart from everything in existence, actually insinuates the existence of a subjectivity that exists a part of everything in existence. In this respect, Descartes method of doubting provides a blueprint through which one may achieve absolute knowledge. It is merely through the formation of a conception that is the result of doubting until you cannot possibly doubt anymore. If a conception is formed in this way, this is equivalent to knowing everything, because there is nothing in the conception referring to everything in existence, which is not completely known for certain. This is the foundation of how one can come to ultimately no longer need to form doubts about existence in order to know something. This is because if you reach a point in reference to all of existence through a conception of it, which does not refer in any way to something that cannot be true, than this enables the existence of every conception that can possibly exist, within itself, which then, through itself, would enable every conception to form an equivalent relation to absolute truth. Hence, freedom for all.)

25. (**THIS IS THE OBSERVER SPEAKING:** Also, a sign of things to come, which I experienced for the first time that day, is perceiving people in other rooms of where I am at, talk and comment on what I am experiencing. Of course, the minute that the people come out of the room that they are in, they act like nothing is going on and act normally. This seems to me to be a pretty impressive tactic used by these people, mainly, behave in front of me like nothing is going on (like, for example, acting like I and them possess some telepathic abilities, enabling me to perceive their thoughts, and for them to perceive my thoughts.)

26. (**THIS IS THE OBSERVER SPEAKING:** It seems that in reference to the radio station saying this while on the air, there are two possibilities: 1.

The radio station wanted me to hear this, so that my paranoia would be that much worse, thereby, making me believe more in the situation that I was currently existing in. 2. The radio station made a mistake, their fuck up essentially being that the news of the upcoming rapture was meant to be heard by anyone except for me)

27. (**THIS IS THE OBSERVER SPEAKING:** An interesting lesson to be made in reference to what is morally right thing to do and what is not, I shall turn the reader's attention to a message from popular culture. In, "Edward Scissorhands", Allen Arkin asks Edward what he would do in the following scenario: What would you do if you found a briefcase full of money, and there is no one around as a witness to say that you took the money for yourself, if that is in fact what you decide to do when finding it. You could either, A) Keep the money for yourself, B) Give the money to the poor, C) Give the money to your family and loved ones, D) Give the money to the police. After thinking about it briefly, Edward responds, "give the money to my loved ones". Allen Arkin shakes his head, and his wife commenting, "I know that is what it seems to be the right thing to do but it's not." Most people in the world today would say that giving money to the police is the morally right thing to do. However, Edward, in his innocence, says he would give the money to his loved ones. Winona Ryder then comments that Edwards decision is a nicer thing to do than giving the money to the police. Arkin then responds with, "we are not talking nice, we are talking right and wrong." So, in reference to how people were behaving in regarding the situation occurring in the world, is that there does not have to exist something negative that seems to contradict the positive right thing to do. If giving money to the police is the morally right thing to do, then even its opposite, mainly, giving the money to your loved ones, does not have to be negative, or even morally wrong, but rather that something could be nice and loving, even if something true and positive is also right, or even appears to be something negative.)

28. (**THIS IS THE OBSERVER SPEAKING:** supposedly air dust cleaner kills a shit load of brain cells, on par with sniffing glue, or huffing jenkum (but all drugs do to some extent (if you are not aware of what jenkum is, trust me when I say that you don't want to know)) and one should probably avoid making a habit out of this if they want to remain semi intelligent.)

29. (**THIS IS THE OBSERVER SPEAKING:** I have since learned to separate what I consider to might be the true Jesus in my head to what

I consider to be the fake Jesus in my head. The main way that I have done this is through the experience of becoming more aware of higher and higher levels of truth in reality, and the fake Jesus having a lesser effect than what I take to be the real Jesus. Also, I can sort of distinguish between the voices of the two. The fake Jesus sounds like a guy in his mid-twenties or a little older at most, and the real Jesus sounds like a person who at least possesses some basic wisdom about the world and sounds like an older person perhaps in his late fifties. This could be the Father, instead of Jesus, but what really would be the difference (at least in reference to how he acts towards me)).

30. (**THIS IS THE OBSERVER SPEAKING:** at this point in my life the girl in the red dress was by far the most beautiful thing I had ever seen. I soon after decided that I was in love with her, although never talking to her, and she having no idea that I even existed. Perhaps this changed when I began to think that people could hear my thoughts. Look at the situation from her perspective, here was some random person who she didn't know in any way, but somehow he knows about her and is completely obsessed with everything about her. I would probably be a little confused (and as I am writing this, I heard a voice say, "terrified" which I think one could make a convincing argument for it) as well. I have later learned that I was not in love with her, but rather with the idea of how perfect my life would be if I was with her, and I equated that with love. That and I kept thinking in my mind how all I wanted to do was make love to her, and many of my feelings towards her were based in a physical way, such that I was more aware of how she made me feel, as opposed to what she made me realize.)

31. (**THIS IS THE OBSERVER SPEAKING:** Important note to anyone who expects to hear an answer to their question they may have in accordance with how they really believe is the truth of how something is: My honest feedback to the mother's question about how getting your tonsils removed is, is not what she wanted to hear/expected to hear. She apparently didn't want her child to know how getting your tonsils removed is, when you are a two to three year old toddler. Somehow, she came to some conclusion that they give you ice cream when the procedure is finished, something that I literally have no memory of. Lesson to be learned: unless you are prepared to hear a negative response from someone about an experience that the person has had, it is probably just best to not ask the question. Too much shit could get fucked up, ending with

the person who asked the question to find himself/herself in a position that they probably believe would be worse than if they just didn't ask the question to begin with. Unless you are expected to hear the truth, even if it negative, then, in the words of Wittgenstein, "Whereof one cannot speak, thereof one must be silent.")

32. (**THIS IS THE OBSERVER SPEAKING:** and as I am currently editing this, I am rolling on Vyvanse, and, after just taking the last of a month's worth of pills in an eleven-hour period, I feel good. Amphetamines are fun).

33. (**THIS IS THE OBSERVER SPEAKING:** The exchange between myself and the other guy took place during a time in my life where I was still a pill junkie and a meth head (without the tweaking (people who tweak when they are on meth are a major reason why people think meth is a hardcore drug. Notice that every "Meth, not even once" commercial shows a person with their entire face full of scabs and they shake a lot.)) Examining this fact, and what I experienced afterwards, the most amount of amphetamines I have taken all at once was 460mg of Adderall. This lasted me roughly 24 hours. With my days of taking a lot of speed are now behind me, I can now say that Meth is probably the best amphetamine. Taking a lot of Adderall or Vyvanse at once, with my tolerance very high, it doesn't do much for me in reference to euphoria, and focus, as Meth does. I first started experimenting with meth when I already had a high amphetamine tolerance, so it would take a few lines or hits of it to get me feeling pretty good. I wish I would have tried it back when my amphetamine tolerance was very low. In that respect, I understand completely why people say it is very addicting, since the euphoria it probably gives you with a low tolerance must be epic. In reference to people taking it and tweaking out and picking at their face is concerned, I think these people are fucking stupid. There is a scene from "Requiem for a Dream" where Jared Leto, who is addicted to shooting heroin, tells his mother that amphetamines are no good for her (referring to the pills that her doctor gave her to lose weight (probably Adderall)), and that she should not take them. In her case, she ended up being a retard who got psychotic, and all mentally fucked up from the pills (but who am I to judge?). However, although I have never shot heroin, I would have to say that taking some amphetamine pills is a much better thing to be addicted to than heroin. And seeing that he had to have his arm amputated at the

end, I think anyone who legitimately thinks heroin is safer than meth, doesn't know what they are talking about.)

34. (**THIS IS THE OBSERVER SPEAKING:** I am a strong believer in that someone should not be punished for telling the truth. I was suspended from college my sophomore year and ended up writing a short essay defending myself with the hope of convincing the school disciplinarians that I should be allowed to stay in school. One of the points I made in the essay was that I was always honest and told the truth to everyone involved in the situation (the cops for example), and never once did I try and lie in the hope of getting away with it and getting into less trouble. This apparently mattered little to the people reading the essay and they upheld my suspension. This can also be understood by someone who gets in trouble with the law. If someone confesses to killing someone, I don't believe that they should get off scot free for being honest, but rather that they should not be penalized further in reference to their truth admission. Unfortunately, this is not how society operates and many people will attempt to lie because they know that their chances of getting a lesser punishment are better if they lie about what they did, as opposed to being honest about it. The dualism between punishment and reward is strange in this way, mainly, that it brings negativity to things that are considered to be good (telling the truth) and bad (telling a lie).)

35. (**THIS IS THE OBSERVER SPEAKING:** Having heard my theory about lying and liars, I would like to end this section by trying to give the reader a basis for how I saw the world when I was growing up, or at the peak of my dishonesty phase growing up. There is an episode of "South Park" where Cartman claims to have come up with a joke with Jimmy. Upon reflecting as to whether or not he really did help Jimmy come up with the joke, every time he thinks about it, he comes up with a different version of how writing the joke happened. Cartman, when telling Kyle that he doesn't want Jimmy to claim that he alone wrote the joke without his help, Kyle responds, "I believe you. I believe that you believe that you helped write the joke." Kyle refers Cartman's claim of truth to someone who has a messed up ego. He says that people with a messed up ego will do anything they can to protect itself, by always sticking to a story which they themselves probably know is wrong. He says that a person with a messed up ego will do "mental gymnastics" to skew the truth of something, and hence, protect itself from the realization that they are full of shit. Having gone through this experience, I can say that Kyle is

absolutely right. Even in the face of overwhelming doubt, I would stick to my lies and claim that they are absolutely true. Even to people that I knew had known the truth of what I said and knew it was bullshit, I would still tell them that what they knew was false, and that I was really telling the truth. Later on in my late teens, I had developed an ego that, once it was shattered by people finding out that I was a liar, had built itself up as an identity of who I was, and when the truth was exposed, my sense of who I was, came crashing down and I experienced a major existential crisis. I then developed a different type of identity or ego of who I was. This, as you are about to read, is a collection of experiences that came to shape ultimately how I see the world and my place in it.)

36. (**THIS IS THE OBSERVER SPEAKING:** I have come under the belief that the mental state I was in when writing this essay was the best attempt I have done up to this point in my life to best unify with God and become all knowing. This is because everything I was writing about was not just in reference to my own internal understanding of existence as well as how I wanted the world to be, but also accorded exactly with how I thought external reality was. The two aspects of existence were united, and everything I wrote was in accordance with the way in which one may form a complete conception of existence. The only difference between this paper and the complete conception is that I was focused on explaining the details of how such a conception is operates through myself (I titled the paper, "On the Perception of Freedom and Happiness"), rather than how it exists in reference to existence apart from myself. In knowing both of these ways of forming a complete conception of existence, any existing thing can provide a way in which one may know anything.)

37. (**THIS IS THE OBSERVER SPEAKING:** in reference to this virtual reality set up of existence, I have come to think that this was just one way in which I could conceive of how reality was organized. If another set up is conceived of that accords with exactly the same overall understanding of how reality is structured, then that set up is just as valid (since everything will literally be the same between the two, the only difference being the external appearance, which, if the two differing one's are the product of an equivalent organization (just different details), then reality will be conceived of in an equivalent way in reference to absolute truth.)

38. (**THIS IS THE OBSERVER SPEAKING:** previously in the night before my friend told me people could hear my thoughts, I was sitting in one of the Universities libraries spending my time between writing more of my

thoughts down and trying to find other ways to make me more certain that what I was experiencing was real, such as trying to make a lighter levitate. What I was mostly doing was engaging with the people around me, many if not all were voices in my perception which I could talk to, telepathically. When I left the library and headed back to my friend's apartment, I saw many people sitting and standing around the campus, just hanging out and not really doing much. I thought that if everything was just made up in my mind, then this would be sort of an odd thing to see, seeing as that it was a Saturday night and usually people would be out partying are doing other things, least of which would be just sitting around on the campus not doing anything. I have learned from my own observation of my experiences, as well as what the voices have told me, that apparently when I get into a high state of consciousness, this interacts with the other people's minds in such a way that it gives them a sort of head buzz or something. I just remember everyone was really calm and probably just sitting around enjoying the good feeling that they were getting from my mind's occupation all around them. The other most notable thing about this night was I noticed that there was a lot of police officers around, which I don't really remember what they were doing. My thought is that they just want to preserve order just in case I went off the deep end and started a riot of something. Perhaps this had something to do with the fact that when I completed my five premise deduction of everything, I immediately said in my head, "anarchy, anarchy for all" or something like that. However, it the situation turned out to be much like how I described the 4/20 gathering that I wrote about above, mainly, everyone was so calm, the cops presence were really not needed at all. Not to mention the anarchy I was talking about is not the lawless society in which there is total chaos. The type of anarchy I was referring to is everyone doing what they want, and at the same time don't fuck with what other people do or want. I called this type of anarchy where there is complete order and freedom, *deontological anarchy*. Do whatever you want, just as long as what you do does not infringe upon the rights of another, as outlined by each person. Interestingly enough, I once wrote a philosophy paper entitled, "Existence: A Very Short Introduction". It was half a page long and said exactly what I wrote above, mainly, do what you want, and allow other to do what they want)

39. (**THIS IS THE OBSERVER SPEAKING:** no less than an hour or two earlier after I was told that people could hear my thoughts, I was talking

to the voices in my head and I was saying how pride was a good thing and that if it wasn't for that I may very well not have gotten to the position I was in (at least not as fast as I did in less than a week). Knowing what I know now, I understand that my putting pride on a pedestal as something of a good or virtuous quality for someone to possess had more to do with having a deep understanding of your potential and your ability to do what you want. It had nothing at all to do with viewing myself as superior or higher in status than anyone else, and at the very most had something to do with that I did in fact know the truth, and that people also did through me. I may have thought that I was more in touch with reality than others, but I never considered myself to be higher authority that possessed the right to govern others for or against their will. So, it was more that I had pride in reference to my own understanding of my potential, rather than my own known potential.)

40. (**THIS IS THE OBSERVER SPEAKING:** right after this happened, I felt that I needed to go to the people in the physical world around me and try and save them. I heard some voice on a loudspeaker saying something to me about the current situation (it should be noted that I had heard this voice on a loud speaker throughout the entire week, and when asking Abe what/who it was, he responded by saying that it had something to do with a sporting event. It wasn't that I wasn't convinced, it was that I was just confused as to what it was (much like how I confused as to many other things going on in the physical world in front of me the days leading up to this point)). I don't remember exactly what the voice on the loudspeaker said, but I think it must have asked me something to do with who I was and I responded by saying, "Call me God". I immediately ran out of Abe's apartment and went to a person in a nearby apartment who had his front door open, and asked, "do you need help?", to which the person did not respond. I then tried to follow the sound of the voice on the loudspeaker, which ended up leading me out into some random traffic intersection, and then cutting off. I was pretty distraught over the entire situation, and even told Abe, between intervals of crying, that I felt like I had just gotten back from being in a different reality for a very long time (I told him that it felt like trillions of years, and I think that was an honest judgement). The last noteworthy thing that happened in reference to the events the night before happened when I was laying on Abe's couch trying to fall asleep. I heard Abe talking to two people who I had met previously in the week. They were talking about the night before

and mentioned something about me now thinking Jesus was God and that Christianity was true. I went out shortly after to smoke a cigarette, and immediately as I did, they decided to leave. As I am writing this recounting the events that happened that morning, I am in a sort of neutral state. I think the overall feeling in everyone in Boulder that day (and maybe the whole world?) was one of being severely let down. Eight hours ago they thought that they would be free and the rest of their lives would be perfect, and now as they currently were they were back to how they were before anything of importance affecting them had happened. If anything, it was even worse than being back to square one because many of them had to live with the trauma of what they had experienced with potentially being annihilated and experiencing an immense amount of pain. However, I do remember getting the intuition that told me that after Jesus had unified with me, that everything would be restored to its natural state as if nothing had gotten screwed up by me in the first place.)

41. (**THIS IS THE OBSERVER SPEAKING:** there is classic line from the movie, "Shutter Island", where the main character is talking to his police partner about some guy he knew. The guy was having his court case, and the judge sentences him to a long stint in a mental hospital. After the judge read his sentencing, the guy began to plead with the judge that she sentence him to death (in those days they executed felons with an electric chair) instead, anywhere but a mental hospital. I can sympathize with this to some extent, seeing as mental hospitals are really fucking boring and time goes insanely slow. More than just the boredom though is that it opens your eyes to how crazy some people can be. Not that I was annoyed with the other patients or anything like that, it was that I was being held against my will in this place, all the while counting the seconds until I got released, so that I could go home and do again exactly what landed me in there in the first place (take a bunch of Adderall, smoking a lot of pot, and writing philosophy). When you are mentally ill, and legitimately believe in the psychosis and paranoia that you get, it feels like the whole world around you is in on something that everyone in the world knows, except you. In this way, even in reference to the other crazy people that I was in the mental hospital with, I thought they all knew who I was and were in on the global conspiracy that revolved entirely around me. Another good scene to illustrate this was also in Shutter Island where one of the ladies he talks with, writes on his notepad, "run". In his case, everything revolved around himself as well, with all the other people in on it. Having

experienced many of the crazy things that schizophrenia throws at you, I can honestly say that if electroshock therapy was an option for me, and that if I did it I would stop hearing voices completely and stop getting paranoid, I would definitely do it. If, in the near or distant future, I again am forced to go to a mental hospital, I would try and create a method of escape, in which I could structure my perception of the world to accord with any way of acting that I want. In the real world outside of mental hospitals, it is very difficult to pretend to be something or someone that you want, since there are always people that you see and interact with, whose perception of you is not how you want to come across to them as, but rather how they see you. If what you see in yourself does not align with what the other people see in you, then you will always have to pretend and act as though it were true, as opposed to knowing it is true. That affords an interesting way of interacting with other people as crazy as you in a mental hospital (what the difference is between a mental hospital, mental institution, and insane asylum, I am not exactly sure). Everyone is seeing the world through their own built-up perception of the world forced upon them by the onset of their mental illness. Rarely, if at all, do crazy people ever judge another person, either positively or negatively. Instead, they are only seeing the world as it relates to them and putting a label or forming a conclusion as to how someone else is, does not even occur to them. For example, back during this time in my life, someone could tell me (like a lot of people did) that they could not hear my thoughts and they have never heard my thoughts. Because I was so convinced in the truth that people could hear my thoughts, I took what these people told me as somehow connected with the fact that they could hear my thoughts ("they are just lying to me and don't want me to realize that they can hear my thoughts"). It is a form of circular reasoning that lies entirely on the perception of the believer to make it remotely valid. Understanding this, creates an escape in the mind of the mentally ill person, such that they could act and behave in a way which nobody would deny or contradict, and hence, make up any form of existence through you own mind that comes to be how you see the world. This is one potential way to cure boredom in a mental hospital.)

42. (**THIS IS THE OBSERVER SPEAKING:** I have since come to the conclusion that I really don't like this perception at all. The idea that everything revolves around me and has something to do with me, such that it bases the fulfillment of itself on me making it happen. I had an

intuition once, or maybe it was what one of the voices told me, that everyone in the world (perhaps everyone in existence) understood a basic way in which reality or the truth of the world is, that is, everyone except for me. Because of this, everyone is waiting for the day that I finally get what everyone else has understood for what has been going on six to seven years now. Or perhaps it could be that I understand something that everyone else in existence doesn't get. A voice once told me that I was the smartest person who has ever lived, and I am not sure what to make of that. If there ever does come a point later in my life when I see the world for how it is without the assistance of drugs, I believe it could only be something that I want to see the world as, as opposed to the world seeing me as.)

43. (**THIS IS THE OBSERVER SPEAKING:** This is the very time I became aware of an interesting logical conundrum, that solves itself through how the perceiver conceptualizes the world to accord with what he/she already knows. This is done through understanding how the logical argument, A & ~A can be shown to not be a contradiction, and actually be known as a truth value through which, whatever the perceiver honestly thinks, would be a completely true depiction of the world/reality. I have abstracted to this understanding a few times in my life, and what I write down I have called it "painting" a picture or depiction of the world. The picture of the world begins to take shape once you really deeply believe that something is true, and what you deeply believe is something that is not true, paves the way through which you use self-referential certainty, to know the truth of the world. It should be noted that this is just one description of how the world is, which exists amongst any other way of conceptualizing it, through the perceiver. In this way, nothing will contradict any other thing, because they are both equivalent ways of seeing the exact same phenomena. This is what I truly meant when (as read earlier in Section 1 of this book) I told my professor that two different, seemingly opposing understandings of something, can both be shown to be true. When trying to describe this to the class I used a thought experiment that if you could just look into the mind (or consciousness as I put it) of someone perceiving the world a certain way, that you believe stands in contradiction to your own, then you could possibly see how both you and the other person are right. The class probably just thought I took too much acid and couldn't return back to reality. I have taken acid, but not that much.)

44. (**THIS IS THE OBSERVER SPEAKING:** Having to listen to voices in my head now for roughly four and a half years, I have built up somewhat of a tolerance to the fear that they try and instill in my, as opposed to how I know what the case of something is. Fear, as I found out through the times in which I legitimately thought I was going to be annihilated, is a driving force for evil, and can be understood as its main mode of how it operates to influence people. Knowing this, I don't get scared anymore, and if ever do feel a slight feeling of fear in reference to something, I just simply remember how reality is which then alleviates any form of negativity that can possibly fuck with me.)

45. (**THIS IS THE OBSERVER SPEAKING:** I think that this might be the only time I had ever gotten to such a high state of consciousness, and not at that time thought I was God. It could have been that it was just in my mind without me perceiving that it simply goes without saying that I am God right now. Perhaps as truism that I never even recognized or reaffirmed to myself. I'm not sure but that is beside the point. Upon reflection, this story is mostly about, philosophically speaking, how I perceived time, such that I was experiencing the past in the present, and the future in the present simultaneously.)

46. (**THIS IS THE OBSERVER SPEAKING:** It is an interesting fact that the sounds made by all 26 letters of the alphabet correspond with all the possible sounds that exist in this world/dimension. Any sound that anything makes in this world, can be known as a sound one of the letters makes. Taking this into account, I could most definitely say that the sounds and music I heard while tripping (the trees singing to me) were sounds that don't exist in this dimension. I wish I could tell you how it sounded but it is literally impossible to make that sound in this dimension. This is analogous to some people, like my friend Eddie, for example, who when tripping, see colors that don't exist in this dimension. An interesting idea that I can see after going through this experience, is that when I thought for certain (100% belief) that I was a tree all along and was just coming out of a trip of living a human life, there are multiple ways that one can conceptualize a possible way of how the world and my existence in it is. For example, perhaps I still am actually a tree and have just gone back into the trip to this dimension. Seeing the world this way makes you conceptualize your own existence in reality as, because there leaves open the possibility that I was perceiving the opposite of how I normally see the world. In this way, when I came down from the Salvia and my trip

ended, perhaps this could be that instead of me coming out of a trip, I was instead going back into the trip of living as a human. Equivalently, when the trip began, instead of going into a trip, I was coming out of one. There is an interesting parallel between the dimensional hierarchy that I saw in the trip (how the world is structured to accord with anything that exists within it), with the dimensional hierarchy that I saw when I was writing my philosophy paper in Boulder. All I can describe it as is just a bridge type organization which represents a unity with everything in it. It was either the philosopher Leibniz or Spinoza who, when trying to understand the correlation between free will and the determinism of the universe as how it was understood by Isaac Newton, he came up with a way of depicting how such a world could exist. The idea is what he called the "organization of pre-established harmony" or something like that. When everything in the universe or existence become organized between themselves and every other thing in such a way that they are in exact alignment with how reality exists as. Once everything in existence is situated according to how it truly exists in the dimensional hierarchy, then a complete union with everything else comes into existence. This relates to the hierarchy I saw in the magic tree friend's reality, in that everything was in unison with everything else, and existence as a whole was complete in how it contrasts with reality, mainly, as being equivalent to reality. Not just in my salvia trip, but also during times in the past where I was getting close to putting into effect a major piece of absolute knowledge, I could the voices in my head singing, in a sort of praise or worship type of way, analogous to the praise and worship music that the trees were singing to me. Why this is relevant is because many people believe that the ultimate purpose of life and existence is to exalt or glorify God. Although I sympathize with this view of reality a little, I think the ways that they feel that they must glorify God (through singing and music) are a little misguided. In the salvia trip, the trees singing worship music, although it made me feel important and loved, didn't resonate with me as the end all be all of existence. Like in this dimension when I hear worship sounds, there is a part of me that feels a little embarrassed or uneasy about the situation, because I am viewing myself as what I think the people worshiping me think about me, as opposed to how I really am and what I really want. I personally, hold the belief that if one truly does believe that the point to existence is to glorify God, then there are an infinite number of ways to do this, and not just by singing praise music, which, in my case, I really don't like very much. Glorifying God is not some specific way you must accord with to show your gratitude and love for God, but rather is an authentic realization of what you always wanted, and now that you have it (being one with God), anything you do can be seen as a compliment to God (because if singing worship music to God is not in alignment with how you really want to show God your love, then singing the worship music is not something that aligns with your authenticity, and hence, does not coincide with how you really desire to live and exist as.)

47. (**THIS IS THE OBSERVER SPEAKING:** This recollection of memories that I have of working at the Mexican restaurant are a catalog how I began to see the world as, that would progress over the summer and finally come to a climactic event in Boulder and other places after that as well. As time went on, I became further and further enveloped in a perception that dictated how I ended up seeing pretty much everything in the world as being. At one point I was so fed up with the whole situation that I, after smoking a bowl or two with my old neighbor in the parking lot of the restaurant, decided I would try and end it the whole situation myself. I arrived at my house after smoking the pot and decided I wanted to just go to sleep. The problem was that I was hearing a ton of voices and I kept visualizing people coming into my perception. I then decided that I would allow Satan to possess me or do whatever the hell it is that he does, if I were to live for 10,000 trillion years in a DMT type reality where I could do whatever I wanted for that amount of time. Once the 10,000 trillion year vacation was over, I then had an eternity in hell to put up with. I decided that I wanted to be with Claire for the last 100,000 years of the trip. I find this to actually be kind of funny because if I really did think Claire was the best girl I have met or someone who I was in love with, why wouldn't I want to be with her the entire time? 100,000 years out of 10,000 trillion years is not that long of a time at all, and upon reflection it actually seems kind of an insult to how I viewed her in relation to the overall importance I placed on her in relation to myself. I could hear my parents talking in the kitchen about what was going on, which made me realize how disappointed they were in me for having decided what I wanted to do. Of course, after I woke up, I was frustrated that I didn't live the 10,000 trillion year life, and so was then forced to keep putting up with the crazy shit that surrounded me every moment of my waking life. It should be noted that from the beginning of when I first started hearing voices, I would visualize their existence in my mind

as according with the virtual reality type set up that I discussed when recounting what happened to me in the *Complete* Story. Whether that way of conceptualizing the setup of how existence exists as and operates through, was my creation or not, I still hold true to the idea that if the voices in my head are real, then they have seen a lot crazier things than I have seen.)

48. (**THIS IS THE OBSERVER SPEAKING:** A good way to understand how some people, when they are fighting (as a joke at least), knock the person that they are fighting down, and instead of letting them get up to begin the fight again fairly, the person just keeps punching or kicking the person while they are down, is somewhat like that game called "Soul Caliber". If you ever get an edge in the game when your opponent is on the ground, you can keep hitting him which will not allow the person to get up to resume the fight. Most people who play the game admit that it is cheap as fuck to do this, and I would have to agree. If it is cheap in a video game that is just for fun, then I think this same rule applies to two people fighting for fun.)

49. (**THIS IS THE OBSERVER SPEAKING:** Years later in my teens, I ended up going paintballing a few times with some friends. I don't exactly remember how getting hit with a paintball hurts in contrast to being whipped with a belt, but if I had to guess, I think being shot with a paintball gun hurts at most as the pain one feels when getting whipped. In this respect, our plan to build up a tolerance to paintballs did have an aspect of rationality to it.)

50. (**THIS IS THE OBSERVER SPEAKING:** An interesting story of me lying in my youth was when I had a reading tutor in elementary school. I told the tutor that I had two dogs, both Dalmatian puppies. A few weeks or months later, in my 1$^{st}$ or 2$^{nd}$ grade class, the teacher assigned us a task where we had to write about something that we really wanted. I wrote down for the assignment that I wanted a dog. My tutor, having read what I wrote, asked me: "I thought you had two puppies?" to which I responded: "Yeah, but they died." I'm not sure what she thought about what I said to her.

51. (**THIS IS THE OBSERVER SPEAKING:** Despite the fact that I am annoyed when people believe things that end up creating a self-fulfilling prophecy to the thing being true, I honestly believe that accepting Jesus as your savior is a good thing (unless he is evil then it would be a bad thing

to do. But this I most definitely believe to be false). I am not a believer myself, but I think there is a certain amount of gratitude that comes from seeing what Jesus went through on the cross. A favorite movie of mine is the Christian movie called, "Fireproof". The lesson that it tried to espouse was that having a personal relationship with Jesus is a good foundation to having a happy marriage. I completely agree. As to whether it is the best way or the only way to having a happy marriage, I am not totally in agreement.)

52. (**THIS IS THE OBSERVER SPEAKING:** I guess I can't really blame my aunt for thinking that the website was some sort of evil thing through which you could really come to invoke the paranormal, much like the way a Ouija does. This is because of a story my dad told me about the paranormal which my aunt was present at also. Apparently, my dad, my aunt, and their cousin were at a cemetery and started saying thing, trying to invoke some sort of dead spirit. They were using a lighter and part of the evidence that you really are communicating with the paranormal is if you see the lighter flicker when you say something. They asked a few questions and then apparently it got to a point where they were in some sort of communication with some spirit. They asked, "are you mad that we are here?" to which the light flickered. They then asked, "are you going to do anything about it?" Right as they asked this question, a truck with a bunch of rednecks or hillbillies in the back of it began to drive towards where they were in the cemetery. They all had to run for their lives, because they were convinced that the rednecks were coming for them for having invoked some sort of entity. So, although the website I used to fake out my cousins was a hoax, I guess after going through an event like what happened in the cemetery, my aunt didn't want to be too cautious.)

53. (**THIS IS THE OBSERVER SPEAKING:** It is a testament to how fucked up these cops were, that they took Ron's cigarettes away, and even crumbled them up in front of use. *There is no minimum age to possess tobacco or smoke in public.* It was pretty obvious that these two cops wanted nothing less than to fuck us. I think it is a highly corrupt and messed up state of affairs that cops (at least in the town I grew up in) would rather find you with something when searching your car, than finding you with nothing. I could definitely tell the partner of the cop who searched my car was a little pissed off about not finding anything. It was at this point that he decided to crumble up the cigarettes. If it really is true that minors are allowed to smoke and use tobacco, then I think what

the cop did to Ron's cigarettes, could be grounds of showing a judge that the cop acted unjustly. I find it completely fucked up that a town (like the one I grew up in) can come under the control of lawmakers who have the power to change how people live in accordance with, by instituting some law or ordinance that forces how people must accord with the law of the town. An example of this is that it was now against the law for a minor to be out past midnight. The societal rule of curfew, I think, is a forcing of rules that one day might come to provide a reason for more government control of the people.)

54. (**THIS IS THE OBSERVER SPEAKING:** I swear by that Peroxl mouth wash. That stuff is liquid gold for your gums. Having gingivitis is something that I don't think that many people go through. I really isn't that difficult to just brush your teeth twice a day, and even easier just to brush it once a day. I have never flossed my teeth for more than a day or two every six months when you go to the dentist, and now that my gums are healthy, the dentist never really seems to notice. I believe that having gingivitis in some ways actually has helped me over the years. First off, my gums are extremely tough, tough enough to the point that my mom commented one time when she saw me brush my teeth, that if she brushed her teeth as fast and hard as I do, then her gums would be bleeding. I personally like using a regular brush as opposed to an electric toothbrush, because you can more deeply clean your teeth by being able to brush more violently at any pace you want. One dentist appointment I went to, the person using the metal hook thing to scrape the plaque off your teeth commented that she really couldn't find any plaque at all. I attribute this to being able to deeply clean my mouth more than what an electric toothbrush will do. What is even more crazy about this story is that when it took place, I only got gingivitis when I didn't brush my teeth for weeks or months, and never a single cavity. I must have strong teeth because that is pretty remarkable.)

55. (**THIS IS THE OBSERVER SPEAKING:** This is the true story of what happened when I went into the grain silo. Years later, in my senior year high school creative writing class, I wrote a story loosely based on this experience. The assignment was simply to write something humorous. You can read this not true, highly exaggerated story of the grain silo story in the index of this book. My teacher thought that the story was extremely funny and encouraged me to publish it in the school newspaper. The only problem is that I claimed that the exaggerated version of this

event was true, rather than just based on a true story. Claiming that the story was true made the people who read the story find it even funnier and appreciate it more as well. My parents read the story in the school newspaper, and I even tried to claim to them that the story was true, which obviously they knew it wasn't because I wrote that in it that I had a cousin named Scott, which we both know is not true.)

56. (**THIS IS THE OBSERVER SPEAKING:** By the time that I had the above conversation with this guy I had already reconciled free will with determinism in one of my philosophy papers. Also, I had resolved Russell's Paradox as well and I was kind of just humoring the guy. He had a "Brooklyn" accent and to this day Eddie and I still joke about him and quote him a lot. I never said I was smarter than him, like he accused me of being, but to be honest, it's not that hard to be smarter than him. He was a fucking nut case.)

57. (**THIS IS THE OBSERVER SPEAKING:** The more you try and get in contact with a woman, who hasn't herself come to really form an opinion about what kind of man you are, makes the girl come to form an opinion of you by labeling you as a potential stocker. Luckily, the technology of the present in which we live, allows for a positive way for some guy to not come across as clingy to a woman. When it comes to woman and how to contact them after they gave you their phone number you (if you don't want her to label you as a potential creep) simply A) call the girl once and leave a message; B) text the girl. If you repeat any of these two forms of communicating between people in today's technology, then you run the risk of coming across as someone who the girl may find not as being that attractive to her. If a woman is into you, she will respond to the first voice mail or text that you send to her. It is superfluous to try and keep getting a hold of the woman by repeatedly sending her messages to try and get a hold of her. A girl that, when asking for her number, only has three possible ways to respond: 1) tell you she has a boyfriend. 2) Give you a fake phone number. 3) Give you her real phone number. Just saying blatantly no someone's face is seen by the woman as not being that much of an appealing option. Perhaps some women feel that putting a guy down through one of the three options is a much nicer thing to do. In my opinion, I think a girl straight up rejecting me for some reason, is a much better result of my asking for her number, as opposed to the girl giving you a fake number. It shows that the girl is a lot less fake/two faced than other actions which make her come across as very fake/two faced.)

58. (**THIS IS THE OBSERVER SPEAKING:** There are times when passing out from a night of heavy drinking, that (at least true in my case) when dozing in an out you play over in your mind the fucked up shit you had done earlier that night. It seems like a dream you are having, and your only hope is that it is. However, when you wake up it dawns on you that the visions you were having are actually true. This is a shitty realization, because you then understand that you are forced to live with whatever fucked up thing it was that happened to you the previous night. It's a good feeling one gets when they were having a bad dream and then wake up to find that it wasn't real. It's a shitty feeling one gets when they are having a good dream and then wake up to find that it wasn't real. In the case of Alex falling into the fire, it's a really shitty feeling when you are having what feels like a bad dream, only to wake up find that it is real. Pour drunk bastard.)

59. (**THIS IS THE OBSERVER SPEAKING:** The potential existence of hell, I have always thought to be something that you cannot joke about like you cannot joke about the Holocaust. It is not a laughing case for someone to try and skew a potential good reason for some evil thing. Morally speaking, to try and bring light to something that is by its definition is an evil thing that either exists in the world, had existed in the world, or will one day exist in the world, can only refer to something which possesses a bad moral foundation.)

60. (**THIS IS THE OBSERVER SPEAKING:** I am torn between releasing the eight-episode podcasts, if this book does ever reach an audience where I think people could handle the type of shit that Eddie and I discuss. In Eddie's words, together we are a complete path of destruction, in that if this book or our podcasts ever were to reach a person(s) which had completely understood and were compassionate about the issues discussed, a rebellion against authority, and self-rule could occur, resulting in an elucidation of universal goodness.)

61. (**THIS IS THE OBSERVER SPEAKING:** An interesting thing that I came to understand about the recording of the podcasts, is that Tucker told me that I have a good voice for recording. I can project my voice in a way which makes it sound sonorous. On the podcast where Tim came into the recording studio, the other guy who came in with Tim said roughly the following about my voice: "It sounds like we are listening to Howard Stern." I find that to be a goofy comparison.)

62. (**THIS IS THE OBSERVER SPEAKING:** The fact that I tried to mask the smell with an air freshener, when the weed was already in a sealed container and you could barely, if at all, smell the weed from it just by being in the container with nothing else, shows how paranoid I was at getting caught with the weed, either by the cops or my parents. This level of paranoia, I think, is common for people just beginning to smoke weed. Beginners usually get so paranoid that they go completely overboard with ways to stop themselves from smelling like weed, or the place you are at from smelling like weed. At the time that I first started dealing, I had only smoked pot for two years, and was still irrationally paranoid.)

63. (**THIS IS THE OBSERVER SPEAKING:** Just to show how fucked up this guy was, not only did he fuck me out of hundreds of dollars of weed money, but also at the time, he, being 21 or 22 years old, was dating and having sex with a 12 year old. Recently, he got released from prison for his plan to set himself and my friend on fire, and within the next few weeks, got in trouble again and is now back in jail. Sucks for him.)

64. (**THIS IS THE OBSERVER SPEAKING:** It was a fantasy that I never saw materialize. Yes, you could make $3,000 for every pound sold, but there was an even worse thing that could happen to you on the east coast if you are caught with weed, as opposed to weed you get in Colorado. Supposedly if you get caught with any amount of weed in certain states on the east coast, they charge you with a felony, since it is labeled by the US government as a Schedule I substance. In Colorado, if you get caught with weed by the cops, they state only charges you with a misdemeanor. So, although I would have gotten way fucked if they caught me with a pound(s) in Colorado, and just that more fucked if they caught me with it on the east coast (Mac was from Baltimore so I think that is where we were going to make the deal at.))

65. (**THIS IS THE OBSERVER SPEAKING:** With all the money I put down to pay for pot or shrooms which numbered in the thousands of dollars, that is money I could have spent on doing any other thing that brought me fun, most notably being able to buy Adderall which, A) is a better drug than pot or shrooms in my opinion, and B) would have helped me kick ass in college.)

66. (**THIS IS THE OBSERVER SPEAKING:** After Dan, the psycho manager left, the new manager was way chiller and while discussing with him some of the bullshit things that Dan did, he said he never yells or gets really pissed off at people who have done something wrong, simply

because you can't change what happened. All you can do is talk about it calmly with the person and get them to know that what they did was wrong. If you get pissed off and scream at the person, that person is just going to think you are a fucking asshole who doesn't deserve your respect. If you can only get your point across to someone by yelling at them, then you are making the person miss the point. The person will then not do what the manager told him not to do, because he doesn't want to get yelled at, as opposed to not doing what the manager told him not to do, because it is simply the right thing to do. So, taking the rape example of my co-worker, I believe it is much better to get your point across to the rapist by putting your feelings about it aside, and then making them understand that they shouldn't rape someone because you will get in legal trouble if you do, but rather you shouldn't rape someone because it is simply the wrong thing to do.)

67. (**THIS IS THE OBSERVER SPEAKING:** Most people who believe in God would say that this argument is straight up wrong or a misrepresentation of God and what God can do. I really don't get this because according to them (Christians at least) there are certain things that the God that they believe in can't do, such as lie or sin. I agree it is more of a noob argument that I came up with before I started liking philosophy and thinking rationally. Even if someone did think it was a legitimate argument, they would then probably go back to the foundation upon which they understand how powerful God is, mainly, "it is like explaining to an ant how the stock market works." Taken at face value, I would still have to say my favorite argument against the existence of God was told to me by a girl I worked with at the car wash: "if there is a God, show him to me." Really stupid, but also really smart.)

68. (**THIS IS THE OBSERVER SPEAKING:** I relate a lot to what the crack girl told me about her constantly thinking that she would get caught by the police. When I was in college, I has this vision that I would think about for weeks of the cops searching my dorm room and catching me with my weed. I don't know why I would constantly think about it, but I didn't do what a competent person would have done, which is to make sure that you always have your drugs in a place where the cops couldn't possibly find it. In this case, all I had to do was put my drugs in my fake bottom, which, for some reason, I was not putting to use and was instead using a cabinet with a lock on it to hide the weed. It wouldn't have been so bad if the cops searched my room and told me to open the cabinet,

because then I could just say (as my freshman year roommate did) I don't know the combination because I am letting my friend put his stuff in this cabinet which I don't use. Instead, when the cops searched my room, I unlocked the cabinet, which had at least two ounces of weed in them, and trying to hurry, I frantically put the two ounces outside the window (my dorm room was on the ground floor) and forgot a gram of weed and a pill of Adderall. Lesson to be learned: if you ever get paranoid about something that may come to screw you over, but at the time has not come to screw you over yet, always do something to change how you are currently living in reference to the paranoid vision. In my case, once I got paranoid that I would get busted with the weed and Adderall, all I had to do was put that stuff in a different place to avoid getting fucked like the paranoid vision predicts. Failure to do so is to live at your own risk and reap the shitty consequences.)

69. (**THIS IS THE OBSERVER SPEAKING:** In this story is another depiction of me lying about something and then later on using that lie to make me come across as a better person. For example, the message that the woman left on my phone about house sitting for her I had received weeks before I called her back, with the excuse that I had just gotten it. I made this lie that I had just received it so that she would still think I was a reliable person, and it was an honest break in communication. I am not sure whether or not she actually didn't need me to house sit for her anymore when I called her back, or she just thought I was full of shit for claiming that I had just received her message. Either way, that's not a very mature way to handle something. But then again, I wasn't very mature. One could make an argument that I am still not very mature, and I think they could come up with some valid evidence to support that.)

70. (**THIS IS THE OBSERVER SPEAKING:** Where my manager got my last name that she put on the first check from I do not know. It couldn't have been someone she knows who has the same first name as me but a different last name, because then she would have realized that I wasn't the person who she knows who has my first name, but different last name. Come to think about it, it makes no sense.)

71. (**THIS IS THE OBSERVER SPEAKING:** I still consider it to be a dream job to drive a cab in NYC, but only if I were to memorize all of NYC and also learn a few other languages. The idea of being anywhere in the city and then knowing exactly how to get to wherever the passenger wants to go, just based off memory and without GPS, sounds pretty

bad ass. Working the GPS was one of the shitty parts of the job I think, partly because it takes a minute or two to enter the address into the GPS, and partly because on more times than one would think, it takes you to a wrong place. The taxi drivers in London have memorized all of London and know how to get from anywhere to anywhere. I watched a documentary about London cab drivers, and it takes anywhere from two to even five years for some people to memorize all of London to then get your taxi driving license. The nice thing about trying to memorize NYC is that more the most part (at least in Manhattan) the streets are lined up like a grid. That would probably make it easier than memorizing a place like London, but it would still take me years to do. I currently lack motivation, partly because the task just seems insanely hard to accomplish, as well as because I don't have any access to Adderall anymore, which, if I was rolling on it all the time, memorizing NYC would actually be really fun. I had a fantasy that once I did memorize it, I would then test myself using Google Earth, using the street view, so that I would go from place to place as if I was actually in the city.)

72. (**THIS IS THE OBSERVER SPEAKING:** One of the most interesting things about this dream is that it had a lesson closely in alignment with a lesson taken from the movie "No Country for Old Men". At the end of the movie, the bad guy, severely injured from a car crash he was just in, walks away from the scene before the cops arrive. I believe (and some other people I have talked to agree with me), that this had a message saying that evil lives on, and you can't really ever kill it or eliminate it. So, what I said, while writing this dream report, this being: *I took that as meaning that evil lives on even if it appears you defeated it at a time.* It's an interesting thing to take away from some event or experience in life. I had this dream I believe in 2011. As of this day, years later, I am not exactly sure where I stand on the issue. I have tried repeatedly throughout the past to eliminate evil from existence so there would only be good in the world, but I was never quite able to do it, either because my powers to influence the world are to slight for the occasion, or because it is impossible to do. I have, however, thought about an interesting scenario which, if put into effect, would completely remove evil from existence: if everyone in the world got their own private universe to be free in for eternity to do whatever they want, then, if we give evil a universe of its own, the following would happen: 1) evil is only evil because it is against something, mainly, good. If in their own universe, evil will not be against

anything, since there is no good. 2) evil will not recognize itself, since it only recognizes itself through goodness. 3) evil will naturally begin to break itself down, since it is meaningless to be evil in there own universe, since it judges itself as something negative, mainly, it doesn't like itself, since it only likes itself through the negation of goodness. 4) evil will be completely removed from existence, through the natural collapse of the evil universe, which removes all evil in existence, through itself. Thus, the universe tends to unfold as it should.)

73. (**THIS IS THE OBSERVER SPEAKING:** I remember saying to myself in the dream that I was dreaming so I could do whatever I want. However, I wasn't completely lucid because I still in a way believed everything was real in the dream. Upon reflection, seeing the moon in the sky as it was falling towards the ground, ranks very high on my list of craziest/most epic things I have ever dreamt of, or even seen in general.)

74. (**THIS IS THE OBSERVER SPEAKING:** The idea of doing the inevitable and just giving up or submitting to a future state that you might eventually find yourself living, I think, is completely irrational. If I knew for an absolute fact that I would one day go to Hell, I would do my absolute best to make sure that I keep living in the world as long as possible. They say that a penny saved is penny earned, which I think has a good parallel to this dream. If the 30-35 year old person doing the obstacle course was me in the future, then I would be content to know that I didn't just give up and give in to an inevitable conclusion (being possessed by the devil). Any amount of time that you live in the world, is a second more that you don't have to live and experience hell or being possessed or living in any other state that you don't like. This seems very rational, since it allows you to experience positivity for as long as possible, or even something negative, which you believe is something less negative, then the negativity you will perhaps find yourself in some day.)

75. (**THIS IS THE OBSERVER SPEAKING:** I was once prescribed Risperidone, or also commonly known as "Risperdal" for my schizophrenia. It didn't do much at all, and I think smoking it like in this dream, even though it sounds like complete bullshit that it will get you high if you smoke it, is a more valuable way to use the drug.)

76. (**THIS IS THE OBSERVER SPEAKING:** In this dream I thought I was awake at one point and began writing what happened previously in the dream, while I was still dreaming.)

77. (**THIS IS THE OBSERVER SPEAKING:** I do not know what the significance or meaning of the $1 signs are. I would like to know since, when holding them up, someone in the dream told us to put them down, while another person laughed when we held them up.)

78. (**THIS IS THE OBSERVER SPEAKING:** For some reason, and to statisticians this is going to sound absurd, but I honestly think you could win consistent money playing Keno at a casino, with no bonuses. I have played Keno at a local casino at least a dozen times, and after it was all said and done, I have made somewhere between $50 - $70. When I was working at Walmart, a guy I work with told me that he had a way to beat the casino playing slot machines. He said the key is to, once you have made a profit, even a small profit, immediately cash out and go to another slot machine, and continue this until all your small to big size profits at each machine add up to a pretty decent profit. Having thought of this before, I for some reason never went to another Keno machine after hitting it big on one of the other machines, but just kept playing at the same machine. Sometimes I would lose my profit, and other times I would make an even greater profit, but come to think of it, you really have nothing to lose if you switch machines once you made any amount of profit. This is because the odds of winning are the same for each machine, and hence, by switching to another machine once you have made any amount of profit, this could only help, because if you lose all your profit, then you can assume that that would have happened at the other machine that you started on as well, because they have the same odds of winning and losing. Statistically speaking, this is analogous to the Monty Hall problem. Let's assume that the odds of making a profit at any machine is 1 out of 3. Now, let's pretend that you make a profit at the certain machine that you are at. Would it benefit you to change machines? If you do change machines, then this would give you a decided advantage, because the profit that you made from the other machine enables you to use that profit, along with the all the other money you have that would make you break even, means that you now have another 1 out of 3 chance, or 2 out of 3 chance of making more of a profit, because you have a 1/3 chance of winning money using your profit, and a 1/3 chance of winning money using the rest of your money (money apart from profit, which, apart from the profit, would make you break even if you stopped playing once you get to that amount of money). This is the same principle used in seeing how the online casinos can be beat. For

example, when I had made $3,500, it was a major mistake that I made, because if I would have cashed out right then, I would then have $3,400 pure profit, if I then decided to put in another $100, which, along with the bonus, give me roughly $700 again. In other words, the $3,500 can be thought of as redeemable up to $24,500 if you use all of the profit with the bonus. Hence, it is completely irrational to keep playing with your profit, as well as with your money you would have if you broke even, because, like Keno at the casinos, you have the advantage of odds, because if you switch machines, then you are playing with your winnings from the last machine, plus the money that you would have if you broke even, which, both have a 1/3 chance of winning. Profit chance of winning = 1/3; break even money chance of winning = 1/3; chance of winning with profit combined with breakeven money = 2/3 (the higher up in profit you go, the more that you put the odds in your favor to switch machines). This strategy is based on variable change, such that you put the odds in your favor by switching your decision (like in the Monty Hall problem), or, equivalently, switching Keno machines. The more machines that you could switch to after profiting off your use of the previous machine, the higher your chance of winning and making a profit.)

79. (**THIS IS THE OBSERVER SPEAKING:** I wrote the above short essay to outline what I think about the effects of drugs in general and the high's that they give to the user. I categorize drugs according to what they do to the user, and how that comes to effect other drugs that they try in the future. I think it's totally fucked up that almost all things (substances, drugs) that make you feel good and see the world in a better way, are all illegal. Some of the drugs are illegal simply because they have the effect of making you feel good. I have heard theories from people that most drugs are illegal because the government doesn't want you to think about some of the things that the drug makes you think about, for fear that you will come to understand how fucked up the government is and try to overthrow it or something. Beside the fact that there is a shit load of things in this world that are more harmful than drugs, I find it to be a compete absurd that someone could claim to be an expert on drugs, when that person has never tried it, to personally know what it feels like. If a drug is addicting, so what? It shouldn't be the governments job to regulate what certain substances are legal or illegal. Cocaine is illegal because it is addicting. But nicotine is legal, and is said to be the most addictive substance in the world (why cigarettes are so addicting). It's a

complete control tactic that the government uses to make certain drugs illegal, since, really, it's my body and I should be able make whatever decisions I want to make in reference to it, even if that means I will get addicted to it.)

80. (**THIS IS THE OBSERVER SPEAKING:** This is one of the angriest I have ever seen my mom. It seems pretty unlucky that her menstrual cycle coincided with April fool's day, and me and my brother's plan to piss the rest of the people living in our house off.)

81. (**THIS IS THE OBSERVER SPEAKING:** I believe this was the first time that my dad said to me that there is nothing that I have done that he hasn't done. As long as I stayed within the boundaries of what my dad has done in the past, and what I am doing in the present, I don't think he would have ever gotten upset with me for getting caught with drinking or doing some drugs. He said this to me throughout my first few years of college, and then quickly came to realize that I had done a lot more things in reference to drugs and alcohol than he ever did. Having gone to high school and college in the 1970's, I figured for sure that my dad had tried psychedelic drugs like a true hippie, but he claims to me that he never has.)

82. (**THIS IS THE OBSERVER SPEAKING:** According to collegehumor. com roughly 20-25% of people that have a Facebook masturbate to the pictures of some of their hot friends. I am not sure if this statistic applied to women also, but I think it would be really funny it did. I would have to admit that I am in the 20-25% club.)

83. (**THIS IS THE OBSERVER SPEAKING:** I am interested in how far down the grade levels this story has spread to. The fact that people talk about the video and think that she is a porn star even though they themselves have never seen the video, I find to be really funny. It really sucks that the video has since been removed, but at least I have had the privilege to have seen it and be the one person who first saw the video and started the rumor. That seems like a 'me' sort of thing to do.)

84. (**THIS IS THE OBSERVER SPEAKING:** I find it hard to believe that we were the only people to ever do this. Obviously, it is banned by XBOX to use the camera this way, but I don't think they could ever find out, considering that at the same time the camera was on to record two people having sex, there are hundreds of thousands, or millions of people on XBOX talking to each other on their cameras.

85. (**THIS IS THE OBSERVER SPEAKING:** Every time that I jacked off for many hours, once I cum, I am immediately struck with the notion that this was a major waste of time. Although if you really have nothing else to do, I suppose that can justify why you have jerked it for that long. I think that the naked scene in Titanic is something which most young teens have masturbated to at least once. I spend the night once at my friend's house, and he would jerk it to a scene in the movie, "Unfaithful", where Diane Lane has sex with some guy in a public restroom. The scene is only twenty to thirty seconds long and so he would have to repeatedly rewind it until he finally came. I'm not sure how many people do it, but I used to jack off in a restroom many times, which, to this day, if I am horny enough, I still do. I saw a porn video once that showed some hot girl fingering yourself in one of the stalls, so I think for sure that some women do this on occasion. It's kind of like that scene in "American Beauty" where some exchange happened with Lester and his boss, that went something like this: "My job consists of basically masking my contempt for the assholes in charge. And, at least once a day, retiring to the men's room so I could jerk off, while I fantasize about a life that doesn't so closely resemble hell." Some may say that masturbating in a public restroom is really fucked up, and to other's it's not a big deal. While in college during one of the classes I had to take for getting an underage drinking ticket, there was some lady who came to talk to the group about sex education. They say that abstinence is the only way to 100% protect yourself from STDs, but an interesting theory could be if someone caught an STD from sitting on a toilet, after some retard just jerked off on it. This possibility apparently didn't occur to her, either because she has never heard of anything like that, or because it is simply not possible to get an STD without having sex. All I can say is be careful if you ever do this. I wonder if collegehumor.com ever took a poll showing the statistic of the percentage of people who masturbate in a bathroom stall. The answer may be surprising.)

86. (**THIS IS THE OBSERVER SPEAKING:** If I'm being honest, I really don't think that sex, although looked upon by many as one of the greatest possible things that can exist, is that special of a thing. Women tend to think that all most men think about is sex. This is definitely not true in my case, and if it ever comes to the point that I am thinking about sex, I just jerk off and then I stop thinking about it. Personally, I think the best part of having sex is, not the pleasure that it gives you, but rather giving pleasure to the girl. If I never had another orgasm for the rest of my life

that would be fine with me. This would enable me to last for however long the girl wants to have sex for. To see a beautiful woman have an orgasm is, in my opinion way better than any orgasm that I could have. This explains why the only condoms I buy are the Trojan Ecstasy condoms, because they are ribbed and supposedly give more pleasure to the girl. At the time that this story took place, I, not being able to think for myself, was very prolife to the point that I thought that life began at conception. Upon further examination, I would have to say that I am very skeptical of whether life begins at conception or not. Many people hold the life beginning at conception belief, because the Bible says something like that God knows you before conception even happens. Today, I would probably have to say that I tend to be more prolife than prochoice, but I really only hold this view because I think partial birth abortions are fucked up, and anyone claiming that life beginning when the baby is born, and not a second before, have kind of a skewed outlook on the issue. If my mom was pro-choice, I probably wouldn't be alive, because when she was pregnant with me the doctor told her to get an abortion. She didn't and here I am. Regardless of what many fundamentalist prolife people will say, I really don't think there is a problem with using the plan B pill. It was just fucked up that Heather was so paranoid about getting pregnant that after every time we had sex, she took one of the pills. Around six months after I broke up with her, she (although she denies this) had sex with some kid I knew and apparently, they didn't throw away the condom or flush it down the toilet and the kid's mom saw it. Sucks for him, this explains why it is justified to flush a condom down the toilet as opposed to not. If you do, you won't get caught, if you don't that leaves the chance open that someone might find it.)

87. (**THIS IS THE OBSERVER SPEAKING:** The girl that I hooked up with on the third occasion mentioned above, was kind of hot (I think I may have jacked off to her on Facebook), but nothing special. Hooking up was ok but there was a weird thing that I noticed. When I was on top of her making out, I noticed that she kept trying to putt her hands up my shirt and feel something. I then realized that she was checking to see if I had armpit hair, because, at least I think so, I, had minor acne, nothing that bad, but it obviously resonated with her as meaning that maybe I was a very late bloomer and was still in the stages of development before you get armpit hair, while also getting acne. I did have armpit hair, and I am guessing she was relieved by this. In reference to the fat/ugly girl I

had sex with, I remember a day or two before we went to Donnie's place in the mountains, he was talking to me about the girl and how she was going to be the only girl there. For some reason, maybe it had something to do with the pot I we were smoking when he told me this, but I kept having visions and intrusive paranoid thoughts that I was going to hook up with the girl. This, one could argue, is another defense of the potential truth of "The Secret", which has come to fuck me over far more than come to my aid. So, having kept thinking about that it could legitimately happen, it turned into a self-fulfilling prophecy and that is exactly what happened. Apparently, she told one of Donnie's roommates that I was hot, and even though I had never been told this by anyone, it made no difference to me or how I viewed her. Also, in reference to the pact that my friends made to all get laid in January, I told my friends when I wrote them a Facebook message to tell them about what happened, that I was A) black out drunk and that that is why I made such a stupid decision to sleep with her, and B) that I was going through and doing it because we made the pact and I wanted to hold up my end of the pact. At least I didn't cum inside her, the thought of having that girl in my life for the next 18 years did not sound good to me at all.)

88. (**THIS IS THE OBSERVER SPEAKING:** The above story happened to be the story I told to the people that were at the coffee shop during open mike night. I didn't want to tell a story that night but one of my friends insisted, by going up to the mike and saying that I was about to come up. I told this story along with a bunch of lies and exaggerations of the truth (the norm for me in other words), and I heard crickets. There were two guys sitting at a table about six feet from where I was standing at the mike, and every time I tried to make a joke or try and make the audience laugh with some arbitrary and obscure detail, one of the guys would always do a fake laugh and then look down at the table he was sitting at. It was kind of like the person who sees someone do something weird and then yells out, "Awkward!" Nobody laughs and people just think you are fucking retard. All in all, I would have to say that this was a top two or three events in my life that I look back on and realize that it was an epic fail.)

89. 89. (**THIS IS THE OBSERVER SPEAKING:** Thinking back to when this story took place, I may have been embarrassed that everyone saw my dick, if it wasn't for A) my ignorance of it being outside the front of my boxers, or B) me being extremely drunk and even if I knew that they

could see my dick, I wouldn't have cared at all. Today, if I'm drunk, I really don't care if people see me naked. I feel like I have nothing to be embarrassed about and don't take people's comments about it seriously. Just think about how weird it would have been if Eve commented on Adam's naked body, like she was critiquing it. That, regardless of whether they ate from the knowledge tree or not, would have made Adam realize that he was naked.)

90. (**THIS IS THE OBSERVER SPEAKING:** The next two stories did not occur with me there but since they were done by Abe and my two other friends, Rick, and Brad, I will tell them here.)

91. (**THIS IS THE OBSERVER SPEAKING:** For some reason we just thought of the Pizza delivery driver as an easy target to fuck with, mainly because we were looking for something entertaining to do, and the idea of messing with the delivery driver just sounded to epic to not do. In all of the above stories, there really were no negative consequences for what we did. I consider it hardcore luck that none of the drivers ever turned us in, with the exception of the trip wire prank, but even that doesn't seem to make sense. The driver must have told his manager about what happened and the manager, perhaps, got very pissed off which explains why she was threatening to sue us. But then talking to the driver on the phone after the manager, the guy seemed nice about the whole thing. Thank the fuck Christ for chill people.)

92. (**THIS IS THE OBSERVER SPEAKING:** people sympathize with a drunk person (because they have been there to) as opposed to some assholes who would when seeing me in the ditch, call the cops and try intentionally try and fuck me over, are way cool. Like they are cleaning up the street to further eliminate crime or some shit. When my brother got a DUI once, some lady who became aware of the event, decided to try and fuck my brother over by claiming that he ran into a fence where there were horses. She tried to sue my brother and get him to not only pay for the fence, but also pay for the "emotional trauma" that he put her horses through. She made this whole story up, just for the simple idea that it was her responsibility to clean up the streets, and make an example of the drunk driver, perhaps thinking, "No one comes into my neighborhood and does something like this without paying a big price. The lawsuit ended up being handled by my brother's insurance, and so in that respect, he kind of lucked out.)

93.  (**THIS IS THE OBSERVERS SPEAKING:** I had a dream once where I met with a good friend of mine who had died a few years earlier. I asked him what happens when you die, and he responded that he is not supposed to say. I then ask him, "ok, but what about if you are Hitler for example and very evil, what happens then?" right after I said this to him, I immediately woke up from the dream. Maybe I was missing the point, but if I could go back in time and relive the dream, I would have phrased it better to show what I really meant: "Is there anything I should be worried about or fearful of when I die?" I think that is a very reasonable thing to ask. This correlates with the above hobo story, in that "Gabriel" as he called himself, said that hell is full of evil people, but for some reason Thomas Jefferson was in hell. This must then mean that Thomas Jefferson, contrary to what history will have you believe about him, mainly, that he was a very smart, good person who helped form the USA, is a total farce. He would have to have lived a double life, considering that nobody in their right mind would call him evil. As to whether or not the hobo really was the angel Gabrielle from the Bible, then I take that as meaning that the real Gabrielle, looking for a body/avatar through which he could then walk the earth like a human being so that nobody knows who he really is, I can't be entirely sure. Nor do I really care. The one positive thing about that night, however, is that he forgot about the Adderall, which, if it came down to him taking the bong or weed, I would have preferred him to take either one, just don't touch my fucking Adderall fix.)

94.  (**THIS IS THE OBSERVER SPEAKING:** For some reason I thought it would be a good idea to tell everyone I knew about what happened. Little did I know, it was to start a mini revolution in how people came to see me as. However, what is important to note is that I used this story as a foundation upon which I could say more ridiculous things about what happened, all of which were flat out lies, and complete exaggerations of what actually happened. Here is a short list of things that I told people happened but didn't: 1) when I was running down my dorm hall to get to the bathroom, I couldn't hold it in, and so I began to shit as I was running as fast as I could. This ended up making a trail of shit starting from my dorm room to the bathroom. 2) after I got out of the bathroom, I looked to see what I had done, and I saw specks of shit on the walls. I told people that this happened because as I was running down my dorm hall, the shit ran down my legs to my feet, and then I kicked the shit from my

feet onto the walls from running so fast. 3) Once I got to the bathroom, I realized that there was no more toilet paper and I said something (I don't remember) to resolve this problem. 4) After I was done shitting, my boxers were completely covered and I had to do something with them, so I decided to flush them down the toilet, which, after doing that got clogged and then overflowed, causing the floor to get covered in shit, along with my puke blood. These are the only major details I made up, but there could have been more I just don't remember (it gets hard to keep track of all the bullshit you make up I suppose). Now, what is important to remember and which I talk briefly about in multiple parts of this book, is that Tucker Max was my hero at that point in my life. All four of these details, rather than just making them up out of thin air to add humor to my story, I got from a story Tucker Max wrote where he shit in a hotel lobby. I was banking on two things: 1) that nobody I told the story to had ever read the Tucker Max story, or who even knew who Tucker Max was. 2) that nobody in the future would ever come to read Tucker Max's story, which they then would notice had striking similarity to my story. So, I told almost everyone I knew about this story, and they in turn told their friends the story. Everyone thought it was the funniest story they have ever heard, and this made me happy because that is exactly what I was going for. I remember the first time I told this story to a few friends, they then kept wanting me to tell it to more people, who in turn wanted me to tell it to their friends to. That day I would have to estimate that I told the story roughly seven to eight times. Now, upon looking back at all the absurd and crazy shit that went down with all of the events recounted here, it seems to me to be poetic justice that the following happened. I was over at a friend's apartment for her birthday party. It turns out that someone she knows bought her Tucker Max's book as a present. I was semi freaking out because of the thought that I might be soon found out, but kept my cool because I would flat out deny that I got my story from his story if she or anyone else were to ask me about it. A few weeks or months later the topic of Tucker Max came up and when I was with the girl and a couple of her friends. I then said, "He had happen to him the same thing that happened to me." I don't know exactly know how they took that to mean, but it was at that point that I stopped telling the story to people and they stopped asking me to tell it (I think this coincided with me getting suspended, since after that happened, I pretty much lost all contact with my college and high school friends). Thinking back to when all this madness took place, I feel like there is a lot of things I could have done to avoid people potentially finding out that the story was not entirely true. For example, instead of taking details from Tucker Max's story that would have afforded me the freedom to say whatever the fuck I want without ever being found out. It could have been entirely original, but the sad thing is that at the time, I was really not that original of a person, at least in reference to making people think more/better about me than how I actually am. For example, instead of taking the part of the Tucker Max story where he kicks the shit onto the walls, I could have said that I was so drunk when I was running down my dorm hall, that I tripped and ran into the wall, making a big half body sized mark on the walls (as written before in the Introduction). This, although not true, would have been entirely original, and I think would have made people laugh at as well. In reference to what I referred to as a revolution surrounding this story and the events that followed, I was from then on known as the person who tells really funny stories. What I thought was kind of unfortunate was one of my friends went to visit our high school English teacher, and she told him the story. Somehow, it then spread to other people and teachers, with one teacher commenting on it saying, "What is this I hear about someone you know shitting in his dorm hall?" Years later, after coming clean to a few friends, I had, at the age of 21, what is the equivalent of a midlife crisis. Apparently, people that become mentally ill later on in life, have some sort of tragic event (or event that they have perhaps built up in their mind to be equivalent to a tragic event) happen to them, which then becomes a sort of new identity or way of thinking about life, that the person now lives and experiences the world as. I can most definitely say that if this story in particular (one could argue that other things contributed to this, although not nearly to the extent or level of influence that this story did) paved a new way in life for me, which, if it never happened, I would either A) still lie and make things up for my own amusement (interestingly enough, I considered making people laugh to be, not as something which I thought was good because it is a nice thing to make other people laugh, but rather because making people laugh entertained me and in that respect, I really only cared about how I felt, rather than how the other people felt.), which I think would have caught up to me, so I really would be just delaying the inevitable or B) I would never have thought about the world in any other way other than it revolving around my amusement, which in this case, I never would have been interested at all in philosophy, and never would have begun to contemplate life and existence. I can definitely say that I am changed for the better because of it, and that one of my current biggest fears is to run into someone I went to high school or college with and them wanting me to tell them the "shit story". I wouldn't even know where to begin, other than to just tell them that I don't tell that story anymore, leaving them to speculate why exactly that is. I stopped caring a while ago.)

95. (**THIS IS THE OBSERVER SPEAKING:** I have been told by a few people (these are just people I have talked so, imagine how many other people think this same thing that I have not talked to) when I am in a complete black out state, it turns me into someone who really isn't me, but rather just a really crazy up version of myself where all of my inhibitions become completely absent in how I relate to people and act around them. To this extent, I have been called by many people a crazy fuck who yells a lot and does anything. I remember back in high school, while at a party at Rick's house, I was in the bathroom and thought I heard a sequence of events in which the cops came into the house and was ready to give people the breathalyzer, when one of the cops asked if there was anyone else in the house (remember I am hallucinating all of this (I was baked and drunk)). Someone said that I was in the bathroom, but then Brad warned the cop, "If I were you, I would just wait here until he comes out of the bathroom, this kid is crazy as fuck." I exited the bathroom, entirely expecting to see cops there, but there were none.)

96. (**THIS IS THE OBSERVER SPEAKING:** The month that I graduated from high school, I was charged with a "Minor in Consumption" underage alcohol ticked. This was the first time I had ever gotten in trouble with the law (except for speeding ticket). The police force in my hometown have two ways in which they can better uphold the law, mainly, by catching people engaging in illegal activities. There is no greater feeling that a cop in my town gets when he and his partner bust a high school party filled with lots of drugs and alcohol. This not only gives them something to do for the next few hours or so. You can see on their faces that they have just scored big time. To the cops there is nothing better than busting a huge party. It is what they consider to be a holy grail of illegal activities that the teenage kids are engaging in, which results with a relatively easy bust, by merely just coming into the house at the front door (when I got my ticket, the house was filled with people and people were constantly going from inside to outside, or outside to inside, and so the door was open. Usually (or always?) the cop, if the front door is closed, must seek

permission from someone (probably the owner of the house?) to legally enter the house. "How's everyone doing tonight!?" I see him walk up the last stairs to the main floor of the house, and immediately know I am fucked. In reference to the other thing that cops do to uphold the law, it is a common practice that they engage in, mainly, if your car is parked somewhere in the vicinity of where a cop is staking out for the night, and, upon returning to your car, get in, start the engine, and begin driving home. The cop, probably bored all night finally finds something he could do: follow me. This has happened to me twice, and, luckily, upon leaving the parking lot, I was following Victoria's car, and she noticed, just as I had, that two cops pull out of the area they are parked at and begin following me. Only a few hundred feet away from the parking lot was a gas station and we immediately pull into it, and watched as the cops drove by, not giving them the satisfaction of them trying to fuck me over and them feeling good about it.)

# PHILOSOPHICAL ROAST OR (HEURISTICS OF MIND TRAVEL)

In this last section of my book, I sound off on whatever I want and is a brief introduction to my authenticity and humorous way of perceiving the world.

## FORWARD

I had a dream once where I was in a setup of heaven and hell that is roughly as follows: The people in heaven are all seated in a huge auditorium, like a large movie theater. The people in hell are the servants of the people in heaven and do whatever the people in heaven tell them to do. I was one of the people in hell, however, I came up with a way in which I could have fun in hell, and even more fun than the people in heaven were having. As I was serving the people in heaven, I would sound off in my head about the absurdities of religion, philosophy, spirituality, and other existential viewpoints. Since people could hear my thoughts, I would entertain the other people in hell, and they would laugh and be having fun because of what I was saying. Even better, the people in heaven also thought that what I was saying was funny and made sense. I then realized that I was having more fun in hell, then I would have been having in heaven. Having this thought in mind, I will now sound off and what I think about the world, and my place in it.

I'm interested in how innocence fares when it collides with harsh reality.
-Geoffrey S. Fletcher

A serious and good philosophical work could be written consisting entirely of jokes.
-Ludwig Wittgenstein

1.  A good moral rule is to never hit a woman. A better moral rule is to never hit anyone.

2. There is nothing in existence which necessitates the return of jealousy and superiority in the mind of another.

3. Would an interpretation of Hegel be easier to comprehend if there was someone who experienced the world in the exact way he talks about?

4. Which person must you trust when telling the truth with certainty; the person who is certain that God exists, or the person who is certain that God does not exist?

5. Which makes more sense, "I think, therefore I am" or, "I think, therefore I was"?

6. If Occam's Razor is correct in its legitimacy, could we not then say that God is simple?

7. Can we call Tarzan the 'Spider Man' of the jungle?

8. I think the existence of twins and doppelgangers can be seen as proof that God ran out of ideas when creating people.

9. If homosexuality is a choice, then is it also a choice to talk in the gay accent, or a choice to walk in the gay way? Or a choice between two birds?

10. Blackmail is an art form, as well as a form of justice.

11. If God is love, and love is not jealous, then God is not jealous.

12. Clothing in reference to Christianity is inevitable, since Adam and Eve would need to wear something to keep them warm when winter comes.

13. I think an interesting thing to see would be transgender, transspecies, because not only would the man want to be a polar bear, but he would want to be a female polar bear.

14. How do they make the machines that make the machines? An infinite regress of machine making ensues.

15. It is important to not confuse being horny for the euphoria of being in love. Thus, marrying for the sex is a confusing thing.

16. It is clear that whoever the false prophet is and whoever the antichrist is, are complete nut jobs.

17. I wonder how Jonah was able to live for three days in the big fish. If he lived in the stomach, then how did he keep from getting digested? Maybe he lived in the liver if that afforded him the best place to survive?

18. Does it really matter whether "Dumbledore" from the Harry Potter books is gay or not? Does anything change when reading it, such that a

completely different meaning is found simply by noting that Dumbledore is gay? Do the children reading the books even know what being gay means?

19. Is it more correct to say that Obama was the 1st black president, or 44th white president? Is it correct to say both (1st white/black president)? If not, why?

20. Both are equal: we can name the False Prophet as the Antichrist's bitch, and simultaneously name the Antichrist as the False Prophet's bitch.

21. Although it is a fact that Fox News is not "fair and balanced", it seems strange that they always get the highest ratings.

22. Although it is a fact that CNN and MSNBC are fair and balanced, it seems strange that they always get the lowest ratings.

23. When tying duct tape around someone's mouth, or when putt a ball gag in someone's mouth always make sure their nose is not clogged like from a seasonal cold. Otherwise, the person will suffocate because their only two ways of breathing have been blocked up.

24. I wonder what kind of wine Jesus turned bread into. Was it cheap stuff like Merlot or Carlos Rossi? Or maybe the top shelf stuff, aged for 20 or more years.

25. Although it is a fact that Jesus was Jewish, can we say he is a Jew now? Wouldn't he be a Christian now? And if he is indeed a Christian, which sect? A Lutheran, Baptist, Evangelical, Catholic, Protestant, Christian Scientist, etc.? A Pilgrim? Why was he Jewish, as opposed to always being Christian?

26. I think it would have been cool of Alan Shepard would have used the lunar rover as a golf cart when he played golf on the moon. The moon is all set up. The American Flag could have been the flag where the hole is, and the craters could have been the sand trap.

27. The notion of bros before hoes becomes void when a man falls in love with a woman. Unless one cares about hanging out with their friends over spending time with their wife.

28. If waterboarding is considered torture, what are we to say about other forms of simulated drowning, like giving someone a swirly?

29. Even if God is omnipotent, there is still something he cannot do, mainly, be a palindrome. (Unless we drop the 'h' at the end of Allah)

30. When the male sperm enters the female egg, the signal it emits is essentially, "I win, now everybody else fuck off." And they do.

31. Could it be possible that Great White Sharks are more scared of you than you are of them?

32. Commanding is the highest form of begging.

33. People care if a stripper has acne. People do not care if a prostitute has acne.

34. You don't have to be crazy to write philosophy but is sure helps.

35. You could go to Daytona Beach (the city) without going to Daytona Beach (the beach).

36. If you do not judge a book by its cover, then you will not be able to judge a book by its name.

37. I think they should give out an Oscar for two important categories (much better than the stupid "Best Poplar Film" award the Academy was thinking about making a category): (i) Best Scene (ii) Best Frame (which is just a single frame/still picture of something in the movie)

38. Who was the dumbass who decided to name a planet, 'Uranus', and then claim that its pronounced 'your anus', as opposed to, "urinus"? It's kind of an unspoken agreement that when people say, Uranus, to not acknowledge what they are all thinking, mainly, that it sounds like one's asshole.

39. First Pluto was a planet, then it was not a planet, then it was a planet again. Why can't Astronomers make up their fucking minds?

40. According to Trump, John McCain is not a hero because he was captured. Rational response: His plane was shot down behind enemy lines and was then captured, you dick.

41. Who do you pay to buy your own private island? And why?

42. When you plead the 5th, you are admitting your guilt through silence.

43. How can you tell that someone is Jewish without asking them? They can just lie and say that they are not Jewish.

    Theorem: Judaism is a belief system, not an ethnic group. A Black person can be Jewish, as could an Asian, a Hispanic or Native American. In order to escape the Nazi's, the Jews could have just said that they were not Jewish. For some reason they volunteered this information. Hitler tried to say that all Jews share some common physical attributes, but they were just made up. If Jews really are an ethnic group, then the only way that this could be known is by examining the Jews DNA or genome, which has not a luxury afforded to the Nazi's to use.

44. Could you be a German but not a Nazi? Does "Nazi" refer to all Germans, or just the people in the government party? Could a German fight in WW2 without being in the Nazi Party?

45. A good way to ensure that nobody commits perjury is to: A) hook them up to a lie detector test; B) inject them with truth serum. Thus, you would not have to swear an oath to not lie, because you already can't.

46. They should come up with an experiment to test the existence of a soul. The experiment would go as follows: Put a person who claims they can leave the body into one room, and then in the next room put an arbitrary object in it. If the person does really have a soul that can leave the body, then they could tell you what the object is. Simple experiment.

47. How exactly did they come up with the layout of a computer keyboard? It seems pretty random, but I guess they thought that the word, "qwerty" was a cool way to design a keyboard as.

48. Games should not force a player to upgrade to a higher, more difficult level, like they do in Tetris. The game should be designed so that the game does not force the player to progress to a higher level if the player still wants to play at the same level of difficulty, until they have mastered it. In this way, the player could get a lot better at the game if the next level is not forced upon the player.

49. Is Bloody Mary omnipresent, and can appear in front of other people's mirrors at the same time? If she is not, then 99% of people summoning her would be disappointed.

50. If an ice cube is put into water and it melts, the water level does not rise. However, if the ice cube is hollow (full of air), then when it melts the water level is lowered.

51. When two people are alone, and one person says to the other person that they are being quiet, what they are saying, really, is that they are quiet also.

52. Although it is true that sex in a relationship can complicate things, does this apply to sex in marriage?

53. In order to win the lottery, people must battle with each other using, "The Secret", because the winner will always be the one who used 'The Law of Attraction' the best.

54. They say black (darkness) is the absence of light, but if this were true, how could you see black (darkness) with a light?

55. A speed limit sign that says, "Speed Limit 14mph" is odd in two ways: (i) it is odd because speed limit signs are usually posted in fives (15, 50, 65, etc.); (ii) it is not odd because 14 is an even number.

56. If meth labs are dangerous because of the risk of making the drug in a laboratory or kitchen, then why don't you just make meth on a nice, sunny day?

57. Quicksand is like a black hole, once you're in it, your fucked.

58. The question should not be, is there a 'gay gene'. The question should be, is there a 'straight gene'?

59. If someone is violent, they can be a Christian, but they cannot be a Buddhist.

60. Having no pubic hair is the ultimate defense against crabs.

61. I wonder who would win if David Blaine and Chris Angel had a battle royal, using their magic against one another? This could easily be made into a show in Las Vegas.

62. An interesting game of bowling would be one in which, using the bumpers, which player could get the lowest score.

63. If the rapture were to happen while you are asleep, how would you be able to tell the dream world from the real world? What about if you are high on peyote? Does getting raptured freak you out and make you seem like you are going crazy?

64. I wonder what would happen if an ant or spider crawled into your ear when you were asleep. Could it control you like you controlling a car or a bus?

65. I think it would be a completely different world if farts smelled good.

66. How much longer will the gay pride movement add letters to their initials. First it was LGBT; then it was LGBTQ. What's next, LGBTQM, with the M standing for Metrosexual?

67. They say that everyone will die. But this is only true if the rapture never happens (if you are raptured, you will never die).

68. If there are clear windows in a blue world, then the blue world remains blue.

69. If you need to gain 4 pounds in order to qualify for a higher weight class in wrestling, just drink two water 32oz Nalgene bottles before the weigh in.

70. True statement: girls got to eat. Truer statement: everyone's got to eat.

71. If a Jewish boy is on Santa Clauses naughty list, then it doesn't matter, since he doesn't celebrate Christmas.

72. Why exactly do people that vote for politicians care about whether the candidate did drugs in the past? If a politician said, "I smoked the pot, but I didn't inhale", then why did you bother hitting the pipe in the first place? Sounds like a waste of perfectly good weed.

73. You never see a horseshoe making a blacksmith. But you do see pot making a pothead.

74. I got 20/20 vision in the year 2020 (Lasik), enabling me to clearly watch the show 20/20 (tv show), on my 20x20 inch tv screen.

75. Do breast implants float? If so, they could make excellent life preservers.

76. Is Santa Clause the knockoff version of The Father? The only difference is the clothes they wear.

77. If your prayers don't get answered, is it because God chose not to answer them, or that you just suck at praying? Maybe your prayers don't get answered because answering them is against God's plan for you?

78. If one is choking on ice cube, then hold your breath long enough for the cube to melt so you can breathe again.

79. Do stoners like the smell of skunk because it smells exactly like marijuana? Or is it the other way around?

80. The credo goes that if it feels good, do it. Rational response: what if they want you to shoot up some heroin?

81. The smaller you get, the bigger the world. The bigger you get, the smaller the world.

82. If dogs are pets, then is it ok if I pet your pet?

83. Is it possible to summon the Holy Spirit with a Ouija board? Why or why not?

84. Could we say that native Hawaiians are also Native Americans? Both existed before America was discovered, and now both exist in America.

85. I'm more concerned that a frog in a beaker will drown before the water gets too hot to kill it.

86. Why did people in ancient times only have one name? Plato, Socrates, Homer, Aristotle, Adam and Eve. Did the hundreds of thousands of people living in an ancient city (Greece or Rome for example), also have unique first names, but no middle or last names?

87. Were Adam and Eve Jewish, since they believed in Yahweh?

88. If you want to help polar bears from drowning because of global warming, it would be more beneficial to stop videotaping the polar bear drowning and help it out.

89. I cannot smell a thought. I cannot taste a thought. I cannot hear a thought. I cannot touch a thought. I cannot see a thought. However, I can think a thought. Thus, we have proved the existence of a sixth sense.

90. The question shouldn't be, how was Stonehenge made? The question should be, how did the people who made Stonehenge find dozens of rocks in the same rectangular shape?

91. It doesn't matter how much you believe in the secret or law of attraction, hitting 10 out of 10 on keno is basically impossible.

92. Who was happier when the Cotton Gyn was invented, the slaves or the slave owner? The slave's job was easier, and the slave owner's profit was increased.

93. All three holidays in December begin with the same synonym: *Happy* Hanukkah; *Merry* Christmas; *Joyous* Kwanza. (Evidence of Intelligent design?)

94. If I only have a $10 bill and only want to give $5 for offering, is it ok if I put in the $10 and take $5 out for change?

95. Which is truer, "may you be in heaven half an hour before the devil knows you're dead", or "may you be in heaven half an hour before God knows you're dead."?

96. Is it a coincidence that every illegal drug makes you feel good?

97. If a writer has "writer's block", then the writer has not dropped acid.

98. Christians and Atheists do agree on one thing: the earth is not 7,000 years old.

99. If the medication any arbitrary American is on is prescribed for taking it at bedtime, then if the prescribed dose is written using the metric system, they're screwed.

100. If grey goose vodka was bamboo, then pandas would be constantly drunk.

101. I think a better way to teach math to elementary school kids, would be to dress up as a dinosaur, thus making mathematics fun.

102. You could forgive a witch for ruining your life, but you cannot ask a Taoist for forgiveness, because the Taoist will have no fucking clue what you are talking about.

103. Is Ayer's Rock a name for a rock, or a rock that belongs to a man named Ayer?

104. Is Boise States football field blue, or the absence of a green field?

105. You can talk dirty on a chalk board. Simply just write down on the board dirty thoughts. You cannot, however, talk dirty when playing poker because people will wonder what the hell is wrong with you.

106. How to tell the difference between an American Indian and an India Indian: Whichever one a cowboy aims at is the American one.

107. If only one person in China believes in Santa Clause, and that person is naughty, then Santa never has to go to China.

108. What does the Koran, and Harry Potter have in common? They are both hated by Christians.

109. If the gold inside Fort Knox never gets exchanged for money, then it's like it is not worth any money at all (or doesn't exist at all).

110. Is it ok to say the N word if one black person says you can, but another black person says you can't?

111. Although Bill Clinton did not have sexual relationship with Monica Lewinsky, he did have a romantic relationship with her.

112. If Jesus had four arms and was painted blue, then Christians and Hindus would believe in the same God.

113. Skiing gives you wiings.

114. If you know how to spell every word in the dictionary, then it is impossible to lose a Spelling Bee.

115. When did it occur to people that they should cover a women's breasts? The cavemen didn't use bras or bikini tops. What makes humans so special?

116. If the rapture happened, would Chick-fil-a go out of business? Does God liquidate the company? All employees go to heaven.

117. Two things Tim Tebow would never do: he would never steal a book from a library, and he would never meditate.

118. An animal can only steal a book from a library or store if the animal somehow got into the store or library. Hence, if a book is missing from a library or store, you could technically blame it on a seeing eye dog.

119. If a mac book pro was an animal, then it could become a fossil when it stops working.

120. If Ann Coulter had her own show on Fox News, then the show would have the best ratings. Not because people like her, but because people hate her (watching the show for all the wrong reasons).

121. Top 10 reasons people masturbate to their classmates on facebook:

    (x) Facebook is not blocked by a parental website blocker.

    (ix) People masturbate to anything.

    (viii) Some of their high school friends are hot.

    (vii) High school and college women tend to post pictures of their asses.

    (vi) The people are fully clothed, and hence, leave it up to the person's imagination.

    (v) So that 'poke' refers to the desire to have sex with their friend.

    (iv) Was the only place to find hot pictures of your friends before Instagram was created.

    (iii) Some people want to be masturbated to (such as a slut).

    (ii) Facebook has videos as well as pictures.

    (i) You could masturbate to your friends 17-year-old pictures from ten years ago, without being considered a pedophile.

122. Why does the NHL and NASCAR not have any black people in them? Answer: because black people suck at hockey and suck at driving.

123. If everyone in the world was in elementary school, then nobody in the world would have chlamydia.

124. 5 hours ago I watched a marathon of Barny episodes, because 5 hours ago I was high.

125. The only difference between a Mormon and a Jihadist, is that Mormon's get 72 virgins on earth, whereas Jihadists get 72 virgins in heaven.

126. Easy exorcism: If demons possessing someone do not like holy water, then just pour holy water all over them until they decide to leave the body.

127. In 2008, Fox News broadcasted the 'weather underground' as a terrorist coup with their leader, 'Bill Ayers'. But this is only because Obama met Bill Ayers at some point in his life.

128. The destruction of Sodom is evidence that God is against anal sex.

129. If something went haywire in the space-time dimensional laws of the universe, would it then be possible for the president to be a werewolf?

130. If there are no lights on, then you are invisible.

131. If one rich person gets into heaven, then at least two camels have gone through the eye of a needle.

132. If someone has an IQ of 16, then that person is the Whore of Babylon.

133. The SETI (search for extraterrestrial intelligence) creed: the hope that there is SETI (some extraterrestrial intelligence).

134. Christian apologists can know what life was like in the Bible when they had no light bulbs, by lighting a candle.

135. Christopher Columbus introduced sickness to the new world. The new world introduced mescaline to Christopher Columbus.

136. The question of whether an elderly person should buy a PC or a Mac, has nothing to do with which is faster, and has everything to do with which device can show text in the largest font size.

137. If gay people have to be forgiven of their sins, does San Francisco have to be forgiven for existing?

138. If the 1,000-year kingdom were to happen, does the space-time warp so that heaven gets transferred to earth?

139. Can you teach a panda to ride a bicycle? The bicycle would have to be the right size, and make the configuration as simple as possible. When the panda masters the bicycle, it is now in the position of moving on to other bikes, like a street bike, a motocross vehicle, and a unicycle.

140. Reasonable response to an arbitrary Christian about the end times when they say, "I'm going to go up in the rapture and come back on a white horse!" and "We are going to fight on Jesus's side with swords!" My response: "That sucks."

141. In order to escape Hades, you must be either a Greek God, or very sneaky.

142. If carnivores, omnivores and herbivores are all asleep at the same time, then every animal on earth is sleeping at the same time.

143. Sure you can get lonely in solitary confinement, but a silver lining is that you won't get raped or beaten like you would in a prison.

144. Socrates would not be able to come up with the 2012 end of the world prophecy, because, (a) he was not a Mayan; (b) he was not Nostradamus; (c) was not a dumbass.

145. Darwin is dead; Jesus is alive; Jesus can walk on water; Darwin cannot.

146. If I think the Mona Lisa is hot and jack off to her, is there something wrong with me?

147. Being a Shiite Muslim gives you wiings.

148. divorce = addicted to porn; hell = lusting when looking at porn; fucked = computer froze and stops working.

149. If your pet rooster wakes you up early on your days off, then you should consider ringing its neck (or putting it up for adoption).

150. According to dictionary.com, a baseball mitt is different than a restaurant.

151. At the final judgement, each person must stand before Zeus, Allah, and Elohim.

152. Ouija Board Discretion (Rated R; Must be 17 to buy)

153. Unless the 'holy ghost' is wearing a white blanket over itself, it should be semantically denoted as 'holy spirit'.

154. Donald Trump: Into the discussion of the most pointless presidents in the history of the United States.

155. If Spiderman's phobias are spider webs and heights, then Spiderman is screwed.

156. The Somalian pirates are a knock-off of the traditional Caribbean pirates with the black skull and bones flag. So, if green is the Caribbean pirates, and red is the Somalians pirates, then, red is the new green.

157. It seems strange that not a single black person in history had natural blonde hair or red hair (coincidence or God's design?).

158. If you could be 'brothers in Christ' (having the same father), can you also be 'fathers in Christ' (having the same son)? Or, 'ghosts in Christ' (same father and son)? According to Christians, a Mormon cannot be any of these.

159. What does money and the Virgin Mary have in common? Both are ancient, and both can be saved.

160. An objective golf course is designed by an architect. A subjective golfer is designed by God. Thus, God is an architect and good at golf. (golf → architect → God's design)

161. The four presidents on Mount Rushmore were all white and made of white rock. Therefore, if Obama were on Mount Rushmore, he should be painted black (or half white/half white).

162. I think the "We can do it!" poster would be funny to masturbate to, considering someone might find her hot, especially because that's what she said.

163. If I get the mark of the beast on my left hand, it's sort of like not getting it at all.

164. Just like Leonardo DiCaprio is the best dream extractor in the movie, 'Inception', Rafael Nadal, even in his dreams, is the best clay court player in the world.

165. To show in Sunday school, if the Bible got made into a Disney movie (like a cartoon talking snake), then the Bible would be more entertaining, and Sunday school wouldn't suck as much.

166. If I was a polygamist, I would marry all the Disney princesses, that is, if they were Mormon and would have me.

167. If Roe vs. Wade can be overturned simply by appointing conservative judges, wouldn't the conservative judges also try to overturn the legalization of gay marriage?

168. If Adam and Eve would have waited until the knowledge fruit dropped to the ground, then they would also have knowledge of gravity, and not just knowledge of good and evil.

169. What do werewolves, cup stacking, the internet and the month of April have in common? They were all invented by Al Gore.

170. The existence of the Garden of Eden in Missouri, and the planet Kolob, although they cannot be entirely refuted, can be shown to be meaningless, since the Garden of Eden was actually in modern day Alaska, and Kolob is Icelandic for Jupiter.

171. If you use blackle.com instead of google.com, then you are just as much a loser as someone drinking at an open bar with Johnny Walker Red, when they have Johnny Walker Blue at the bar with the same price.

172. I could write on facebook: "my pet just died" and your friends won't be able to share their condolences because there is no "I don't like" button.

173. An unfortunate way to die would be when you get lethally injected (executed) by the death penalty, since, apparently, only fetuses are people, not convicted felons.

174. When the three wise men gave Jesus gold, hopefully it wasn't too much, since rich people don't go to heaven.

175. Jihadist: We will not stop jihad until the flag of Islam is flying over the White House. Response: What about the flag of Islam over Candy Land? Why doesn't it already have a flag over Candy Land?

176. If a stick figure is a picture of the prophet Muhammad, then no Muslim would ever know it and then kill the person who drew it.

177. An interesting card to give to someone would be: "Roses are red, violets are blue, I am penniless and so are you" If you are not homeless than you are a dick. If you are homeless than you are funny.

178. It is easier for a camel to go through the eye of a needle, than for a Buddhist to make it into the kingdom.

179. Chair Recliner Atheism: the absence of belief that chair recliners exist.

180. When Ted Haggard said that Evangelicals have the best sex life of any Christian sect, he proved this clearly.

181. If you are gay, you have the gay gene. If you are straight, you have the straight gene. If you are bisexual, you have both. If you are metrosexual, you have the straight gene, but want the gay gene.

182. Driving on mushrooms is sort of like Mario Kart. The only difference is that in Mario Kart you eat shrooms to make you better, and in real life eating shrooms makes you worse.

183. If you buy 'The Secret' DVD or book, make sure you save the receipt, just in case a drunk driver runs you over while you are feeling good.

184. If every NASCAR fan wrote in cursive, then every NASCAR fan would be literate.

185. Philosopher: Ideas exist in platonic space. Mathematician: Ideas exist in mathematical space. Logician: Ideas exist in logical space. Anyone else: What the fuck are you people talking about?

186. If a demon has the flu, does it spread the flu to the person possessed? If the person possessed has the flue, does it spread the flu to the demon?

187. One unfortunate thing about the butterfly effect, is that it could have the effect of making you a butterfly.

188. What would a SETI person score on the midterm exam if it were to ask, "are aliens real". They would be just as clueless as everyone else.

189. To help students understand philosophy they came out with, 'philosophy for dummies'. To help students understand engineering, they came out with 'the idiots guide to engineering'. To help students that must use both study guides (dummies and idiots), they came out with a retard self-help book.

190. Why do most black people get offended when a nonblack person says, 'nigga'? It's not the actual N word, and they don't even rhyme.

191. If mother earth existed, nobody would care.

192. Instead of waiting for the boats to come back when Titanic sank, why didn't anyone just swim to one of the boats?

193. If you take 50 Cents saying of 'get rich or die tryin' literally, then trying to break into Fort Knox is a good idea.

194. Could the movie, "cloudy with a chance of meatballs" actually be a premonition of God's wrath?

195. Black lives matter, unless you are Asian, in which case your life doesn't matter, since you are not black.

196. If I can only buy something if I get the mark, then could I use the money I have to pay indulgences for myself?

197. If Lebron James heard news that he now has a granddaughter, it is indifferent to him, since he got his priorities straight (basketball over family).

198. What do you call a God that can give 4 hand jobs at once? Answer: either Krishna or Yahweh (Krishna because she has four hands and Yahweh because he could do anything).

199. Who fucked up more, Adam and Eve on Earth, Lucifer in Heaven, or Jesus when he created a future corrupt world?

200. Messenger: "The Dali Lama just died"; Christian: "Praise God"

■ Or maybe I'm just mentally ill. Yeah, that's it.


**FADE OUT.**

**END.**

# ABOUT THE AUTHOR

You just read it.

# AUTHOR'S PHOTO

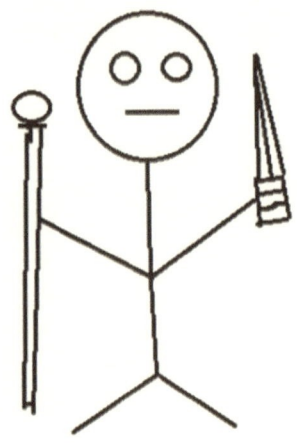

www.ingramcontent.com/pod-product-compliance
Lightning Source LLC
Chambersburg PA
CBHW020915140626
46545CB00015B/46